TALKING ABOUT FILMS

A Discussion Guide
by Robert Selinske

For Bonnie

ACKNOWLEDGMENTS

I'd like to thank David Chamberlin for editing my introductory essay, eliminating some of the more blatant exaggerations and generalizations. Mr. Chamberlin also wrote the discussion questions for *High Noon* and *The Last Picture Show*.

I'm deeply indebted to Norma Withrow for creating the section dividers and for advising me on typography, and to Lynne Hubenette for helping with the graphics.

Colin Higgins took time away from his new film to write a brief note granting permission to reprint stills from *Harold and Maude*. For permission to reprint stills, I'd also like to thank: Ian Birnie (Janus Films), R.M. Ford (Les Artistes Associes), Peter J. Meyer (Corinth Films), Tim Meyers (Analysis Films), Sara Risher and Tom Hoskins (New Line Cinema), Ruth Robbins (Cinema 5), John W. Schouweiler (New World Pictures), Jarold Sole (New Yorker Films), and P.Ray Swank (Swank Films). These very generous, enlightened distributors know that it's in their own interest to encourage film scholarship. Not so, Hollywood! Several of the major studios referred my inquiry to their lawyers, who barraged me with forms, legalities, and demands for astronomical royalties. It's fortunate that so few of their films contain ideas worth discussing.

Unlike George Lucas, who may have been too busy counting his profits from *Star Wars* dolls and T-shirts, Ingmar Bergman responded to my request for permission with an encouraging personal note written from his retreat on the island of Faro. Not only is Mr. Bergman the greatest creative genius in film today. He also has a lot of class.

Finally, this book would not have been possible without the encouragement of my parents and the insightful conversation of my friends and former students. I'd especially like to acknowledge my personal and intellectual debt to the following people: Jamie Armstrong, Stephen Carrier, Saul Chaikin, Lee Clements, David Colbert, Paul Harrod, Jonathan Horton, Beth Johnson, Barbara Lawrence, Mary Rose Warner, and Steven Westly.

CONTENTS

APPROACHES TO FILM

THE FILMS

I
APPROACHES TO FILM

The purpose of this book is to suggest guidelines for discussing films without resorting to plot summary, technical jargon or gossip about the "stars." By selecting one hundred films for analysis, I mean to imply a hierarchy of taste, a basis for judgment about Quality in cinema. The ultimate judge is time: if a film can stand up to analysis after twenty years, we may use it as a touchstone to identify aesthetic elements in more recent films. Whether films are old or new, comic or tragic, cinematic masterpieces have certain features in common.

By examining basic principles of film aesthetics, we can ignore fashion and academy awards and identify these features. Although many fine films lack a traditional plot, they do have a *structure*. The "rounded" characters who populate Victorian novels are not necessary either, but all good films have *patterns* of characters that we may discuss as "polarities" or as "webs of relationships." The setting is also very important; it should reflect the inner lives of the characters. The very best filmmakers project their own personal conflicts onto universal characters. Hence, it is often possible to analyze both the structure of a film and its system of characters by alluding to mythological and psychological archetypes. Finally, what is a film but a montage of images and symbols? The images in good films are not merely visual, but visionary. They force us to look into human nature and draw imaginative conclusions about our own motivations. By structuring characters, settings, and symbols, a filmmaker expresses a world-view whether he intends to or not, and it is on this he will eventually be judged as an artist.

I STRUCTURES OF REALITY

The differences between "open" and "closed" structures in dramatic art have been significant since the time of Sophocles. *Oedipus Rex,* for instance, is a typical "closed-structure" play. It has a tightly composed plot—literally a conspiracy involving fate and the hero's tragic flaw, which gradually enmeshes him until any choice he makes will destroy him. In such a closely woven drama, there are no irrelevant incidents or characters. Sophocles thinks that although life may be tragic, it *does* make sense both morally and psychologically because everything is governed by laws of cause and effect. We can see the opposite view of life in the "open-structured" plays of Shakespeare. Writing after the chaotic War of the Roses, Shakespeare yearns for order but finds life too complicated to describe in Aristotelian terms. Hamlet's motivations don't conform to Aristotle's rules; strictly speaking, Shakespeare doesn't organize the play with a plot, but with a loose *narrative* of contrasting episodes building toward a climax. Instead of concentrating on the interaction of three characters, Shakespeare fills his stage with people expressing every possible point of view. As the bodies drop to the stage, he explores all of life's contradictions until truth emerges from the warring philosophies.

The same contrast between Sophoclean *plot* and Shakespearean *narrative* can be seen in the early history of film by comparing two early masters, D.W. Griffith and Sergei Eisenstein, and by tracing their influence on other directors throughout the century. Griffith effectively translated the plot of Victorian melodrama into cinematic terms, inventing nearly every technical and dramatic device used by Hollywood directors today. Though hardly a Sophocles, Griffith could weave a plot that stretched to paranoia in *Birth of a Nation,* a melodrama that implies an intrigue between abolitionists and southern reformers to pollute the "racial purity" of the South. The narrative tradition of Shakespeare finds its way into

---

The continuum of humanity in the Dance of Death that concludes Bergman's *Seventh Seal.* This famous shot also alludes to *The Great Chain of Being,* another medieval metaphor for the structure of reality. (Photo courtesy of Ingmar Bergman.)

the cinema through the work of Eisenstein, the inventor of "montage"—a technique that juxataposes contrasting shots to create dramatic tension. In *Potemkin* he uses montage not merely as a structural device, but as a symbol of the revolution itself. Hence, Eisenstein embodies all the Soviet cliches about revolutionary struggle and the victory of the proletariat as surely as Griffith represents the conservatism and sentimentality of American soap opera. For both directors, structure and content are closely related.

As laughable as most modern audiences find the intellectual content of *Birth of a Nation* and *Potemkin,* anyone sensitive to artistic structures will notice that the greatest directors have followed either Griffith or Eisenstein in composing their films. Americans generally feel more comfortable with closed-structure films: French classics by Renoir, for instance, and the psychological studies of Ingmar Bergman. There are few Americans who dislike Chaplin or Hitchcock, because the intrigue of their tightly woven plots reflects our cultural and political assumptions. Filmgoers with more revolutionary tastes often prefer films that are episodic and open-structured. This is why films originally considered aimless and confusing, like *A Clockwork Orange* and *O Lucky Man,* now gather admirers. The acceptance of open-structured films has also led to recognition of two of the greatest modern directors, Luis Bunuel and Federico Fellini, whose nightmare visions of contemporary life are slowly beginning to look like reality.

STYLE—CLASSIC VS. ROMANTIC

An artist's structure reveals his vision of reality. But within his open or closed structure, a director works in a style that is either Classic or Romantic. Jean Renoir and Ingmar Bergman, for instance, are both "closed-structure" directors whose styles nevertheless express opposing spirits. Renoir, the father of poetic realism, works in a subtle, clean visual style designed *not* to be noticed. Bergman borrows the expressionistic style of Lang and Sternberg, utilizing dramatic visual effects that call attention to themselves—theatrical shadows and sharp contrasts between light and dark, instead of the natural sunlight of Renoir. Renoir uses the *scene* as his unit of composition, rather than the *shot.* His films depend on naturalistic acting, and he considers acting important in itself. Bergman, on the other hand, relies on camera-work and editing to achieve his dramatic effects. The acting in Bergman's films

The child-wife climbs onto Daddy's knee in Bergman's Oedipal comedy, *Smiles of a Summer Night*. (Photo courtesy of Ingmar Bergman.)

tends to be stiff and choreographed, for his actors serve mainly as symbols of his own self-absorbed, Romantic consciousness. Renoir's smooth, Classic style assumes a basic order in the world, a natural rhythm that will emerge with the disappearance of the "Grand Illusions" of the weak, corrupt aristocrats who regard war as a game and life as just another rabbit hunt. Bergman is not so optimistic. In his mystical, guilt-ridden depictions of persecuted artists, he finds evil in the structure of the universe itself, reflected in the indifference of the human soul.

This philosophical and stylistic contrast is clear even when Bergman imitates Renoir's *Rules of the Game* in one of his rare comedies, *Smiles of a Summer Night*. Both films offer us a comic version of an Oedipal triangle—a young hero competing with an older sophisticated aristocrat for the love of his young wife. Both directors refer constantly to eighteenth century music and the "comedy of manners" to stress the shallowness of modern society, while sympathizing with the feelings of the naive young lover. The difference is that Renoir is concerned primarily with social questions like the death of individualism and the decay of the forces that supposedly govern us. Uninterested in social issues, Bergman conceives of this same Oedipal triangle as a religious allegory. His father-figure represents God—a cheerfully cynical god who thinks he's in control, but really isn't. His artistic young son suffers from guilt and masochistic passion unimaginable in the Classic characters of Renoir. Bergman communicates all this irony and anguish with melodramatic camera-work, lingering on reflections in mirrors and mud-puddles, and punctuating the civilized comic dialogue with flashes of Romantic anger.

As Renoir's successor as the Sophocles of the cinema, Bergman occupies the opposite end of the cinematic spectrum from Federico Fellini, whose style is Shakespearean and open-structured. Like Shakespeare, Fellini tries to "get everything in." His anti-hero in *La Dolce Vita* wanders through the same chaos as Shakespeare's warriors in the War of the Roses. His Hamlet—an indecisive filmmaker in *8½*—ponders the meaning of his life, dreaming restlessly of his mother and of the women who have taken her place. His Othello is Zampano, the circus strongman in *La Strada,* whose violence and jealousy drive his delicate mistress into insanity.

That Bergman and Fellini are opposites is clear when we compare their most similar films. Bergman's "circus" film, *Sawdust and Tinsel,* released just before *La Strada,* resembles it in several ways. The main characters in both films, Albert and Zampano, are macho strongmen with dependent mistresses. Both films focus on a love triangle; both explore the artist's relationship with society; both are self-parodies, revealing the director's own doubts about the importance of his art. But although Bergman and Fellini use the same metaphor to express their vision of reality, they work in opposite artistic traditions, and they are concerned with different questions.

Bergman's circus is the human heart. He has inherited the Romantic, claustrophobic world of August Strindberg, whose famous play *Miss Julie* dissects the love-hate relationships that Bergman has carried to such an extreme in recent films like *Cries and Whispers* and *Autumn Sonata*. Bergman uses self-lacerating loves exactly as Strindberg does: to reflect the relationship of Man and God. Although Fellini also draws religious parallels in *La Strada* by juxtaposing circus parades and religious processions, his intent is mainly social, Classical, and neo-realist. His characters are frigid rather than tormented, and it is their *society* that is the circus, not their hearts. Instead of concentrating on the emotional intrigue of his characters, Fellini depicts them as stunned observers of their fragmented culture. They drive from town to town, occasionally glimpsing reality between their tired performances, but Zampano refuses to think about the meaning of his life and Gelsomina is too fragile to bear this knowledge alone.

Fellini records Zampano and Gelsomina's wanderings like a Classical satirist—that is, without any regard for plot. He adopts the picaresque structure of *Don Quixote*, focusing on each incident for its own sake, accumulating symbols and ironies until the audience is finally overwhelmed by the truth of his vision. Avoiding Bergman's melodramatic coincidences, Fellini follows the neo-realist tradition of depicting people's lives as they really are. Not as theatrical and articulate as Bergman's characters, Zampano and Gelsomina grope for words, try to understand each other, and fail. Their life together is a hopeless circle full of anti-climaxes. Gelsomina's death remains hidden from Zampano until several years after he abandons her. And even then, the meaning of his loss eludes him until he finds himself on the beach, alone in the darkness.

CINEMATIC STRUCTURE

SOPHOCLEAN
CLOSED STRUCTURE
(PLOT)

SHAKESPEAREAN
OPEN STRUCTURE
(NARRATIVE)

D.W. GRIFFITH

CLASSICAL STYLE	ROMANTIC STYLE

Charles
Chaplin

EXPRESSIONISM
Josef Sternberg
Fritz Lang
F.W. Murnau

The Blue Angel

SERGEI EISENSTEIN

CLASSICAL STYLE	ROMANTIC STYLE

Carl Dreyer
*The Passion
of
Joan of Arc*

Un Chien Andalou

Alfred
Hitchcock

CLASSIC
FRENCH CINEMA:
Jean Renoir

Orson Welles
Citizen Kane

ITALIAN
NEO REALISM

KUROSAWA	BERGMAN	FELLINI	BUNUEL

PERSONAE

There is an apocryphal story that when Fellini and his wife, Giulietta Massina, saw *La Strada* together for the first time, he wept and asked her forgiveness. Some critics do, in fact, see Zampano as a self-parody of Fellini. There is also a strong temptation among filmgoers to think that actors really *are* the roles they play, just as many readers assume that the narrator in a novel speaks for the author. This is a mistaken notion. In both novels and films the characters are *personae,* various *masks* an artist uses to project his own conflicts. Hence, Fellini is only *part* Zampano; the Fool and Gelsomina also represent facets of this very complicated man.

Although it's entertaining to speculate about "who represents whom" in our favorite films, this is not interpretation. The function of film criticism is not to gossip about personalities, but to detect patterns of characterization that occur in film-art in general. Some filmmakers define characters in terms of "polarities;" others are concerned with "webs of relationships." These two approaches to characterization reveal completely different attitudes toward life.

Artists who think of characters as polarities, as pairs of opposites with an occasional catalyst included to complete the triangle, regard life as a balance of forces. This is the view of Greek tragedy, with its conflict between Apollo and Dionysus, and of all Classical theatre from Moliere through Ibsen and Shaw. Even Romantic directors like Ingmar Bergman see life in terms of polarities, and some picaresque novels and films, such as *Don Quixote* and *The Seventh Seal,* hang together by focusing on the basic contrast between Knight and Squire. The idea that life is a balance between soul and body, intellect and emotion, idealism and practicality, is also the theme of Sherlock Holmes movies like *They Might Be Giants* and of Jekyll-Hyde films like *The Ruling Class.*

Perhaps the most significant character relationship based on polarities is what Walt Disney calls "The Lady and the Tramp." If we compare *The African Queen, A Streetcar Named Desire, The Taming of the Shrew,* and *Swept Away,* we can detect a shift in attitude toward what it means to be a Man or a Woman. *The African Queen* satirizes the idea that a "real man" is dirty and crude and drinks a lot, while a woman is "above all that." Her job is to read her bible, keep the boat tidy, and "civilize" the man so he won't drink quite so much gin. *A Streetcar Named Desire* shatters this traditional ideal by showing that Blanche Dubois' inability to reconcile sex and spirituality have driven her crazy. What is

Persona: Ingmar Bergman frequently projects the conflicting sides of his own nature onto female characters. (Photo courtesy of Ingmar Bergman.)

charming eccentricity in Katherine Hepburn becomes neurosis in Vivien Leigh when she can't admit to herself that Stanley Kowalski's animal sexuality is what she really wants.

Since the sexual liberation of the sixties, "The Lady and the Tramp" have continued to battle—although the Lady is no longer so pristine and repressed. The fight becomes more savage with Zeffirelli's *Taming of the Shrew,* in which Shakespeare's heroine is very much a feminist, terrorizing all the passive men who surround her. Katherine the Shrew is the direct ancestor of Raffaela in Lina Wertmuller's *Swept Away,* a brilliant allegory about a rich lady and a communist sailor who are marooned on a desert island. The point of both films is that a woman who is power-hungry and loves to fight can only be happy with a man who beats her into submission. If this is true, the "Lady-Tramp" polarity will not disappear merely because modern women are "liberated."

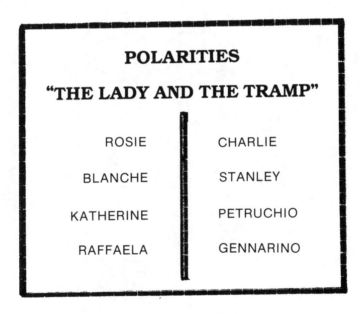

POLARITIES

"THE LADY AND THE TRAMP"

ROSIE	CHARLIE
BLANCHE	STANLEY
KATHERINE	PETRUCHIO
RAFFAELA	GENNARINO

Of course, not all filmmakers see life as a pattern of polarized conflicts. Since the sixties, Fellini and many other directors have made open-structured films that concentrate on a single character

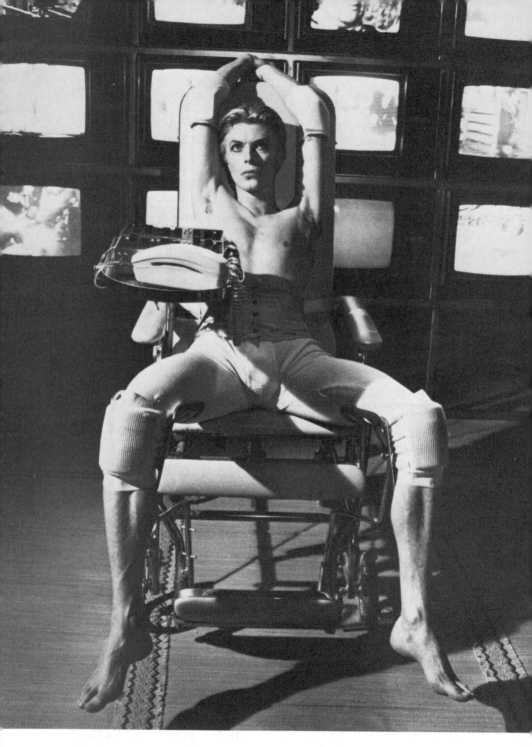

David Bowie as a "media-made man" in Nicholas Roeg's *Man Who Fell To Earth*. (Photo courtesy of Cinema 5.)

and his wanderings. After *La Strada*, the typical Fellini *persona* becomes a "blank," a victim who gets entangled in webs of relationships over which he has no control. In *La Dolce Vita*, a young newspaperman bounces around from woman to woman, each of whom reveals a different aspect of his shallowness. Marcello's parasitic relationships with Emma, Maddalena, and Sylvia reflect the corrupt society on which he feeds. There is also a fourth lady, an innocent young girl dressed in white, who calls to him on the beach while the tide rushes between them, drowning out her words. He turns away from her to inspect a grotesque sting-ray that has been washed up on the shore—a mirror image of his inner life.

The isolated grotesque becomes a whole parade in Fellini's *8½* and *Juliet of the Spirits*. In *8½*, Guido is so empty and confused, one wonders how he could have become a famous director in the first place. Juliet has a more serious problem: her environment is such a circus, she can no longer distinguish fantasy from reality. In Fellini's more recent films, like *Satyricon* and *Casanova,* the fantasies of his wanderers become so intense that even the audience feels like it's trapped in some unpleasant hallucination. By making Casanova himself grotesque, Fellini forces *us* to be his anti-heroic observers.

Fellini's blank *personae*, blundering through the circus of life, have influenced younger filmmakers enormously. In Mike Nichols' *The Graduate,* Dustin Hoffman plays a glazed young man who zombies his way from mother to daughter without thinking too much about what it all means. Bertolucci's *Conformist* is about a man who will do anything to fit in, even murder his teacher to please his fascist friends. David Bowie, Nicholas Roeg's *Man Who Fell To Earth,* drops like an apple from the tree of knowledge. By the time "Mr. Newton has had enough," he too is just another passive victim, daydreaming about a lost wife who has long since started over.

In all these films, the *persona* is a passive observer, the reflectionless shadow of his society. He is very different from the polarized heroes of *African Queen* and *Swept Away,* characters who possess values and a central core of identity. A filmmaker who characterizes in "polarities" usually believes that people create their society, or at least rebel against it. His characters *act,* for better or worse. Characterizing in "webs of relationships" implies a different concept of human nature. Insisting that society has absorbed any individuality we might have had, Fellini and his followers depict modern man as a voyeur surrounded by freaks. Like Woody Allen in *Play It Again Sam* or Peter Sellers in *Being There,* the modern anti-hero has no identity—he only has an *image.*

2 DREAMSCAPES

To locate the site of the action, nearly every commercial film begins with an "establishing shot"—usually right out of the can. Hollywood film libraries stock helicopter shots of New York and San Francisco specifically for this purpose. In any good film, however, the setting should relate directly to the inner lives of the characters. The best illustration of this idea is the opening sequence from *Citizen Kane,* in which a dark castle contrasts with a parabolic slow-motion shot of a glass ball rolling from Kane's hand and shattering on the steps. The castle represents Kane's ego and his worldly accomplishments. The glass ball, a crystal circle of perfection enclosing a tiny cabin shrouded in snow, symbolizes Kane's soul—something he lost when his mother sent him away to become rich and famous. As he whispers "Rosebud" and dies, Kane realizes that his castle is a poor substitute for the cabin of his childhood, and that the climb to power isn't worth a single sleigh ride.

METAPHORS OF EXPERIENCE:

Kane's childhood image provides a key to understanding the two approaches filmmakers take to the inner world. According to Freud, "the child is father to the man." From early childhood, every person establishes a basic pattern of perception and behavior, which he then repeats continually throughout his life. Consciously or not, an intelligent child discovers early that he can "conduct" his life, or that he can "paint" it. As he gets older, he may even shape his life like a symphony or a miniature medieval painting. To use two ancient metaphors, he may picture his ideal as a *rainbow* or as a *circle of perfection.*

Inner landscape in *The Cabinet of Doctor Caligari.*

The differences between the two metaphors are significant. A composer/conductor like Beethoven strings out rainbows of harmony in the Ninth Symphony. Beethoven creates a splendid edifice *outside* of himself. As he generates musical rainbows, he takes a godlike stance, observing his macrocosm. The listener either appreciates the harmonic structure, or he doesn't. This is rather different from the "circle of perfection," which recalls medieval painters creating tiny enclosed worlds full of meticulous details. The fifteenth century painter Jan Van Eyck puts himself in the heart of his artistic microcosm by reflecting his image in a round mirror in the very center of the "Arnolfini Wedding." He takes a vulnerable stance, inviting the participation of the viewer in his small but perfect world, which is a projection of his own inwardness.

By the same analogy, some filmmakers *conduct* their dreamscapes in an elaborate counterpoint between inner and outer worlds. Others explore from the inside-out, like medieval miniaturists focusing on the circle of perfection. Akira Kurosawa stands apart from his characters, whom he depicts objectively, framed against a visionary landscape to which their souls correspond. The opposite tendency—exemplified by Ingmar Bergman—is to begin with the soul and redefine space and time from the perspective of the microcosm. The distinction between "objective" and "subjective" approaches to the dreamscape will be clear if we compare two groups of films that develop the concept of "Lost Eden."

COUNTERPOINT:

A director who visualizes the dreamscape in musical terms—as "counterpoint"—would agree with Lawrence Durrell's statement that we are the "children of our landscape." It forms us to the degree that we're responsive to it. This is the theme of Nicholas Roeg's beautiful film *Walkabout,* which describes the encounter between two protected white schoolchildren and a young aborigine who leads them to safety across the Australian desert. Although the white children wear the uniforms of their strict private schools, and are presumably well-educated, inwardly they are as barren emotionally as the desert in which they are lost. They survive only because the aborigine finds them lying half-conscious beside a dried oasis, a setting that effectively symbolizes their souls. In a parallel setting later in the film, the three young people swim nude in a beautiful jungle pool. The girl is curiously unmoved by this experience and oblivious to the aborigine's love for her—until years later. While her husband chatters about business, she absently reflects on her "land of lost content."

Loss of Eden—and of a corresponding inner paradise—is also the theme of Terrence Malick's *Days of Heaven.* Malick's settings shimmer in the same blinding light as paintings by Edward Hopper. Like Hopper's couples, Malick's young migrant workers don't relate to each other and fail to notice the beauty that surrounds them. Richard Gere, whose face is as pretty as the landscape, is nevertheless completely cold inside. He pushes his girlfriend into a marriage with a rich young farmer, who will presumably die soon from some unnamed disease. The farmer does not die, however, and hell breaks loose in Eden with a swarm of locusts and a firestorm that mirror the repressed passions of the three main characters.

"Some say the world will end in fire, some say in ice." More likely, suggests Satyajit Ray, we will eventually die of famine as all the food is taken to feed the world's armies. Ray's film *Distant Thunder,* set during the man-made famine of 1943, emphasizes the irony of five million people starving to death in a landscape so fertile and beautiful. The embodiments of this heavenly landscape are a young brahmin and his angelic wife, symbolized by two orange butterflies nestling together on a sea of caked mud. In the beginning of the film, the brahmin is very much like the migrant worker in *Days of Heaven*—selfish, calculating, and insensitive to the feelings of others. Because he's a brahmin, he thinks he's better than his poorer neighbors. Through the influence of his wife, however, he grows toward an eventual identification with his people and his land.

In general, oriental films emphasize this kind of identification. Unlike western civilizations, which strive to conquer nature, oriental cultures have always stressed the symbiotic relation between man and his environment. The union of man and nature is the theme of *Dersu Uzala,* Kurosawa's exploration of the relationship of two men whose lives symbolize east and west, old and new, nature and civilization. The film's frame is set during the early years of this century, when the old ideal of "living off the land" has already died. Not only has it died—its remains can't even be found. As the Russian captain searches for the grave of his friend Dersu in what used to be a forest, he can find nothing but an enormous stump—a powerful symbol that moves him to reflect on the meaning of their friendship. The unsentimental flashback that follows astonishes us with one brilliant image after another. The most striking is a shot of

A premonition of death in Kurosawa's *Dersu Uzala:* Dersu the Hunter caught in the rapids, symbol of the onrush of civilization that dooms his way of life. (Photo courtesy of New World Pictures.)

the two men standing on the edge of a vast wilderness, with the sun on one side of the sky and the moon on the other. They stand in silence, for they have come face to face with themselves. The sun and the moon symbolize the polarity in the relationship of the rational young captain and Dersu the hunter, who represents the unconscious world of myth.

THE MICROCOSM:

Not all filmmakers agree that man is merely an extension of his landscape, or that human consciousness is subordinate to environment. For this second group of visionaries, who begin with the microcosm and work outward, the main purpose of film is to externalize our inner worlds, to redefine space and time as we experience them unconsciously. The first major film to create this kind of subjective dreamscape was *The Cabinet of Doctor Caligari*, in which the distorted setting finally makes "sense" as a projection of the hero's fevered imagination. By the end of the film, however, we have long since identified with the hero's view of reality, and the final reversal does not calm our unconscious fear that the director of the asylum may indeed be the real lunatic. During the reign of Kaiser Wilhelm—just before the rise of Hitler—this is not an altogether absurd idea. The paradox of *Caligari*, and of German Expressionism in general, is that the visual distortions actually reflect a malady of soul in the national consciousness.

A more recent example of inner landscape is Ingmar Bergman's *Cries and Whispers*, which begins with an expressionistic setting in a *red room*. Why a red room? Bergman may have been thinking of Poe's "Masque of the Red Death." His film also relates emotionally to Edvard Munch's painting "Virginia Creeper," which depicts several anxious figures over whom hovers a breathing house, smothered by a menacing red stain. Like Munch, the central character in *Cries and Whispers* suffers from tuberculosis, and the red room makes us feel like we're living inside her lung. This is not actually the organ in question, however. Bergman's "Lost Eden" is the soul—or the womb. He once said that in his dreams he conceived of the soul as a "moist red membrane." And the film's most vivid image is of the heroine's sister mutilating herself sexually with a piece of broken wine glass, declaring, "It's just a tissue of lies." If *The Cabinet of Doctor Caligari* is about a lost paradise of the mind, Bergman's red room in *Cries and Whispers* symbolizes a loss that is even more primal.

What Bergman does to our sense of space, Alain Resnais does to our sense of time. His films are ironic renderings of the medieval "circle of perfection," in which dreamlike characters wander lost in an eternal present. In *Hiroshima Mon Amour,* Resnais' heroine experiences this microcosmic sense of time for a split second when she looks at the twitching hand of her sleeping Japanese lover, and he suddenly transforms under her gaze into her young German who had been killed by the French Resistance twenty years before. From that moment, she finds herself adrift in time, unable to think of her two lovers as different men. As both Proust and Joyce have shown, this is not a unique experience. The mere taste of a tea-cake was enough to shock the hypersensitive Proust into a hallucinatory memory of his youth. In Joyce's *Portrait of the Artist,* the "stream of consciousness" pulls Stephen Dedalus back and forth in time during the course of a muddy football game. Nor does one have to be Proust or Joyce to experience this relativistic sense of time. We all do it regularly in our dreams, and it is the truth of dream-time that makes films like *Hiroshima Mon Amour* so powerful.

Since the release of *Hiroshima Mon Amour* in 1959, atomic physicists have corroborated Einstein's relativistic view of time, demonstrating that a positron (for instance) is merely an electron going *backwards* in time. That this concept should find its way into several recent films is not surprising, since cinema is concerned in a very basic way with the nature of time—with its repetition, expansion, and condensation through editing. Philosophically, the possibility of exploring the dreamscape in terms of *time* as well as space is therefore only one step away, a step taken very boldly in *Catch-22* and *Slaughterhouse Five.* Yossarian, the crazed bomber pilot of *Catch-22,* has the impression that his life is one big circle of carnage. Billy Pilgrim in *Slaughterhouse Five* is less fortunate in that he can't stop the world and get off. Every time he opens his eyes or steps through a door, he has no idea whether he will emerge in the past, present, or future. If we look out the window of our "Yellow Submarine," we can even wave to ourselves as we watch our doubles in the world of anti-matter plunge into the past.

The Beatles to the contrary, an artist's journey through inner space is often frightening. Unlike the Hollywood Dream Machine, serious filmmakers explore their dreamscapes to discover what has gone *wrong* with the metaphors of our experience. What has happened to the American pursuit of the Rainbow? Why has the world become a Circle of *Im*perfection—a Global Ghetto, rather than the Global Village predicted by Marshall McLuhan?

Visionaries like Kurosawa and Bergman deal with these questions as opposite human problems. A composer-artist "objectively" portraying man in his environment as a rainbow of harmonies must cope with the dissonance of the modern world. Like the conductor in Fellini's *Orchestra Rehearsal,* he starts from the standpoint of his own alienation. A "subjective" artist, on the other hand, is prone to the paranoia that afflicts Franz Kafka and Francis Bacon, and other great meditative writers and painters. Like Roman Polanski in *The Tenant,* his constant temptation is to hurl himself, soul first, from a sixth floor window. To find positive answers to the twin problems of alienation and paranoia, we must approach film from a different perspective: as myth.

3 MYTHOLOGIES

Scientists and children often regard myths as mere fairy tales, amusing stories concocted by primitive people ignorant of worldly "facts" commonly known by any graduate of one of our modern diploma mills. Some film critics also use the word "myth" to describe the stereotypes in westerns and space fantasies, implying that the characters in *Shane* and *Star Wars* are unreal. This is a naive argument, however, since no film is "real." Neo-realist films like *The Bicycle Thief* use characters as symbols, and even documentaries are edited to convince us of some particular vision of human nature.

One of the main purposes of cinema is to present us with alternative self-images, based on ideal models. Consequently, all films may be studied as "myths." Stripped of details, the most naturalistic films repeat situations and characters that are *archetypal,* descended from ancient sources in Greek drama and medieval romance. Even in "low-life" films of the fifties, the setting for *A Streetcar Named Desire* is the "Elysian Fields," and the adventures of Bogart and Hepburn in *The African Queen* echo those of Odysseus. So do the exotic wanderings of James Bond, whose name-brand accessories ironically mimic Homer's epic catalogues. Note also that Bond's nemesis Goldfinger is a modern King Midas, while the other villains and goons who threaten him are like the monsters of myth and romance. The medieval Faust legend has inspired films as different as *Bedazzled* and *Phantom of the Paradise.* The modern search for identity is also basically medieval, with Peter Fonda and Dennis Hopper in *Easy Rider* fitfully resurrecting Galahad, Parsifal, and Don Quixote. Several critics have pointed out that the *Star Wars* saga alludes to the Arthurian legends. And the "liberated woman" so popular in recent films used to be known (in less "enlightened" times) as the "unwomanly woman." Her ancestors include Hedda Gabler and Lady MacBeth,

The Woman in White: Symbol of the poetic imagination in Fellini's *8½*. (Photo courtesy of Corinth Films.)

as well as Medea, Antigone, and Clytemnestra. There seem to be no new myths, just variations on old ones.

Modern filmmakers, like medieval scribes and Greek poets, do not regard their myths as *lies*. Medieval romance was a civilizing force, intended to provide moral patterns of behavior for knights who were more violent and barbaric than the crudest western outlaws. The Greeks, inhabiting a more sophisticated and relativistic world, thought of myths as models for psychological understanding. Unlike modern scientists, they were not particularly interested in external facts—only in inner truths. This is also the key to understanding cinematic myth-makers like Bergman and Fellini, whose fantasies reflect eternal problems.

APOLLO AND DIONYSUS:

In Greek mythology, the polarity between Apollo and Dionysus represents the most basic division in human psychology, the schism between reason and emotion. With Apollonian sunlight we associate abstract qualities like rationality and idealism, as opposed to the earthier passions generated by the wine of Dionysus. This contrast may recall the "Platonic split"—Plato's idea that the soul is good and the body evil—an idea that also infiltrates Christianity during the century after the crucifixion. But the older myth-makers differ from the Platonic/Christian view in considering Dionysus an important, positive force. He provides an earthy balance for the intellect, which would otherwise become sterile and neurotic.

One of the best films to explore the psychological problems involved in "balancing one's gods" is *Zorba the Greek,* based on the novel by Nikos Kazantzakis. The novel describes the most basic problem confronting us today, the dissociation of mind and feelings. We are so appalled by our primitive or passionate impulses that instead of confronting them directly we project them as "devils"— and then spend enormous amounts of time and money seeking priests, psychotherapists, or politicians who can exorcise them. It would be healthier, Kazantzakis thinks, for us to learn to *dance* with our devils, sublimating them in Dionysian ritual. This is what his young hero (known only as "The Boss") learns in the course of the film. In the beginning, however, he is alienated from his emotions. The Boss is a pure Apollonian, a man whose blood is "very snow broth." His intellect has left him frozen in space, incapable of relating to other people on the simplest emotional level. Not until his

Anthony Quinn in *Zorba the Greek* taking a Dionysian bite out of life. (Photo courtesy of Twentieth Century Fox.)

whole life has fallen apart does the young man thaw enough to see the wisdom of joining Zorba in his Cosmic Dance.

THE MADONNA AND THE MEDUSA:

Mythical polarities are not always positive ways of seeing human nature. Jung points out that in many cultures, women are pictured as extremes: as Virgin Mary, the idealistic all-nourishing mother-figure—or as the snaky-haired temptress who coldly uses sex to dominate men, drain them of their strength, and destroy them. The contrast is especially common in nineteenth century novels, Hollywood movies, and TV soap operas.

What is the source of this recurrent myth? Why do so many young men grow up thinking of women in extreme terms? Jung provides an answer by suggesting that every man has a female side, a "woman within" called the *anima* whom he must learn to accept. If a man rejects the qualities he has inherited from his mother, projecting them outward as alien to his self, he will fail to treat women as people. This failure, which expresses itself in alternating feelings of adoration and detestation, leads to self-destruction.

The best illustration of Jung's theory is *The Blue Angel,* a classic film about a high school teacher who is destroyed by the passion he has repressed all his life. Although Marlene Dietrich, as Lola-Lola, is an archetypal temptress, it is more accurate to see her as Dr. Rath's "anima"—the projection of unconscious lust that he hypocritically condemns in his students. Because he is so naive about women and so rigidly Teutonic in his moral attitudes, he has no understanding of her world. Paradoxically, since he hates what she represents, he "loves" her. Like most tragic heroes, he is self-deluded.

The same confusion, Jung says, awaits any woman who cannot acknowledge her *animus,* the male component of her psyche. This is the basic situation in Jean Cocteau's surreal fantasy *Beauty and the Beast.* As every child knows, the Beast falls hopelessly in love with Beauty, who finds it impossible to return his love—not merely because he looks so repulsive, but because she is deeply attached to the platonic love of her father. Only when Beauty learns to love the goodness hidden beneath the Beast's wild appearance does she outgrow her childlike dependence on her father and transform her savage dream-lover into a handsome prince.

Richard Pryor would say it bites . . . Marlene Dietrich as the Jungian
"anima" in Sternberg's *Blonde Venus*. (Photo courtesy of Swank
Films.)

ALLEGORY: THE GOSPEL OF KONG— ACCORDING TO JUNG, FREUD, AND MARX:

An even more powerful depiction of a woman in the grip of her *animus* is the classic American film *King Kong*. Made in 1933, the original film is a monument, an accidental work of genius understood *least* by the Hollywood hacks who directed and starred in it. Merian Cooper's macho persona, Carl Denham, wants to make a film reinterpreting the myth of Beauty and the Beast. His idea is that a Real Man—who naturally hates women—will become completely enslaved at the mere sight of superficial physical beauty. This is exactly what happens, not only to the film's conventional hero, but also to Kong, who represents the kind of animalistic passion that Cooper regards as evil. Cooper and his director, Ernest Schoedsack, even cast themselves as the "heroic" pilot and machine-gunner who blast Kong off the top of the Empire State Building.

Fortunately, a work of art often maintains a life of its own in spite of the limitations of its creators. *King Kong*'s power derives from the ironic gap between what it intends to say and what it actually tells us about ourselves, both psychologically and socially. Instead of admiring the director and the hero, audiences have always related more to the figure of Kong himself, who represents our deepest feelings.

Kong may even express what Jung calls the "collective unconscious" of American life. Jung thinks that when we dream, we all inhabit the same place—a surreal landscape in which we share common symbols, passions, and fears—another world governed by laws different from those in our waking life. His point is that we share this other world *collectively,* not only with each other but with everyone who has ever lived. One of these shared images is a dark godlike creature who fights fierce monsters and smashes through bolted gates to reach the lady he loves. When Kong climbs the Empire State Building with Fay Wray in his hand, he transcends the thirties and becomes eternal. His passion is Promethean—nobler and more admirable than the sentimental love offered by the film's conventional human hero. Kong represents the raw, primitive power that many people find frightful and attractive, and it is the nightmarish quality of his love that makes him so real. When he reaches through Fay Wray's window and draws her to him, bed and all, it is as though her *animus*—the dreamlike man within—is forcing her to acknowledge his existence within her own heart. But unlike Cocteau's Beauty, who finally accepts her *animus,* Fay Wray can do nothing but shriek when confronted by the projection of her own animal passions.

Aside from symbolizing the savage power of love, Kong unintentionally reflects many unconscious American values and fears. The Empire State Building epitomizes our culture's obsession with phallic dominance—our belief that we must conquer the earth with our technology and build childlike towers to celebrate our national ego. The film is also so full of warlike sentiments and racist stereotypes that one need not be a Marxist to conclude that Kong's fall symbolizes the fate of the Black man in America. And when the director declares, "He's always been king of his world, but we'll teach him fear," there is no sign that Merian Cooper sympathizes with this fate.

The following diagram is useful in discussing *King Kong* as a three-leveled allegory:

KING KONG

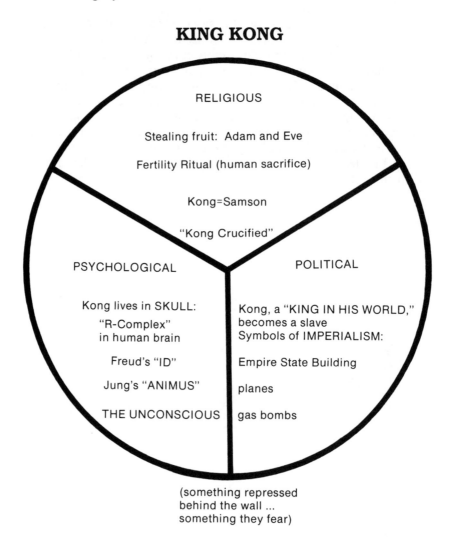

RELIGIOUS

Stealing fruit: Adam and Eve

Fertility Ritual (human sacrifice)

Kong=Samson

"Kong Crucified"

PSYCHOLOGICAL

Kong lives in SKULL:
"R-Complex"
in human brain

Freud's "ID"

Jung's "ANIMUS"

THE UNCONSCIOUS

POLITICAL

Kong, a "KING IN HIS WORLD,"
becomes a slave
Symbols of IMPERIALISM:

Empire State Building

planes

gas bombs

(something repressed
behind the wall ...
something they fear)

Aside from *King Kong* and the beautiful fantasy by Jean Cocteau, three other films that deal with the "Beauty/Beast" archetype may also be analyzed as allegories: *Morgan, Walkabout,* and *Phantom of the Paradise.*

Isabelle Adjani and Klaus Kinski in *Nosferatu*. Werner Herzog's mystical allegory portrays Dracula as a lonely, alienated Beast who longs for death. (Photo courtesy of Twentieth Century Fox.)

4 PROJECTIONS

By its very nature, cinema is a *cubist* medium that examines reality from several conflicting points of view. A filmmaker who understands this principle will often project his own conflicts onto several characters. If he is honest with himself, he will make it very difficult for his audience to determine where reality lies.

The masterpiece of philosophical ambiguity is Akira Kurosawa's *Rashomon,* in which we are asked to compare several wildly conflicting versions of an incident involving rape and murder. All we know for certain is that a bandit led a samurai and his wife into a trap, tying up the man and raping the woman. After that, the samurai is stabbed to death—by whom, it is difficult to say. According to the bandit, he killed the husband in a furious battle after the wife insisted that they fight for her love. The wife, on the other hand, claims that *she* killed her husband in a "fit of insanity" after he refused to kill her to expiate her disgrace. Through a medium, the husband's ghost declares that he killed *himself* after his wife's disgraceful conduct with the bandit. That leaves the only "objective" witness, the woodcutter, who observed the entire scene from hiding. He describes a clumsy, cowardly fight between the two men, ending with the bandit stabbing the samurai as he lies defenseless in the bushes. The only problem with this story is that the woodcutter is lying also—to hide the fact that he took the woman's pearl-handled dagger. Where does truth lie? Anyone who thinks he knows has been tricked by Kurosawa into projecting his own values onto the witnesses.

THE ETERNAL FOUR:

A director can create convincing characters only by projecting a genuine part of his own nature onto each of them. Is there a

---

It's difficult to predict the future, in film or in life . . . Those who believe that "the Force is with us" should bear in mind the warning of Emperor Ming in *Flash Gordon:* "The universe is *not* what we imagine." In fact, it's probably the opposite of what we imagine. (Photo courtesy of Swank Films and Universal 16.)

Toshiro Mifune and Machiko Kyo represent the Body and the Heart in *Rashomon*, Akira Kurosawa's exploration of the nature of Truth. (Photo courtesy of Janus Films.)

universal pattern in these projections? There are several possibilities. We have already seen how important polarities are in the world of film. In *Rashomon,* it appears that the samurai and the bandit are polar opposites. On closer inspection, however, it is clear that the real conflict is between husband and wife, with the bandit acting merely as a catalyst.

This suggests the possibility of understanding *Rashomon* as a sexual triangle, analyzing it according to Freud's division of the personality into *ego, id,* and *superego.* Indeed, there are strong religious and psychological reasons for westerners to think in "threes," and some of our finest love films are based on triangles— notably Truffaut's *Jules and Jim* and Fellini's *La Strada.* The problem is that *Rashomon* is not a love film, and that this interpretation ignores the importance of the woodcutter, whose redemption at the end is the point of the film. Besides, *Rashomon* is oriental, not western, and the most important number in oriental philosophy is not three, but *four*—the number that reflects the elements and the seasons.

The number *four* is also buried deep in western consciousness, emerging occasionally in Yeats' cyclical theory of history and in Plato's concept of the human psyche. Before Plato, as William Irwin Thompson has pointed out, the "eternal four" may be rooted in primitive anthropology. In John Marshall's film *The Hunters,* a primitive hunting party consists of Headman, Hunter, Shaman, and Clown—four highly symbolic characters who (Thompson claims) prefigure the structure of modern civilization. By a leap of the imagination, we may see that the four men have evolved into the government, the military, the university, and the media. Whether or not the reader accepts this analogy, it is far more significant to speculate about why these four particular men would have been chosen to form the hunting party in the first place. One possible reason, according to Jung, is that they represent the four aspects of the human personality, and thus can act together as a "whole man."

It is Jung's analysis of the personality, rather than Freud's, that reflects the structure of *Rashomon*—and possibly of the sound era of film as a whole. The important difference between the two psychologists is that Jung adds a fourth element to Freud's three-part model of the psyche: the concept of *self* as an entity separate from Freud's rational *ego.* This "self" is the equivalent of Plato's "soul," the existence of which Freud would strenuously deny. Freud claims that the mind *is* the self. Jung takes a more spiritual view of the personality, insisting that mere rationality is insufficient to cope with reality. Without arguing about the truth of these conflicting

RASHOMON

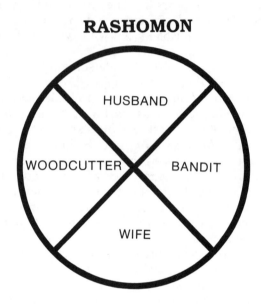

PLATO   JUNG

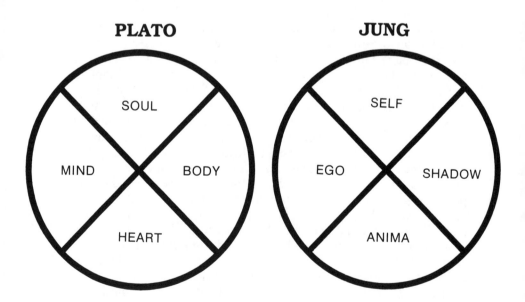

models, we may see that Jung and Plato are more applicable to the pattern of projections in *Rashomon* if we compare the adjacent diagram. In Platonic terms, the husband's *soul* testifies, since he himself is dead. His wife is driven exclusively by her emotions. The bandit, who scratches himself constantly and carries on like a baboon, is entirely physical. And the woodcutter's "objective" testimony supposedly symbolizes human reason. But also note that each diagram suggests *two* polar relationships that intersect and conflict. Jung would say that the husband and wife represent each other's *animus* and *anima,* respectively. The woodcutter falsely expresses the voice of "reason," denying his own ulterior motives, which are embodied in his "shadow," the bandit. For is he not also a thief?

A THEORY OF MODES:

The following theory, which is strongly influenced by Northrop Frye, is unabashedly Jungian. I present such an elaborate scheme knowing well that it does not account for *every* film in any particular period. Granting hundreds of exceptions—including some films that are totally unique, and others that are ahead of their time—I merely offer this model as a means of categorizing the *general tone* of each decade. During the sound era, the film medium itself—like *Rashomon*—has evolved through four distinct modes or *phases:*

```
(1) MYTHICAL (1930s)
(2) ROMANTIC (1940s)
(3) INTELLECTUAL (1950s)
(4) POLITICAL (1960s)
```

Curiously, these phases correspond to Jung's model of the human personality. The thirties, in both Germany and the United States, revealed the film industry's "shadow" and its compulsion to generate soothing myths. The heart, at peace and at war, was the main theme of the forties. The silent generation of the fifties retreated into existentialism and intellectual alienation. And political revolt, associated with a new emphasis on finding the Self, characterized the most important films of the sixties. These are broad generalizations, of course, but the weight of evidence suggests a cycle we should consider.

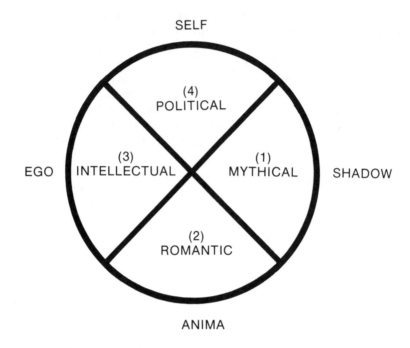

(1) THE MYTHICAL PHASE:

In the thirties, largely because of the Depression, cinema entered its "Mythical" phase. *King Kong* was made by men who were literally afraid of their own "shadow." In westerns like John Ford's *Stagecoach* and in countless Tarzan movies, the Good Guys cheerfully blew away the evil natives with bravado that would impress any medieval knight. At the same time, Superman was born, and Walt Disney emerged as America's main mythmaker, expressing our unspoken values in films like *Snow White* and *Pinocchio*. In *Modern Times,* Charles Chaplin and Paulette Goddard defined the American Dream: a simple cottage, and fruit falling from the trees.

But the film that best expresses the American myth of the search for the rainbow is *The Wizard of Oz.* This brilliant film is full of mythical absolutes, with the Wizard symbolizing both Big Government and Nietzsche's "Dead God," and with pairings of good and evil witches as in medieval morality plays. Most important, Judy Garland (as Dorothy) represents the thirties concept of the Self, with her three friends reflecting different aspects of her nature. The Lion, Tin Man, and Scarecrow are Jungian projections of Dorothy's body, heart, and mind. Like most myths, the films ends with a simple moral lesson—that courage, love, and intelligence are merely functions of *will,* and that happiness waits in one's own backyard.

(2) THE ROMANTIC PHASE:

European films like Jean Renoir's *Grand Illusion* and *Rules of the Game* predicted the death of such optimistic old myths. The disappearance of childlike fantasies, however, makes real love possible. Many critics think that the forties brought us the masterpiece of pure cinematic artistry and sophisticated romance in *Children of Paradise.* In this complicated intrigue, a mysterious lady named Garance symbolizes the "Naked Truth." She is loved and pursued by four men, each of whom represents a contrasting aspect of the psyche and a different approach to love. Lacenaire, the thief, is her "shadow," a man whose elegant exterior conceals dark, murderous impulses. Frederick, a rather overblown Shakespearean actor, is all ego and chatter. The aristocratic Count de Montray is self-obsessed and a total snob. The man Garance really loves is Baptiste, a mime who symbolizes the *heart*—an appropriate choice in a film that epitomizes the Romantic phase of cinema. Also, since the film ends in tragedy, Jung would say that Baptiste and Garance act as each other's *animus* and *anima,* leading to the destruction of their love as the "Naked Truth" again vanishes into the crowd.

(3) THE INTELLECTUAL PHASE:

The Lonely Crowd and mankind's alienation are the main themes of cinema in the fifties, when the best films were existential in philosophy and intensely intellectual. Rene Clement cast a cynical eye on World War Two with *Forbidden Games,* while American directors like Elia Kazan filmed their working-class heroes in smoky, brooding black and white. In this "Intellectual" phase, the giant of the cinema of ideas is Ingmar Bergman. All of Bergman's films confront the philosophical "Problem of Evil," an ancient question best described in a diagram:

$$\text{If GOD is} \begin{cases} \text{omnipotent} \\ \text{omniscient} \\ \text{all-loving} \end{cases} \text{how can EVIL exist?}$$

Mythical films like *The Wizard of Oz* answer the question by projecting all the evil in the world onto a witch—and then dissolving her into a puddle. *Children of Paradise* and other romantic films allude to the idea of "tragic flaw," suggesting that a villain is merely a hero who has gone too far.

But Bergman does not believe in Romantic Heroes or mythical supermen. In *The Seventh Seal,* he uses a mythical structure—a questing knight playing chess with Death—but he characterizes the knight as a modern, ironic anti-hero. Like Don Quixote and Sancho Panza, the knight and his earthy squire wander through a country that has lost its chivalric ideals. They suffer every human ill: as the squire declares in a mock-litany, they have been "bitten by insects, poisoned by bad wine, infected by women—all for the glory of God." The disillusioned crusaders also encounter every form of human cruelty—flagellation, witch-burning, the general stupidity of soldiers—in short, all the terrible things done in the Middle Ages in the name of Religion, that are done now in the name of Patriotism. Bergman photographs this morality play in stark black and white. He bluntly juxtaposes allegorical characters like the corrupt seminarian against Mary and Joseph, the naive circus acrobats whose love for their child redeems mankind from the general curse. Bergman's symbols are no less blatant: a *pig* roots around in a filthy tavern while his brother is roasted on a spit. Meanwhile, the plague hovers over Bergman's peasants with the inevitability of atomic war.

Despite the simplicity of his allegory, Bergman himself is a complicated man. He projects himself as both knight and squire, as self-tormented idealist and as existential man of action. Bergman also identifies with his "shadow"—depicted literally as Death—and with his clown, the juggler who does the "impossible trick." Like Joseph the Juggler, Bergman wants to "make a ball stand still in the air"—his metaphor for making a film that momentarily defeats death by grasping the total meaning of life and projecting his vision on a screen for the whole world to understand.

(4) THE POLITICAL PHASE:

Hiroshima Mon Amour, a landmark film that closed the fifties, set the tone for what was to follow. To Bergman's philosophical concern with the suffering of the innocent, Alain Resnais attached a strident, anti-social, activist message that shocked many audiences during the early years of the Viet Nam War. As the tensions of the decade intensified, and Resnais' images of Hiroshima horror became commonplace on TV newscasts, filmmakers responded to his artistic challenge in one of two ways. Directors like Truffaut and Fellini decided that the only way to cope with a society that has become a madhouse is to revolt by turning inward, focusing on the "search for the self." This is the theme of the two best films of the sixties, *Jules and Jim* and *8½*, which have influenced a whole generation of young directors in Britain, France, and America. The result has been many fine films like *Morgan, King of Hearts*, and *The Graduate*, all of which echo Truffaut's active camera technique and Fellini's idea that the real grotesques and lunatics are the people who govern us.

The other strong tendency in sixties films is to assert the Self by becoming frankly revolutionary and political. Most of the radical activists are British "angry young men," like Tony Richardson, whose *Loneliness of the Long Distance Runner* suggests analogies between prison and the British public schools, a theme that Lindsay Anderson carries even further in *If*. Formerly "Romantic" war movies also undergo a cynical transformation in Joseph Losey's *King and Country* and in Stanley Kubrick's brilliant satire, *Doctor Strangelove*. Finally, Peter Brook—creator of the Royal Shakespeare Company's production of *Marat-Sade*—combines Fellini's "search for the self" with the new radical politics.

In Brook's film version of William Golding's *Lord of the Flies*, he echoes Bergman's theme of the Problem of Evil, while adding his own political twist. The question of *Lord of the Flies* is whether children's cruel games reflect the values of their society, or some dark force buried deep in human nature. Brook discreetly avoids a simplistic answer by eliminating the Lord of the Flies' speech to Simon. Instead, he concentrates on the Island on which the boys are stranded as a microcosm of government. As in John Marshall's film *The Hunters*, there are four main characters: Hunter, Shaman, Headman, and Clown—all of whom differ in their attitude toward the "Beast." Jack, the Hunter, provides the standard military answer: the Beast adopts thousands of disguises, and they should spend all their time making weapons to *kill* it. Piggy, a modern corruption of the Shaman, is a parody of scientific liberalism. He doesn't believe in the Beast's existence any more than educated adults believe in the Devil—otherwise, he says, "things wouldn't make sense." Ralph, the Headman, is a true politician. He doesn't understand any of the arguments, but he thinks he can settle the Problem of Evil by majority vote. That leaves Simon, the Clown, the strange little kid who lives in his own poetic, mystical world.

Although everyone ignores him, he is the only one whose heart and intuition can solve the riddle of the Beast. When Simon and Piggy die, Ralph is left in the position of any moderate third-world leader, unable to resist the power of the totalitarian Jack. Understood as a political allegory, the film's supposed happy ending—with the Man in White coming to "save" them—implies the ultimate tragedy.

(5) THE ETERNAL RETURN:

The main critical question now is, where can film go after the radicalism of the sixties? An artist can't live forever on irony and revolt. He can wallow in soap opera like Bergman, drown in sentimentality like Truffaut, or lose himself in narcissistic dreams like Fellini. The alternative is to create new myths that give life positive meaning. This is why many filmmakers in the seventies have gone full-circle, returning to film's original "Mythical" phase. Hence the campy rebirth of Superman and Flash Gordon, as well as more significant allegories like Kubrick's *Clockwork Orange,* Herzog's *Aguirre,* De Palma's *Phantom of the Paradise,* and Blier's *Get Out Your Handkerchiefs.* Linda Wertmuller's *Swept Away* may also be interpreted as myth, and there is no better explanation for the re-blossoming of Luis Bunuel, whose *Obscure Object of Desire* recalls the surrealism of the thirties.

The most obvious return to the Mythical phase is the most popular film of the seventies, *Star Wars,* which literally restates the world-view of the thirties with its evil monsters and squeaky-clean heroes. According to one interpretation, Luke and Han Solo are little blond crypto-nazis who relish wiping out the "inferior races" in barroom shoot-outs; their Princess is the Wagnerian ideal, Obi Wan Kenobi represents Nietzsche, and Darth Vader symbolizes Stalin's collectivist tyranny. While refraining from pushing an analysis quite that far, I would nevertheless insist that the main characters do conform to Jungian archetypes. Luke (or Han Solo, the hero for those in the audience over the age of twelve) does symbolize the Self, the seventies ideal, whose hair is never messed. Princess Leia, the liberated woman who shoots a gun as well as any man, is very much his *anima* in a cold, sexless sort of way. Obi-Wan Kenobi, with his Silicon Valley Religion, is supposed to be the film's intellectual philosopher. And Darth Vader, all in black, turns out to be Luke's "shadow" in a recognition scene that would cause Freud to howl with laughter.

How seriously should we take all of this? Not very. Perhaps the only unnerving element in *Star Wars* is the ending, the final procession that echoes Leni Riefenstahl's *Olympia.* If history, like cinema, moves in cyclic phases, I hesitate to imagine what lies in store for us in the near future. Let's hope that the Force is *not* with us.

THE ETERNAL FOUR

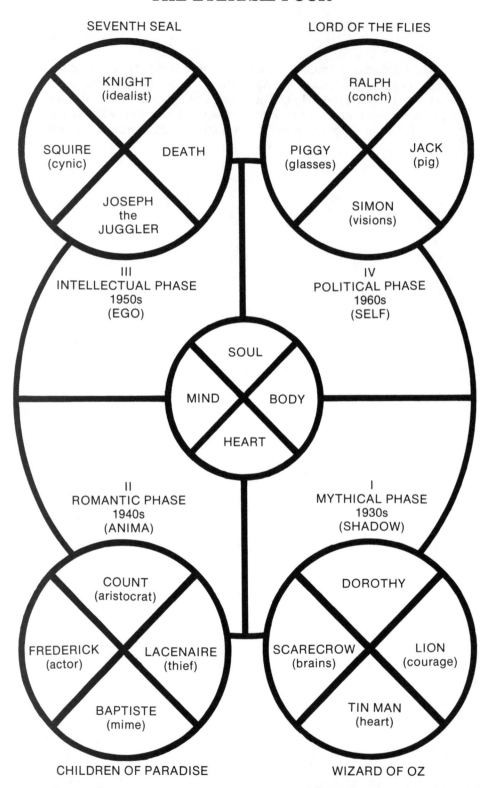

SEVENTH SEAL

LORD OF THE FLIES

KNIGHT
(idealist)

SQUIRE
(cynic)

DEATH

JOSEPH
the
JUGGLER

RALPH
(conch)

PIGGY
(glasses)

JACK
(pig)

SIMON
(visions)

III
INTELLECTUAL PHASE
1950s
(EGO)

IV
POLITICAL PHASE
1960s
(SELF)

SOUL

MIND

BODY

HEART

II
ROMANTIC PHASE
1940s
(ANIMA)

I
MYTHICAL PHASE
1930s
(SHADOW)

COUNT
(aristocrat)

FREDERICK
(actor)

LACENAIRE
(thief)

BAPTISTE
(mime)

DOROTHY

SCARECROW
(brains)

LION
(courage)

TIN MAN
(heart)

CHILDREN OF PARADISE

WIZARD OF OZ

The thirties come full-circle with Isabelle Huppert in Claude Chabrol's dark comedy, *Violette*. (Photo courtesy of New Yorker Films.)

II
THE FILMS

Our first reaction to a film is usually subjective, based on our personal identification with its characters and plot. There is nothing wrong with this, of course, except that we have been conditioned by TV to identify with stereotypes, to confuse one-liners with wit, and to accept materialism as a legitimate philosophy. If, as Woody Allen says, TV has systematically lowered our standards, can we really trust our critical faculties? And is there any way to get beyond opinion, to make aesthetic judgments about film? Yes, if instead of merely empathizing, we interpret the films we see by *questioning* their values.

In all the arts, the right answers are never as important as the right questions. This principle excludes fact-oriented trivia, especially the multiple-choice questions so popular in our schools. Traditionally, teachers have asked their students questions like this:

"In the film of *Hamlet,* Laurence Olivier's *hair* is (a) blond (b) black-and-white (c) prematurely orange."

Or they might probe the meaning of *King Kong* with a fill-in-the-blank question:

"When Kong pulls Fay Wray through her bedroom window, she S_____!"

After years of public education, any fool can learn to handle such "objective" questions as long as he can:

(1) memorize as many meaningless facts as possible,

(2) parrot his teacher's prejudices, and

(3) keep his mind relatively unclouded by drugs so that when he fills in the bubbles on his IBM card, he won't go over the edge (so to speak).

The best questions are unanswerable—or at least they provoke discussion. They reflect what was probably going on in the mind of the filmmaker when he created the film. As Albert Elsen says, the greatness of any artist depends on the problems that haunt him and the seriousness of the questions he asks. By putting ourselves in the filmmaker's place while we watch his creation unfold, we should be able to ask the same questions he did. In keeping with this approach to film, I have framed several *types* of questions that attempt to re-create the artistic process:

(1) *Thematic* questions are the most basic. All films contain ideas and express values, whether they intend to or not. Sometimes these ideas are *ironic:* that is, they mean the opposite of what they say, or they operate simultaneously on two levels of meaning. The first task of analysis is to interpret what a film is telling us about ourselves.

(2) *Psychological motivations:* Another basic question to ask about any film is not what its characters do, but *why* they do it. Why does

Citizen Kane waste his time collecting art objects he doesn't really want? Why does the Knight in *The Seventh Seal* trade his life to help a young family escape death? Why does the rich old man in Bunuel's *Obscure Object of Desire* chase after a young lady who gives him such a hard time?

(3) *Imagery* and *symbolism:* Unlike TV, which relies on "talking heads" to convey its themes, film is primarily visual. When a film's pictures merely evoke a mood, we call them *images*. If these images connote various ideas, we may question what they *symbolize*. The hallucinatory setting of *Elvira Madigan* is imagistic, as opposed to the symbolic landscape of *Swept Away*, which suggests both the island of Robinson Crusoe and the Garden of Eden. In most Hollywood films, a room is merely a room; but for Roman Polanski a room may symbolize hell, or it may stand as a metaphor for a body that entraps a claustrophobic soul.

(4) *Allegory* begins with an abstract idea, then searches for an image to embody it—unlike symbolism, which always starts with the object. Allegory also differs from symbolism by suggesting a 1:1 correspondence rather than a variety of meanings. Allegorical films draw precise parallels with religion, psychology, or politics. Bunuel's *Viridiana,* for example, is an allegory about the relationship of church and state. *Woman in the Dunes* compares modern sexual relationships to life in a sand pit. And Fassbinder's *Maria Braun* corresponds very deliberately to the economic recovery of post-war Germany.

(5) *Myths* and *archetypes:* A myth is a symbolic story, usually intended to convey a moral view of the world. The characters in the myth are often *archetypal* figures who occur throughout history whenever the myth reappears. To understand conflicting views of human nature, we should always ask how the characters in films compare with their ancestors in other cultures. For instance, how is John Gielgud (in Resnais' *Providence*) like an Old Testament God? Or how does Klaus Kinski (in Herzog's *Nosferatu*) differ from the traditional Dracula?

(6) *Analogies:* Creativity begins when we look at one thing and think of something else. The richer a film is, the more parallels we may draw to the other arts. *Jules and Jim* recalls the Don Quixote-Sancho Panza polarity so common in literature. Bunuel's *Discreet Charm of the Bourgeoisie* is constructed according to the musical principle of "theme and variation." We may also discuss film as a "cubist" medium that looks at reality from different perspectives, just as Picasso does. This is especially true of *Citizen Kane, Rashomon,* and Fellini's *8½.*

(7) *Juxtapositions:* Most films consist of "montage"—sequences of contrasting shots edited to comment on each other. The source of these juxtapositions may be unconscious, but their execution is never accidental. After all, editing is the most deliberate process in filmmaking. Therefore, we should ask why Alain Resnais (in *Mon Oncle D'Amerique*) would cut from a man leaving his wife and fleeing from his mistress—to a white rat running back and forth between compartments to avoid being shocked. Or why he intercuts shots from forties films whenever his characters face a crisis.

(8) *Vision of Reality:* The most important questions we can ask are philosophical. With Wertmuller and Bertolucci we must deal with their ideology and how it affects their vision of society. But whether or not a filmmaker is political, all artists express a life attitude and a concept of human nature in their work. For Kurosawa, whose *Kagemusha* is the most beautiful philosophical film in recent years, the main question is very basic: "Who is wicked?" If a king and a thief condemned to crucifixion can change places without causing a single ripple in the government, what can we conclude about human nature?

The following films have been selected because they focus on questions about human nature. Some of my choices may seem obscure or even alien to our world-view. They share no single philosophy and illustrate no fashionable critical theory. Few of them have made their producers rich. What do they have in common? Intelligence and style.

It would be easy to list another hundred great films that are *not* recommended here for discussion. This includes a number of famous classics—by Visconti, Godard, and Antonioni, for instance—that traditionally put students to sleep. I have also omitted several great films from the thirties and forties because their excellence depends on *acting* rather than on filmic qualities. *Casablanca* and *Gone With The Wind* are both wonderful movies—but there isn't much to say about them that goes beyond character analysis. Nor have I chosen to include any films by Hitchcock, a talented stylist whose technique merely creates suspense, without much thematic content.

Finally, the purpose of this book is to instruct, not just to entertain. I have therefore avoided Hollywood blockbusters as much as possible. It would be silly to discuss *Jaws* as social allegory, or to solemnize *The Godfather's* parallels between the Mafia and Corporate America. As for all the recent space fantasies and horror flicks that revel in new ways to make people's heads explode, what can we say except that this sort of Roman entertainment is technically very adept? But a great film must be more than slick and entertaining. It must also express a vision of life that is intellectually defensible. Otherwise it will never be a true classic—a work of art that will be as provocative in the year 2001 as it is now.

THE BIRTH OF A NATION (1915—American) Directed by D.W. Griffith; with Lillian Gish. Distributed by Audio-Brandon.

1. In what ways is Ben Cameron, "The Little Colonel," the typical Griffith hero?

2. "In the Slave Quarters"—The slaves all dance happily to welcome the master. Why does Griffith include this scene before introducing the war theme and the separation of the young lovers?

3. Why does Griffith shoot several "historical fascimiles" based on old photographs? What does this imply about his story?

4. "Viciousness, common to all races, is brought forth by war." Why does Griffith insert this disclaimer?

5. While the war rages, Ben Cameron moons over the picture of Elsie Stoneman, whom he has never met. How does this typify Griffith's view of love?

6. Why are the battle scenes famous? What is the significance of Ben's leading the charge against the forces of his best friend?

7. After Lincoln's assassination, Senator Stoneman's servant says, "Now you are the most powerful man in America." What does Stoneman symbolize?

8. Stoneman's protege, Silas Lynch, is depicted as a mulatto. What is the significance of this, and how does it relate to Griffith's obsession with the "evils" of inter-marriage?

9. Ben refuses to shake hands with Lynch when he and Stoneman visit the Cameron home. What is Griffith's attitude toward this refusal?

10. What is Griffith's attitude toward allowing Blacks to vote? What details suggest this?

11. Note that the love scene in the garden between Ben and Elsie is *backlighted*. What is the effect of this?

12. Phil Stoneman also declares his love for Ben's sister. Why does she reject him, and what does her rejection symbolize?

13. "Celebrating their victory at the polls"—While the Blacks celebrate outside, Lynch eyes Stoneman's daughter. What is this blatant juxtaposition supposed to suggest?

14. How does Griffith characterize the first meeting of the all-Black legislature?

15. Ben gets the bright idea for starting the Ku Klux Klan while watching some children play with a white sheet. Why is this unintentionally ironic?

16. Ben's little sister goes to the spring. What does the setting symbolize?

> "I'm a captain now, and I want to get married..." What does Gus the Renegade symbolize?

> Note the closeup of her *bucket* on the edge of the spring after she jumps from the cliff. What does the bucket symbolize? What is the significance of her leap from the cliff?

17. The blacksmith searches for Gus in the local gin-mill, where he beats up all the Blacks (until someone shoots him in the back). How does Griffith use the setting and the action to convey his racial stereotypes?

18. The trial is brief. The Klansmen dump Gus' body on the steps of Stoneman's mansion. What is Griffith's attitude toward this, and toward their childish flag-dipping ceremony?

19. While Mr. Cameron is being taunted by his former slaves, the "Faithful Souls" help him escape. Griffith referred to scenes like this to prove he wasn't a racist. Why, in fact, does it prove the opposite?

20. "A Little Cabin" defended by two union veterans offers the Camerons protection against a whole army of Black soldiers. What does the setting symbolize?

21. In a cross-cut, Elsie pleads with Lynch for help. What is the significance of his plans for her? How is this reflected in the cross-cuts to the rioting mob outside?

22. Griffith cuts again to the summoning of the Klan. Note Griffith's brilliant intercutting . . . also the cavalry charge filmed from the rear of a truck. Why does this shot no longer have its original dramatic effect?

23. Stoneman congratulates Lynch on his desire to marry a White woman . . . until he discovers it's his own daughter! What racist cliche does this illustrate?

24. While the Klan rides down the street, shooting everyone in sight, the Camerons hold off a whole army in their little cabin. What is Griffith's attitude toward this primitive frontier violence?

> Note Wagner's "Ride of the Valkyries" thundering in the background. Why were both Griffith and Hitler fond of Wagner?

THE CABINET OF DOCTOR CALIGARI (1919—German)
Directed by Robert Wiene. Distributed by Janus Films.

1. How does the film relate to the Expressionist movement in early twentieth century German art?

2. Note the lack of right angles, especially in Caligari's shack. Why does the director use a *stage* setting with surrealistic distortions? How does the set reflect what Freud and Jung call the "world of the unconscious?"

3. What is the structural significance of the opening conversation? (The old man speaks of the "evil spirits" that have driven him from his home. As the girl walks by in a trance, Francis says she is his fiancee).

4. What is the symbolic purpose of the *Dionysian carnival* whirling in the background as Caligari enters?

5. Caligari's somnabulist kills people like the town clerk, who have displeased him. Politically and psychologically, what does this sleepwalker symbolize?

6. The poet, Alan, asks Caesare how long he will live. What does Alan's interest in Caesare signify?

7. According to Francis, "There is something frightful in our midst." What are the various meanings of this line?

8. Caligari beckons the girl into his shack, and insinuatingly flicks open Caesare's coffin. What does this gesture symbolize, and why is she so horrified?

9. Caesare later goes to the girl's room to stab her. What is the significance of his reaction to seeing her face? How does this illustrate the Beauty/Beast archetype?

10. What is the significance of the pursuit through the twisted landscape, which winds up in the *lunatic asylum?* How is this asylum like a painting by Giorgio De Chirico?

11. What is the irony in Francis' asking if the asylum has a patient named Caligari? What is the allegorical meaning of the answer? What is the effect of the white lines converging on the figure of Dr. Caligari seated in the *director's* chair?

12. Dr. Caligari wants to test his theory that "a sleepwalker can be compelled to do things that he would shrink from in his normal waking state." What does this experiment symbolize?

13. "It's not me, it's the director who is mad!" Does this ending "explain" the distortions in the setting as the projection of a diseased imagination— or has Wiene merely imposed this structure to avoid German censorship?

THE GOLD RUSH (1925-American) Directed by Charles Chaplin; with Georgia Hale and Mack Swain. Distributed by Janus Films.

1. Why is Chaplin considered "important?" How does he express both the aspirations of the nineteenth century and the realities of the twentieth? In what ways does this "lone prospector" symbolize the condition of modern man?

2. Al Capp claims that "all comedy is based on man's delight in man's inhumanity to man." How does *The Gold Rush* illustrate this idea?

3. The opening: The *iris-out* on the train of miners struggling in the snow looks like a documentary. Why does the film start with such a serious sequence? How does this relate to the main themes of the film? How does it reveal Chaplin's view of Man and of Man's relation to Nature?

4. Why does Chaplin juxtapose the dramatic, romantic panorama of the mountains against his entrance, teetering on the edge of the abyss? What does his "loss of direction" symbolize?

5. What is the symbolic significance of Chaplin's being blown out of the cabin?

6. Big Jim and Black Larsen wrestle with the gun, which keeps pointing at Chaplin. How does this symbolize his relationships with other people?

7. Note how meticulous Chaplin is in cooking the boot. Why is the eating scene funny? What *visual puns* are involved in this sequence?

8. What is the significance of Chaplin's transformation into a chicken?

9. Except for Chaplin, the characters in this film are all engulfed in *fur coats,* making them look like wild animals. What does this imply about human nature? How does Chaplin's grabbing the bear's leg underscore this idea?

10. The scene between Georgia and Jack the Ladies' Man is followed by Chaplin's bedraggled entrance. What is the effect of this juxtaposition?

Georgia: "I'm bored. I wish I could meet someone worthwhile. I'm so tired of this place." What does this reveal about her character?

Why does she dance with Chaplin, and why would he misunderstand? What does the business with the *dog* symbolize?

What is ironic about Chaplin's thinking he has knocked out the bully? What does the *clock* symbolize?

11. Why is Chaplin's relationship with Georgia funny? When she visits him with her friends, how do his *hot-foot* and getting hit in the face with *snow* comment symbolically on their relationship?

12. In order to earn money to make dinner for Georgia, Chaplin *shovels snow.* How is this task a metaphor for love?

13. What is the tone of Chaplin's New Year's Eve dinner? What does the "Oceana Roll" symbolize? What is the significance of Georgia's not showing up, and how does this continue the film's *food* metaphor?

14. How does the shot of Chaplin looking through the window into the dance hall stress his image as the "eternal outsider?"

15. Why is Georgia's love letter ironic?

16. "Fate guided them to a spot where all was calm." Why is this ironic? What does the cabin shifting on the edge of the cliff symbolize? How does this satirize D.W. Griffith's "cliff-hangers?"

Note how Chaplin and Big Jim climb on each other to escape. How does this reflect Chaplin's view of human nature?

17. What is the significance of the costume change in the last scene? Dressed like a tramp, Chaplin will be thrown off the ship. What does this imply about the nature of Reality?

18. Chaplin finds Georgia again: How is his fall into the coil of rope symbolic? How does this modify the tone of the ending?

Thinking him still a tramp, Georgia offers to pay his fare. Does this complicate the ending? Or do you consider the action unreal, in terms of her character?

What is the significance of her marrying him? How is this different from the usual ending of a Chaplin film? What is the double-meaning in the photographer's saying, "You've spoiled the picture!"?

19. Chaplin thinks that becoming a millionaire is entirely a matter of *chance.* How does this idea connect the "Gold Rush" theme with the film's romantic theme? What is the parallel between gold mines and love?

POTEMKIN (1925—Russian) Directed by Sergei Eisenstein. Distributed by Audio-Brandon.

The German philosopher Hegel theorized that history evolves through conflict, with the ruling idea of each civilization giving birth to its opposite. The dialectical struggle between *thesis* and *antithesis* results in a new *synthesis,* a blending of old and new which eventually generates yet another contradiction. The cycle continues until mankind presumably achieves perfection. That Sergei Eisenstein, as a good communist, would believe in Hegel's theory of history should come as no surprise. It is a mark of his genius, however, that he could dramatize his philosophy in visual terms by inventing *montage,* one of the most important technical discoveries in the history of film.

The best way to understand montage is to distinguish it from its opposite, *collage,* which collects similar images to illustrate a theme. The essence of montage is not comparison, but *contrast*—the collision of images that creates dramatic tension. In *Potemkin,* Eisenstein experiments with several types of montage, contrasting shapes, textures, and directions of movement. He cuts from closeups to long shots, and from symbols to people. In "tonal" montage he juxtaposes atmospheres—the backlighted ship, for instance, against the stoic swing of the sailors' hammocks. In the famous Odessa Steps sequence, he creates "metric" montage by repeating motifs at regular intervals, as in music. As the baby carriage hurtles down the steps, he shortens each succeeding shot, moving the audience toward an eye-slashing climax. By intercutting sharply different shots, Eisenstein found that he could not only intensify the drama, but that he could manipulate our concept of time and even the nature of reality itself.

Aside from Hegelian visions of reality, Eisenstein's invention of montage may owe even more to his study of Chinese art and philosophy. The lines in the *I Ching*, he realized, mean nothing except in the context of a particular hexagram; with the alternation of a single line, the configuration may convey the opposite meaning. Similarly, Eisenstein found that any individual shot is neutral until it is combined with other shots in its sequence. The emotional and psychological totality of montage is thus greater than the sum of its fragments. Only artistic editing re-integrates a director's "hieroglyphs" to express his vision of reality.

***

1. Although *Potemkin's* five-part structure invites comparison with Brecht, Shakespeare, and the Greeks, how does the film's *moral view* distinguish it from classical tragedy? In what sense is *Potemkin* actually a "Marxist Fairy Tale?"

PART ONE: MEN AND MAGGOTS

2. In the opening shot, how do the waves crashing on the breakwater symbolize both *Potemkin's* central conflict and the Russian Revolution in general?

3. The boatswain, tangled in the maze of hammocks, strikes a sleeping sailor. How does this capricious violence symbolize the treatment of the Russian masses by their leaders?

4. Although Eisenstein avoids focusing on a central character, note that Vakulinchuk *does* look like Joseph Stalin (!) How does the martyred sailor differ from the tragic hero of classical tragedy?

5. "These are not maggots..." What does the *rotten meat* symbolize? Despite his magnified view of the problem, Dr. Smirnov declares the meat edible. What is the significance of his denial of reality, and how does this reflect on the Russian scientific establishment?

6. "Give us this day our daily bread..." Why does the young dishwasher smash the plate, and what does his action symbolize? How does Eisenstein expand the nature of time in this sequence? How does this reflect the experiments of the *cubists* in modern art?

> Why would Solzhenitsyn refer to this incident in *One Day in the Life of Ivan Denisovich,* his famous novel about life in Siberian labor camps?

PART TWO: DRAMA ON THE QUARTERDECK

7. Note that the captain on this "ship of state" looks like Czar Nicholas. What is the effect of the low-angle shot that silhouettes him against the sky?

> Why does Eisenstein cut from the yardarm "cross" and the apparition of the hanging bodies to the face of the old sailor?

> What is the purpose of the closeups of one of the marines in the firing squad?

8. How is the tarpaulin used for the mass execution like a giant *blindfold?* What does this metaphor imply about the Russian people?

9. "Lord, reveal Thyself to the unruly . . . " Why does Eisenstein intercut the shots of the firing squad with the archetypal Russian monk? How does the old man with his billowing mane recall Rasputin, and what is the significance of this?

> How does the monk's tapping the cross in his palm reveal Eisenstein's attitude toward religion?

10. During the ensuing struggle, note that the cross sticks in the deck like a dagger. What does this symbolize? What is the significance of the closeup of the officer's white shoe crushing the candles and stepping on the keys of the piano?

11. When Dr. Smirnov is thrown into the sea, why does Eisenstein cut first to the maggots, then to the glasses tangled in the rigging? How is this last shot a visual *synechdoche?*

PART THREE: AN APPEAL FROM THE DEAD

12. Eisenstein is famous for his ceremonial processions. How does he compose and edit the shots in the mourning sequence to make a few hundred people look like an endless sea of humanity?

13. During the harangue of the Lady in Black, how do the intercut shots of the *clenched fist* represent the feeling of the crowd?

> "Down with the Jews!" cries a well-dressed onlooker. What force in Russian society does he represent? Considering the current Soviet attitude toward Jews, why is his fate ironic?

PART FOUR: THE ODESSA STEPS

14. Before the slaughter on the Odessa Steps, why does Eisenstein include the poetic montage of the boats sailing to meet the Potemkin?

15. In the closeups of the waving citizens, how do the veiled lady, the woman wearing pince-nez, and the legless cripple represent a cross-section of Russian society?

16. How does the peasant carrying her dead son up the steps symbolize "Mother Russia?"

17. Why does Eisenstein avoid showing the faces of the soldiers? Why does he emphasize their shadows and the mechanical rhythm of their march?

18. "Let us appeal to them..." What does the lady wearing pince-nez symbolize, and what is the significance of her fate?

19. How does Eisenstein lengthen the sense of time as the baby carriage rolls down the steps?

20. The headquarters of the generals is the Odessa Theatre. How does the baroque sculpture of the goddess and her cherubs symbolize the Old Regime? What does the montage of the three stone lions symbolize?

PART FIVE: MEETING THE SQUADRON

21. Why does Eisenstein juxtapose the formal composition of the cannons and rigging against the abstract dance of moonbeams on the sea? How does this contrast reflect the inner state of the sleeping sailors?

22. What is the dramatic purpose of all the closeups of the Potemkin's machinery (especially the whirling pistons)?

23. In the final shot of the film, the Potemkin's prow passes right over the audience. How does this symbolic gesture affirm the Russian Revolution in general?

THE BLUE ANGEL (1930—German) Directed by Josef von Sternberg; with Marlene Dietrich and Emil Jannings. Distributed by Janus Films.

General Themes:

1. How is *The Blue Angel* similar to other "temptation stories?"

2. How is *The Blue Angel* different from traditional Faust, Don Juan, and Don Giovanni legends?

3. Do you regard *The Blue Angel* as a "tragedy?" If so, how does it differ from classical tragedy?

4. What does the film tell us about life in Germany in the 1920s? How does it reflect "expressionist" ideas in art? How does it relate to the plays of Bertolt Brecht and the music of Kurt Weill?

5. The recent film *Cabaret* is a variation on the "Blue Angel" theme. What are the similarities and differences between the two films?

6. Although *The Blue Angel* is a "sound" film, very little of its dramatic impact is due to the dialogue, which is mostly improvised. What visual effects does Sternberg use to convey character and theme?

7. Why is Sternberg's lighting so theatrical? What is the effect of the frequent musical performances, and how do they relate to the off-stage action?

***

Important Details in Individual Scenes:

1. Note Rath's treatment of the dead songbird, which the maid then throws into the stove. How does this incident relate symbolically to the rest of the film?

2. In class: How does Rath's *nose-blowing* ritual characterize him? What does his "cleaning the glasses" so frequently symbolize? How does the

student's attempts to recite, "To Be or Not To Be" foreshadow Rath's inner conflict?

3. Rath peers into the Blue Angel through a dirty window—then gets caught in ropes and netting as he tries to enter. As he pursues the student, Rath collides with the clown, who stares at him throughout the film...How do these symbols relate?

4. Note the spiral staircase to Lola's bedroom...the trained bear...the business with Lola's panties...How do these symbols predict Rath's entrapment?

5. To Rath's disgust, Kiefert—"Professor of Magic"—regards him as a "colleague." What does this imply?

6. What is the symbolic significance of the *cellar* in which the students—and later Rath—hide?

7. Rath confronts his students, one of whom lights a cigarette..."Same as you." Why is this confrontation ironic?

> To make Rath feel better, Kiefert mixes him a "prescription." What does this drink symbolize?

8. Lola strikes her famous pose to sing for Rath, who sits in the box seat above her. What does his position symbolize? What do the *life preservers* imply? How is the *clown* staring up at him Rath's "double?"

9. Note the interaction of the symbols: As Lola's bird chirps in its cage, Rath awakens from his hangover holding Lola's doll. She drops sugar in his coffee, insinuating "You could have this every day." He looks up guiltily as the clock chimes for school. How do the gargoyles passing in front of the clock reveal Rath's "unconscious?"

10. The riot in the classroom ends with the principal's entrance. Why is riot and repression a typical pattern in European schools? How does it also reflect Rath's inner nature?

11. Why does Lola laugh hysterically when Rath asks her to marry him? Cut to the wedding feast, at which Kiefert conjures an egg from Rath's nose. Lola makes chicken noises, and Rath crows like a rooster...How does this barnyard symbolism foreshadow the film's tragic climax?

12. Rath picks up Lola's suitcase, which opens dumping pictures of her on the floor. She cajoles him into picking them up. Cut to Rath sitting

drunkenly, smoking a cigarette. What is the significance of his now selling her picture?

13. Lola pares an apple, waiting for Rath to return after their argument. She orders him to help her on with her stockings. He cools the curling iron on calendar pages, which burst into flame... How do the symbols relate?

14. Four years later... Cut to Rath at a dressing table, making up as a clown, putting on a false nose (cf. earlier nose-blowing). What does his transformation symbolize?

15. "Great International Magic Act": What is the significance of Rath's performance, a variation on the *egg* business? What does his metamorphosis into a rooster symbolize?

16. In the final scene, Lola straddles the chair, singing: "Men cluster to me like moths around a flame/ And if their wings burn, I know I'm not to blame..." How does Lola illustrate the Jungian *archetype* known as the "*anima?*"

How do the gargoyles passing again in front of the clock establish the action of the film as a *mythical cycle?*

CITY LIGHTS (1931—American) Directed by Charles Chaplin. Distributed by RBC Films and Films Inc., by arrangement with Roy Export Co.

1. How does Chaplin's performance with the statues reflect his relationship with society? How does it foreshadow his relationship with the Blind Girl and the Rich Drunk?

The Mayor's speech: why the gibberish? Why is "Peace and Prosperity" ironic?

2. How are the newsboys characterized and what do they represent? Despite his obvious sentimentality, why doesn't Chaplin always sentimentalize children and poor people?

3. How does Chaplin's peeking at the nude sculpture characterize him? How does the sinking sidewalk symbolize his love-life?

4. Chaplin meets the BLIND FLOWER GIRL after climbing through the rich man's car. What does her blindness symbolize?

> When the car drives off, she thinks he has gone ... How does her throwing water in his face foreshadow the outcome of their relationship?

5. Dissolve to Grandma making tea. The Blind Girl gropes her way to the phonograph and puts on a record. What does this symbolize? As her neighbor is picked up for a date, what does the look on her face mean?

6. The RICH DRUNK prepares to drown himself. How do you know he's rich? When Chaplin tries to persuade him not to kill himself, he throws his noose over both of them and winds up throwing *Chaplin* in the water. What does this symbolize? What is the significance of their falling in several times? How does this foreshadow their relationship? (I'M CURED! YOU'RE MY FRIEND FOR LIFE!"—Why is this ironic?)

7. They go to the Rich Drunk's mansion. What is the significance of the way the butler treats Chaplin? What is the symbolic significance of the bottle that keeps pouring down the front of Chaplin's pants?

8. THE NIGHTCLUB SCENE is full of Chaplin's usual slapstick. Note that the following details are *metaphorical,* illuminating Chaplin's character and the themes of the film:

> How is his slipping all over the dance floor symbolic?

> What does the business with the chairs symbolize?

> Each time he tries to light his cigar, it is the Rich Drunk's cigar that is lighted.

> A lady sits on the lighted cigar. Chaplin pats her behind, then sprays her with seltzer.

> The Apache Dance: Why would Chaplin intervene to "save" the lady?

> As he tries to eat the spaghetti, it gets tangled in the streamers. Why does Chaplin include visual puns about *food* in all his films?

Chaplin grabs the lady and dances with her, finally winding up in a mad dance with the waiter. How does this frenzy reflect his love-life?

By 1931, the entire country had been engulfed by the Depression. Why would Chaplin include a scene showing a crowd of rich fools wining and dining?

9. The drive home: How is *cutting corners* a metaphor for the Rich Drunk's life? ("Am *I* driving?")

10. As Chaplin sits on the steps after the butler has slammed the door in his face, the Blind Girl walks by with her flowers. Meanwhile, the drunk wants his "friend." Why does the butler humor him, but treat Chaplin badly behind his master's back?

11. Chaplin gives the flowers to the butler and drives the girl home. Why does Chaplin's treatment of the butler impress her, and what does this reveal about her character?

As Chaplin stands in a trance after kissing her hand, the *cat* knocks a flower pot on his head. How does this foreshadow the end of the film?

He tips the rain-barrel over on the neighbor. What does this symbolize?

12. THE RICH DRUNK AWAKENS, puzzled about the flowers in his lap. What is the significance of this?

After being thrown out by the butler, Chaplin drives around in the Rolls, looking for a cigar butt. What is the significance of his knocking over the other hobo in order to get it?

When he drives the car home, the Rich Drunk—now sober—doesn't even recognize him. What is the point of this?

13. Chaplin again meets his drunk friend, who embraces him and takes him home for a party. After the way he's been treated, why does Chaplin go with him?

Note the man whose bald head looks like a gelatin salad. What does this visual pun suggest about human intelligence?

A girl thumps him on the chest, causing him to swallow his whistle. How does this characterize his relationships with women?

Chaplin can't stop "whistling" during the singer's performance, causing him to be the focal point of dogs and taxi drivers. What does this imply about "culture?"

14. THE MORNING AFTER...The Rich Drunk awakens to find Chaplin in his bed(!) What is the symbolic significance of his non-recognition? How does this reflect Chaplin's relationship with the Blind Girl?

Chaplin squirts the butler with a grapefruit and stuffs a banana in his pants. What are the connotations of these actions?

15. Chaplin discovers that the girl is sick...What is the significance of his job as a *street sweeper*. What does this metaphor suggest about the nature of love? Why does he throw up his hands when he sees the elephant?

16. Victorian Melodrama: the landlord's letter of eviction...Meanwhile, the Blind Girl fantasizes about Chaplin—"He isn't just rich...he's more than that." Why is this ironic?

17. Lunchtime: How does the business with the *soap* continue the film's *food* metaphor?

18. Without the millionaire, Chaplin continues to "play the part of a gentleman." Why does he persist in perpetuating this illusion?

When he tells the girl about the doctor in Vienna, she exclaims, "How wonderful—then I'll be able to see you!" Why is this ironic?

What is the symbolic significance of her unraveling his underwear?

19. THE BOXING MATCH—"WINNER TAKE ALL": Thematically, how does the boxing match relate to the rest of the film? Why does Chaplin use *visual puns* to connect boxing with making love? Note the following details:

Chaplin's "flirtation" causes the Bully to undress in the closet...

They "dance" and "embrace" in the ring...

While the trainers are slapping his thighs and wiping his brow, Chaplin fantasizes that the Blind Girl is caressing him.

20. What is the significance of Chaplin's being a sneaky fighter?

21. The boxing match is organized according to the *musical* principle of "theme and variation," with Chaplin and the Bully taking turns rising from the count. How does this reflect Chaplin's relationships with the Blind Girl and the Rich Drunk?

>What is the significance of Chaplin's neck getting entwined in the bell rope?

22. After getting knocked out, Chaplin again runs into the Rich Drunk, who has just returned from Europe. In the scene with the burglars, he promises to "take care of the girl." What is the significance of his forgetting when he regains consciousness? What does this represent in society?

>"WHO IS THIS MAN?"—What is the significance of Chaplin's being accused of stealing the money?

23. Chaplin gives the girl the money and cranks the record player once more before he goes. What does this gesture symbolize?

24. SIX MONTHS LATER... The girl has her own florist shop. What is the significance of the handsome young millionaire who comes into her shop? ("I thought he had returned.") Why is it unlikely that a man who looks like this would even give her a second glance?

25. The newsboys shoot at Chaplin with a pea-shooter and pull at his rags when he bends to the gutter to pick up a discarded flower. Inside, the girl laughs. What is the significance of their confrontation through the glass?

26. Chaplin starts to run away when she comes outside to give him a flower. Why does he come back?

>"You?" (She puts her hand to her face in shock.)
>"You can see now?"
>"Yes, I can see now."

>Why is this ironic? What do the last two closeups imply?

27. Apparently, Chaplin thinks that men are stupid, and that women are blind. This is a *tragic* idea. What makes his treatment of this theme *funny?*

M. (1931—German) Directed by Fritz Lang; with Peter Lorre. Distributed by Janus Films.

1. *M* opens with a circle of children playing a typical gory game: "The nasty man in black will come, and with a little chopper he will chop you up." Why does Lang emphasize the violence in children's games?

2. A little girl walks home from school. As she bounces her ball against the "wanted" poster, Peter Lorre's shadow appears. Why do expressionistic films dwell on *shadows?* Psychologically, how does Peter Lorre represent Jung's "Shadow" and Freud's "Subconscious?"

3. The Nice Man buys little Elsie a balloon. What does the Blind Balloon Man symbolize? What are the mythical connotations of Peter Lorre's whistling Grieg's "In the Hall of the Mountain King"?

4. Cut from Elsie's mother calling her name . . . to a ball rolling out of the bushes and a balloon caught on the telephone wires. Why does Lang use symbols instead of just showing the murder?

5. "Any man on the street could be the guilty one . . ." Why does Lang include the "respectable" men fighting over the cafe table, and the thug harassing the little old man? How does this foreshadow Peter Lorre's trial at the end of the film?

6. Note how clinical and scientific the police are, projecting huge fingerprints and drawing circles on their map radiating from the discovery of a candy wrapper. How do the authority figures in *M* symbolize the Weimar government?

7. How is the head criminal characterized by his black leather coat and gloves? What is the implication of his describing their mob as a "union?"

> "Our reputation suffers," he complains, "because the cops are looking for the murderer in our ranks." Besides, increased police activity impedes "normal business." How does this echo Brecht's concept of crooks as *businessmen?*

8. What do the intercut shots of the gangsters and the police planning their strategy imply about the values of both groups? What is the effect of all the *smoke* that fills the two rooms?

9. Why do the gangsters decide that they'll have to catch the murderer themselves? How are they like the nazis in the early thirties?

10. What is ironic about the gangsters' watching over all the children in the city? Why do they enlist Berlin's beggars as their spies? Why is it ironic that all the beggars have *union* numbers?

11. What is the significance of the landlady's deafness? While the detective inspects the table, Mr. Becker munches *fruit*. What does this symbolize?

> In the store window he sees the reflection of a little girl. Why does Lang repeat the "Hall of the Mountain King" motif?
>
> The little girl's mother reaches her just in time. Note the pinwheel and the arrow going up and down in the store window. How do they comment on Becker's state of mind?

12. The Blind Balloon Man hears a familiar theme. Cut to Becker buying candy for a little girl. What is the effect of his whipping out a switchblade to slice an orange?

13. If this film is a social allegory, how does the "M" branded on Becker's back connect him with the Jews in pre-war Germany? In theological terms, how does the "M" echo the mark of Cain?

14. Becker and the girl step in front of a doll store. What does the puppet dancing in the window symbolize? What is the symbolic meaning of the brilliant shot of him staring at his reflection in the glass—and noticing the "M" imprinted on his back?

15. Pursued by the beggars, Becker scurries into an office building. He hides in the loft, which is divided into wooden-barred compartments. What do these Kafkaesque compartments symbolize?

16. The criminals unlock the gate and invade the building. While Becker digs at the bolts of his cage with his broken knife, the criminals burrow through the floor to reach him. How does this *animal imagery* reflect Lang's view of human nature?

> Note the shot of the safecracker emerging from his hole in the glare of police flashlights. How does his predicament parallel Becker's?

17. Why the low-angle shot of Inspector Lohman's crotch? As Lohman hints to Franz the burglar that the watchman has died, why does Lang cut to the watchman swilling beer and spearing sausages? What is the purpose of this comic scene?

18. THE TRIAL: After Becker tumbles shrieking down the steps, what is the effect of the silent panorama of all the criminals staring at him?

> WHAT MORAL ISSUES DOES THE TRIAL RAISE? HOW IS IT LIKE A "LAST JUDGMENT?"

> The Blind Balloon Man suddenly siezes Becker's shoulder. What are the symbolic connotations of this dreamlike action?

> Why does everyone laugh when Becker demands that he be turned over to the police? Why do the criminals refuse to trust the justice of the court?

> "I can't help what I do," Becker weeps. "You are criminals because you *want* to be, but what choice do I have?" What is the difference between Becker and his judges?

> Becker describes his life as a nightmare: "It's me pursuing myself..." Why does Lang cut to an old man nodding in agreement? On the other hand, why are most of the criminals outraged? Why don't they accept any of his defenses?

19. Why the *deus ex machina* ending when it's obvious that Becker is going to be torn to pieces? Why does Lang add the pious epilogue in which the grieving mothers weep that punishing him won't bring their children back?

THE THREEPENNY OPERA (1931—German) Directed by G.W. Pabst; based on the play by Bertolt Brecht and Kurt Weill. Distributed by Janus Films.

1. How does the opening tune set the mood of the film? What is Brecht's view of human nature? How does the imagery of the opening song establish this?

2. Note the shot of Polly Peachum looking at the wedding dress . . . MacHeath's reflection suddenly appears in the window. What is the effect of this shot? What is its purpose?

3. How is Mack characterized in the beer-hall scene? Note that he doesn't say a word for a long time . . . he only glowers and laughs harshly. His first words we merely *see* through the smoky window. What is the effect of this?

4. How does Brecht characterize the chief of police, Tiger Brown? What does Brecht imply in having Mack invite him to the wedding?

5. What is the point of having the wedding in an abandoned *warehouse?* How does Brecht regard the institution of marriage?

6. Note that Peachum has catalogued his beggars' rags according to type, each psychologically calculated to "touch the human heart." In what other ways does Peachum represent the Business Establishment? What is Brecht's attitude toward capitalism? Why does he have Peachum constantly quote the Bible?

7. "A mother-in-law should know where her son-in-law can be arrested." What is Brecht's view of human relationships?

8. Instead of escaping from the police, Mack spends his "regular Thursday night" at the Sporting House. How does this characterize him?

9. In the "Pirate Jenny" song, what does the *ship* symbolize? Why does Jenny betray Mack? Why does she later change her mind?

10. Introduced by the Beggar, all of Mack's former gang members appear as "Gentlemen of the Board" . . . "One can rob a bank, or one can rob others *through* a bank." Why is the latter method of becoming rich more practical?

11. When Peachum hears that Mack has become a bank president, he tries in vain to stop his beggars from marching on the coronation. Ignoring him, they march on in a silent flood. What is the significance of this?

12. Mack and Tiger Brown sing a happy tune about how much fun it was shooting natives back in their army days. What does this contribute to the theme of this film?

13. At the end, Mack joins forces with Peachum and Tiger Brown. What is the significance of this?

MODERN TIMES (1936—American) Directed by Charles Chaplin; with Paulette Goddard. Distributed by RBC Films and Films Inc., by arrangement with the Roy Export Co.

Charles Chaplin is a great artist because his comedy springs from tragedy. When the little tramp in *Modern Times* is gobbled up by a machine, we laugh—even if we know that the source of this comic food-metaphor is Upton Sinclair's *The Jungle,* in which workers who fall into the machinery are literally transformed into canned meat. Paradoxically, conservative industrialists were less upset with Sinclair for detailing their atrocities than with Chaplin for laughing at them. Robber-barons don't mind being regarded as monsters, but they definitely resent being portrayed as clowns.

***

1. The opening caption tells us that *Modern Times* is a story of capital and labor working hand in hand. What is the effect of the cut to a herd of sheep? How does the following dissolve to a stream of factory workers reveal Chaplin's actual attitude toward capitalism?

2. How is the president characterized by playing with a crossword puzzle and reading the comic strips? How does his observing the workers on a huge TV screen predict George Orwell's "Big Brother" in *1984?*

> As the boss snaps, "Section five—speed her up!" cut to Chaplin on an assembly line tightening bolts. What is the significance of his twitching hands as he takes his break?

3. What does the automatic feeding machine symbolize? How does Chaplin's meal epitomize what industry has done to its workers? What are the sexual connotations of the corn-feeder going wild? What is the significance of the machine's breakdown?

4. The afternoon speed-up causes Chaplin to go berserk. How is his being swallowed by the machine symbolic?

> How is his "Pan" act a self-parody? (Note the secretary's buttons and the fat lady on the street!)

Returning to the factory, Chaplin performs an elaborate comic ballet amidst the machinery, squirting everyone with an oilcan. Why is his Errol Flynn act funny?

5. Fresh out of the hospital, Chaplin picks up a red flag that has fallen off a truck—and suddenly finds an army of striking workers behind him! What is the effect of the music (the Communist Internationale)? How is this sequence a self-parody of Chaplin's political beliefs? What is the significance of the brutal way the police treat the protesters?

6. We first see Paulette Goddard stealing bananas from a boat. What are the erotic connotations of this activity? How does she parody Tarzan movies of the thirties?

Her father is one of the unemployed. Why does Chaplin include this tragic subplot?

7. Held as a communist leader, Chaplin languishes in jail. What is the symbolic purpose of the *eating* scene? Why does Chaplin insert the "nose-powder" joke?

8. After Paulette's father is shot by the police, the Law takes charge of the orphans. Why does Chaplin juxtapose the tea-drinking sequence with the minister's snooty wife? What do their gurgling stomachs symbolize? How does this comic analogue reinforce Chaplin's attitude toward authority figures?

9. With the sheriff's recommendation, Chaplin gets a job in a shipyard. How does the business with the boat reflect his life in general?

10. Alone and hungry, Paulette steals a loaf of bread . . . and meets Chaplin rather abruptly while trying to escape. When a "respectable" lady tells the police, why does Chaplin take the blame? Why does he *want* to go back to jail?

11. Chaplin meets Paulette again in the paddy wagon. Why is she so surprised at his gallantry? Why does Chaplin counter this sentimental moment by sitting in the fat lady's lap?

12. Chaplin and Paulette sit on the street fantasizing about the American Dream. Why does he include the shot of the man and his wife kissing goodbye? How do the shots of the grapes and the cow satirize the California Myth? What is the significance of a cop interrupting their fantasy?

13. Again using the sheriff's recommendation, Chaplin gets a job as a night watchman in a department store. How does Paulette's slipping into the store at night satirize the American Dream?

> ## WHAT DOES CHAPLIN'S SKATING (BLINDFOLDED!) ON THE EDGE OF THE ABYSS SYMBOLIZE?

14. "Stay where you are!" the robber commands. What is the significance of the business with the escalator, and of Chaplin's accidentally getting saturated with rum?

> "We ain't burglars—we're hungry," his old friend Bill claims. Why does Chaplin insert serious lines like this in otherwise comic scenes?

15. The next morning, Paulette wakes to find the store about to open. What is the significance of Chaplin's winding up in the "remainders" bin?

16. Chaplin gets out of jail to find Paulette waiting... She has found them a home. What does their crumbling house symbolize? What is the significance of the beam that keeps hitting him on the head? What are the connotations of his sleeping in the "dog house?" Note what happens when Chaplin dives into the bay to bathe. How is this a metaphor for his life?

17. Chaplin finally finds work as a mechanic's assistant. How does the tool box caught in the gears reflect Chaplin's purpose in making this film? Why is he so matter-of-fact about the mechanic's getting stuck in the machine? When the workers go on strike again, why do Chaplin and the mechanic react by scratching their heads?

18. Paulette gets Chaplin a job at her nightclub as a singing waiter. What does his performance with the *duck* on the crowded dance floor symbolize? Why does he include the *football* metaphor? How does the "shafted" duck reflect Chaplin himself?

19. "I hope you can *sing!*" his boss threatens. How does this sequence reveal Chaplin's attitude toward the new sound medium? What is the significance of his inability to remember his words?

> How is the song itself (about "a pretty girl and a gay old man") a self-parody?

20. What does Chaplin think of the juvenile officers' desire to "protect" Paulette from the evils of the working world?

21. On the Road Again... What is the significance of Chaplin's undying optimism? What does their walking on the white line up the middle of route one symbolize?

GRAND ILLUSION (1937—French) Directed by Jean Renoir; with Erich von Stroheim, Pierre Fresnay, and Jean Gabin. Distributed by Janus Films.

1. Capt. de Boeldieu and Lt. Marechal are shot down and captured by a German commander, von Rauffenstein: "If they are officers, invite them in for lunch." What is his attitude toward war, and how does this relate to the title "Grand Illusion?" What other details in this scene set the tone of the film and characterize Boeldieu and Rauffenstein?

2. In the Prison Camp: The French prisoners eat in style, thanks to Rosenthal's unending supply of canned delicacies. What is the significance of this?

3. As the French rehearse their performance, Boeldieu comments on the German military exercises: "On one side children play like soldiers, on the other soldiers play like children." What is Renoir's implication?

4. The French Variety Show, complete with "girls," is wildly applauded by the German officers... until Marechal announces the German military loss. Why does Renoir include this absurd "drag" show? What is the effect of the French "girls" taking off their wigs to sing the French national anthem? If this entire episode is a metaphor for World War One, how does Renoir view the nature of war?

5. What is the symbolic importance of Rauffenstein's being put in command of the castle? How does the setting characterize him? Note his obsession with white gloves. Also, what is the significance of his head being held in place by a silver plate and brace?

6. "Everyone would die of the disease of his class, if war didn't equalize all microbes." Boeldieu observes that syphilis, gout, and cancer are aristocratic diseases, but war is democratizing them, like everything else. What is the point of this conversation?

7. When Boeldieu asks, "Why do you accept my word and not theirs?" Rauffenstein replies with a sneer, "The word of a Rosenthal and a Marechal?" Although Rauffenstein is polite to the other two officers, he obviously dislikes and despises them. Why? Why is he so attentive to Boeldieu's needs and opinions?

8. When Boeldieu mentions that an aristocratic acquaintance "lost a leg in the war and married a rich woman," Rauffenstein exclaims, "What a fine career!" What does this reveal about the aristocratic view of war?

9. Rauffenstein mourns the fact that he is no longer a combatant, but a mere functionary. How does he symbolize the fate of the German aristocracy?

10. "I don't know who will win this war, but it will mean the end of the Rauffensteins and the Boeldieus." What does Rauffenstein mean by this?

11. What does Rauffenstein's *geranium* ("the only flower in the castle") symbolize?

12. Why does Boeldieu sacrifice himself to help Marechal and Rosenthal escape? What does his sacrifice symbolize?

> Why does Boeldieu wash his white gloves before going out to die? Why doesn't Marechal understand?

> British playwright Harold Pinter thinks that "all aristocrats are in love with death." What do you think of this idea?

13. Boeldieu plays his flute alone, up in the rafters. What does this symbolize? What is the tragedy implied in Rauffenstein's having to shoot him off the roof?

14. At Boeldieu's deathbed, Rauffenstein apologizes for his bad aim. Boeldieu comforts him with the philosophical assertion that "for an ordinary man to die in war is terrible . . . for us it's a good solution." What does he mean?

15. As the snow falls outside the window, Rauffenstein snips his geranium and places it on Boeldieu's body. What does this gesture symbolize?

16. A contrasting scene: Framed against the beautiful mountains, Marechal and Rosenthal quarrel bitterly, then become friends again. How are the two escapees characterized, and how do they represent twentieth century man?

17. Why does Renoir include the love scenes between Marechal and the German widow? "Lotte has blue eyes"—Why is this phrase repeated? What is the significance of his learning phrases of German and teaching her French?

18. Marechal's conversation with the cow: "You're a poor cow, and I'm a poor soldier." What is the point of this?

20. What is the effect of the last shot, showing Marechal and Rosenthal's struggling figures, surrounded by vast fields of snow? (One critic has observed that they are "stumbling into the twentieth century." How is this so?)

THE RULES OF THE GAME (1939—French) Directed by Jean Renoir; distributed by Janus Films.

1. Why does Renoir preface the film with a quotation from Beaumarchais and a theme from Mozart? How do they set the tone of the film? Although the film is obviously a social and political satire, why does Renoir insist that it contains no social criticism?

2. "I flew the Atlantic for her"—How does this characterize Andre? Why doesn't Christine show up for his landing? ("She's a society woman, and society has strict rules.")

3. How does Christine's husband, La Chesnay, differ from Andre in his attitude toward love? What is the significance of his collecting mechanical birds and music boxes?

4. Schumacher and the gamekeepers at La Coliniere spend all their time shooting rabbits. How does this relate to the central action of the film? In the course of the film, what do *rabbits* come to symbolize?

5. Why does Christine make a public speech about her friendship with Andre? Why does her husband congratulate her on her speech?

6. How are the aristocrats characterized by their pheasant hunt? How does this activity symbolize the sexual intrigue in the film, as well as the political and social assumptions of the upper class?

7. How do the *masquerade party* and the dance of the skeletons relate to the love intrigue? (cf. ending of Mozart's *Marriage of Figaro*)

8. What is the significance of Octave's being stuck in his bear costume? How does this characterize him? Why does Renoir play this part?

9. As La Chesnay presents his prize music box, Renoir cuts to the two pairs of lovers. What is the point of this juxtaposition?

10. Why does Renoir include the kitchen intrigue between Marceau and Lisette? What is the significance of his being a *poacher?* How does her constantly eating *apples* characterize her? Why would Lisette rather "stay with madame" than go with her husband, and what is the political significance of this?

11. Why does Andre insist on talking with La Chesnay before eloping with Christine? Why does she balk at this? How do his "rules" differ from hers?

12. While everyone dances drunkenly, Schumacher runs wild through the chateau, firing his pistol. How do the aristocrats react, and how does this reflect the values of the ruling class?

13. What does Christine's "wearing Lisette's cloak" symbolize, and what is the significance of the ensuing confusion of identities?

14. How does La Chesnay's final speech reflect society's attitude toward its artists, lovers, and heroes?

THE WIZARD OF OZ (1939—American) Directed by Victor Fleming; with Judy Garland, Ray Bolger, and Bert Lahr. An MGM Film, distributed by Films Inc.

1. What is the significance of Dorothy's attachment to Toto?

2. "Somewhere Over the Rainbow"—How does this relate to the American Myth of Happiness? What is ironic about Judy Garland's dying later of alcoholism?

3. What does Professor Marvel represent? What is the significance of his later transformation into the Wizard of Oz?

4. Why does Fleming cut from Dorothy's spinning head to the house flying through the air?

5. Note the "dream effects" passing by the window, especially the rear-screen projection of Miss Gulch, whose bicycle turns into a broomstick. What social and political force does she represent?

6. When the house lands, what is the effect of the sudden shift to color film? Why are the colors so psychedelic? What do the plastic plants symbolize? What is the effect of Dorothy's understated reaction? ("I have a feeling we're not in Kansas anymore.")

7. How does Munchkinland symbolize California, delivered from the "Wicked Witch of the East?"

8. What is the significance of the witch's obsession with the *red shoes?*

9. Glinda tells Dorothy to "follow the Yellow Brick Road" to the Emerald City where the mysterious wizard lives. What does this road symbolize? How does Dorothy's journey to the Emerald City reflect the migration of farmworkers to New York?

10. The farmworkers are transformed into three symbolic allies: The Scarecrow, hung up in space, complains, "I can't make up my mind. I don't have a brain." The Tin Man is rusted stiff because he has no heart; he's "all hollow." The Lion is all bluster, but he lacks courage. How do these transformations relate to their characters in the opening scene?

> "I feel like I've known you all along." How do the three reflect different parts of Dorothy's psyche? What does her release of them signify?

> What is the political significance of their thinking that "the Wizard will fix everything?"

11. The Witch plans to put them to sleep with *poppies*. What does this mythological reference symbolize? (cf. Odysseus in the Land of the Lotus Eaters)

12. As Dorothy and her friends dance their way to the Emerald City, they sing, "You're out of the woods/ You're into the light." How do these metaphors express the thirties attitude toward The City?

13. People who live in this futuristic utopia do nothing but laugh all day. How is Oz like heaven, or like Huxley's "Brave New World?"

14. What is the significance of the fact that no one has ever *seen* the Great Oz?

15. How does the Lion's song about being king of the forest satirize traditional images of power? Why is it *operatic* in style?

16. What is the implication of Oz, the new authority figure, being a *projection?* How does this predict the modern concept of "media presidents?"

17. Oz demands, "WHO are YOU?" How does this relate to the film's theme?

18. Their quest: They must bring the witch's *broomstick* before the Wizard will grant their requests. What does this ritual symbolize?

19. What does the haunted forest symbolize? The witch's soldiers are *flying monkeys.* Why is this appropriate during the rise of Hitler? (Notice the rear-screen projection and the brilliant animation during this sequence.)

20. Toto escapes and leads Dorothy's friends back across the cubist landscape to rescue her. What is the significance of the *Scarecrow* devising the plan to get into the castle by disguising as soldiers?

21. The confrontation with the Witch: What is the significance of her being destroyed by *water?*

22. "If you were really great and powerful, you'd keep your promises." How does this reveal the general American suspicion about politics and religion? As Toto opens the curtain, the unveiled Oz admits, "There's no other wizard except me." What are the political and theological implications of this?"

23. The Wizard gives the Scarecrow a diploma, the Lion a medal, and the Tin Man a testimonial watch. What is the significance of his observations?

24. After leaving the Scarecrow to rule, aided by the Tin Man and the Lion, Oz takes off in a balloon. What does his departure symbolize? ("I can't come back—I don't know how it works!")

25. Glinda: "You always *had* the power to return to Kansas." Why didn't Glinda tell her this in the first place?

"What have you learned, Dorothy?" What is the significance of the moral, and of the fact that she had to learn it for herself?

CITIZEN KANE (1941—American) Directed by Orson Welles; with Joseph Cotten and Agnes Moorehead; music by Bernard Herrmann. Distributed by Janus Films/Films Inc.

1. Note the free movement of the camera in the opening shot of the fence. How does this series of forward-tracking shots, each dissolving into the next, set the tone for Welles' analysis of Kane's character?

> What do details like the "No Trespassing" sign and the shot of the monkeys in a cage symbolize?

> Cross-fade to *snow* and an extreme closeup of the *glass ball*...Kane whispers "ROSEBUD" and dies as the glass ball slips from his hand and shatters on the steps. How do these symbols relate to each other and to the film's theme?

2. Cut to the parody-newsreel, which speaks of Xanadu as a collection of "everything...the loot of the world...so big it can't be catalogued...the costliest monument a man has built to himself." In what ways are Kane and Xanadu symbols of America itself?

> What is the purpose of this "objective" history of Kane's life?

3. Susan Alexander, drunk, is seen first through a rainy skylight. How does this remarkable shot illuminate her character?

4. Thatcher Library: What is the effect of the cold granite, pierced by shafts of light? Of the echo in the librarian's voice? Why do we only see Thompson from the rear?

5. *FLASHBACK* to Kane's childhood: He is seen through the window while his parents argue over entrusting him to Thatcher. Notice how often Welles contrasts dramatic action between background and foreground.

Kane clutches his sleigh and refuses to leave his mother. What is the purpose of the lingering shot of snow burying the abandoned sleigh?

6. Uninterested in his inheritance, Kane only wants to run a newspaper because "it might be fun." What is the significance of his wanting to be a newspaperman? How does his attitude toward reality change in the course of the film, and why?

7. What are some of the ironies in his confrontation with Thatcher, who resents his muckraking activities? (end of flashback)

8. Thompson interviews Bernstein, whose wealth has made him very content. Why is he different from Kane in this respect?

9. *FLASHBACK* to the opening of the *Inquirer,* which is being run by a group of inefficient old fogies. What is symbolic about Kane's moving his furniture into the editor's office? Why does Leland decide to keep the original copy of Kane's "Declaration of Principles?" ("No special interests will interfere with the truth.") Given Kane's character, why is this principle impossible?

Kane wants to make his newspaper "as necessary as the *gas* in the lamp." Why is this ironic?

Cut from photo of rival newsmen to celebration after Kane has bought them... Why does this bother Leland?

What is symbolic about Kane's returning from his European "Art Collecting" trip with a fiancee? (end of flashback)

10. Thompson visits Leland in a convalescent hospital. What do you think of Leland's analysis of Kane's character? Might Leland have any ulterior motive?

11. *FLASHBACK* to Kane's marriage with Emily: How does Welles suggest both character development and the passage of time in the quick succession of quarrels over the breakfast table?

12. Splattered with mud, Kane is taken home by Susan Alexander. Why is he attracted to her? How do the *mud* and her *toothache* foreshadow the result of their relationship? What is the effect of the dissolve of Susan at the piano to another, richer, room?

13. What are some of the ironies in Kane's political campaign as champion of the underprivileged?

14. Kane is forced by his wife to go with her to Susan's apartment, where his political rival is waiting. Why does he decide to stay with Susan?

15. Kane loses the election. Leland accuses him of trying to buy people's love, demanding love on his own terms. What is the effect of shooting this scene from a low angle?

16. Why does Kane marry Susan and sponsor her operatic career? What is the effect of the *pan up* from her singing on the stage to the stagehands above?

17. Why does Kane complete Leland's critical review of Susan's performance? Why would he then fire Leland? (End of flashback)

18. Leland: "He was disappointed with the world, so he built one of his own." How is this idea reflected throughout the film?

19. Thompson visits Susan again:

20. *FLASHBACK* to Susan's singing lesson: Despite her lack of talent, why is Kane determined to have Susan succeed as a singer? How does this reflect his world-view? Or his role as a newspaperman?

21. Susan's performance: What is the effect of the cuts from the prompter's cringing face, to the grimly determined Kane, to Leland making paper dolls of his program?

22. In the midst of Kane's confrontation with Susan, Leland returns Kane's check—along with his "Declaration of Principles." How does this account differ from Leland's own story of his firing?

> Kane insists that she keep singing—why? What is the effect of his shadow looming over her?

> As she continues, drowned in phony publicity, what is the effect of the newspaper headlines juxtaposed against the sound of her voice?

23. Why does Susan take an overdose? (Note again the contrast between foreground and background.)

24. Years later, we see Kane and Susan at Xanadu. They talk in echoes about what time it is. She wants to return to New York. Why does she hate living there?

> What is the effect of the enormous *fireplace* that dwarfs them? What do her jig-saw puzzles symbolize?

25. Kane and Susan go on a little "picnic." What is the effect of the zoom from the closeup of them to the endless caravan of cars?

> Susan complains that Kane has "never given her anything that *meant* something." She accuses him of demanding love in exchange for *things*. How does Welles intend this as a criticism of the American character and of America itself?

26. When Susan packs her bags to leave, what is the significance of Kane's reaction? ("You can't do this to me.") (end of flashback)

27. Thompson interviews the butler at Xanadu, who tells him about "ROSEBUD." Why is the butler the last person in the world who could understand Kane's obsession?

28. *FLASHBACK* to Kane's reaction to Susan's departure: He tears the room to pieces, then stops when he comes upon the glass ball and whispers "ROSEBUD." He finally marches silently past his servants, reflected to infinity in his mirrors. What does the setting symbolize? (end of flashback)

29. The survey of all the artwork in Xanadu: "He never threw anything away." What is the significance of Kane's obsession with *collecting?*

> "If you put all this together, what would it spell?" Rosebud? America?

> What is the effect of the camera zooming back to show all the piled crates?

30. As workmen throw junk into the furnace, the revelation about ROSEBUD is not as simple as it may seem . . . But what *is* the only reason a little boy climbs a hill?

31. Why does Welles conclude with a final shot of the *fence* and the "No Trespassing" sign?

***

Brilliant as he is, Orson Welles has never made a film as good as *Citizen Kane,* his first film, which he shot when he was in his twenties. Why might this be so? Why is his study of William Randolph Hearst so sensitive and effective?

CHILDREN OF PARADISE (1945—French) Directed by Marcel Carne; with Jean-Louis Barrault, Arletty, and Pierre Brasseur; written by Jacques Prevert. Distributed by Janus Films/Films Inc.

1. Garance as "The Naked Truth": What does she symbolize?

2. Frederick tries to pick up Garance... "Paris is small for lovers like us." How is he characterized by using the same approach on the next lady who passes by?

3. What is ironic about Lacenaire's writing *love letters* for a living? Why would someone with his "education" be "at war with society?" He brags about loving no one, about being alone... Do you believe him?

4. The theft of the watch: What is the significance of Baptiste's relationship with his father?

5. AT THE FUNAMBULES: Jericho predicts that Nathalie will marry the man she loves. What does Jericho symbolize?

> While the actors battle, the audience goes wild. What does the audience symbolize? Why are they called "Children of Paradise?"

6. As Nathalie admires herself in the mirror, Baptiste enters smelling the rose Garance gave him. Why does Nathalie keep saying, "I have such faith in you?" Why doesn't Baptiste love her?

7. In the bar, Baptiste and Frederick discuss their art. How are the two men characterized? What is the significance of Baptiste's "speaking with his legs," while Frederick is a man of *words?* How do they differ in their view of themselves and their attitude toward their audience? ("Their lives are very small, but their dreams are very big.")

8. As Frederick flirts with Madame Hermine, the landlady, Baptiste encounters the "Blind Man." What is the purpose of this juxtaposition?

9. At the Red Throat Tavern, Lacenaire and his gang joke about beheadings and deride actors ("The church used to bury them at night.")

When Avril throws Baptiste through the window, what is the significance of his return?

10. Baptiste takes Garance home. How does his attitude toward love differ from hers? ("Life...Dreams...It's all the same.") In what symbolic sense does their first kiss lead to lightning and thunder?

> In her room: Why does he hesitate to make love with her, despite her hints about not being sleepy?

11. As Baptiste runs in panic from Garance's room, Frederick lies in bed reading *Othello:* "She must die, else she'll betray more men." What is the significance of this juxtaposition? How does it foreshadow the end of the film?

> "Did you lock your door, my love?"
> "What could a thief take from me?"
> Frederick and Garance *seem* to have the same view of love...or do they?

12. BAPTISTE'S PANTOMIME: What does his worship of the goddess Diana (=the moon) symbolize? Harlequin, played by Frederick, takes his flowers while he sleeps and goes off with the goddess. What is the significance of this performance? In describing the relationship between Art and Life, why would an artist portray *painful* personal experiences? Why would Baptiste have his father play the *cop?*

13. In the SUICIDE BALLET, Nathalie uses Baptiste's rope as a clothesline...What does this imply about marriage? Why does Baptiste suddenly stop when he looks offstage and sees Frederick talking with Garance? Why does Baptiste still deny the reality of their affair? ("They aren't living together...they're only pretending to live.")

14. In Garance's dressing room, Frederick chatters about love. Why does Garance insist that she and Frederick don't really love each other?

15. The Count de Montray sends a mountain of flowers to announce his visit. What is the significance of Garance's reaction? ("Somebody's dead?") Why doesn't she like his proposal to "change her life?" What is the significance of his fondling a cardboard *turkey* as he spouts platitudes about falling in love?

16. As the count leaves, Baptiste enters..."A funeral? Mine perhaps." What is the significance of Baptiste's obsession with death? Why does he destroy the flowers? Why does he X his reflection in the mirror? ("I hate Frederick, I hate myself!")

17. Nathalie breaks in on them, insisting that no one could love Baptiste as much as she does. How does Garance react to her ideas about love?

18. Several years later, Frederick is a successful actor, with a girl on each arm. Why does Carne include that awful melodrama for Frederick to make fun of?

19. Why does Lacenaire appear in Frederick's dressing room? Why do they wind up liking each other? How are they alike?

20. The Duel: Note the melodramatic fog. What is the effect of Frederick and his friends staggering drunk from their carriage?

21. The wounded Frederick visits the Funambules to see Baptiste's performance. The mysterious lady in the box turns out to be Garance... Why does she come to see Baptiste perform every night without letting him know she's there?

22. Baptiste's Performance: He is thrown out when he tries to get into the Ball. How does this reveal his self-image and define his relationship to society? What is the significance of his "killing" Jericho, who is portrayed by his father?

23. Why does Jericho tell Nathalie that Garance is waiting for Baptiste in her box. Why does Nathalie send her little boy to speak to her?

> Baptiste (again) stops dead in the middle of a performance
> and runs to her box... Why has she left?

24. Lacenaire tells Garance he hoped to find her changed—"stupefied by money." Why? How would this allow him to hang onto his idea of human nature?

> When the count asks "who he is," Lacenaire replies with a
> lecture on how no one ever reveals his true self. What is the
> significance of this conversation being set *on the stairs?*

25. Montray confronts Garance: What does he really want from her? Why is his polite, formal tone ironic? Why is their conversation shot in the *mirror?*

26. Why does Baptiste take refuge in his old room, where he "sleeps and dreams" and refuses to eat?

> "Love is so simple"/ "I made conditions." What has he
> realized?

27. What is the significance of *OTHELLO* as the backdrop for the climactic encounter? Why do the count and his friends insult Shakespeare? Why does Lacenaire draw the curtain on the "farce?"

28. Baptiste and Garance return to her old room. What is the significance of its remaining the same?

29. Lacenaire and his friend weave through the carnival to find the count. What is the significance of the murder being performed in the *bath?* What is the connotation of Montray's Roman *toga?* Why doesn't Carne show the actual stabbing? Why does Lacenaire remain to face execution?

30. Nathalie confronts Baptiste and Garance in her bedroom. Where do your sympathies lie in this scene? ("You go and you return, beautified by memory.")

31. What is the significance of Baptiste's being engulfed in the crowd as he struggles to reach Garance's carriage?

BEAUTY AND THE BEAST (1946—French) Directed by Jean Cocteau; with Jean Marais and Josette Day. Distributed by Janus Films.

1. Aside from "Filthy Beastly Lust," what does the Beast symbolize?

> "At times, he's almost noble... At times, he seems stricken with infirmity." How does the Beast reflect Cocteau's self-image?

> "Everything I have comes by magic." How does the Beast represent the Romantic concept of the artist?

2. At first, Beauty is horrified by the Beast. Why does she finally change her mind, and what is the significance of her growing to love him?

3. Why does the Beast tell Beauty never to look into his eyes? Why does she have so much control over the Beast... or does she? How does the Beast compare with King Kong in this respect?

What is the importance of the scene in which the Beast drinks from Beauty's hands?

4. The Beast tells Beauty that he'll meet her for dinner each night at seven. What is the symbolic function of this ritual?

5. What are the connotations of the other important symbols in the film: the sculptures, the rose, the mirror, the glove, the Beast's smoking hands...?

How has Cocteau's choice of symbols been influenced by the surrealist painters?

6. Why does the Beast give Beauty the key to Diana's Pavillion? How does this pavillion relate to Beauty's inner life?

7. The Beast sends Beauty his horse and mirror. As she looks into the mirror, her face changes into that of the suffering Beast. What is the significance of this? How does it foreshadow the ending?

8. Avenant and Beauty's brother plan to kill the Beast. What social and psychological forces do they represent?

9. As the Beast lies dying by the waterhole, Avenant breaks into the pavillion. What does the breaking of the skylight symbolize?

10. "You resemble someone I know..." What is the significance of the final "switch?" What is the *tone* of the "Superman" ending?

(The most interesting analysis of Beauty and the Beast is in Carl Jung's *Man and His Symbols*.)

THE RED SHOES (1948—English) Directed by Michael Powell and Emeric Pressburger; with Moira Shearer, Anton Walbrook, and Marius Goring; music by Brian Easdale. Distributed by Walter Reade 16.

1. Note the polarity in the characterization of the rivals for Victoria's love: Julian is blond, English, and romantic in the tradition of the chain-smoking forties hero. Lermontov is dark, European, and icily intellectual.

Clearly, they "love" her in very different ways. What are the cultural implications of their rivalry? How are both men *archetypes?*

2. The opening: The students burst through the doors to fill the balcony for the Ballet Lermontov. Julian Kraster, sitting in the front row, is shocked to realize that Professor Palmer has stolen *his* music for *Heart of Fire.* How is he characterized by storming out of the theater?

> Why does Brian Easdale echo Stravinsky in this opening ballet? How is Boris Lermontov like Serge Diaghilev, founder of the Ballets Russes?

> Why does Powell show us only Lermontov's *hand* refusing the party invitation? Why does he change his mind when Palmer tells him Lady Neston is a "patron of the arts?"

3. For Lermontov, ballet is a "religion." Why, then, does he decline to see Victoria dance?

> Embarassed at meeting "the Horror" face to face, Lermontov asks, "Why do you want to dance?" Victoria snaps, "Why do you want to live?" In light of the film's ending, why is this exchange ironic? Why does Lermontov change his mind and decide to audition her?

4. When Julian barges in to apologize for his impulsive letter, why does Lermontov advise him to destroy the letter and forget about *Heart of Fire?* ("It is more disheartening to have to steal then to be stolen from.") Why does he offer the young man a job?

5. Why does Lermontov vanish without a word when his prima ballerina announces that she has just gotten married? How does his dismissal of her parallel the main action of the film?

6. Lermontov tells Julian the story of the Red Shoes: "Life rushes by, but the red shoes dance on." What is symbolic about his assigning the music of this ballet to Julian? In what sense is *The Red Shoes* a "temptation myth?"

7. "You cannot have it both ways," Lermontov tells Ljubov. "A dancer who relies on doubtful human love will never be a great dancer." Why does he insist on "ignoring human nature?" Why does Powell focus on Victoria's face during Lermontov's speech?

8. Monte Carlo: Lermontov sends his car to call for Victoria. How does her ascent up the steps of his villa echo Cocteau's *Beauty and the Beast?*

9. Unable to sleep because of their excitement over *The Red Shoes*, Julian and Victoria meet on the balcony. What is ironic about Lermontov's "sending them both to bed?" How does the train passing beneath them foreshadow the film's ending?

10. Victoria complains that the tempo of the music is too fast. How does this classic *agon* between Music and Dance anticipate the tragic conflict?

11. Lermontov calms Victoria's stagefright by reminding her of the rainy night he saw her dance in London. Why does he suddenly drop her hands and walk off stiffly?

12. THE BALLET OF THE RED SHOES: The demonic shoemaker lures Victoria away from her lover with a reflection of her dancing in the Red Shoes. How does this seduction reflect the film's theme?

Victoria's lover is carried away... What is the meaning of her whirling dance with the sailors and the businessmen?

Her mother tries in vain to restrain her... Why does Victoria superimpose the images of Lermontov and Julian on the figure of the shoemaker?

What is the meaning of the transformation of the stage setting into a hallucinatory dreamscape?

Why does Victoria imagine Julian coming up onto the stage to dance with her? What does her vision of the ocean waves symbolize?

Why does Powell juxtapose the church procession? What is the meaning of Victoria's inability to remove the shoes as her lover, dressed as a priest, backs away and enters the church with the others?

In the blatant symbolic conclusion, the lover returns too late... He removes her shoes and carries her body into the church as the shoemaker dances off with the shoes. How is this entire ballet sequence a thematic analogue to the main action of the film?

13. Lermontov brushes everyone away so he can talk with Victoria: "What do you want from life?" Without hesitation, she replies, "To dance." How does this scene reveal Lermontov's "Pygmalion complex?" How does her performance as the puppet comment on their relationship?

14. If Lermontov doesn't love Victoria himself, why the tight little smile on his face when his colleagues announce her romance with Julian?

15. Why does Powell dissolve from Victoria and Julian's love scene in the

carriage to Lermontov sitting alone in his box? How do the two settings contrast? Why is Lermontov outraged that Victoria would smile at Julian while she's dancing? ("Dreaming is a luxury I've never permitted in my company!")

16. Despite the opinion of his colleagues, why does Lermontov reject Julian's latest score as "childish, vulgar, and insignificant?"

17. Victoria confronts Lermontov to ask why he broke with Julian. When he offers to make her "one of the greatest dancers the world has ever known," what is the significance of her response?

18. "Fool" is Lermontov's reaction to the announcement of Victoria and Julian's wedding. Why does he smash his image in the mirror?

19. Julian slips out of bed to play his piano . . . What does this imply about their relationship? Why does Victoria stop to fondle her ballet slippers before running to embrace him? After reading about this incident in their letters, why does Lermontov decide to write to her? Why does he tear up the letter when his aide informs him that she will be in town next week?

20. Lermontov meets Victoria at the railroad station . . . "Would Julian give up his opera if you asked him to?" Why does she succumb to his plea to "put on the red shoes and dance for us again?"

21. Cut to the announcement of Julian's opera opening at Covent Garden. What is the significance of Julian's sudden "illness?" Why does he insist that Victoria not perform? In their confrontation with Lermontov, why is her position tragic?

22. Why does Victoria hallucinate that she is wearing the Red Shoes? What does her plunge from the balcony symbolize?

23. In its portrayal of relationships, how does *The Red Shoes* differ from *The Turning Point* and other feminist films of the late seventies?

THE BICYCLE THIEF (1949—Italian) Directed by Vittorio De Sica. Distributed by Corinth Films.

To audiences raised on the montage sequences of "new wave" films and commercial TV, the long tracking shots in *The Bicycle Thief* may seem tedious and primitive. Why does De Sica turn his back on twenty-five years of film technique? Because he regards montage as manipulative and dishonest. Although the film is about a "cycle"—in a double sense—De Sica is not likely to roll it down the Spanish Steps in imitation of Eisenstein. Such trickery is not necessary to convey the poverty and suffering of post-war Rome. Instead, he details the odyssey of an ordinary man, magnifying his mishap into a universal tragedy and forcing us to identify with him. By the end of the film, a stolen bicycle symbolizes the shattered hopes and the spiritual deprivation of the entire human race.

***

1. A major Hollywood studio reportedly offered Vittorio De Sica a fortune and a fancy technicolor production—provided that he cast Cary Grant in the lead role of *The Bicycle Thief.* Why would De Sica refuse, preferring to film "non-actors" in simple black-and-white?

2. Pleading for work, the unemployed mob a government contractor. Why does De Sica begin the film with this bleak image of poverty and unemployment? Why does he stress that Ricci's survival depends on his bicycle?

3. What is the effect of the *barbed wire* as Ricci interrupts his wife at the well? What do the two buckets of water symbolize?

4. What does Maria's pawning their *wedding sheets* symbolize? As Ricci redeems his precious bicycle, what is the significance of the whole line of bikes and the surreal warehouse full of pawned wedding sheets?

5. Marie visits the Santona ("the one who sees".) What are the mythical connotations of this visit? Does De Sica regard the fortune teller as a mere charlatan, preying on the superstition of her neighbors—or does she serve some symbolic purpose?

6. Ricci's job is to paste up Rita Hayworth posters. Why is this ironic? What does De Sica think of glamorous Hollywood movies?

> Why does he juxtapose Ricci's comic attempts to smooth Rita Hayworth's lumps (!) against the tragic theft of the bicycle?

7. How does the police station, with its shelves of disintegrating documents, recall the mountain of pawned wedding sheets. How do both images comment on modern governments?

> Since the problem is "just a bicycle," the police captain tells Ricci to look for it himself. What is the significance of his indifference?

8. Why does De Sica include the vaudeville act with the singer who keeps hitting the wrong note? How does this performance reflect the film's tragic theme?

9. At the market, Ricci and his friends find thousands of bicycles in pieces. What does this mass dis-assembly symbolize? What is the effect of all the long tracking shots?

> "It's hopeless! Come Sunday, it rains"—What is the symbolic function of the weather as Ricci and Bruno search?

10. As the rain clears, Ricci briefly spots the bicycle thief talking with an old man, whom he pursues into the soup-kitchen of a mission. Why does De Sica set their confrontation in a church? Why does he include the rich ladies with their fancy hats and the well-scrubbed young men who pause to genuflect while chasing Ricci through the church?

11. When the old man escapes, why does Ricci hit his son? How does this incident illustrate De Sica's use of "parallel structure?"

> While Ricci searches by the river, why does De Sica juxtapose the cries of the crowd trying to save a drowning boy?

12. Ricci makes up with Bruno over a pizza and a bottle of wine. Why does De Sica include the pampered rich boy at the next table? What is the effect of the cheerful violin music while Ricci and Bruno calculate how much money they *could* have made if the bicycle hadn't been stolen?

13. Why does Ricci return to the fortune teller? Why does De Sica include the sequence with the homely young man? How does the oracle's advice

("Put your seeds in another field") also apply to Ricci's pursuit of his elusive bicycle?

14. The thief turns out to be epileptic. Why does De Sica imply that he too is a victim? Why do the boy's neighbors—who *must* know he's a thief—gang up on Ricci?

15. What is the effect of all the *cheering* as Ricci spots an unattended bicycle by the stadium? Why is his action ironic? What is De Sica saying about poverty and crime?

ORPHEUS (1949—French) Directed by Jean Cocteau; with Jean Marais. Distributed by Janus Films.

1. What is a "myth?" What is the purpose of myth?

2. In the ancient Greek myth, Orpheus is a skilled musician who pursues his dead wife, Eurydice, to the Underworld. He plays such beautiful music for Dis, god of the Underworld, that he is allowed to take his wife back to Earth—on condition that he does not look back at her during their journey. Unable to resist looking, he turns, and she is snatched back to the land of the dead. Shortly afterward, Orpheus himself is torn apart by the Bacchantes (a primitive Women's Lib group), resulting in his metamorphosis into a constellation.

What are some of the symbolic meanings of this myth? In what ways does Orpheus prefigure Christ? How does Orpheus epitomize the Artist?

3. What is the *tone* of Cocteau's version of the Orpheus myth? Is it a serious commentary on the idea of death and rebirth? A satirical comparison of modern life with the civilization of ancient Greece? Both of these?

4. Several modern French playwrights—including Sartre, Anouilh, Giraudoux, and Cocteau—have adapted Greek myths and dramas. What are the artistic advantages of basing a modern film or play on an ancient myth?

***

5. The film opens in a Paris cafe. Why is Orpheus unwelcome among the avant-garde poets there?

> What is the significance of Death arriving in a Rolls Royce?
> Of Death's agents riding motorcycles?

6. The Journey to Death's Mansion... "Sleeping or waking, the dreamer must accept his dreams." What does this reveal about Cocteau's view of "Reality?"

> What is the significance of Death entering and exiting through *mirrors?* What do mirrors symbolize for Cocteau? What does his obsession with mirrors reveal about his approach to art?

> "Silence goes better backwards... A single glass of water lights the world."—Significance of these radio messages? Is this a platonic view of the origin of poetry? Or is Cocteau implying something negative about modern poetry, and about modern life in general?

> The poets and the press consider Orpheus responsible for Cegeste's disappearance. Symbolic significance of this?

> Significance of Orpheus accompanying Cegeste's body? How do Orpheus and Cegeste represent two sides of Cocteau himself?

7. Returning from his strange evening with Death, Orpheus is upset and impatient with his wife. How does this differ from the original Greek myth?

> Why does Cocteau portray Eurydice as a very "ordinary" woman?

> Aglaonice's "League of Women"= the Bacchantes

8. Orpheus spends all his time sitting in the Rolls Royce, listening to radio messages, while Eurydice sits neglected. What is the meaning of this metaphor?

> "Just like a woman... One discovers a new world, and all she talks about is bottles and babies."

> "It's not that talking car I fear—it's what he seeks." What *does* the poet seek, according to Cocteau?

9. "Every night, the Death of Orpheus entered his room and watched him sleep."—Why does Cocteau depict Death as a woman?

> What are the symbolic associations of Death's *rubber gloves?*

10. Heurtebise: "Mirrors are the doors through which Death comes and goes . . . Look in a mirror all your life, and you will see Death at work, like bees in a hive of glass."

11. The Journey to the Underworld: "Here are men's memories, and the ruins of their beliefs."

> Note the details: The glazier, the wind, the ruins. (The "old lady" seated on the window ledge is actually Cocteau.) What is the effect of the setting?

12. The Judges sit in a stark, ruined room, reminiscent of the setting in Kafka's *Trial.* They accuse Death of taking a woman whose time hadn't come. What does this imply about the powers of Death? What is Cocteau's view of the force that rules the universe?

> In the Greek myth, Orpheus is allowed to take his wife back to Earth because his music charms the ruler of the Underworld. What is the difference here?

> When Orpheus says he wants to appeal to the Source of all the "orders," Death replies: "He exists nowhere. Some say he sleeps, and we are his bad dreams."

13. What is the irony in Orpheus' being forbidden to look at his wife? What is the symbolic significance of his accidentally glimpsing her in the rear-view mirror of the car?

14. What is the significance of the mob's attack? What is Cocteau saying about the relationship of artist and public?

> Orpheus: "Life sculpts me . . . I am hewn like marble." How does this relate to what society usually does to its artists and saviors?

15. Note the special effects during Orpheus' second journey to the Underworld.

> Why does Death order Heurtebise to strangle Orpheus?

"The death of a poet requires a sacrifice to render him immortal."

By what strange logic does Orpheus then walk backwards through the corridor of death to reappear back on Earth?

16. Eurydice awakens from her nightmare... Why does Cocteau use this dream framework? How does his treatment of this device differ from the usual cliche?

Note that while Orpheus and Eurydice talk, Heurtebise backs through the mirror.

17. Why are Death and Heurtebise taken away by the police? What do you make of Heurtebise's final cryptic comment—"They had to return to their mire"—?

LOS OLVIDADOS (1950—Spanish) Directed by Luis Bunuel. Distributed by Audio-Brandon.

Like the Italian "neo-realist" films, *Los Olvidados* is almost documentary in tone. Bunuel shot the film in the streets of Mexico, rather than in a studio, using non-actors instead of professionals. Rejecting the Dickensian idea of the "virtuous poor," Bunuel shows what actually happens to souls that have been transformed by poverty. His "clean window" camera style emphasizes the truth of his vision, drawing the audience into the lives of real people, instead of attracting attention to itself by elaborate tricks. There are still some reminders, however, of Bunuel's earlier surrealist style—the same dreamlike violence as *Un Chien Andalou*, the allegorical figures of *L'Age d'Or*, and the Freudian idea of the unconscious that has been typical of his films from 1928 to the present.

1. What are the differences between Bunuel's depiction of juvenile delinquency and the usual Hollywood version starring Sal Mineo or Marlon Brando?

2. Although Bunuel claims to offer no solutions to the problem of juvenile delinquency, what are some of the *causes* he implies?

3. What is the symbolic purpose of the *bullfight* that the children pantomime?

4. Why do the other boys idolize Jaibo? Why doesn't Bunuel sentimentalize him?

5. Why does Bunuel include the episode of the legless beggar?

6. What does Julian's death symbolize?

7. PEDRO'S DREAM: Note the double-exposure of Pedro rising from his bed. A chicken floats down from the ceiling... He finds the dead Julian under his bed, laughing at him... His mother floats over to him ("Why don't you ever kiss me?")... She gives him an enormous slice of meat... Then Julian emerges from under the bed and grabs it. WHAT DOES THIS DREAM MEAN?

8. In Pedro's wanderings, he encounters the pervert in the street, quarrels with the ragpickers, and winds up pushing the merry-go-round for pesos. What is the symbolic importance of these incidents, and how do they relate to the theme?

9. While the *trained dogs* dance in the street, Jaibo and Pedro's mother go to bed. What is the implication of this juxtaposition? How does it reflect on the way she treats her own son? Why is it ironic that she is morally outraged when Pedro returns after wandering for days?

10. What is ironic in her committing Pedro to a reformatory?

11. When the social worker asks, "Don't you love your son?" Pedro's mother replies, "How could I? When I was a girl, his father deceived me." How does this imply a *cycle* in the life of the poor?

12. Although he is being blamed and punished, why won't Pedro reveal that Jaibo stole the knife?

13. At the reformatory, Pedro kills the chickens. Why? How does this relate to the theme of the film?

14. Instead of punishing Pedro, the director gives him fifty pesos and sends him on an errand. Why does Pedro fail, and what is the significance of this?

15. THE BLIND MAN'S SOLUTION TO JUVENILE DELINQUENCY: "They should hang all those criminals. Under my General, they used to hang people for stealing a loaf of bread." What force in society does the Blind Man represent? Why doesn't Bunuel agree with this approach to solving crime?

16. What is the significance of the *chickens* that cluck around Pedro's dead body?

17. Jaibo's dying vision: "Careful—here comes the mangy dog." What does this symbolize, and how does it explain Jaibo's behavior?

18. Why does Bunuel include the Blind Man's reaction: "One less. Better to kill them before they're born.?"

19. What is the significance of the way Pedro's body is disposed of?

THE AFRICAN QUEEN (1951—American) Directed by John Huston; with Humphrey Bogart, Katharine Hepburn, Robert Morley, Peter Bull, and Theo Bikel; screenplay by James Agee. Produced by United Artists.

1. In the 1940s, Humphrey Bogart represented what it meant to be a Man: tough, chauvinistic, and hard-drinking. And of course, Katharine Hepburn symbolized glamour and femininity. In this film, they have aged and degenerated into faded stereotypes of their former selves. What does this symbolize?

2. What is the significance of the *off-key* church service? What does the Reverend represent, and what is Huston suggesting about missionaries?

3. As Hepburn pumps her organ, Bogart blows his whistle. How do these contrasting symbols characterize them?

4. What does the AFRICAN QUEEN symbolize? What is the significance of its being a creaking old tub? How does it reflect Charlie's character? How does his assertion that he's the "only man who can get up a head of steam on the African Queen" foreshadow his relationship with Rose?

5. The natives scramble over Charlie's cigar butt. Is this a racial stereotype, or is Huston satirizing the depiction of natives in older films?

6. Tea-time: "What do you suppose makes a man's stomach carry on like this?" Why does Huston juxtapose Charlie's rumbling stomach against "Holy, Holy?"

7. As Rose and the Reverend kneel in prayer, the Germans enter and burn the village. How does this illustrate the "Problem of Evil?" Why does the Reverend go crazy, and what is the significance of his death?

8. What is the significance of Charlie's excessive politeness? Why are he and Rose so formal with each other, addressing each other as "Mr." and "Miss?"

9. How is Charlie's personality reflected in his "leaky steam engine" that he has to kick occasionally?

10. Why is Rose hesitant to "take the tiller," and how does this characterize her?

11. How do the contrasting symbols, *gin* and *tea,* illustrate the film's basic conflict between nature and civilization?

12. What is the significance of Charlie's having to sleep in the rain? Why does Rose change her mind? What does her *umbrella* symbolize?

13. When Charlie gets drunk and tells Rose she's a "crazy, psalm-singing old spinster," she retaliates by pouring his gin overboard. Why does he then shave and clean himself up? What is the effect of the *animal cries* while she sits reading her bible, ignoring his complaint?

14. "Nature is what we were put in this world to rise above." Why is this line *funny* to a modern audience? How have public attitudes changed since 1951?

15. How is GOING DOWN THE RAPIDS a metapor for love? After Rose and Charlie embrace, why do they suddenly back away from each other? What does flinging her hat overboard symbolize?

16. How is the growth of their love suggested by the following symbolic acts: his putting more wood on the fire, and her pumping the bilges and removing a thorn from his foot?

17. What is the significance of their conversation about the *flowers?* ("They probably don't have a name because no one has ever seen them before.")

18. Note that immediately after their love scene, the boat becomes tidy. She even serves him breakfast in bed. What does this symbolize?

19. What does making faces at the hippos suggest about Charlie's nature? Why does Huston include this comic scene before plunging them into the rapids again?

20. As the river "changes its name" from Ulanga to Bora, it becomes peaceful and swampy. What does this change symbolize in their relationship? How does the imagery here relate to Shakespeare's idea of love in *Antony and Cleopatra?*

21. Rose and Charlie now face an opposite set of perils: a swarm of biting flies, and a swampy labyrinth infested with leeches. Finally they wind up stranded on a mud flat. How do these problems reflect the difficulties of sustaining a love relationship? In what sense are their trials *mythical,* like the adventures of Ulysses?

22. God apparently answers Rose's prayer and sends rain that floats them over to the channel. How does this balance the view of God in the beginning of the film?

23. "You at the tiller and me at the engine"—how is this a metaphor for marriage?

24. Note that when they *try* to torpedo the Luisa, their boat sinks. What is the significance of their victory being accidental?

25. The film's most famous line: "I now pronounce you man and wife...Proceed with the execution." What does this imply about marriage?

FORBIDDEN GAMES (1951—French) Directed by Rene Clement; with Brigitte Fossey; music by Narciso Yepes. Distributed by Janus Films.

1. Judging from the way the refugees treat each other, what is Clement's view of human nature?

2. Note the sign on the wall behind the dead parents: "Masters of Mystery." What is the significance of this?

3. What is the point of the little girl's attachment to her dead dog?

4. Why does Clement present Paulette as having absolutely no knowledge of religion?

5. How does Clement characterize the Dolles and the Gouards? What social forces do they represent? What does their feud symbolize?

6. How does the setting, especially the bridge between their property, characterize them?

7. What does the children's *graveyard* symbolize? How do they reflect their parents and French culture in general? What is the symbolic significance of their killing animals to fill their graveyard?

8. What is the importance of the death of Michel's brother, and of the care his family expends on his funeral? (Note that they don't even bother to call a doctor when he's sick and suffering.)

9. What is the symbolic and psychological significance of the children's fascination with crosses?

10. As the children push their wheelbarrow full of crosses, bombs explode overhead. What is the visual effect of this? How do the children represent the entire human race?

11. What is the symbolic significance of the two fathers fighting over the grave in the cemetary, smashing each other's crosses?

12. What is the effect of the beautiful guitar music as the camera pans over the children's graveyard?

13. What is ironic about the adults being so outraged over the children's stealing crosses?

14. Why does Michel agree to tell his father where the crosses are? What is the significance of his father's broken promise?

RASHOMON (1951—Japanese) Directed by Akira Kurosawa; with Toshiro Mifune and Machiko Kyo. Distributed by Janus Films.

1. *The Introduction:* Rashomon Gate in the pouring rain, with two miserable creatures huddled at the base of an enormous pillar ... What is the symbolic significance of this setting?

1. "It all makes no sense"... "My faith in men may be destroyed." What is the thematic significance of these statements? In a world in which violence is commonplace, in which heads hang from the Rashomon Gate, why would this particular murder trouble the two men?

2. Notice Kurosawa's love of textures and lighting effects, and his repeated use of triangular motifs, during the Woodcutter's introduction. This is the Woodcutter's romanticized vision of the woods, complete with an exotic musical background. How does this prepare the audience for the stories to follow?

3. Why do we never see or hear the judge presiding over the trial? Why do the actors speak directly into the camera?

4. What is the significance of the *wind* that blows so fiercely throughout the trial? How does this wind comment symbolically on the testimony?

II. The Bandit pictures himself riding silhouetted against a dramatic sky. Also note the shot in which he lies beneath the tree, slowly drawing the sword up the side of his leg. How do these shots help characterize him?

1. He says that since he's going to die, his story is the truth. Why isn't this necessarily so?

2. *The Bandit's Story:* The wife pulls a knife on him and bites his wrist... which greatly excites him. After leading her around a tree, he wrestles the knife out of her hand and kisses her passionately until she succumbs to him. She then demands that he kill her husband—or else fight with him—and she'll take the one who survives. Untying the husband, the bandit takes the offensive in a ferocious battle, finally trapping him in the underbrush and killing him.

3. Why does the Bandit insist on the Husband's excellent swordsmanship? What does the Bandit's story reveal about his image of himself?

III. The young priest relates *the Wife's story:* After her "ordeal," she runs weeping to her husband, still tied up, who stares at her with a "cold steely gleam." Because he despises her pleas to kill her, she [... kills him in a fit of insanity?] She "passed out," she claims, waking to find her dagger in her husband's chest. She then tries to kill herself and fails... "But what can a poor woman do?"

Why would the priest be sympathetic to her story? What does this reveal about his own nature?

IV. *The Husband's Story:* After raping the Wife, the Bandit persuades her to go away with him. The Wife not only agrees, but orders the Bandit to kill the defenseless Husband. Horrified at this suggestion, the Bandit strikes the Wife to the ground and asks the Husband if he should kill her instead. In the confusion, the Wife escapes. "Hours" after pursuing the Wife, the Bandit returns to untie the Husband, who (it is implied) kills himself with her pearl-handled dagger. The last thing he feels is someone approaching quietly and withdrawing the dagger from his chest.

> Why does the Woodcutter interrupt angrily, insisting that the Husband was killed with a *sword*... that no dagger was found?

V. Nervously declaring that he "doesn't want to be involved," the Woodsman nevertheless tells his version of the story. (Note that he also related the Bandit's story.):

The Bandit begs the Wife to forgive him for assaulting her, invoking her beauty and pleading with her to go with him. Outraged, she unties her Husband, assuming that he'll protect her. Instead he scorns her and suggests that she either kill herself or go with the Bandit. As she lies sobbing at their feet, the Bandit decides that he doesn't want her after all; whereupon she rises, challenges them both, and laughs in their faces... thus forcing them to fight, which they do in a most clumsy and cowardly fashion. After much hacking and slashing, in which they miss each other completely, the Bandit stabs the Husband as he lies defenseless in the bushes. The Wife runs away in terror, as the Bandit trips over his own feet pursuing her. The Bandit then withdraws the sword from the Husband's chest and limps off, trembling with fear.

VI. *The Conclusion:* If you were to list the four stories in the order in which you believe them, your conclusion would merely reveal your own values. Why does Kurosawa do this? Why doesn't he intend us to figure out the "truth?"

1. The three men at the gate debate the meaning of the case, the priest insisting that men must trust each other. What forces in life do these three men represent?

2. The Commoner, hearing the cry of the abandoned baby, goes to steal its clothes. Why is the woodsman so shocked at the Commoner's "selfishness?"

3. How does Kurosawa characterize the priest, as opposed to the Common Man? While the Commoner walks laughing into the rain, the young priest clutches the baby. What is the significance of this?

4. Why does the young priest entrust the baby to the Woodcutter? What is the symbolic significance of this? How does the Rashomon Gate relate to this symbolic ending?

A STREETCAR NAMED DESIRE (1951—American) Directed by Elia Kazan; with Marlon Brando, Vivien Leigh, Kim Hunter, and Karl Malden; based on the play by Tennessee Williams. Produced by Warner Bros.

1. Blanche emerges from the *smoke* of a locomotive and approaches a young sailor for directions. How does this symbolic entrance characterize her? What is the double-meaning implied in her looking for the "streetcar named desire?"

> Why is it ironic that Stanley and Stella live at the "Elysian Fields?"

2. How is Stanley characterized by his bowling?

3. What is the significance of the filmy dresses Blanche wears?

4. Blanche tells Stella that "BELLE REVE" (=Beautiful Dream) has been *lost*. What does this symbolize?

5. As the cat yowls, Blanche grabs Stanley's arm. What is the effect of this juxtaposition?

6. "You were married once, weren't you?" What is the purpose of the echo effect?

7. What is the psychological significance of Blanche's frequent *baths?*

8. Blanche touches Stanley's shoulder, exclaiming, "My sister has married a *man.*" Why does Stanley get angry at Blanche's flirtation?

9. Blanche: "A woman's charm is fifty percent illusion." How does this relate to the theme of the film?

10. Why does Blanche go berserk when Stanley grabs her love letters?

11. The Card Game: Blanche meets Mitch as he emerges from the bathroom. How is he characterized by the *wet towel* in his hands? Why would Blanche consider him "superior to the others?"

   Why does Blanche peek at them through the curtain?

   Mitch's cigarette case: "And if God choose, I shall love thee better after death." Why is Blanche moved by this?

12. Blanche says, "I can't stand a *naked* light bulb." What is the significance of her choice of words? What does her Chinese lamp shade symbolize?

13. "WE'VE CREATED ENCHANTMENT." What is the significance of Stanley's throwing the *radio* out the window? How does this characterize the "Natural Man's" reaction to modern media?

14. Stanley shouts for Stella to come back down. Why does she, and what does this say about their relationship? What does the wrought-iron stairway symbolize?

15. Blanche runs into Mitch at the bottom of the stair. He sits there with a *burning match* in his fingers. How does this foreshadow his relationship with her?

16. Why does Blanche disapprove of Stella's relationship with Stanley, whom she describes as a "survivor of the stone age?"

   "We're a long way from being made in God's image..."
   Why is her chatter about art and poetry hypocritical?

17. The minute Stanley enters, Stella disentangles herself from her sister and flings herself at him. Why? Why does Stanley look at Blanche over Stella's shoulder?

18. Why does Stanley complain about Blanche's house-keeping?

19. Why would Blanche insist that the Flamingo Hotel isn't a place where a respectable woman would be seen?

   Why does she immediately question Stella about "unkind gossip?"

   What is the purpose of the shot of Blanche against the rainy window?

Why does Blanche freak out when the beer glass foams over?

20. Blanche: "I want to deceive him just enough to make him want me." *Does* she want Mitch? Why does she add, "I want a rest?"

21. WHAT DOES "THE BOY FROM THE *EVENING STAR*" SYMBOLIZE? Why does she entice him, and then act like such a prude with Mitch? What does this reveal about her past?

22 Mitch bounds through the door just as the boy leaves. How is Mitch characterized by his polka-dot bow tie? Why would he *ask* if he can kiss her?

> Why does Blanche *laugh* when he says he has never met anyone like her? Why is this ironic?

> Why does she chatter in French and pretend they're in Paris?

> They talk about his coat and about how he *sweats* (!) How does this characterize him?

> Why does she push him away, insisting that she has "old fashioned ideas?"

> Why does she ask Mitch what Stanley has said about her?

23. Blanche talks about her dead young husband . . . In the middle of the dance floor, she announced to the whole crowd that he was "weak" (a fifties euphemism for *homosexual*) . . . and he went outside and shot himself. Why does she tell Mitch about this? How does this incident motivate Blanche's promiscuity, as well as her inability to grasp reality?

24. What is the effect of the cross-cut to Stanley and Mitch in the shop about to fight? Why isn't the cause of their quarrel explained?

25. Cross-cut to Blanche in the bathtub singing happily, "But it wouldn't be make-believe, if you believe in me . . . " What is the thematic function of this lyric?

> While Blanche bathes, Stanley tells Stella what he found out about Blanche. What is hypocritical about Stanley's outrage over Blanche's involvement with a seventeen year old boy?

26. While they have dinner, Blanche waits in vain for Mitch to come. Why does Stanley clear the table as he does, and how does this symbolize what he has done to their lives? ("What do you think you are, a pair of queens?")

27. Stanley tells Stella how happy they were because he "pulled her down from those white columns and got them colored lights going." What does he mean by this mixed metaphor? Why does he blame Blanche for their estrangement?

28. Mitch shows up . . . Why does he turn on the *light*, and what does this symbolize? Why does Blanche insist that she doesn't want realism, she wants "magic?"

29. "FLOWERS FOR THE DEAD"—What does the flower-lady symbolize? How does her dreamlike entrance foreshadow the end of the film?

> When Blanche kisses Mitch and asks him to marry her, he replies that she isn't clean enough. How does this characterize him?

30. As Blanche is in the middle of fantasizing about one of her southern balls, Stanley enters. She tells him a telegram arrived—an "invitation." Why does she make this up?

> Blanche's soliloquy about desire—is it addressed to Stanley?

> Why is he determined to shatter her fantasy?

31. THE "LOVE" SCENE: What do the *broken bottle* and the *shattered mirror* symbolize? Why does Kazan cut to a shot of garbage being washed down the gutter, followed by a shot of Stella's baby? What is the symbolic function of these shots? Why doesn't Kazan merely show Stanley raping Blanche?

32. While the men play cards, Blanche goes crazy. Why does Kazan depict Stanley back at his old routine?

> How does Blanche's insanity affect Mitch, and why?

33. "Someone is calling for Blanche"—The final scene contains some of the most beautiful and ironic lines in the film:

> "Please don't get up—I'm only passing through."

> "You are not the gentleman I was expecting."

> "Whoever you are, I have always depended on the kindness of strangers."

What is the effect of these understatements?

Why does Blanche take the doctor's arm so calmly, and what does this gesture symbolize?

34. Stella grabs the baby and runs upstairs, ignoring Stanley's pleas to return. In Tennessee Williams' original play, Stanley again fondles Stella until she give in and takes his word against Blanche's. Which ending do you consider more pessimistic?

HIGH NOON (1952—American) Directed by Fred Zinnemann; with Gary Cooper, Grace Kelly, Lloyd Bridges, Katy Jurado, and Lon Chaney; music by Dmitri Tiomkin. Produced by United Artists; distributed by Swank Films.

1. When the wedding ceremony is over, Will takes Amy into the next room and vows to try hard to make the marriage work. Why should there be any special problem with a marshall marrying a Quaker?

2. In terms of traditional western stereotypes, what are the differences between Amy and Helen Ramirez?

3. Will and Amy both have loyalties to abstract ideals. What are they?

4. The children are let out of church early. How does their tug-of-war game comment on the debate inside?

5. The minister says "Thou shalt not kill," but is honest enough to admit that doesn't solve the immediate problem. How do the hymn ("Battle Hymn of the Republic") and the scripture reading (Malachi 4:1) ironically undercut the commandment?

6. How does the famous rapid editing sequence that climaxes at noon involve all the townspeople in Frank Miller's arrival? What is the purpose of the triangular composition in the shots of the railroad tracks pointing to the apex of Frank Miller, the church aisles and pews, and the three men standing in the bar?

7. Why is the town named Hadleyville? How does it recall the "respectable" little town in Mark Twain's story, "The Man Who Corrupted Hadleyburg"?

> Why is the marshall named *Kane?* How is he like the hero of Orson Welles' *Citizen Kane?*

8. Why do both Will and Amy ultimately forsake their ideals? What is ironic in her shooting Ben Miller in the Back? Why does Will drop the "tin star" in the dust?

9. *High Noon* can be interpreted as a comment on the "House Un-American Activities Committee" hearings that went on during the five years before its release. What are the parallels?

SAWDUST AND TINSEL/THE NAKED NIGHT (1953—

Swedish) Directed by Ingmar Bergman; with Harriet Andersson and Ake Gronberg; cinematography by Sven Nykvist. Distributed by Janus Films.

1. The entire film seems like a rainstorm, with wheels grinding in the mud. How does this setting communicate the theme and mood of the film?

2. *FROST AND ALMA:* Why does Bergman flash back to the scene of Frost's humiliation? How does this episode relate thematically to the main drama of Albert and Anne's relationship?

3. Why is this flashback shot in the style of a twenties war film? What is the effect of the montage of shots of Alma flirting and the cannons firing?

4. What is the symbolic importance of the landscape in this scene? (Note the sun and the barren, rocky shore. Also note that the procession up the hill predates the famous shot at the end of *The Seventh Seal*—What is the connection?)

5. *THE VISIT TO THE THEATRE:* What forces in society—and in the human personality—are symbolized by the *circus* and the *theatre?*

6. "A pure heart is a woman's most cherished possession"—How does this play-within-a-play relate to the main drama?

7. Why does Sjuberg, the theatre director, despise Albert? Why is this ironic? How do the two characters represent the split in Bergman's own nature?

8. Frans, the young actor, declares his "love" in a scene that sounds much like a rehearsal. What is Bergman's attitude toward Romantic Love, and what details in the scene suggest this?

9. Albert visits his wife Agda, who declares, "I got away from the circus I always hated. What does the circus symbolize for her, in contrast with the tobacco shop she now owns?

10. Meanwhile, "in this farce of dark shadows," Anne visits the actor. Why is she fascinated with the theatre? What does it represent to her? (Note how impressed she is with Frans' performance of Romantic Suicide.)

11. As Anne walks through the theatre, how does the play of light on masks and mirrors prepare us for the love scene?

12. How does this differ from a Hollywood love scene? How is Frans characterized by small details, like offering Anne some of his perfume?

13. Anne anticipates her escape from the circus: Albert will come home to find "no bareback rider, no young lady in tights for a drunkard to saw in two." How is this a metaphor for their life together?

14. Why does Bergman shoot the dialogue between Frans and Anne in a *mirror?*

15. What is the symbolic significance of the *jewel* Frans gives Anne?

16. Meanwhile, Albert's wife stitches the button on his coat. What is the effect of this transitional shot? How does it relate to the previous scene?

17. Albert wants to quit the circus and work in the shop. What does this symbolize?

18. Bergman cuts to Anne and Frans. Outside, two monkeys dance to the tune of an organ grinder. What is the purpose of this juxtaposition?

19. As Albert watches Anne leave the jewelry shop, Bergman cuts from the expression on his face to a closeup of Anne playing cards. What is the symbolic implication of this closeup? Why does Bergman also shoot this conversation in a mirror?

20. "We're stuck in the circus . . . we're stuck in hell." At this moment, Frost the Clown enters. What is the purpose of this entrance? How does it tie the film together?

21. Albert and Frost drink to their "brotherhood." In what sense does Bergman mean this? Why does he depict them alternately pointing guns at their heads and rolling in the hay?

22. THE CIRCUS PERFORMANCE begins with Frost and another clown kicking each other in the rear and knocking each other down. What does this act symbolize, and how does it foreshadow Albert's performance later in the scene?

23. How does the trained bear, tied to a stake, reflect Albert?

24. What does Anne's bareback ride symbolize?

25. How is Frans and Albert's battle in the ring a *metaphor?* How does it reflect on the nature of love? How does it reveal Bergman's view of human nature?

26. After the fight, Albert stares in the mirror, contemplating suicide. Why does he shoot the bear? What does this symbolize?

27. What is the thematic significance of Frost's dream? How does it relate to the final shot of Albert and Anne walking off together into the gloom?

28. How does *Sawdust and Tinsel* differ from Fellini's *La Strada*, which also uses the *circus* as a metaphor for life?

UGETSU MONOGATARI/TALES OF MIST AND MOONLIGHT (1953—Japanese) Directed by Kenji Mizoguchi. Distributed by Janus Films.

1. Why does Mizoguchi use *two* main characters rather than one to develop this beautiful allegory about the nature of Reality? How is this film similar to *Don Quixote, King Lear*, and other works that use parallel structure and *thematic analogue* to convey their ideas?

2. What forces in life do TOBEI (the would-be warrior) and GENJURO (the artist-hustler) represent?

3. Like Brecht's Mother Courage, Genjuro and Tobei both believe that "War Is Business." Why is this ironic? How is it relevant to the recent history of South East Asia?

4. Genjuro is obsessed with selling his pots; Tobei thinks he'll be a samurai if only he can get a spear and some armor. What is the relationship between their greed and the fate of their wives?

5. Why does Mizoguchi include the sequence of the boat edging through the fog? What does this symbolize, and how does it relate to the film's main idea?

6. After pretending that he has beheaded an enemy general, Tobei is given a horse and a command. At the height of his glory, he runs into his wife in a highly unexpected place... "So now you've become the samurai of your dreams," she says. What is the significance of this?

7. What does the Kutsuki Mansion symbolize? Lady Wakasa, the "highborn lady" who cherishes Genjuro's art and invites him to stay with her, turns out to be something very strange indeed . . . What does her courting of him symbolize?

8. After Genjuro is left in the ruins of the Kutsuki Mansion, stripped of all he has, he returns to his wife and son... What is the point of the ending? What does this ending imply about the relationship of dreams and reality?

9. How does this film illustrate the Taoist ideal of "wu wei?" (= "doing nothing," a much misunderstood phrase in the West!)

10. How does the film relate to the philosophical problem of "personal space?"

11. The hero in a tragedy is supposed to achieve an important realization as a result of his suffering. How is this idea illustrated in the film?

GATE OF HELL (1954—Japanese) Directed by Teinosuke Kinugasa; with Machiko Kyo and Kazuo Hasegawa. Distributed by Janus Films.

Note the incredible colors of the costumes and draperies... After studying color technique at the Eastman Laboratories and at Warner Brothers, Kinugasa returned to Japan, where he showed his American teachers how they could use color for artistic effect, as an integral part of the drama. As in the traditional Japanese Noh, the power of *Gate of Hell* derives from the tension between external and internal: between classical values expressed in formal choreography, controlled compositions, and delicate colors—and the romantic inner turmoil of the main characters, which threatens to tear this polite, ceremonial world to pieces.

***

1. Although *Gate of Hell* is based on a twelfth century chronicle, what are the *modern* elements in the film that make the tragedy relevant and universal?

2. Why does Lady Kesa volunteer to impersonate the queen? Why would this action inspire Moritoh's love for her?

3. "A master is a master"—How does Moritoh's argument with his brother characterize him?

4. Why does the film keep returning to the "Gate of Hell?" What does this setting symbolize? What is the significance of Moritoh's again meeting Lady Kesa there?

5. How is Wataru, Kesa's husband, characterized? How does he differ from Moritoh? Why might Kesa be seriously attracted to *both* men?

6. Why does Wataru react so calmly to Moritoh's love for his wife? Why does he insist that Kesa accept Lord Kiyomori's invitation, knowing full well that its purpose is a meeting with Moritoh?

7. What is Lord Kiyomori's attitude toward Moritoh's passion, and how does this characterize him? How is he like a modern political leader?

8. Note Moritoh's reaction to Kesa's virtuosity on the koto. What does this gesture symbolize?

9. What does the *horse race* symbolize? Why does Kesa want Wataru to keep out of the race? Why does Wataru insist that it's just a game, and it doesn't matter who wins? Why does the race end as it does, and what is Wataru's motive?

10. At the feast: Why is Wataru's desire for peace impossible?

11. Although Moritoh is the kind of man who kicks dogs, smashes kotos, and threatens to kill old ladies—how is he still admirable, compared with the other men in the drama?

12. What is Kesa's motive in getting Wataru drunk? Why does she agree to aid Moritoh in his plan, and why is her choice *tragic?*

13. When Moritoh threatens to kill Wataru, why doesn't Kesa simply tell her husband so he'll be prepared to defend himself?

14. Not even once does Kesa tell her husband or the audience what she *feels* about Moritoh. Why not?

15. The murder scene: What is the effect of the moonlit veils blowing gently in the breeze? How does this comment on the central action?

16. A tragedy is supposed to end with Knowledge. What do the two men learn about themselves, their lady, and their male code of honor?

17. In a tragedy, the hero's best quality ("arete") and his tragic flaw are the same. How is this true of all three characters in the film? How does Kesa's courageous impersonation of the queen in the beginning foreshadow the ironic ending of the film?

18. In Greek tragedy, the hero falls because he fails to find the Golden Mean between the two extremes of Reason and Emotion. How is this similar to the Taoist ideal of the harmony of "yin" and "yang"? How are both ideas reflected in this film?

LA STRADA (1954—Italian) Directed by Federico Fellini; with Anthony Quinn, Giulietta Masina, and Richard Basehart; music by Nino Rota. Distributed by Janus Films.

1. What is the *irony* in Zampano's being a "strongman?"

2. Like Fellini's other films, *La Strada* is a narrative, an "open structured" work with no plot. Its action is episodic, with Zampano performing his "act" over and over. What is the significance of this? How does the film's structure reveal Fellini's view of life? How does his world-view differ from Ingmar Bergman's?

3. Zampano teaches Gelsomina to play the drum as though he were training a dog. What is the significance of this?

4. Note that Fellini is fascinated with circuses and with the Catholic church. What does this reveal about his world-view? How does his religious procession differ from Bergman's in *The Seventh Seal?* What is the purpose of details like the *butchered pig* and the *bar sign?*

5. The Fool appears, walking a tight-rope while eating a plate of spaghetti. Why does Fellini juxtapose this scene against the religious procession? What force in society does the Fool represent? How is he like the Fool in Shakespeare's *King Lear?*

6. How do Gelsomina, Zampano, and the Fool represent the different sides of the human personality? Why do Zampano and the Fool hate each other, and what does their hatred symbolize?

7. Why does Gelsomina stay with Zampano, considering how badly he treats her?

8. In the main philosophical scene in the film, Gelsomina asks, "What am I here for on this earth?" The Fool replies, "Everything in this world serves a purpose—even this stone." What is the point of the Fool's speech about the stone?

9. Back on the road again...What is the significance of Gelsomina's fascination with the *sea?* What does the sea symbolize for Fellini? How does this sequence foreshadow the film's final scene?

10. At the convent, the nun declares, "We both travel—You follow your husband, I follow mine." What does this comparison imply about the relationship of God and Man?

11. When Gelsomina asks Zampano what he "thinks," he replies that there's no point in "thinking," because there's nothing to think about. What is the point of this conversation? How does it relate to their life on the road?

12. What does the Fool's death symbolize?

13. What is the importance of the little theme Gelsomina plays on her trumpet?

14. What is the meaning of Zampano's final scene on the beach?

ON THE WATERFRONT (1954—American) Directed by Elia Kazan; with Marlon Brando, Rod Steiger, Eva Marie Saint, Lee J. Cobb, and Karl Malden; screenplay by Budd Schulberg; music by Leonard Bernstein. Produced by Columbia Pictures; distributed by Swank Films.

1. What does Joey Doyle's fall from the roof symbolize? Why does Kazan avoid showing us his face, focusing instead on the reactions of Terry and the gangsters standing below?

2. Why is Johnny Friendly's *name* ironic?

3. Terry *loses count* of the money. How does this reflect his inner state?

4. "Stooling is when you rat on your friends"—Why does the priest have such a hard time getting someone to talk?

5. Edie: "Which side are *you* with?"
   Terry: "Me, I'm with me." Throughout the film, Kazan emphasizes the necessity of taking sides. What does this reveal about his world-view? Why

is it ironic that he testified against his idealistic colleagues in the HUAC witch-hunt?

6. Terry: "My brother Charlie is a very brainy guy—he had a couple years of college." Edie: "It isn't just brains—it's how you use them." What is the dramatic purpose of the Edie/Charlie polarity?

7. Why does Pop Doyle insist that his daughter return to the nuns? What is the meaning of her refusal? ("I've seen things that are so wrong. How can I go back to school and keep my mind on books?")

8. Edie: "I wouldn't think you'd be interested in pigeons."
    Terry: "You know, this city is full of hawks." What is the double-meaning here? What do *pigeons* come to symbolize in the course of the film?

9. In the bar, Edie insists that "Everybody is part of everybody else." Terry counters with "Do it to him before he does it to you." Why do they have so much trouble understanding each other? How do their world-views differ?

10. How does Edie's attraction to Terry perpetuate the American myth of "the Lady and the Tramp?"

11. Charlie and Johnny Friendly demand that Terry stop seeing Edie because, as Charlie declares, "It's an unhealthy relationship." Why is this ironic?

12. What does *Joey's jacket* symbolize? (Note that it is given first to Dugan, then to Terry when Dugan is killed.) What is ironic about Dugan's death by a sudden overdose of Irish whiskey?

13. "You're asking me to put the finger on my own brother ... And Johnny Friendly used to take me to ball games when I was a kid." Why is the priest so impatient with Terry's conflict?

14. What does Fr. Barry think will happen when Terry tells Edie that he caused Joey's death?

15. As Terry tells Edie the truth, what is the symbolic function of the railroad whistle that drowns out their words?

16. "You were a Golden Warrior once—You started the gang." What is the double-meaning here?

17. Defending his brother, Charlie pleads, "This girl and the Father have their hooks in the kid so deep, he doesn't know which end is up anymore." Why is this ironic?

18. The scene in the car is justly famous for the realism of its acting. How does Kazan use *sound* symbolically throughout this sequence? Also, what is the effect of the *light* flickering through the venetian blinds on the rear window of the car?

> "It was *you,* Charlie . . . I could've had class, I could've been a contender." In what sense is this a tragic realization? Why does Charlie let Terry go?

19. When Terry barges into Edie's room, she'll have nothing to do with him. How does this undercut Fr. Barry's insistence (and Edie's too!) that Terry simply tell the truth? What is ironic about his method of persuading this high-minded lady to forgive him?

20. When Terry and Edie find Charlie again, how is Charlie's position symbolic?

21. Why does the priest insist that Terry get rid of the gun?

22. "Who's your friend?" says Terry's neighbor to the cop. Note how the police themselves react to Terry's testimony. What does this imply about cops and gangsters?

> When Terry complains, "My friends won't talk to me," Edie replies, "Are you sure they're your friends?" What is Kazan suggesting about the problem of "friends?" To what extent is this problem universal? Why is it particularly intense in a ghetto environment?

23. Why does the boy kill the pigeons? ("A pigeon for a pigeon")

24. Why don't the longshoremen go down the gangplank to help Terry? What does Pop Doyle's long-repressed action symbolize?

25. Why is it important that Terry *walk* up the gangplank? How does this action assert him as a Christ-figure?

SMILES OF A SUMMER NIGHT (1955—Swedish) Directed by
Ingmar Bergman; with Gunnar Bjornstrand, Harriet Andersson, and Bibi Andersson; cinematography by Gunnar Fischer. Distributed by Janus Films.

1. Comedies, like tragedies, often deal with an "Oedipal Triangle"—the competition between father and son over a woman. What makes Bergman's treatment of this theme *funny?*

2. This is a comedy about sexual frustration ... What do the *filled cannons* symbolize?

3. What are some of the differences between Frederick and his son, Henrik? Why does Henrik resent his father?

4. All of Bergman's films, including this one, are about death and about man's alienation from God. In what sense does the conflict between Henrik and Frederick mirror the *tragic* conflict between Man and God?

5. Note Desiree's speech on the stage about "Man's Dignity": Love is a "juggling act." How does this metaphor foreshadow the action of the film? How does Desiree differ from Anne in her attitude toward love?

6. Henrik reads Martin Luther's words on "Virtue" and "Temptation" to both Anne and Petra. Why is this ironic?

7. Frederick slips out in the middle of the night to visit Desiree at the theatre. What is the purpose of the shots in the *mirror*, with the two gas lamps burning behind them?

> Note their reflections in the water as they walk along the street. What does his falling in the *puddle* symbolize?

8. What is the significance of the *polite tone* in the confrontation between Frederick and Count Malcolm? How does this establish the film as a traditional "Comedy of Manners?"

9. Why does Desiree want to bring the Egermans together with Count Malcolm and his wife at her mother's chateau?

10. What is the significance of the *target practice* during Malcolm's conversation with his wife? How does this characterize their marriage?

> "I can bear my wife's deceiving me, but if anyone touches my mistress I become a tiger." Why is Malcolm basically a *comic* character?

11. No one ever makes much sense out of the scene in which Petra and Anne giggle and roll around on the bed(!) Why does Bergman include this scene? Why is it obvious that *both* girls are virgins?

12. After being kicked out of the kitchen, Anne goes upstairs to bully Henrik... Why?

13. Anne interrupts Frederick's studies. How is she like Nora in Ibsen's *Doll's House?*

14. Why does Charlotte tell Anne about Frederick's traipsing around town in his nightshirt? If Malcolm is just an arrogant brute who talks about nothing but his horses, his women, and his duels, why does Charlotte "love" him?

15. Frederick finds Anne's pictures in his son's theology text. Why does this confuse him?

16. Why is it predictable that a tease like Petra can *only* be seduced by someone like Frid the coachman?

17. At the Chateau: As Desiree and Charlotte plot, the men play croquet very aggressively. How does this juxtaposition distinguish women from men? What does *croquet* symbolize? (The idea is to keep your ball on the field, while knocking everyone else's *off...*)

18. At dinner, the old matriarch tells her guests about the *magic drop* in the wine. What does this symbolize? (cf. *Tristan*)

> What is the significance of their reactions—especially Henrik's harangue, Anne's sudden flash of sympathy, and Frederick's realization?

19. What is funny about Henrik's attempt to hang himself? Apparently, God answers his prayer... Why would he think that he has died and gone to heaven?

20. How is *Russian Roulette* a metaphor for love?

21. What does the *windmill* symbolize?

THE SEVENTH SEAL (1956—Swedish) Directed by Ingmar Bergman; with Max von Sydow, Gunnar Bjornstrand, Bibi Andersson, and Nils Poppe; cinematography by Gunnar Fischer. Distributed by Janus Films.

1. It is obvious that modern and medieval attitudes toward the existence of God are very different. Why, then, would Bergman risk setting a serious philosophical film in the fourteenth century? What are the similarities between the middle ages and the twentieth century?

2. *Oedipus Rex* and *The Seventh Seal* both focus on a tragic hero who seeks *knowledge,* since mere faith seems insufficient to explain the Problem of Evil. For both men, this search is connected with their own identity and with their need for meaningful action. Despite these similarities, how do Sophocles and Bergman differ in their moral beliefs and in their approach to tragedy?

3. The opening shot: A stormy sky. On a chord of music, a white bird is suddenly illuminated, frozen in mid-air. How does this establish the film as an allegory? Why does Bergman stress the contrast between black and white throughout the film?

4. The Knight and his Squire sleep on the rocky shore. Why does Bergman make them look like they're dead? Note the rear-screen projection as the Knight prays... What is the purpose of the theatrical lighting?

5. The Knight is probably praying for a sign of God's existence... What is the significance of Death's sudden appearance? Why does Bergman launch right into the Knight's conversation with Death without any exposition or motivation? What does their *chess game* symbolize?

6. "Between a strumpet's legs I lie/That's the life for which I sigh"—How does Jons the Squire differ from his master? How are they like Don Quixote and Sancho Panza?

7. After Jons approaches the "sleeping man" to ask directions, the Knight asks, "Did he show you the way?" Why is this ironic?

8. As the Knight and his Squire ride past Joseph and Mary's wagon, note the change in the light. Why does Bergman deliberately overexpose the sequences with Joseph and Mary?

9. Joseph and Mary (with their baby son) are obviously the archetypal Holy Family. Why does Bergman balance Joseph's visions against his clownishness?

10. What is the significance of Joseph's being a *juggler?* How does Joseph's desire to see his son do the "impossible trick"—to make a ball stand still in the air—reflect the Knight's purpose in playing chess with Death? How does Joseph also represent Bergman himself as a filmmaker?

11. What is ironic about Skat the Ladies' Man playing the part of Death? How does this comic scene mirror the theme of the film ?

12. The Painter declares, "A skull is more interesting than a naked woman... I paint things as they are. People can do whatever they like." How does the Painter represent Bergman himself? How does the crude painting of the Dance of Death foreshadow both the procession of the flagellants and the famous silhouette at the end of the film?

13. In the confession scene, what does Bergman imply by having Death masquerade as a priest? Why does he stress the Knight's emptiness and indifference?

> "I call out to God in the dark," says the Knight, "but no one seems to be there."
> "Perhaps no one *is* there," Death replies.
> "Then life is a meaningless horror. No one can live with Death, knowing that all is nothingness." Why does Bergman emphasize God's *silence?* What is the theological implication of the Knight's assertion?

> The Knight complains that his whole life has been a "meaningless search." How does his desire to do "one meaningful deed" motivate his sacrifice later to save the young family? In his emphasis on *action,* how is he like an existential philosopher?

14. Why does Bergman cut from this serious philosophical scene to Jons' drunken, cynical comments about the crusade? Note Jons' self-portrait: "This is Squire Jons. He grins at Death, mocks the Lord, laughs at himself, and leers at the girls. His world is absurd and exists only for himself— meaningless to heaven and of no interest to hell." How does Jons represent one side of Bergman's nature?

15. A young girl in the stocks is accused of causing the plague by having sex with the Devil(!) How does the priest's "soup" symbolize Bergman's view of religion?

16. Why is it appropriate that the seminarian who sent the Knight on his crusade now loots the bodies of the dead?

17. The performance: Note that Joseph and Mary's song is about Death ("the Black One squatting on the shore.") How do the lyrics and the animal noises in the song correspond to the action as Skat cavorts with the "chicken eater?"

18. What is the effect of the sudden entrance of the procession of flagellants? What does this interruption symbolize? How does the masochism of the penitents reflect the Knight's psychological torment? As the procession leaves, why does Bergman dissolve them into the sand?

> Note Jons' reaction: "Do they really expect modern people
> to believe in such nonsense?" Why does Bergman put these
> words in the mouth of a fourteenth century cynic?

19. The blacksmith interrogates Jons about his missing wife (the "chicken eater"). How are Plog and Lisa like Hephaestus and Aphrodite in Greek myth?

20. The Inn: Note the pig rooting around under the tables while another pig roasts on a spit. How does this symbolism comment on the superstitious dialogue about the plague?

> Plog and the corrupt seminarian force Joseph to dance like a
> bear. How does his performance symbolize the treatment of
> the artist by society?

21. Note the intense light in the sequence in which Mary and Joseph share their *wild strawberries* and cream with the Knight and his Squire. What do the strawberries symbolize? How is this scene like a communion ritual? What is the effect of the *death mask* peering over Joseph's shoulder while he plays the lute?

22. After partaking of the strawberries, the Knight rejoins Death at the chessboard. Why does he look cheerful when Death "takes his knight?" Why does his mood change when Death asks him if he's escorting Joseph and Mary through the forest?

23. In Jons' comic conversation with Plog, who still blubbers over his missing wife, what is the implication of his describing love as "the blackest of all plagues?"

"It's hell with women, and hell without them." How is this a comic analogy for the Knight's concern with the Problem of Evil?

24. As the Knight and his friends enter the forest, what does the *silence* symbolize? Note the fog and the melodramatic lighting.

> What is the effect of the sudden tumult as the cart gets stuck in the stream? It is the witch being brought to execution... What is the significance of *this* being the answer to their prayer to hear some human voice beside their own?

> When Jons observes that they are "brave men" to burn a little girl possessed by the Devil, the soldier replies, "Well, we've been paid." What does Bergman think of the military and the Church?

25. The scene with the witch: When the Knight asks, "Why have you crushed her hands?" Death replies, "Don't you ever stop asking questions?" Why does Bergman again have Death play the part of the priest?

> As the smoke billows, Jons exclaims, "Who watches over that child? Is it the angels, or God, or the Devil, or only Emptiness? Emptiness, my lord!" How does this sequence illustrate the philosophical Problem of Evil? (Note the girl's crucified position... Why is this ironic?)

26. As the travelers continue through the forest, they meet Skat and Lisa. Why is Skat's "romantic suicide" ironic? What does Death's cutting down his tree symbolize? Why does Bergman include the shot of the squirrel?

27. As the heat hangs over the travelers like a smothering blanket, they worry that something terrible is going to happen to them. How do the shrieks of the dying seminarian comment on their fear? As the ex-priest dies in convulsions, what is the symbolic function of the setting—a huge fallen tree that divides the light from the darkness?

> Why would Jons "console" his lady by asserting "it's useless"?

28. As the Knight plays his final move with Death, what is the significance of Joseph being the only one to "see" them? What does the Knight hope to gain by upsetting the chessboard?

29. When the Knight asks Death to reveal his secrets, Death says simply, "I have no secrets." Why would Death's having "nothing to tell" be the ultimate terror for Bergman?

30. As the Knight and his friends sit around the table, his wife Karin reads the description of the end of the world from the Book of *Revelations*. How is this mystic vision relevant to the modern world? When Death enters to claim them, how do their reactions express the different sides of Bergman's nature?

> Jons: "I'll be silent, but under protest."
> His lady, who speaks for the first time, has the final word: "It is finished."

31. What is the effect of the sudden sunshine as Joseph and Mary emerge from their wagon? What does their temporary salvation symbolize?

> What is the significance of Joseph's final vision? ("I see them! Over there against the dark, stormy sky. They are all there. The smith and Lisa and the Knight and Raval and Jons and Skat. And Death, the severe master, invites them to dance...") Why doesn't Bergman include the Knight's wife and Jons' lady in the lineup?

> Why does Bergman give Mary the last word? ("You and your visions!")

THRONE OF BLOOD (1957—Japanese) Directed by Akira Kurosawa; with Toshiro Mifune and Machiko Kyo. Distributed by Audio-Brandon.

1. Throughout the film, the actors look like tiny insects scurrying around in a sandstorm. How does this image convey Kurosawa's attitude toward human pride and ambition?

2. What is the significance of the *wind* and the *fog* in the opening sequence?

3. Why is it ironic that Washizu boasts of his ability as an *archer?*

4. What is the symbolic significance of the emperor's describing the forest as a *labyrinth?* How does it correspond to the human heart?

5. What is the symbolic purpose of all the shots through the *twisted branches?*

6. The Witch: "Would you not want to be Lord of the Forest?" How has Kurosawa expanded the *meaning* of the forest beyond what it means in Shakespeare?

7. How does the witch's *spinning* recall the Greek concept of Fate?

8. "There is the castle, and finally we have come out of the forest." What does their riding around in circles symbolize?

9. Miki: "We dream of what we wish." Freud couldn't have put it better. How does this explain the appearance of the witch?

10. "North Castle is a Paradise after life at the fort." What are the theological implications of this line? What is the importance of the peacefulness at North Castle when Washizu begins his command there?

11. Tempted by his wife, Washizu answers. "No, I am satisfied with myself as I am." Do you believe him? How does this relate to a basic Shakespearean theme?

12. Asaji: "This is a wicked world. To save yourself, you must often kill first." What would Kurosawa (and Shakespeare) think of her world-view?

13. "Without ambition, man is not a man." Why is Washizu's wife so certain that ambition lies in his heart? How is Kurosawa's idea of "what it is to be a man" similar to Shakespeare's?

14. What is the significance of the "forbidden room," with the bloodstain that won't wash off? How does this foreshadow Lady Asaji's guilt?

15. Lady Asaji tells Washizu that if he leads the attack against Inui, "arrows will find him not only from the front, but from behind." Why is this ironic? How does it foreshadow the end of the film?

16. Washizu's men look down at North Castle from Forest Castle: "We have climbed high with Lord Washizu ... Our luck would be complete if only he had an heir." How does this "if only" reveal the main defect of ambition?

17. Lady Asaji: "I did not stain my hands with blood to forward Yoshiteru, Miki's son." How does this perverted reasoning motivate the plot against Miki?

18. Before the banquet, Miki's horse won't let itself be saddled. How does this echo Hollywood westerns?

19. The entertainment at the banquet: "All of you wicked, listen while I tell of a vain man who couldn't escape his punishment." Why does Washizu stop the dancer from finishing his tale?

20. When Washizu sees Miki's ghost, Asaji attributes his erratic behavior to drunkenness. Also, she says, "His lordship's death still hangs heavily on his mind." Why is this ironic?

21. After the revelation of Miki's death, Washizu's men have another symbolic conversation: "What a wind! The whole castle is shaking. The foundation has long been rotting... I cannot believe that this castle is as strong as it once was." What does this imply? How does it recall Shakespeare's idea of "correspondence theory?"

22. What is the significance of Asaji's baby being still-born?

23. The second scene with the witch: "If you choose ambition, Lord, then choose it honestly with cruelty... If you would shed blood, let it run like a river." How does this Machiavellian advice indicate Washizu's main shortcoming as a villain? What does the pile of skulls symbolize?

24. The rebellion: The enemy is led by Noriyasu, who "knows the forest well." What does this symbolize?

25. What is the significance of all the *birds*—e.g. the crows that caw when the servants enter the "forbidden room," and while Washizu and Asaji plan the murder? Also note the birds that fly into the castle during the siege.

26. How is the end, with all the arrows, foreshadowed in the beginning of the film? Why this particular kind of death? Note that Washizu collapses shrouded in *fog*... What is the significance of this?

27. The epilogue: "Within this desolate place there once stood a mighty fortress." How does the setting reflect Washizu himself?

WILD STRAWBERRIES (1957—Swedish) Directed by Ingmar Bergman; with Victor Sjostrom, Ingrid Thulin, Bibi Andersson, and Gunnar Bjornstrand; cinematography by Gunnar Fischer. Distributed by Janus Films.

This very sensitive film is about one day in the life of an old man, Dr. Isak Borg, who finds himself "unstuck in time," unclear about what is real, and uncertain about what his life is worth.

1. Dr. Borg's self-examination is prompted by a dream set in an empty street lined with ruined houses—a nightmare that foreshadows his approaching death. How do the dream's symbols (the watch without hands, the man with the melted face, the body in the coffin) relate to the basic problems in his life?

2. Dr. Borg is a successful, humane, cultivated man. Why does his daughter-in-law Marianne feel sorry for him?

3. Marianne and Dr. Borg stop at the summer home where he had spent his youth. What does the strawberry patch symbolize?

4. As Dr. Borg wanders through his memories, he suddenly sees Sara, the love of his youth, picking strawberries. She is pretending to fend off the advances of his brother Sigfrid, who undoubtedly has other sorts of fruits on his mind. Psychologically, what is going on in this scene? Why does Sara prefer Sigfrid to Isak? ("Isak is so good, so moral and sensitive . . . He wants us to read poetry together and play duets on the piano . . . ")

5. As he watches the Sara of his dreams run down the path, Dr. Borg is suddenly jolted into the present by a girl's voice. How is the "modern" Sara (also played by Bibi Andersson) like the Sara of his past? What is the effect of this on Dr. Borg's sense of reality?

6. Dr. Borg and the young hitch-hikers pick up a middle-aged couple, who amuse themselves by ridiculing and tormenting each other. Why does Bergman include this episode? How does their rivalry differ from the teasing arguments of the teenagers in the back seat?

7. The gas station attendant (Max von Sydow) and his wife thank Dr. Borg very warmly for his past kindnesses. How does this modify our view of the doctor's character?

8. As Dr. Borg, Marianne, and the hitch-hikers sip wine, the two young men argue about God and Death. Why does Bergman include this philosophical dispute? How does their relationship with Sara reflect the love-conflict of Dr. Borg's youth?

9. Dr. Borg visits his mother, who unearths the family remembrances, including *the father's gold watch with no hands.* How is she like her son, and how does this symbol link them?

10. On the road again, Dr. Borg dreams of flights of birds and of a very traumatic conversation with Sara. How does the following progression of images develop our sense of his inner life?

> (a) Sara holds up a *mirror* for him to see how old he is: "As professor emeritus you ought to know why it hurts, but you don't."

> (b) As the birds shriek overhead, she takes the baby from its cradle and runs to Sigfrid...

> (c) As Isak peers through the window, Sara plays the piano... Sigfrid bends to kiss her...

> (d) Isak pounds on the door, accidentally piercing his palm on a stray nail. How does this serve as a transitional device to introduce the next scene?

11. What is the significance of the "trial" that follows? How is it similar to the philosophical and psychological trials in the stories of Franz Kafka? (Some critics have also found theological implications in this scene because of its allusions to the Last Judgment.)

12. The man who opens the door for Dr. Borg looks exactly like the Quarrelsome Husband he met earlier in the day. Why does this particular character reappear to act as Dr. Borg's judge? What is the symbolic significance of the three tests he gives Dr. Borg?

> (a) The doctor looks through a microscope, but he can't see anything but his own eye.

> (b) He vainly tries to decipher "A Doctor's First Duty," which is written in a strange foreign language. (Answer: "To Ask Forgiveness.")

(c) He diagnoses as "dead" a young female patient, who then opens her eyes and laughs at him.

How do the three tests relate to Dr. Borg's inner problem?

13. After telling Dr. Borg that his dead wife also accuses him, the Judge leads him into the forest, where he observes his wife being seduced. Why does it bother her that Isak always "understands" and never accuses or blames her for anything? ("Now I will go home and tell this to Isak, and I know exactly what he'll say: 'Poor little girl, how I pity you.' As if he were God himself...Then I'll cry and ask him if he can forgive me. And then he'll say, 'You shouldn't ask forgiveness from me. I have nothing to forgive.' But he doesn't mean a word of it because he's completely cold. And then he'll suddenly be very tender, and I'll yell at him that he's not really sane and that such hypocritical nobility is sickening. And then he'll say that he understands everything and that he'll bring me a sedative. And then I'll say that it's his fault that I am the way I am, and then he'll look very sad and will say that he is to blame. But he doesn't care about anything because he's completely cold.")

What are the theological implications of this guilt-ridden speech?

14. The verdict: guilty
    The punishment: loneliness

15. Dr. Borg realizes that his dreams are trying to tell him something he won't hear when he's awake: that he's dead, although he's still alive. Why does this remind Marianne of her husband Evald? In what ways are father and son alike?

16. Flashback: Evald and Marianne argue in the rain. What is the effect of the setting? Why is Evald unwilling to have children? How does this relate to the psychological and philosophical theme?

17. Marianne describes Dr. Borg's mother as "cold as ice." Why does this worry her when she reflects on her husband? (This may also relate to Bergman's view of Swedish culture and of human nature in general. Cf. Henrik Ibsen's view of Norway in *Ghosts*.)

18. As Dr. Borg loses himself in this gloomy conversation, the young hitch-hikers approach singing, with a bouquet of flowers: "It's always you I've loved." What is the importance of this scene?

19. How have Dr. Borg's memories and experiences of the day changed his relationship with his son and his daughter-in-law?

20. Why does Bergman include the gentle comic scene between Dr. Borg and Agda, his housekeeper? How has their relationship changed since the opening scene of the film? What does their new understanding add to the general pattern of love relationships in the film?

21. As Dr. Borg tosses on his bed, he has one last memory: "Isak, there are no strawberries left..." He and Sara walk hand-in-hand through the fields, down to the water where he encounters a gentle memory of his parents fishing. In the context of the entire film, what is the tone of these images and what are their symbolic implications?

22. Note the beautiful cross-fade from one closeup of Isak's face to the other. What is the effect of this? How does it relate to the film's juxtapositions of reality?

THE MAGICIAN (1958—Swedish) Directed by Ingmar Bergman; with Max von Sydow, Gunnar Bjornstrand, Ingrid Thulin, and Bibi Andersson; cinematography by Gunnar Fischer. Distributed by Janus Films.

In this early allegory, Bergman establishes the theme that haunts him throughout the sixties: the relationship of the artist and his society. Bergman's attitude toward his artist-figure is ambivalent. Vogler is persecuted most cruelly by bourgeois philistines. But doesn't he deserve such poor treatment? Like Kafka's "Hunger Artist," the Magician is a charlatan who doesn't even believe in his own tricks, a man terrified of death and incapable of love. He starves only because he never found his proper food.

***

1. On the road: What does the witchy old grandmother represent?

Vogler meets the dying actor, who asks, "Why the makeup? Are you a swindler who must hide his real face?" Why is Vogler so fascinated with the dying actor?

2. What is the significance of Vogler's playing dumb in his interview? How does this establish him as a Christ-figure?

3. Dr. Vergerus observes that Vogler's activities reveal a "remarkable duality." How does Bergman relate to Vogler's being both an idealist and a charlatan?

> The doctor examines Vogler and finds "no scientific reason for his dumbness." He says, "I'd like to do a post-mortem on you—weigh your brain, open your heart, lift out your eyes." Why is it unlikely that scientists will find the secret of creativity by peering at brain cells through a microscope?

> How does the doctor's antagonism toward Vogler reflect the contemporary attitude of scientists toward art and religion?

4. How does Vogler and Company's being told to eat in the *kitchen* reflect society's attitude toward artists?

5. Dr. Vergerus makes a bet with Consul Egerman...Why would he consider it "disastrous if science had to accept the unexplainable?"

6. In the kitchen: Notice how often Bergman cuts from "high characters" to "low characters." How does the subplot relate to the main theme?

> What is the significance of Tubal's "love potion" being rat poison?

> What force in society does Antonsson the coachman represent?

7. Simson and Sara in the laundry room: What does the setting symbolize, and how does this characterize their love?

> Simson pretends to all sorts of experience he doesn't have. How does this relate to the main theme?

8. Unlike Vogler, the old Grandmother really does perform magic: She comes to Sanna in her bed—gives her an ear(!) and sings a bloody battle song. As if under a spell, the drunken actor returns. What is the meaning of his resurrection?

9. Antonsson and Rustan are talking of their hatred for Vogler and of how they'd like to "smash his face" when a "ghost" (the actor) enters, smashes the table with an axe, and steals their whiskey. How does this comic sequence foreshadow the climax in the attic?

10. While Egerman listens from hiding, his wife confesses her "love" for Vogler, pleading with him to help her contact her dead daughter. Why does Vogler look so agonized?

11. The actor tells Vogler about his search for meaning...and promptly dies (for real this time). Why does Bergman include this philosophical sequence? How does it reflect his own preoccupation with death?

> (Note that Vogler hides the body in the coffin he uses in his act.)

12. The doctor visits Aman: What would account for his "unexplainable liking" for her and her husband? What is the implication of his comparing their "tricks" with those of the clergy?

> Like Egerman, Vogler also observes unseen. How does his response differ from Egerman's? What is the significance of the way Vogler and the doctor feel about each other?

13. Very much by surprise, Egerman confronts his wife. How do the psychological complexities of this scene foreshadow marital relationships in more recent Bergman films?

14. During the performance, Tubal is revealed working the wires...Vogler takes revenge on Starbeck by hypnotizing his wife. How does this reveal Bergman's attitude toward authority figures.

> What does Antonsson's being bound by an "invisible chain" symbolize? Why does he respond by strangling Vogler?

15. Why does Bergman shoot the sequence of Vogler's friends pulling out the coffin in a *mirror?* What is the significance of the "body switch" and of the doctor's inability to tell the difference?

16. What does the *attic* symbolize? How is it a metaphor for the human *brain?*

> After examining the body, Dr. Vergerus finds "no peculiarities of interest to science." How is he like a modern behavioral psychologist who denies the existence of qualities that can't be measured by scientific instruments?

17. As the doctor writes his report, how does Bergman prepare for the climax in the attic with the following series of cross-cuts?

(a) Starbeck threatens the Grandmother with "Institution."

(b) The Grandmother passes Antonsson's body hanging in the laundry room. Significance of his death?

(c) Egerman and his wife are artificially posed in their 18th century bedroom. What do they represent in contrast with the Grandmother and the actions of the Magician?

(d) A hand slips around the corner as a voice orders Aman to lock the attic door.

18. Back in the attic: The doctor finds an *eyeball* in his inkwell, and a *severed hand* touches his as he writes his diagnosis. How do the visual effects relate to the theme?

The corpse spits in the doctor's face... Vogler steps on the doctor's glasses... How do these actions symbolize the artist's attitude toward science?

A reflection of Vogler (unbearded) appears behind Dr. Vergerus in the mirror, which then shatters. How does this relate to the "identity" theme?

What is the imagistic effect of Vogler's haunting Dr. Vergerus from the other side of the "bars?"

The doctor falls down the stairs screaming. What does his fall symbolize? When Aman intervenes to save him, why does he deny that he felt any more than a "slight fear of death?"

19. The departure: The unbearded Vogler confronts Mrs. Egerman and asks her for money. What is the significance of her not recognizing someone she previously called her "twin soul?" When Vogler begs *him* for money, why is the doctor so contemptuous?

What does Sara's switching places in Vogler's wagon with the Grandmother and Tubal symbolize?

What is the purpose of the Felliniesque ending, in which a brass band escorts Vogler to perform for the king? Note Vogler's sudden pride... What is the point of his shift from whimpering self-pity to megalomania? How is this ending like the conclusion of Brecht's *Threepenny Opera?*

THE WORLD OF APU (1958—Indian) Directed by Satyajit Ray; with Soumitra Chatterji; music by Ravi Shankar. Distributed by Audio-Brandon.

1. This film is *very* slow to get into. What is Ray's purpose in pacing his film so slowly, dwelling on every detail of Apu's life?

2. Why does Ray use so little dialogue? How do the characters and their talk differ from their counterparts in Hollywood movies?

3. The fragmentary prologue shows Apu looking for a job. Why does Ray start the film this way, instead of just plunging into the credits?

4. Calcutta: Ray emphasizes atmospheric textures by shooting through smoke and falling water. We first see Apu's apartment in a shot through the torn rain-soaked curtain. How does this set the mood and theme of the film? What do we learn about Apu from the setting and the rainstorm of the opening scene?

5. Apu again goes looking for a job...at a primary school...at a factory. What is the effect of these scenes? What impression do they give of Indian life? Why won't anyone give Apu a job?

6. Nightfall...A woman watches Apu through his open window. Troubled, Apu closes his shutter and plays his flute. Why does Ray include this scene? What does it tell us about Apu?

7. Crossing the bridge in the dark with his friend Pulu, Apu recites ecstatic poetry to the Mother Goddess, asking her to fold him in her bosom. When a policeman challenges them, Apu cries, "I am Mainaak, the son of Himalaya, mourning the loss of his wings." What is the purpose of these mythological references?

8. Apu describes his obviously autobiographical novel. Why does Pulu laugh when Apu says that his novel will have "love interest?" Describing his hero's hardships, Apu insists that "what's important is that he doesn't turn his back on life." How is this ironic, in terms of what happens later in the film?

9. The Wedding: Aparna's mother sees Apu as "the God Krishna, complete with his flute." What does this symbolize? What is the point of using so many mythological references to describe very ordinary people? What is Ray's view of human nature?

10. The arrival of the bridegroom: What is the effect of the music ("For He's a Jolly Good Fellow")? How does this reflect on British colonialism?

> Apu lies asleep with his flute as the procession passes...
> What is Ray's purpose in this?

11. The elaborate ceremony is interrupted by the discovery that the bridegroom is insane. How does this tragi-comic disaster reflect what is going wrong with ancient traditions, as symbolized by the "arranged marriage?"

12. What is your reaction to the scene in which the family approaches Apu? Why is Apu confused and astounded at their proposition? How does the setting of the river contribute to the tone of the scene in which Apu ponders his decision?

13. Apu and Aparna speak for the first time on their wedding night. What is the effect of the setting, the bed all decked with streamers and flowers? How is Apu characterized in this scene? How does Aparna's simple answer to his question characterize her?

14. Back in Calcutta: What is Aparna's first reaction to her new abode, and why? (Note the shot of her face through the hole in the torn curtain.)

15. The next scene opens with a shot of a new curtain... What is the effect of this? As Aparna gets out of bed, she finds herself tied to Apu. What is the significance of her reaction? After contemplating Aparna's hairpin, Apu opens his cigarettes, only to find a warning note from her inside. How do these details characterize their marriage?

16. What does the *eating sequence* tell us about their relationship? Why does Ray use so many short sequences to describe their marriage? How does this effect the audience's sense of *time?*

17. Apu and Aparna at the movies: Why does Ray include this scene, parodying the hack melodramas cranked out by the Indian film studios?

18. The conversation in the taxi: What is the significance of the fact that Apu hasn't worked on his novel since they were married? How has marriage changed Apu's life?

19. Apu rides home from work, stealing glimpses of his wife's love-letter. What is the effect of the announcement that awaits him at home? What is the significance of Apu's reaction to the announcement? How does his life change as a result?

20. The clock stops ticking while Apu stares in the tiny mirror. Then a train whistle blows, acting as a transition to the shot of Apu standing beside the railroad track. How do these visual details signify the change in Apu's life?

21. The shot of Apu riding north on the train is juxtaposed against the shot of a baby swinging in a basket. What is the purpose of this cross-cut?

22. Note the powerful shots of Apu standing by the ocean... walking through the woods... gazing down from the mountain. What does Apu's gesture on the mountaintop symbolize? In this sequence, how is Apu like (and unlike) Siddhartha in Hesse's novel?

23. Feet-first, Apu's five-year old son Kajal appears wearing a monster mask and shooting his slingshot at birds. Juxtaposed against Apu's tragic gesture, what is the effect of this scene? How is Kajal characterized? In what ways is he like Apu? In what ways does he resemble his mother?

24. Why won't Apu have anything to do with his son?

25. Persuaded by Pulu, Apu goes to Aparna's house to see his son, only to find the little boy asleep in the bed that had been decked for his wedding. What is the effect of this?

26. Why does Apu change his mind about his son?

27. Why does Kajal react as he does to seeing his father for the first time?

28. Although this is a "neo-realist" film, the action in the final scene is carefully choreographed, creating the impression of a cosmic dance. In what other scenes does Ray use this formal device?

HIROSHIMA MON AMOUR (1959—French) Directed by Alain Resnais; with Emmanuelle Riva and Eiji Okada; screenplay by Marguerite Duras. Distributed by Corinth Films.

1. *Hiroshima Mon Amour* is about a love affair between a French actress and a Japanese architect. Why aren't the characters *named?* Why are they attracted to each other? What is the significance of their professions?

2. Imagistically, what does Hiroshima have to do with her first love affair? How is this idea established by the opening shot of the drenched, dissolving bodies?

3. Why does Okada insist that Riva knows *nothing* about Hiroshima? ("What was there for you to weep over?")

4. Why does Resnais intercut the documentary footage with the shots of them embracing?

5. What do the severe architecture and Fusco's dissonant music contribute to the opening sequence? How do they relate to the imagery of "stones, molten and exploded"?

6. "Just as in love, the illusion exists that it can never be forgotten . . . " Why does Riva identify with his past?

> As Riva says, "Like you, I have struggled against forgetting," Resnais cuts to a smiling Japanese guide in a Hiroshima tour bus. Why? What is Resnais saying about the human capacity to remember?

7. "You destroy me, you're so good for me . . . " How does this chanted dialogue characterize Riva? What is the implication of the cross-cut from the deformed hand to *her* hand caressing his back?

8. As Riva stands in the doorway watching Okada's sleeping body, it momentarily turns into the body of her dead German lover from twenty years before. What is the significance of this?

"Sometimes a person dreams without realizing it." What does this imply about our "waking" lives?

9. Why does Riva keep insisting that she doesn't want to see him again?

10. Riva is staying at the Hotel New Hiroshima. What does this modern, antiseptic hotel symbolize?

11. Okada meets her again at the Peace Parade. As she strokes the cat, he tells her how much he longs for her. Why does Resnais interrupt their love scene with the parade? What is the significance of their having to push their way through the crowd?

12. How does the classical Japanese architecture in Okada's home characterize him?

13. Why do they both insist they're happily married?

14. Why is he so intent on hearing about Nevers? Note that Resnais films *three* replies. Why? What does this suggest about human motivations?

15. In the bar, Okada asks, "When you're in the cellar, am I dead?" Why does he say "I"?

16. In Riva's flashback story, what does the *cellar* symbolize? Why does she rub her hands against the wall until they bleed?

17. Why does Resnais cut from the closeup of her face to the eyes of the cat to the automatic jukebox in the bar playing a French tune?

18. Note the cross-cut from Riva in her mother's arms to an identical embrace in present time. What does this imply about Time and about relationships?

19. When Riva exclaims, "He was my first love!" why does Okada slap her? Why does she smile? Why is he happy that she has never told her husband this story of her past?

20. "Don't things ever stop in Hiroshima?" What does Hiroshima symbolize?

21. After Riva finishes her story, why does she suddenly turn cold and tell him to leave her?

22. Back in her ugly modern hotel, Riva washes her face and accuses herself in the mirror. Why? What does she mean when she says she was searching for an "impossible love"?

23. As Okada follows Riva past all the neon lights, they walk entranced, like sleepwalkers. How does the setting relate to the characters? What is Resnais implying about love in the modern world?

> She says to herself, "He'll kiss me...then I'll be lost." But he doesn't. He turns away. What is the point of this episode?

24. What is the purpose of the intercuts between Hiroshima neon and old French chateaux?

25. What is the significance of the old lady sitting between them in the bus station?

26. Riva goes to a cafe named "Casablanca." Why does Resnais allude to the famous Humphrey Bogart film?

> The other man sits beside Riva and tries to start a conversation in English...while Okada watches from a nearby table. What does this contribute to the dreamlike atmosphere of the film?

27. *Hiroshima Mon Amour* represents a cycle, beginning and ending, "This city was made to the measure of love..." Why does Riva say that *he* is Hiroshima? Why does Okada reply that she is Nevers? What is implied about the nature of war by the identification of the characters with their cities, and by the cycle of their affair?

> I'll think of you as the symbol of love without memory. I'll think of this story as the anguish of forgetting."

SHOOT THE PIANO PLAYER (1960—French) Directed by Francois Truffaut; with Charles Aznavour; music by Georges Delerue; cinematography by Raoul Coutard. Distributed by Janus Films.

1. Truffaut is one of the most important French directors of the "New Wave." What is "new" about this film? How does it differ from the classic French films of Jean Renoir? How has it been influenced by American gangster films?

2. The film begins with a chase down a dark street. What is the effect of the interruption? How does this absurd sequence establish the film's tone?

3. Charlie walks down the street with Lena, uncertain whether or not he should take her hand. What is "real" about this scene? How does it characterize Charlie?

4. How are the two crooks characterized by their driving? How do they differ from gangsters in Hollywood films?

5. The flashback to Charlie's life as a concert pianist: Why do Charlie and his wife play at being "waitress and customer?" How does she react to his success, and why?

6. "Who is Charlie Kohler? We only know him as the Piano Man . . . " How does he represent Truffaut's concept of "Modern Man?" How is he like a character in a novel by Camus or a play by Edward Albee?

7. Why is Charlie's fight with his boss absurd?

8. The gangster tells Fido about all his possessions: "If I'm lying, may my mother drop dead." Why does Truffaut include this sequence? How does it influence the English films of the sixties?

9. Why does Truffaut include the sentimental radio music while Lena and Charlie are escaping to the country?

10. The return to the farm: Why does Truffaut set this scene in the *snow?* What does the setting contribute to the film's meaning?

11. "We're all alike . . . and that includes Fido," says Charlie's brother. This causes Charlie to reflect on where the "wildness" in his family comes from. How does the family symbolize the human race? What is the significance of Charlie's childhood memory of his brothers throwing rocks at the car that was taking him away to the music conservatory?

12. What does Lena's death in the snow symbolize? How does this allude to the philosophical "Problem of Evil"?

13. Why does Charlie return to his piano? How does this reflect Truffaut's view of life?

JULES AND JIM (1961—French) Directed by Francois Truffaut; with Jeanne Moreau, Oskar Werner, and Henri Serre; screenplay by Jean Gruault; cinematography by Raoul Coutard; music by Georges Delerue. Distributed by Janus Films.

To Freud's question, "What does a woman want?" Truffaut would simply answer, "More." In *Jules and Jim,* Truffaut's Catherine is a primitive fertility goddess who will be satisfied with nothing less than total worship. Her two lovers are opposites and best friends who love each other as much as they love her. The resulting *menage a trois* is one of the most sophisticated love relationships in the history of film.

***

1. Why does Truffaut set *Jules and Jim* in 1912 and the war years? How does this period relate to the present time?

2. Why the documentary format for such a zany story?

3. How does Truffaut's camera technique differ from the classic style of Jean Renoir? What is the effect of the constant music? How does this influence English films of the sixties?

4. Truffaut's imagery is highly symbolic. Note the lady with the watch around her ankle ("Next, Jules tried professionals.") Why does Truffaut include Jules' *hour glass* and Therese's *steam engine* act?

5. After viewing Albert's slides of the ancient stone goddess, Jules and Jim embark immediately for the Adriatic. How does their fascination with the idol's smile foreshadow their relationship with Catherine?

6. What is the tone of Jules and Jim's boxing match? How does this relate to the love theme and to the nature of their friendship? In what ways are they opposites?

7. Upon meeting Catherine, Jules proposes a toast: "Instead of linking arms in the usual way, let us touch feet under the table." How is this ritual gesture ironic?

8. What is the thematic significance of Catherine's disguising herself as a boy? What does the race across the bridge symbolize, and what does it reveal about her character? How does it foreshadow the end of the film?

9. While Jim helps Catherine pack, she accidentally sets fire to her dressing gown. How does this foreshadow their tragedy? What does her pouring *vitriol* down the drain symbolize?

10. The house of their dreams: When the three appear at the windows, what is the visual impact of the *triangular composition?*

11. While Catherine chatters to dominate their attention, Jules and Jim are absorbed in a game of *dominoes.* What does this game symbolize? Why does Catherine resent the bond between Jules and Jim?

12. When Catherine asks if someone will "scratch her back," Jules sarcastically replies, "The Lord scratches those who scratch themselves." Why does Catherine slap him? What is the effect of her frozen poses? Note that Jim later gives her a back-scratcher. What does this symbolize?

13. After the performance of the feminist play, Jules attacks with a quote from Baudelaire: "I am astonished that women are allowed in churches. What can they have to say to God?" Why does Catherine respond by jumping in the river? What does her leap symbolize?

14. Jim and Catherine arrange to meet at the cafe to "discuss." What is the significance of their missed date? How does this foreshadow their future relationship?

15. World War One intervenes. What is the significance of Jules and Jim's fighting on opposite sides? What is the effect of alternating newsreel sequences with cross-cuts to Jules and Jim?

16. After the war, they resume their friendship at Jules' chalet... What is the significance of Jules being a bug collector? ("One day I may become famous and write a love novel with insects as its characters.")

> Jules prances around the patio like a horse as his daughter follows him with a riding crop. How does this reflect his relationship with Catherine?

> Expressing his "Buddhistic" side, Jules tells Jim of his fear that Catherine will leave him again ("I am slowly renouncing her and all I had expected from the world.") Why won't Catherine stay with him?

Jim recalls his earliest memories of Catherine: "She leaps at men the way she leaped into the Seine." How does this simile characterize her approach to life? How is she like an Ibsen heroine like Hedda Gabler?

17. Catherine challenges Jim to follow her. Knowing Catherine as well as he does, why does he go after her?

18. Jim tells a very moving story about a young soldier who "fought his own war," becoming engaged to a girl (by correspondence!) in wartime...and dying...without ever having seen her. What does this story imply about the nature of love? How does it foreshadow Jim's own long-distance relationship with Catherine?

19. Accompanied by Albert on the guitar, Catherine sings about a "femme fatale" with rings on every finger. How does this reveal her self-image?

20. Jim and Catherine become lovers. Why isn't he satisfied with his relationship with Gilberte?

Observing them from the balcony, Jules quotes Goethe and asks Catherine to translate it. Shortly afterwards, Jules sends for Jim to bring his copy of Goethe to Catherine. Why all the references to Goethe?

The love scene in front of the window: In silhouette, the insect on the window pane "enters her mouth" just before they kiss. What is the effect of this?

21. As Catherine and Jim kiss, Jules *saws logs*. What does this activity symbolize?

One day as Jim sits rocking in Jules' chair, Catherine decides to spend some time "laughing" with Jules. What is the significance of Jim's reaction?

22. In Paris, Jim again meets the "Steam Engine," who tells him about her marital adventures. How does this digression reflect Jules and Jim's relationship with Catherine?

23. Jim returns to the chalet, only to find that Catherine has left again. Jules lectures him on the necessity of treating Catherine like a goddess, an "irresistible force." How does his worship of her explain her frequent departures?

As Jim is about to leave, Catherine suddenly appears in the window. She later confronts Jim: "You said goodbye to your loves; I said goodbye to mine." How is she like a modern "liberated" woman?

24. Unable to have a child, Jim and Catherine part once more: "We should never be hurt both at once. When you stop suffering, I'll start." What is the significance of their inability to have a child?

25. What is the significance of the missed connections in the series of letters between Jim and Catherine?

26. By accident, Jules and Jim meet again in Paris and get together at another of Jules' incredible houses. While they prepare for a drive, Catherine carefully wraps her pajamas in a parcel. Why?

27. As Jim lies asleep beside Gilberte, Catherine zig-zags through the square, blowing her horn to wake him. How does this act characterize her?

Jim confronts Catherine in her room: "You wanted to invent love, but pioneers must be unselfish." How does this imply a criticism of modern feminism?

28. The trio meet again in a theater during a documentary showing Hitler's nazis burning books. What is the significance of all these accidental meetings?

29. "Catherine suggested a ride, but to where?" What is the significance of her last drive? What does the shattered bridge symbolize? How does this recall the race across the bridge earlier in the film?

30. Why the anti-heroic documentary ending?

"Everyone called them Don Quixote and Sancho Panza." What is the point of this parallel?

"Catherine wanted her ashes to be cast to the winds—but it was not permitted." What is the effect of the understatement? How does it sum up her whole life?

VIRIDIANA (1961—Spanish) Directed by Luis Bunuel; with Sylvia Pinal, Fernando Rey, and Francisco Rabal. Distributed by Audio-Brandon.

1. Why does Bunuel use Handel's "Hallelujah Chorus" as background music during the titles and elsewhere during the film?

2. Our first glimpse of the uncle's estate shows the servant's daughter *skipping rope*. ("She loves the handles.") The jump-rope returns as a leitmotif, possibly a symbol, throughout the film. What are the connotations of this particular game?

3. "Your fields look neglected; the weeds have taken over." How does the uncle's estate symbolize the condition of modern Spain?

4. While Viridiana removes her black stockings and unwraps her religious paraphernalia, Don Jaime plays the organ. Why this surreal juxtaposition? What social and psychological forces do their performances represent?

5. Why does Bunuel cut from Viridiana praying—to a closeup of the servant milking a cow? Notice Viridiana's trembling hand as she grasps the cow's udder. What is the visual effect of this? Why does she hesitate to give it a good squeeze?

6. What is the significance of Don Jaime's estrangement from his son? As he and Viridiana discuss the problem, why does Bunuel focus on a *bee* struggling in the water?

7. To the accompaniment of liturgical music, Don Jaime puts on his dead wife's shoes and corset. What does this ritual imply about Spanish aristocracy?

8. The sleepwalking Viridiana interrupts him . . . What is the meaning of her gathering ashes from the fireplace and scattering them on Don Jaime's bed?

9. Why does Viridiana's uncle ask her to wear his dead wife's wedding dress? How does this reflect Spanish society's attitude toward religion? (Note that although Don Jaime is *obsessed* with Viridiana, he has never shown her any genuine affection, and has in fact ignored her all her life.)

10. How is the coffee-drinking scene a perverted communion ritual? What are the connotations of the little girl's dream about a "big black bull trying to get through the pantry door?"

11. Why does Don Jaime kill himself, and what does his death symbolize? What is the significance of his using the little girl's jump-rope? Why does Bunuel cut from the suicide scene to the girl jumping rope again?

12. Why does Viridiana feel responsible for her uncle's death? How does her guilt establish the film as an allegory about the relationship of church and state in modern Spain?

13. Why does Viridiana open her dead uncle's estate to the town's beggars, and how does this gesture symbolize the role of the Church in the twentieth century? How does Bunuel characterize the beggars? What is his view of human nature?

14. How does Don Jaime's son differ from him? Jorge's first act is to play several chords (off-key) on his father's organ. Why does Bunuel stress his lack of musical talent?

15. Why does Bunuel have one of the beggars use the jump-rope to hold up his pants?

16. Jorge wants to introduce electricity to cultivate the fields. What does this symbolize?

17. The cart with the dog tied behind it: After Jorge buys the dog to release him from his misery, a second cart and dog rattle down the road. What is Bunuel implying about social problems?

18. Jorge on the beggars: "Your kind of charity is outdated. You should throw them out." How does he reflect the middle-class, technocratic attitude toward the poor?

19. As Viridiana and her beggars pray, Jorge's men break rocks, sift stones, pour cement. What do these intercut shots imply about religion?

20. Jorge and the maid inspect the old furniture in the attic. What does the setting symbolize? How is the seduction a *political* act? (Note the cat pouncing on the mouse . . . Bunuel avoids subtlety!)

21. What are the connotations of the Beggars' Banquet? Some important details: (1) the blasphemous tableau, (2) the syphilitic beggar dancing in the wife's wedding veil, (3) the blind beggar smashing the dishes. What do these symbols convey about modern democracy and the nature of man?

22. Jorge and Viridiana arrive as the party breaks up. The blind beggar staggers out, the wedding veil tangled in his feet. As Handel's *Messiah* heralds the Second Coming, Jorge surveys the mess...The jump-rope makes its final appearance: what is the significance of the way the beggars finally treat Viridiana?

23. "I want to put another plug down there." Jorge electrifies the estate, and presumably Viridiana as well. As rock music fills the house, why does Bunuel cut to the burning cross and crown of thorns?

24. "The first day I saw you, I said that my cousin Viridiana would play cards with me some day." How is the card game a sexual and political metaphor?

THE LONELINESS OF THE LONG DISTANCE RUNNER

(1962—English) Directed by Tony Richardson; with Tom Courtenay and Michael Redgrave. Distributed by Audio-Brandon.

Hollywood films like *The Exorcist* and *I Was a Teenage Werewolf* provide a simple explanation for evil: "The Devil made him do it." Or else, like Marlon Brando in *The Wild One,* the black-jacketed thug is really an angel at heart, and the sheriff's daughter just naturally falls in love with him. *The Loneliness of the Long Distance Runner* differs markedly from Hollywood formulas. Like most real-life delinquents, Colin Smith is sullen, unattractive, and simmering with rage. He is not about to be rehabilitated so that psychologists can continue to believe that "there's no such thing as a bad boy." Nor is he a romantic figure like John Travolta or Sylvester Stallone with whom teenagers want to identify. He is the embodiment of working-class resentment, an "angry young man" who mocks all of our sentimental notions about teenagers.

***

1. Why is the "Governor" so intent on having his boys outrace the boys from the school? How does this relate to his view of life?

2. How does life in the prison reflect life in the world outside?

3. "Running has always been a big thing in our family," says Colin. What is the double-meaning here?

4. How do the psychologist and the warden represent the two approaches to rehabilitation in the prison system? Why doesn't either approach work?

5. Why does Richardson cut from Colin working on the assembly line dismantling gas masks to the flashback of his mother collecting the insurance money from her dead husband's factory?

6. Why does Richardson include the absurd concert scene? Note that while the prisoners are singing "Jerusalem," Stacey is being handcuffed and thrown in a cell. Why is this ironic?

7. As Colin runs through the woods, he flashes back to his mother spending his father's insurance money. What is the effect of the cheerful muzac in the department store? Why is Colin disgusted as his mother and sister cluster around the new TV? Why does he burn the money his mother gives him?

8. Colin and his girlfriend run on the beach. How does this scene relate thematically to the rest of the film?

9. Colin and his friend turn off the sound while the TV politician rambles on about England's greatness. How does this relate to the conflict that follows with his mother's lover?

10. As the money trickles out of the drainpipe, Richardson cuts to Colin running through the woods. What does the drainpipe symbolize?

11. The warden tells Colin that the greatest honor a man can receive is to represent his country in the Olympics. What is the social and political significance of his obsession with athletics?

12. The cons and the students compare life in their respective institutions. What similarities and contrasts are immediately apparent?

13. The Big Race: As Colin runs, images flash through his mind—

> the warden's lecture
> his mother: "Everything in this house belongs to me."
> his father: "I won't go to no hospital!"
> the warden: "It's my ambition to see you boys take that cup."
> Stacey: "Keep back, Smith!"
> the cop: "Tell me where that money is."

Various voices jumble in his ears as the crowd chants "RUN!" What is the significance of Colin's reaction?

14. Why does the film end with a shot of Colin back on the assembly line?

15. What are the problems involved in seeing life as a game in which the best man will win—whether he is a convict or a student in a rich private school?

SUNDAYS AND CYBELE (1962—French) Directed by Serge Bourguignon; with Hardy Kruger and Patricia Gozzi; music by Maurice Jarre. Distributed by Swank Films.

Of all the films based on classical mythology, *Sundays and Cybele* is the most beautiful. This strange story of a shell-shocked fighter pilot who falls in love with a twelve year old girl derives its power from the ancient fertility myth of Cybele and Attis. The Romans brought the worship of Cybele, the Great Mother, to their city in 204 B.C when a meteor shower—and the invasion of Hannibal—convinced them that their traditional gods couldn't protect them. With Cybele came Attis, her son and lover, whose death and resurrection were celebrated in a rather barbaric festival at the end of March. In imitation of their god, who castrated himself and metamorphosed into a pine tree, the eunuch-priests of Attis commemorated the spring equinox by cutting a pine tree in the woods, decking it with violets and woolen bands, and slashing themselves with knives to splatter it with blood. Any novice wishing to join the priesthood would also have the honor of castrating himself to show his devotion to Attis and the Great Mother. The symbolism in this myth is obviously relevant to *Sundays and Cybele*. Note Pierre's stones, the tree, the knife, and especially the cock—which is the emblem of the priests of Attis. Also note that Bourguignon has changed the time of his ritual from the end of March to Christmas, undoubtedly to allude to other ancient religions that believe in death and resurrection.

***

1. How does Pierre's love for Cybele relate to the opening sequence, in which his plane crashes, killing a little girl?

Why does Bourguignon use a *solenoid* effect for this sequence? As Pierre whips off his oxygen mask, what is the purpose of the freeze-frame?

How is Pierre's "resurrection" from this plane crash like the death and rebirth of an ancient god?

2. Cut to the train station in Ville D'Avray, where Cybele's father is dragging her to a convent school... "On Sundays I'll come to visit you," he lies. Why is Pierre fascinated with the little girl?

3. Pierre offers her a stone: "It's a piece of a star—it fell from the sky." What does the stone symbolize? How does it recall his own tragic fall? (Note that *Pierre* in French means "stone.")

4. "What does that mean—a wasted life?" What is the significance of Pierre's amnesia?

5. Why is Pierre so turned off by Madeleine, a very beautiful woman who obviously adores him?

6. Pierre helps his friend Carlos, a sculptor, build a cage for birds. What are the mythical connotations of this?

Note the reflection of the trees in the window... "People always hide behind their faces. Trees are different," Carlos claims. Why does he urge Pierre to look at the trees?

What is the significance of Pierre's dizziness when he looks at the water? How is he like the hero of Hitchcock's *Vertigo?*

7. Pierre returns to the school. "My mother ran away with a magician," Cybele tells him. Why does Bourguignon stress her mysterious origin?

The nuns call her Francoise because her name "isn't Christian." Why would they refuse to address her by the name of a Greek fertility goddess?

She'll tell him her real name if he'll get her the cock from the steeple. How does her secrecy reflect the importance of *names* in primitive religions?

8. Cybele and Pierre run in the park... "Look at the circles!" she exclaims as the pebbles drop in the pond. How does their ritual echo the classical idea of the "circle of perfection?"

> Why does Bourguignon dwell on the reflection of the trees in the pond as Cybele plans their "Marriage?"

> What is the significance of Cybele's grandmother being *Greek,* a gypsy with a magic dagger?

> "You're like a lost child," Cybele admonishes him. Indeed, she acts very much like Pierre's mother. What is the significance of their reversal of roles?

9. What is the symbolic function of the middle-aged bicyclist and the handsome man on horseback who pass by while they're playing? Why doesn't Pierre like the man on the horse?

10. Pierre gives Cybele one of his stones. What is the significance of its being a crystal prism that refracts reality?

11. What does their "temple" in the woods symbolize?

12. Why does entering the temple cause Pierre to suffer a sudden dizzy spell? As Cybele says, "When I grow up I'll study medicine and I'll cure you," Bourguignon cuts to Madeleine in her hospital being pursued by a young doctor. How does this irony foreshadow the end of the film?

13. Why does Bourguignon cut from Cybele in class saying her prayer to Pierre in Carlos' cage with *birds* perching on his shoulders? How does this connect him with Attis the Hunter in Greek myth?

14. How do the toy battleship in the pond and the bicyclist fiddling with his earplug symbolize the French middle class?

15. "There, we're home again," Cybele says as they throw a pebble in the pond. What does she mean? Why does she object to the artist painting her tree?

> Cybele plays "blind man's bluff" with the other children. What is the reason for Pierre's violent reaction?

> The horseman rides by. Why does Bourguignon repeat this motif?

> While Pierre carries her, Cybele lies in his arms as though she were dead. What are the mythical connotations of this childlike game?

16. Why does Pierre stop singing when Madeleine enters the apartment?

"If you ever want me again, your slave will be ready," she whines. Why does he keep pushing her away?

17. Why isn't Pierre pleased about Madeleine's "surprise"—a wedding party on Sunday? Why wouldn't her "sexy dress" interest him? As she rattles on about how Bernard flirts with her, why does he just leave without a word?

> When Madeleine worries about Pierre's sudden disappearance, Bernard tells her, "You think too much." How does this characterize him?

18. In the restaurant by the park: Pierre looks at his companions through his *wine glass*. What is the significance of his dreamlike perspective? How does the *wine* symbolism connect him with both Dionysus and Christ?

> Why does he drop one of his stones in the finger-bowl? What is the purpose of the cut to the pond and Cybele's voice over: "Pierre, we're home again"? What is the significance of their apparent telepathy? Or is Pierre merely projecting Cybele's rather erotic pubescent fantasy?

19. As Pierre rubs the frost from the window, why does he imagine Cybele riding with the horseman in the park? While the others get in the car, Pierre wanders off to stare at the horseman and his lady ... who wears the same hat as Cybele. Why does Bourguignon include this dreamlike confusion of identity?

20. Cut to the carnival: What does the carousel symbolize, and how does it relate to the film's imagery? (Note the large rooster!)

> Despite Bernard's scoffing, why is Pierre fascinated with the fortune teller? How does her asserting the "power of destiny" foreshadow the end of the film? During the seance, why does Bourguignon place her huge fishbowl in the foreground? Why does Pierre take her *knife?* ("It's full of vital fluid.")

> The bumper cars: How does this sequence symbolize adult relationships, in contrast with Pierre's relationship with Cybele? As the camera zooms in on Cybele's face, why does Pierre go berserk?

21. The young nun visits Pierre to tell him that Cybele is not well. Why does Cybele lie in bed, refusing to speak? Why would she fear that Pierre has abandoned her?

22. Madeleine looks for Pierre at the grocery store ... where she finds out about "the little girl." While Carlos tries to reassure her, why does Bourguignon focus on the birds in the cages?

> "Is the girl dead? Did I kill her?" Why would the hysterical Pierre repeat what he said in the hospital after his crash?

> Carlos' wife keeps shrieking that Pierre isn't normal. What does Bourguignon think of "normal" people?

> "With that girl he's discovered a world on his own level. He's re-living his childhood." Why is Carlos the only person in the film who understands Pierre and Cybele's relationship?

23. Instead of getting on the train, Madeleine follows Pierre to the boarding school and watches him play with Cybele in the park. Note that nothing interferes with the regularity of a religious ritual or a children's game: Pierre kicks a hole in the ice so they can drop a stone in the pond and be "home" again. Then, as Madeleine watches, Pierre sticks his knife in a tree. What does their listening to the trees symbolize? Why does Madeleine smile?

24. In the cafe: "Will you tell me your real name one day?" Pierre asks. She replies, "And you—will you give me the cock from the steeple?" What are the mythological connotations of this particular request? How is she like the young girl in Ibsen's *Masterbuilder?*

> As Cybele caresses the knife, why does Bourguignon shoot her face through the flames? How is she like the child-priestesses at Delphi?

> "Would you die if I died, or would you forget me with your wife?" Why does she dwell on death? Why does she insist that if she died there would be no name on her tombstone?

25. Note the sculpture of the angel as Pierre stands by Carlos' door. What is the significance of his bashing the door open and taking the Christmas tree? To the accompaniment of church bells, Pierre walks up the street carrying the fully decorated tree ... What is the meaning of his visual "transformation" into a tree, and how does this allude to the Attis myth?

26. Why is Madeleine suddenly afraid as Carlos shows her his broken door?

> Madeleine stops in the bar to use the phone. What is the purpose of the saccharine broadcast about Santa Claus? Why does Bourguignon juxtapose this against the

insensitive customer referring to Pierre as the "cradle snatcher?"

27. While Pierre and Cybele drink champagne to celebrate Christmas in their "temple" in the park, Bourguignon cuts to Bernard meeting Madeleine. Why would he violate her trust and call the police?

> "You're the one who's sick!" she exclaims. What do you think of Bernard's psychoanalytical interpretation of the situation?

28. Cut to Pierre at the top of the steeple unscrewing the cock. What is the significance of his not suffering from vertigo any longer? What is the effect of the organ music during his descent? How does this action establish Pierre as a fertility god, a Christ figure, and a tragic hero?

29. Cut to Madeleine and the ringing phone. Why would Carlos be furious about their calling the police?

> "This is no time for sentiment," Bernard insists, cutting off the phone. How are Carlos and Bernard different? What forces in society do they represent, and how do they function within the framework of the film?

30. Why does Bourguignon place the tragic denouement "offstage?" What is the effect of the cross-cut from Madeleine's cry to Cybele running screaming through the woods?

31. At the end of the film, what does Cybele mean when she says, "I have no name"? What is the purpose of the religious music?

For further information on the mythology, see Sir James G. Fraser's *The Golden Bough.*

DAVID AND LISA (1963—American) Directed by Frank Perry; with Keir Dullea, Janet Margolin, and Howard da Silva. Distributed by Walter Reade 16 and Films Inc.

1. How does the opening shot of *tangled trees* establish the film's theme?

2. "TOUCH CAN KILL"—Why is David afraid of being touched?

> His mother insists that he was never hit as a child. How do her *white gloves* comment on this assertion? What other details of behavior reveal her responsibility for much of David's problem?

> If someone is *deprived* of physical contact as a child, why will he grow up fearing human contact?

3. What is the significance of David's obsession with *clocks,* and of his "clock execution" dream? How does his dream of decapitating Lisa reveal his unconscious desire for her?

4. Why does Lisa talk in *rhyme?* Why does she grow fearful when David tries to talk with her in normal sentences?

5. Lisa draws *circles* on the wall. Psychologically, what does this reveal about her?

6. Why does David dislike psychiatrists? How does the doctor succeed in winning his confidence?

7. Why does David's mother want to take him out of the school?

8. What is the importance of the scene in the train station? ("If you're normal, who wants to be normal?") How does this scene illustrate the theories of R.D. Laing?

9. "Parents don't like you when you're sick. If you get 'well,' they don't like you either." Why would many young people identify with this statement?

10. What do we learn about David's problem from his parents' conversation at the dinner table? How does the shot framing David between the candles establish David's position in this scene?

11. Trying to talk with David, his father stands there with a hand full of *ashes*. What does this symbolize? What does David mean when he describes his father as a "marshmallow?"

12. Why does David run away from home and return to the school?

13. As Dr. Swinford and David talk in front of the window, how do the two boys playing *catch* in the background comment on their conversation?

> What problem is David working out in his story about "George/Georgina"? Why does he decide to put the flowers in his room?

14. How is the scene in which David and Dr. Swinford raid the refrigerator a symbolic *communion* ritual?

15. Why is Lisa fascinated by the sculpture in the museum? What is the significance of the museum guard's reaction?

8½ (1963—Italian) Directed by Federico Fellini; with Marcello Mastroianni, Sandra Milo, Anouk Aimee, and Claudia Cardinale; music by Nino Rota. Distributed by Corinth Films.

1. The opening: What on earth is going on? How is Guido's being trapped in the car a metaphor of *birth?* What does his "ascension" symbolize? Why does Fellini cut to Guido on the beach, tugging on a rope, crying, "Counselor, I've got him"? What does the final plunge into the sea symbolize?

2. Guido's awakening (without transition) in the sanitarium: What does his taking the "cure" symbolize? (Cf. Thomas Mann's *Magic Mountain*)

What is the effect of the music (Wagner's "Ride of the Valkyries" and the overture from Rossini's *Barber of Seville)?* What is the tone of this scene, as the wrinkled old people march up to get their mineral water?

When Guido lowers his dark glasses, the music stops and he has a vision of Claudia. What is the point of the sudden shift to the reality of the waitress serving mineral water?

3. Why does Fellini cut to Daumier criticizing Guido for lacking "poetic inspiration?" "These capricious appearances of the Girl in White... What do they mean? Of all your symbols, this is the worst." How does this allude to the ending of *La Dolce Vita?*

What is Fellini's attitude here toward his *persona?* What justification is there for regarding this scene as self-parody?

4. Guido and Carla in the hotel room: "You want me to put on an act, like those actresses of yours." How does this scene develop our conception of Guido's sense of reality?

What is the significance of Carla's always *eating?*

5. Fade to graveyard scene with Guido's mother and father. Note that something rather unusual happens when he kisses his mother. What is the significance of this? How is his conversation with his father like a scene out of Joyce or Kafka?

6. In the hotel, Guido is besieged by people wanting parts in his film. What is the significance of his being presented with *four* versions of his father? Why can't he make up his mind?

7. In the pavillion: Mario dances with Gloria while Guido hides behind a false nose, ignoring Carla sitting alone at the table opposite. As everyone chatters about religion and politics, why does Guido interject a question about "whether the asparagus is good?" Why does Fellini make this dialogue so disjointed?

"Let's entertain these bores!" How does the magician fit into the structure of the film? How does he relate to Guido himself?

8. "ASA NISI MASA" provokes a cryptic but revealing memory. How does it serve as a transition to the flashback of a childhood scene in which Guido is bathed in wine? What are the symbolic connotations of this wine-bath, and how does this relate to the rest of the film?

9. Back in the hotel, the actress complains, "I feel I'm a complete failure, in my life and in my work." How does she reflect Guido's own self-image? How does Guido's old friend Conocchia compound his problem? ("You need younger people around you . . . But watch out—you're not the man you used to be.")

10. As Guido declares, "Enough of symbolism and these escapist visions," Claudia suddenly appears in his room: "I want to create order . . . " What does she symbolize?

> Claudia vanishes, banished by the buzzing telephone . . .
> Carla is sick from drinking too much mineral water. How
> does this interruption represent stark reality?

11. Guido comforts Carla, who is looking very bloated: "That water is for sick people—why did you drink it?" Why would Guido be involved with such a bovine lady?

12. As Guido thinks about what to say to the Cardinal, Fellini fades to the monastery. Guido is concerned with his hero's upbringing, which has created "certain complexes." Like what? What do you make of the Cardinal's senile response?

13. Guido's attention drifts to the forest, where he observes a rather large lady picking berries. Why does this trigger a flashback to his prep-school humiliation? What is the significance of his dance with Saraghina? Why is the chase done in the style of a silent film? How does the priest's reaction affect Guido's concept of women? How is Saraghina the prototype for Guido's current mistress?

14. In the steam bath: What are some of the visual connotations of the setting? Note that Guido's walk in the bathhouse parallels his walk up the aisle in the previous flashback. What does this imply?

> Cardinal: "Who said we were put on earth to be happy?
> Outside the church, no one will be saved." What does the
> closing window symbolize?

15. Guido's wife Luisa enters. Note her short hair, heavy glasses, and chain-smoking. How do these details characterize her? How is she different from Carla, and how does this contrast explain Guido's problem with women?

16. What does Guido's *space tower* symbolize?

17. The scene with Luisa is very bitter. What is the source of their problem?

18. In the restaurant: Why would Guido hallucinate about Carla and Luisa being friends? How does this lead to the harem scene?

19. How do elements of Guido's childhood reappear in his harem fantasy? How does the tone of this scene change? What is the significance of Jacqueline, the lady who won't go upstairs when she's too old? How does the *whipping scene* symbolize male chauvinism?

> Note Luisa's part in the harem: "I don't bother you any more—I don't make any demands." What is the point of this wish-fulfillment?

20. Cut to theatre for screen tests: "If people like you would pay attention to the world around them, they wouldn't have so many illusions." Why does Guido respond by hallucinating Daumier's *hanging?*

> What is the significance of the different versions of reality presented in the screen tests? Note Guido's dialogue with the screen figure: "Luisa, I love you." Why does the "real" Luisa yawn and walk out?

> What is the visual effect of the repeated images of Carla?

21. When Claudia arrives, why does Guido say, "You came just in time"? Guido describes himself as wanting to "devour and possess everything." How does this relate to the film he has been trying to make—and possibly to Fellini's self-image?

22. Guido and Claudia drive to the ruins of a Roman spring. What does the setting symbolize? Claudia: "This man you describe who doesn't love anyone—I don't have very much sympathy for him." Why does this force Guido to tell her there's no part for her in his film? What is the significance of this admission?

23. The Producer drives up, and Fellini cuts to a press conference. As Guido crawls under the table, his mother suddenly appears: "Guido, where are you running to?" Is the shot real or imaginary? How much of this scene is hallucination?

24. What is the meaning of the final dance? Is this dance Guido's dying vision? Or is it the *shot* that is "imaginary," suggesting that Guido has given up his film and allowed his tower to be torn down? Or did Fellini merely shoot two endings for the film?

KNIFE IN THE WATER (1963—Polish) Directed by Roman Polanski. Distributed by Janus Films.

Roman Polanski's classic Oedipal triangle is laden with mythological imagery and political significance. Speaking of his claustrophobic study of three people on a boat, Polanski says, "The real conflict in the film is between man and wife—the third person is merely a catalyst." Also, the struggle of honor between generations reflects the struggle within Poland itself, with the husband representing the Polish middle class.

1. What is the psychological significance of the *speed* of the husband's driving? (Note his reaction to nearly hitting the hitch-hiker: "... to run over a pup and be tried for killing a man.")

2. The hitch-hiker admires Andrei's *car* and *sailboat*, which is named after his wife Christina. What do these possessions symbolize?

3. "I knew you'd call me back—you want to carry on the game." How does this establish the basic metaphor of the film?

4. What does *sailing* symbolize? Note that the husband emphasizes the necessity of quick reflexes and discipline, while the young man insists, "Sailing is a kid's game. It's when you walk straight ahead that you need a knife."

5. "If two men are on board, *one* is captain." What are the political and psychological connotations of this statement?

6. As the wife looks on admiringly, the young man answers the challenge to his whistling by climbing the mast. Why do young men often climb trees, mountains, etc. to impress women?

7. The young man lies on his back staring at the sky, where he observes "a cloud in the shape of an ass." How does this echo Hamlet's famous conversation with Polonius?

8. What is the symbolic significance of the *hot pot*, which the husband holds with pliers and which the young man tries to hold with his bare hands. How does this symbol reflect the love intrigue?

9. While the young man tries to paddle to shore, the husband deliberately steers the boat in a circle. How is this a political and psychological metaphor?

10. What is the significance of the young man's hanging back, unable to swim, while the husband and wife play in the water with their inflatable crocodile?

11. The young man "walks on water" as he learns to balance the boat. How does this recall the earlier shot of him lying on the deck in a crucified position, with the rope coiled behind him like a halo?

12. Blowing up the air mattresses: Note that the husband makes a contest out of everything, using a *pump* while the young man relies on lung-power. How does this symbolize the differences in their approach to life?

13. What does their game of *pick-up-sticks* symbolize? Note that the husband emphasizes delicacy and rules. As her forfeit, the wife sings a song about emptiness—while her husband listens to the boxing match on the radio with an ear-plug. The young man recites a Romantic poem. A fly buzzes overhead. How do these activities relate?

14. How does the wife feel about her husband's bossing the young man around?

15. What does the young man's *knife* symbolize?

16. Why does the young man pretend to drown? How does this relate to the "game" he speaks of at the beginning of the film?

17. The Wife: "You're just like him...only half his age, weaker, and more stupid." What does this add to our understanding of this basic Oedipal triangle?

18. What is the symbolic significance of the young man's putting on the husband's *robe* to keep warm?

19. Why does Polanski interrupt the attempted love scene with the alarm clock? How does this affect the film's tone?

20. "Why did that sailor jump on the broken glass?"—Christina asks her husband to finish his story. (The sailor hadn't realized that in a year of not working his feet had gotten soft. He could no longer perform the trick he had done many times before.) How does this story reflect the main conflict of the film?

21. The main theme of *Knife in the Water* is generational conflict, an idea that goes back at least as far as Euripides' *Hippolytus*. How has Polanski varied the classical love-triangle to make it more relevant to modern audiences?

LORD OF THE FLIES (1963—English) Directed by Peter Brook; music by Raymond Leppard. Distributed by Walter Reade 16.

1. Despite the lush green and beautiful colors of the tropical island, Brook shot the film in *black-and-white*. Why? In the beginning, why does he use the *stop-frame* technique to suggest atomic war?

2. What is the effect of the *flies* buzzing as Ralph climbs through the bushes? What does the *tangled underbrush* symbolize?

3. How is Piggy characterized? Why are he and Ralph all dressed up in schoolboys' uniforms with jacket, cap, and tie? What does discarding their clothing symbolize?

4. What does the *conch* symbolize?

5. Jack and his choir enter dressed in black, framed against the white sand, singing Raymond Leppard's jazzed-up "Kyrie Eleison." How does this characterize them, and what force in society do they symbolize?

> "Hey, what are you wearing those funny clothes for?" "It's our uniform." What does this imply about the military and the church?

6. While Ralph, Jack, and Simon go exploring, they push the rock down the cliff. What does this foreshadow?

7. Jack tries to stab the pig, but he lacks the nerve. In the next shot, as the flies buzz loudly, he slices the flower Simon is looking at. Why?

8. Jack: "We've got to have rules. We're not savages, we're English. And the English are best at everything." Why is this ironic? Why does Jack stress

punishing anyone who breaks his rules? Why do people who are violent or corrupt always insist on having lots of rules?

9. What do Piggy's *glasses* symbolize? How is he like Robert Oppenheimer, the developer of the atomic bomb—or like any scientist who does war research for the government?

10. What is the point of the *military* maneuvers and commands as Jack's choirboys guard the fire?

11. What do *children's games*—for instance, jousting on the beach and making the sand-crabs fight—suggest about human nature? Or do these games merely reflect adult society? Why does Brook cut to Simon playing gently with a lizard?

12. Flies buzz as the boys go on their first hunt . . . While Jack and his friends are killing the pig, a *plane* passes overhead. What does this juxtaposition imply?

13. What does the fire on the mountaintop symbolize? What is the theological implication of Ralph standing by the dead fire crying "Come back!" at the heavens?

14. Why does Brook make the pig-eating scene so disgusting? What is the point of the ritual dance that follows?

15. Simon: "Maybe there isn't a beast. Maybe it's only *us.*" How does this differ from Jack's view of the beast? Piggy denies that there could be a beast—otherwise, "things wouldn't make sense." What does this imply? In suggesting that they *vote* on the existence of the beast, how does Ralph represent the western, democratic view of reality? What are the problems with this view?

16. As Ralph exclaims, "The rules are the only thing we've got," why does Brook cut to the mob of shrieking boys hunting?

17. What is the significance of Jack and his friends painting their faces?

18. What does the pig's head symbolize? What is the significance of their leaving it as a gift for the Beast? Why does Simon stare at it?

19. Why does Simon's silent communication with the Lord of the Flies cause him to climb the mountain again?

20. What is the effect of the cross-cut from the dancing and swirling flames of the pig-roast to the shot of the low cloud bank as Simon stares at the

dead parachutist? Why does Brook cut back to the boys' distorted, painted faces?

21. What does the dead parachutist represent? What is ironic about his being the "answer" from the heavens, and from the world of grown-ups?

22. What does Simon's death symbolize? What is the effect of the music and the light flashing on the water as his body floats out to sea in a *crucified* posture?

23. Piggy's death: What is the significance of Piggy's blindness? What do the falling boulder and the breaking of the conch symbolize?

24. What does the *Officer in White* symbolize? In Golding's novel, the officer surveys the hollocaust and asks, "Fun and Games?" Why does Brook choose to have the officer remain silent instead? What does the expression on Ralph's face mean? Why does he cry? What is the purpose of the "Kyrie" refrain?

25. If the children on the island had been *girls*—or a mix of boys and girls— would the outcome have been different?

26. What does this film imply about Rousseau's idea of the "Noble Savage"?

DR. STRANGELOVE (1964—American) Directed by Stanley Kubrick; with Peter Sellers, George C. Scott, Sterling Hayden, Slim Pickens, Keenan Wynn, and Peter Bull; screenplay by Terry Southern. Distributed by Swank Films.

Note that Peter Sellers plays three parts in this brilliant black comedy.

1. While the bomber is refueling in mid-air, what does the background music ("Try a Little Tenderness") insinuate about the military?

2. As the "documentary" voice assures us that there is a flight of B-52s in the air to protect us at all times, Kubrick cuts to a bomber pilot reading *Playboy*. What is the effect of this?

3. After Major Kong (!) checks the secret code book, what is the effect of his putting on a *cowboy hat?* How does the music ("When Johnny Comes Marching Home") comment on the action? Why does Kubrick include all the cliched characters from old Howard Hawks films?

4. One of the perks of General Buck Turgidson's position is a secretary who works late. What is the significance of his being "in the powder room" when the emergency call comes from the Pentagon?

> George C. Scott plays his part very broadly, chewing gum and slapping his stomach as he tells his girlfriend, "You start your count-down, and I'll be back before you can say 'Blast-off!' " How do metaphors like this characterize him?

5. What is the effect of the low-angle shot of General Jack D. Ripper chomping on his cigar as he quotes Clemenceau on war ("War is too important to be left to the generals.")?

6. How would Freud explain General Ripper's obsession with preventing the communists from "sapping and impurifying our precious bodily fluids"?

7. Cut to the War Room: "It's beginning to look like General Ripper exceeded his authority." What is the significance of the president's not being able to stop the attack?

8. How does General Turgidson's briefing book ("World Targets in Megadeaths") comment on his speech about our alternatives?

> "We'd stand a good chance of catching them with their pants down." What does this metaphor imply about the nature of war?

9. As the Russian ambassador gets Premier Kissoff on the hot-line, the communist leader is obviously in bed with someone. What is ironic about Turgidson's calling him a "degenerate atheist?"

10. What is funny about the president chiding Turgidson and the ambassador for "fighting in the war room?" How does this emphasize the basic childishness of war?

11. How does the repeated use of the word "fine" made President Merkin Muffly's phone conversation with Premier Kissoff like a dialogue in an absurdist comedy? How is the president a parody of Adlai Stevenson?

12. Why does Kubrick cut from the ambassador announcing the doomsday machine to General Ripper's lecture on "precious bodily fluids?" What is the significance of Ripper's obsession with *fluoridation* as the "most monstrous commie plot?"

> How is Ripper characterized by keeping a machine gun in his golf bag?

13. How is Dr. Strangelove a parody of Henry Kissinger?

14. The marines battle in front of a billboard that declares, "Peace is Our Profession." Why is this ironic?

15. Colonel Batguano accuses Mandrake of "organizing a mutiny of preverts." Why is the business with the telephone ironic? What is the effect of Batguano's deadpan "That's private property . . . You'll have to answer to the Coca-Cola Company"?

16. What does Major Kong's *riding* the bomb symbolize?

17. Just as the bomb hits its target, Kubrick cuts to Dr. Strangelove explaining how they can all live in a mine shaft while waiting for the cobalt radiation to wear off. Why would General Turgidson like Strangelove's idea?

> Why does Dr. Strangelove's hand keep trying to strangle him? What does this symbolize?

18. "We must not allow a mine shaft gap!" Turgidson argues for maintaining a high level of weapons in the mine shafts, in case the Russians try to take them over. Why is this ironic?

19. Why does Kubrick cut from Dr. Strangelove exclaiming, "Mein Fuehrer, I can walk!" to a sequence of silent mushroom clouds? What is the effect of the music ("We'll Meet Again")?

WOMAN IN THE DUNES (1964—Japanese) Directed by Hiroshi Teshigahara; with Eiji Okada and Kyoto Kishida. Distributed by Corinth Films.

1. If this film is an *allegory,* what are some of the possible interpretations of the traveler's situation?

2. What are the symbolic connotations of the *sand pit?* the *ladder?* the *villagers?* What are the political and theological implications of the following lines?

> "Call the man in charge... Isn't there some way to contact them, like beating a can?"

> What are the implications of his saying that "even a monkey can be trained to dig sand"?

> "It's useless! If it wants to, sand can swallow cities, even countries."

> "Don't you feel meaningless? Are you clearing sand to live, or living to clear sand?"

> "We'll soon be trapped forever... And you call them your friends!"

> What is the visual effect of the masked villagers encircling the sand pit, beating drums, wanting him to make love to the woman for their entertainment? How are the villagers like primitive gods?

> What does the woman's being taken up in the basket symbolize?

3. Why does Teshigahara juxtapose bodies and faces against ripples of sand? (e.g. the sand flowing down the hillside during the love scene)

4. How does the woman's attitude toward the sand pit differ from the traveler's? What do his various attempts to escape symbolize?

5. What is the significance of the traveler's being a *bug collector?*

> Speaking of the blister beetle, he says, "I may get my name in the insect book if I find one." Why is this ironic?
>
> As he studies his bottled beetles: "No need to worry—I've got the upper hand." How is he like one of his bugs?
>
> Why does Teshigahara juxtapose the shot of the moth in the glass globe against the aerial shot of them lying on opposite sides of the room?
>
> What does his finally burning his insect collection symbolize?

6. By the end of the film, how has the traveler's attitude toward the sand pit changed? What is the philosophical significance of this?

> In the beginning of the film, he lies on the sand thinking of all the papers and licences he needs. How does the setting comment on modern civilization's obsession with "credentials?"
>
> "If the sand is not cleared in time, my house will be buried." "Let it! Why should it involve me?"
>
> He reads the newspaper used for wrapping food: "A *coup d'etat*—Nothing stays the same." Why is this ironic?
>
> After his ascension to look at the sea, why does he return to the sand pit?
>
> What is the significance of his "crow trap," which accidentally becomes a *well?* Why is he so preoccupied with the well? What is the importance of the final shot of his reflection and the reflection of the little boy?

7. In image and theme, what are some of the similarities between *Woman in the Dunes* and the short stories of Franz Kafka ("The Burrow," "A Hunger Artist," "Metamorphosis," etc.)?

> How is *Woman in the Dunes* also like Camus' *L'Etranger?*

ZORBA THE GREEK (1964—English/Greek) Directed by Michael Cacoyannis; with Anthony Quinn, Alan Bates, Irene Papas, and Lila Kedrova; based on the novel by Nikos Kazantzakis. Distributed by Twentieth Century Fox and Films Inc.

1. According to a famous critic, all modern literature is a variation on the theme of Don Quixote and Sancho Panza. How can this idea be applied to *Zorba the Greek?* What abstract forces do Zorba and the Boss represent?

2. In Greek mythology, the main conflict in life is caused by the tension between Apollo and Dionysus. How is this tension depicted in *Zorba the Greek?*

3. What is the effect of the opening shot, in which Alan Bates runs around in the rain with an umbrella, trying to protect his crate of books? How does this characterize him?

4. What is the symbolic significance of Zorba's first appearance—through the rainy windowpane?

5. When the Boss asks Zorba "why" he should take Zorba with him, Zorba replies, "Will no man ever do something without a 'why'—just like that, for the hell of it?" How does this exchange typify their differing ways of approaching the world?

6. What does the abandoned *mineshaft* symbolize? How is *mining* a metaphor for Zorba's approach to women?

7. What does Zorba's *santuri* symbolize?

8. Why is Zorba upset at the Boss's unexcited reaction to seeing the dolphin? How does this characterize them both?

9. How does the decor of Dame Hortense's bedroom characterize her?

10. The townsmen take the Widow's goat. What is the significance of this? How does it foreshadow the climax of the film?

11. The Boss offers the Widow his umbrella. What does this gesture symbolize, and how does it characterize him?

12. Why is the Widow attracted to the Boss, despite her basic dislike of all the other men in town?

13. What does Zorba's *dance* symbolize? Why is it significant that the Boss doesn't dance? (The Apollonian Voice: "Come inside, Zorba—you'll catch cold.")

14. Why is Zorba determined to get the Boss together with the Widow? ("God has a very big heart, but there is one sin he won't forgive...")

15. "What's so stupid about fighting for your country?" How does Zorba's attitude toward war differ from the Boss's, and why?

16. Why does the Boss tell Dame Hortense that the absent Zorba will marry her when he returns? Why does Zorba decide to go through with the wedding ceremony?

17. When the Boss finally goes to the Widow, why does she cry?

18. The ritual murder on the church steps: Why does Mavrandoni act as he does? What is the significance of the cross-cuts between the church service and the murder? What is the effect of Manolakis' crossing himself as he prepares to stab the widow? How does this scene reveal Kazantzakis' view of human nature?

19. "Why do the young die? Why does anybody die?" Why can't the Boss answer this question to Zorba's satisfaction?

20. What is the significance of the way the "mourners" treat Dame Hortense after her death? How does this relate to Kazantzakis' view of human nature?

21. All that remains of Dame Hortense's cherished belongings after the villagers loot her house is—her *parrot*. What is the significance of this? Why doesn't Zorba stop the looting?

22. What does the final dance symbolize?

JULIET OF THE SPIRITS (1965—Italian) Directed by Federico Fellini; with Giulietta Masina, Sandra Milo, Mario Pisu, Valentina Cortese, Lou Gilbert, and Sylva Koscina. Produced by Rizzoli; distributed by Audio-Brandon.

1. This is a film full of monstrous symbols, elaborate baroque shapes, and startling clashes of color. What does Fellini's bizarre technique contribute to the meaning of the film?

2. Note that the leaves on the trees in the opening shot are *plastic*. Why does Fellini prefer *sets* to natural exteriors?

3. Juliet first appears with her back to the camera, looking in the mirror, trying on wigs. What is the symbolic importance of *wigs* and *mirrors* in this sequence? How does this scene establish the film's theme?

4. Giorgio enters the darkened house, wondering why the lights are out. With him he brings a crowd of freaks. How does this scene foreshadow Juliet's nervous collapse?

5. The seance focuses on a conflict between two opposed spirits. Iris' message: "Love for Everybody." Why does Fellini interrupt this message with Olaf, a less peaceful spirit?

> "You're nothing to anybody...Nobody needs you..." As Juliet recovers from her faint, note the circle of false, smiling faces. How do the seance and its aftermath relate to Juliet's inner conflict?

6. The next morning: Juliet looks out the window to see the grotesquely fat gardener climb out of the pool. What is the visual effect of this? Why does Fellini include such shots?

> Also note the stunning, dreamlike shot through the window as the maid places the table. Why does Juliet tap on the table? What does this reveal about her approach to reality?

7. Cut to the beach, where Juliet's doctor advises her on her hallucinations. How does the doctor's outlook on life differ from Juliet's? How does Juliet's *costume* reveal her personality?

> Juliet tells him that when she was a child, she could summon visions just by closing her eyes. As she does so in illustration, she suddenly sees Iris swinging on a trapeze. What is the psychological significance of this sequence?

> Cut to the laughing face of the doctor, whose solution is that she should (1) go horse-back riding and (2) make love more often with her husband. How does the doctor interpret Juliet's problem?

8. The arrival of Susy's boat seems almost hallucinatory. How does it foreshadow the arrival of the Turkish barge?

9. As Juliet dozes off, the detective emerges from the sea, pulling a rope, which he hands to her. She begins to pull ... A raft appears bearing a dead horse—a horrifying symbol of death reminiscent of Picasso's "Guernica" or Bunuel's "Andalusian Dog." A landing craft full of strangely painted savages follows. As Juliet tries to run, a Turk rises from the sea to throw his spear at her ... Juliet awakes.

> What do the various elements of her dream mean? How is her dream a symbolic reaction to the doctor's advice?

10. Walking in the woods, Juliet meets her mother and sisters. How does Fellini use color to characterize them? How does Juliet contrast with her family? What is the significance of the way they kiss goodbye?

11. What is the visual effect of seeing Georgio in bed, wearing eyeshades and talking in his sleep?

> Bathed in intense white morning light, Giorgio denies knowing any "Gabriella." Juliet strings peppers, wondering who Gabriella is, while the maids chatter enthusiastically about the new Hollywood flick, in which "Robert Mitchum comes back repentant." What are some of the satiric details in this sequence?

12. Valentina takes Juliet to see Bhisma, the "man-woman who knows the secrets of both sexes." What is the significance of the Master's talking through a *tape recorder* about the reality of the *apple*? What is the significance of Bhisma's falling asleep and being carried out by his assistants? How does this satirize faddish Eastern religions?

In her private audience with Bhisma, Juliet sits outlined sharply against a red velvet background, while Bhisma sits in bed veiled in white gauze. What is the visual effect of this setting?

"Women all want to be sirens, but they don't know their trade." What is the gist of Bhisma's advice to Juliet: Why can't Juliet accept ideas from the *Kama Sutra?*

13. Riding in the car, Juliet flashes back to her grandfather's "bareback rider." Remember the details in this sequence—they appear later in Juliet's hallucinations.

Sandra Milo, who plays Susy and Iris, also plays the bareback rider. Psychologically, what does she symbolize?

What does Juliet's grandfather represent for her? How does he relate to the rest of her family, particularly to her mother?

Note the parody of the ending of Bergman's *Seventh Seal:* Grandfather and the Lady run up the skyline to escape in the plane. What does Grandpa's plane symbolize? What is the significance of the family's reaction?

Throughout this scene, note Fellini's love of circuses, freaks, and baroque ornamentation.

14. Home again . . . Jose stands in the garden, quoting Garcia Lorca, the Spanish Romantic poet of love and death. What does Jose symbolize for Juliet? What is the significance of his sangrilla ceremony?

Jose also teaches Juliet the ceremony of the *bullfight*. What is the symbolic significance of what he tells her? ("Thus is the monster defeated.")

As Giorgio aims his telescope through Susy's window, Jose shakes his head disapprovingly. How does this serve as a transition to Juliet's visit to the detective?

15. Examining the photographs of Giorgio, the psychologist declares that he obviously "has great need of his mother." "Who doesn't?" replies the detective. What is the thematic significance of this exchange? What is the tone of the scene as a whole?

16. Juliet visits the sculptress, who assures her that "God is Sex." Juliet responds with a memory from her childhood, in which she was to be

roasted on a grill (!) in a school play. Why does her friend's statement on God prompt this particular memory?

> What is the visual effect of the assembly-line of nuns passing along the angel wings? Also note Laura, a perfect medieval angel, white-on-white.

> Why does Juliet's Grandpa stop the performance? How do the principal and Juliet's mother react to this, and why?

> How does this childhood incident contribute to Juliet's neurosis?

17. Juliet returns Susy's fat Persian cat. What is the difference between their two houses? How does Fellini use the decor of Susy's house to characterize her?

> Why does Fellini include the visit to Arlette, Susy's suicidal younger sister? How does she reflect on Susy's hedonistic life?

> Why does Fellini balance this by having Iris speak to Juliet from the vase of flowers: "Susy is your teacher—listen to her."?

> What is the symbolic significance of Susy's rather odd swimming pool, with its scallop-shell entrance? Juxtaposed against the shell, how does Susy allude to Botticelli's "Birth of Venus"?

18. What does Susy's *tree-house* symbolize? What is the visual effect of the women's costumes in this scene, and of Susy's "ride to the top?"

> While Juliet talks about her marriage, Susy signals the men below with her mirror and drops her slipper for them to retrieve. Why does Juliet decide not to stay?

19. Juliet tells her nieces the ancient Greek myth about the *labyrinth*. How does this symbol relate to Juliet's inner problem? How does this brief sequence serve as a transition between the scene with Susy and Juliet's second visit to the detective's office?

20. The detective shows Juliet films of Giorgio and his girlfriend. "Our view is limited, being objective," he says. "Reality can be something else entirely." How does this "film-within-a-film" scene relate to Fellini's general approach to Reality?

21. Juliet goes to Susy's party. What is the tone of this sequence? Why is Juliet unable to enjoy herself? How do the juxtaposed images and colors convey her discomfort?

> Why does Juliet freak out in the scene with Susy's "Godson?" What is the significance of the image she sees in the mirror above the bed?

> Note the parting shot of the *sculpture* as Juliet flees.

22. What is the effect of the cut to Juliet's nieces *dancing?* How does Giorgio's party differ from Susy's?

> Why do Juliet's visions start invading her "normal" life? Note that the vision in the bathroom combines Susy with Juliet's memory of her dead friend Laura. What is the psychological significance of this?

> Everyone has advice for Juliet...her mother, Jose, her doctor, her lawyer...Why can't their advice help her?

> Dr. Miller suggests psychodrama as a solution to Juliet's problem: i.e. you "relive difficult episodes of your life by projecting them onto someone else." What is ironic in this as a solution to Juliet's problem? Dr. Miller's analysis is that Juliet subconsciously *wants* Giorgio to leave her. What do you think of this theory?

23. After trying (unsuccessfully) to speak with Giorgio's girlfriend, Juliet returns home to find Giorgio packing. She sits watching the tube while Giorgio eats alone in the other room. How does the decor emphasize their alienation?

> What is the significance of the unanswered telephone?

> As Juliet closes the closet door, she flashes back to her wedding day. Why does Fellini cut abruptly to the present with the maid closing the windows black behind her? How do these actions build the mood of the scene?

24. As Giorgio leaves, Juliet's spirits invade in a great army. Note that each figure is a memory from her past. Juliet's vision of the drowned Laura is interrupted by a bizarre collection of juxtaposed images, all giving her advice. Juliet's visions no longer go away when she tells them to. What is the significance of this?

25. In a classic Freudian dream sequence, Juliet asks her blue-haired mother to help her. What is the significance of this final apparition of Juliet's mother?

WHAT DOES THE "CLOSED DOOR" SYMBOLIZE—
AND THE CRYING CHILD BEHIND IT?

What is the psychological importance of the brief exchange between Juliet and her mother? ("Don't open it! Obey me!" "You don't frighten me any more.")

WHAT IS THE SIGNIFICANCE OF JULIET'S RELEASE OF THE "SPIRIT CHILD?" Why do the spirits crawl away in horror? Why does her mother wither and fade? (How is this like the ending of *The Wizard of Oz? Hansel and Gretel?* Other fairy tales?)

26. What does Juliet's reunion with her grandfather symbolize? Why does he refuse to take her along? ("This is an old plane that goes nowhere. It only exists to come here ... ")

27. As Juliet walks out through the gates, she hears whispers: "Now, if you like, we can stay." This is an extremely perplexing ending. Has Juliet flipped out completely? Has she withdrawn from life and feeling? Or has she found some kind of peace?

Why does Fellini leave the ending vague?

28. How does Fellini's portrayal of Juliet's inner life contrast with Hollywood depictions of "neurotic females?"

GEORGY GIRL (1966—English) Directed by Silvio Narizzano; with Lynn Redgrave, Alan Bates, James Mason, and Charlotte Rampling. Produced by Columbia Pictures; distributed by Swank Films.

1. How does the comic Oedipal triangle (old man-woman-young man) establish *Georgy Girl* as a modern *commedia del arte?* How is it also similar to Moliere's *School for Wives?*

2. The film begins with Georgy looking in a window at hairdos. In what sense has she spent her life "window shopping?" Immediately after trying an absurd new hairstyle, she dunks her head in the sink. How does this reflect her relationships with men?

3. Georgy runs a nursery school, in which she plays imaginative games like "Things in Space." What is the significance of her rapport with children?

4. Georgy plays a dissonant wedding march as her father climbs the stairs with a gift for her. Why does she record their conversation? How is her father, the butler, characterized? When James honks, he scuttles—as she plays the "William Tell Overture." What does all the music contribute to this scene?

5. James listens to the tape recording... Why does he laugh? Why does he love Georgy? In contrast, James' wife lies in bed all day with pills and chocolates. How does this characterize her?

6. Meredith gets ready to go out... Why, when she knows Jos is coming? Aside from her obvious good looks, why do men always cluster around a woman like her?

7. Why does Jos always tease Georgy? ("Are you naked under that coat?") Why does Georgy make such an elaborate dinner? What is the significance of Jos' gangster act? How is he like one of the kids in her school? Jos lounges in the bath... Why does he open the door before standing up?

8. Meredith roars up with two guys on motorbikes and immediately climbs on Jos. Why does Georgy peek through the window as they roll on the floor? What is she feeling? Why does she leave the dinner on the table and go out?

9. At James' house, he sits suffering on the couch while the opera blares. What is the effect of the music in the background as he comments on Georgy's clothes, kisses her, and gives her some money? Why is her father's response funny ("Say thank you to Mr. James.")? Why does Georgy climb in bed and pull the covers over her head? How does her dream express a hidden wish (a slow motion parade of children)?

10. How does the cross-cut to Georgy doing animal imitations for Meredith characterize their relationship? As they're about to go out for dinner, Meredith is invited to a party. Why would she just leave Georgy flat and go?

11. Georgy goes to James' birthday party, where her father asks accusingly, "Why can't you be a lady just for once?" Georgy responds with a song: "It takes a whole lot of lovin' to keep this baby happy..." Why would Georgy

do this particular number? What does it reveal about her? What is the significance of the audience's non-reaction?

12. How does James' CONTRACT OFFER characterize him? What is the significance of her being dressed like a floozy? Why does she make fun of him? ("Will we have to have any shareholders?" and "I won't have to wear gymshorts or suck lollypops?") What is the significance of their *glasses* getting entangled when he tries to kiss her?

13. Why would Georgy dress up to have an Italian dinner with a *record player?* Jos interrupts her and takes her to a disco . . . Why does he grin as he dances with his hands on her rump?

14. Back in Georgy's apartment, what is the point of the business with the *lights?* He lies in her lap like a child as she tries to pour tea . . . Why does he back away when she leaps on him? How is he characterized by slobbering over his soup?

15. What is Meredith's psychology in telling Jos she's pregnant? ("I've destroyed two of yours already.")

> They slap each other, then make love. What does this imply
> about their relationship?

16. What is the effect of the cross-cut to Meredith suffering from morning sickness?

17. Georgy goes to James to get "baby equipment." What is the significance of her using him all the time, pushing him away, and calling him a "lovely old thing?"

18. Jos in the playground: How does *going down the slide* characterize him?

19. What is the point of the cross-cut from Meredith playing violin in the orchestra to Georgy and Jos watching childbirth on TV? What is the significance of their reading Dr. Spock together? How does Georgy's attitude toward childbirth differ from Meredith's? ("*We're* like the old married couple!")

20. Georgy goes shopping with James. Why isn't Meredith pleased with all the presents?

21. While pantomiming wedding parades with her children, Georgy continues to elude James, who still waits for his answer. Why?

22. "Mr. James' horse won!"/ His wife is dead ... What is the effect of this juxtaposition?

23. Meredith's reaction to being *very* pregnant: "It's taught me how it feels to look like the back end of a bus and sit around every night." Why does Jos settle the argument by kissing Georgy?

24. In a series of closeups, Jos chases Georgy through London, screaming "I love you." What is the purpose of the cross-cut to James (drunk) reminiscing about his dead wife, whom he describes as "exciting as a half brick"? When the butler jokes, "Who could try it with old Georgy?" what is the effect of the cut back to Jos chasing her and taking off his clothes? How does this public strip characterize him?

25. What is the effect of the cross-cut to *both* their clothes on the floor as they make love? What is the significance of Meredith's being in labor in the hospital at this very moment?

> Jos and Georgy get drunk. What is the effect of his *staggering* as he carries her to the bedroom?

26. In the hospital, Meredith sits *filing her nails*, ignoring the baby. How does this characterize her? While Meredith shrieks at Georgy, Jos reads "Women's Realm." How is this ironic?

27. What is the purpose of the cross-cuts from James cleaning out his wife's pills, to Georgy and Jos bringing the baby home, to Meredith being picked up in a Mercedes by a new boyfriend? What do these actions have in common?

28. Georgy's apartment is a forest of steaming diapers, and Jos is upset at having to go to the movies alone. Why is their relationship not going to work?

29. Why does James plan to fill his dead wife's bedroom with *lace?* What is the effect of the cross-cut from the butler worrying that he's going to bring in a "Fancy Woman" to the shot of Georgy pushing the *baby carriage?* Why is this ironic?

30. James helps Georgy up the stairs with the carriage. What does this symbolize? How does this act foreshadow the end of the film? ("Poor old James.")

31. Jos climbs into bed with Georgy ... Why don't things work for them anymore? (Note the baby between them.)

32. The social worker is interrupted by Jos announcing that he has quit and they can spend all their time in bed. Why is this funny?

33. Sailing up the river: Why does Jos keep playing, even though he's obviously going to leave her?

> What is the significance of his story about the man who drowned? ("You want to save people.")

> Jos declares, "I'm like PETER PAN." How so?

34. WHY DOES GEORGY ACCEPT JAMES' PROPOSAL?

35. WHAT DOES THE FINAL SHOT IMPLY ABOUT THEIR FUTURE RELATIONSHIP? (Note the expression on their faces.)

MORGAN (1966—English) Directed by Karel Reisz; with David Warner, Vanessa Redgrave, and Robert Stephens. Distributed by Cinema 5.

1. Why the documentary introduction about the Lowland Gorilla? What parallels to human behavior does the film suggest? What does it imply about the theory of evolution, and about the primacy of our civilization?

2. As Morgan hallucinates, the workman on the scaffold turns into a monkey. How does this establish Morgan's approach to reality?

3. In court, Leonie tells the judge that Morgan shaved a *hammer and sickle* on her poodle. How does this characterize their marriage?

4. Morgan's attic: Note the portraits of Marx and Trotsky, and the life-sized gorilla. How does this setting reflect his nature?

5. Leonie leaves court with Morgan's mother. How is the mother characterized? Why won't she step aside when the Rolls Royce honks at her? ("They got their car from the sweat of the workers.")

6. Why does Morgan sniff Leonie's pillow? Why does he put the skeleton in her bed?

7. WHAT IS THE SIGNIFICANCE OF LEONIE'S BEING *RICH?* IF MORGAN IS A COMMUNIST, WHY WOULD HE MARRY *HER?*

8. Charles Napier, we are told, is "physically loathesome, mentally retarded, and genetically unsound." Why the constant references to his *greasiness?* ("I can smell him"... "I'll move that greasy art dealer out of our nest...")

9. Leonie tries to take a bath...How does Morgan's *rubber duck* characterize him?

> They chase each other through the house, winding up in the attic; what does their *chest-pounding* act mean?

10. As she lounges in the tub, Leonie calmly says, "I don't want you." Does she mean this, or is she just playing games?

11. Why does Reisz contrast the *fancy table setting* with Morgan eating with his fingers and playing with the electric can opener? How does his *table-cloth act* reveal his attitude toward civilization?

12. Napier's Art Gallery: What is the significance of Morgan's rival being an *art dealer,* while Morgan himself is an artist? Why is Napier so calm? How is he characterized by his *cigarette holder,* and by all the *abstract sculpture* he sells?

> What is the effect of Napier's glib use of *understatement?* ("This is most uncivilized..." "I wish you'd get into the habit of making an appointment.")

13. Morgan's Mother's Cafe: How is her boyfriend, WALLY THE GORILLA, symbolic? What is the significance of her being a communist?

14. In the London Underground: What is the point of Morgan's imaginative transformations? (The lady becomes a peacock, the yawning attendant becomes a hippo.)

15. Why would Morgan dream about swinging through the trees? What is the significance of his sleeping in the car? (note the bananas!)

> How does *playing hopscotch* characterize the cop? Why is he astonished by Morgan's car?

"It's an island of sanity, this car, in a world of pain." Why is this ironic?

16. Why does Morgan admire Trotsky so much, and why does he hate Stalin?

17. Driving with Napier: How is Leonie characterized? What is the significance of her draping her veil over his head?

18. "Is there anything in life that isn't an assault?"

19. Morgan attacks Napier's car when they arrive. Why is Leonie happy to see him? "You'll have to fight him; then the winner can drag me off and have me." What does this reveal about her nature?

20. Morgan climbs the wall as Leonie lies swinging in the yard. He wants to fill the garden with sunflowers and babies . . . How does this foreshadow the end of the film?

WHY DOES HE COMPARE NAPIER TO STALIN?

21. In the cemetary: Morgan's mother describes his father as an "idealist"— he wanted to shoot the royal family. Why is this funny?

> Marx: "Philosophers have tried to understand the world; our problem is to change it." Why would Morgan like this idea? Why does he perform his gorilla act in front of Marx's statue?

> What is the effect of the piggy-back ride through the tombstones?

22. Why does Morgan rig the house for sound?

> "Living with a gifted idiot has its rewards, but the function of the nursery . . . " What do you think of Napier's analysis of Leonie's never having children?

> In bed: What does the *count-down* on the *war sound track* symbolize? ("Go, baby, go!") What is the effect of the *Star Spangled Banner* as Napier confronts Morgan in the closet?

> How does banging on the bedroom door emphasize the *Oedipal* nature of this love-triangle?

23. Morgan goes back to his old bedroom in his mother's house. What is the significance of her tucking him in bed?

24. Morgan dreams that he is in bed, riding on a flatcar, while Leonie rides past on a horse: "Do you love me? Then do something!" Morgan yells back, "Put a skirt on!" What on earth does this dialogue mean? Why are revolutionaries often puritannical and chauvinistic? (cf. Iran)

25. What is the purpose of the cross-cut from Morgan planting a bomb under Leonie's bed to her mother planning a "proper wedding?"

> "I want Charles"/"I want to live the way I used to" What *does* Leonie want?

> What is the significance of Morgan's blowing up Leonie's mother? How is this act a comic analogue to the Russian Revolution?

> What is the significance of the mother throwing the gorilla out the window? How does this allude to the end of *King Kong?*

> As Morgan runs down the street, Leonie's father cries, "By God, he's got my wife—and she's on fire!" How does this foreshadow the end of the film?

26. How does WALLY THE GORILLA being thrown around in the ring reflect what's happening with Morgan?

27. The Kidnap: Why is Leonie unhappy beside a beautiful lake in Wales? What is the effect of the high-speed escape from the tent as she locks herself in the van?

28. Like Katherine Hepburn in *The African Queen,* Leonie floats alone on the raft while Morgan watches her from the shore. What is the significance of his TARZAN FANTASY? (Note Tarzan catching Jane in a net, diving from a cliff, fighting an alligator . . .)

> "NOTHING IN THIS WORLD LIVES UP TO MY BEST FANTASIES—EXCEPT YOU." How does this explain his love for her?

> After she has just said that she'll marry Charles while he's in prison, Morgan and Leonie wind up making love. Why?

29. In court: While the lawyer drones on, Morgan fantasizes about giraffes being pursued. "I DON'T RECOGNIZE THIS COURT AT ALL." Why not?

30. When he gets out of prison, Morgan literally transforms himself into a gorilla. NOTE ALL THE INTF...CUT SHOTS OF MORGAN WATCHING *KING KONG*. WHY DOES HE IDENTIFY?

31. In an elaborate parody of *KING KONG*, Morgan crashes the wedding party. He pushes Napier into the wedding cake, catches fire, steals a motorcycle (which he doesn't know how to drive), and ends up in the river. How are these details symbolic?

32. What is the significance of his winding up in a *junkyard?* How is the mountain of tin cans a symbol of our civilization? How is a rubbish pile a metaphor for history? What is the significance of his not being able to get his mask off?

33. MORGAN'S HALLUCINATION: A crane brings a straight-jacket and the policeman helps him put it on. How does this relate to their earlier conversation ("You want to watch it."/"Yes, but where *is* it?")? What is the significance of Napier's operating the crane?

> How is Morgan's being jacked up into the air a metaphor for insanity and death?

34. Morgan sits in a barber's chair surrounded by portraits of Marx, Lenin, Stalin, and Trotsky. WHAT DOES HIS EXECUTION SYMBOLIZE?

> Peasants emerge with shotguns, and Leonie rides in on a white horse. Although Morgan considers himself a marxist, why is he the kind of person who is always shot *first* after a revolution?

35. What is the purpose of the dreamy shot of Leonie walking through a garden, where Morgan intently plants flowers? The setting is an *asylum,* but in what sense has Morgan died and gone to heaven?

36. When Morgan asks, "Is that my baby?" Leonie smiles and nods yes... What is the effect of the *freeze-frames* of their faces? Why does she quietly walk away?

37. The camera zooms back to reveal his garden in the shape of a *hammer and sickle.*

> In what way have both Morgan and Leonie achieved their desires?

> What does the last shot imply about marxist paradises?

BEDAZZLED (1967—English) Directed by Stanley Donen; with Peter Cook, Dudley Moore, and Eleanor Bron. Produced by Twentieth Century Fox; distributed by Films Inc.

1. *Bedazzled* retells the Faust legend, using the technique of "theme and variation" to describe a modern anti-hero's search for love. What is the significance of Stanley Moon's working as a *hamburger chef* at *Wimpy's,* and how does he differ from the traditional Faust? What is the point of all the contrasting identities that Stanley adopts (Intellectual, Millionaire, Rock Star, Fly, Oxford Student, and Nun)? How does this reflect William Irwin Thompson's idea that the symbol of the modern search for identity is not the novel, but the TV set—with its constantly changing channels?

2. Why is the opening sequence set in a church? As Stanley fantasizes about Margaret Spenser, why does the director cut to the *toaster* popping and a slice of cheese melting on a hamburger? What is the effect of the minister intoning, "May the Lord make clean our hearts"?

3. Why does Stanley decide to kill himself, and why is his suicide attempt funny? As George tells him about the "million pounds," Stanley stands there with his finger in the broken pipe. How does this characterize him? How does it reflect his frustration?

4. What does the Frobisher and Gleason Raspberry Ice Lolly symbolize? "Doing me a favor! I could've done that myself . . . " How does this relate to the film's theme?

> Note that Stanley doesn't get to eat the ice lolly—it melts when George takes him flying. How does this foreshadow the outcome of his next six wishes?

5. In George's Underground Club, he performs routine mischief. What is the significance of George's pettiness, and what does this suggest about the nature of evil in the modern world?

6. Margaret tells the Inspector that Stanley left her his collection of moths(!) His last words? "Heavy on the onions." How does this conversation characterize Stanley's lady-love?

7. As Stanley signs the contract, George asks, "What would you like to be first—Prime Minister? Oh no—I've made that deal already." What is the film's attitude toward politics?

8. WISH #1: THE INTELLECTUALS—Stanley wants to be the kind of person who can use words like "inarticulate," assuming that people who can express their love in words will automatically be successful with the opposite sex. What is the flaw in his reasoning?

9. What do the *monkeys* symbolize? "I could watch them for hours," Margaret says. Stanley replies, "Metaphorically speaking, society creates its own cages." How does this intellectual chit-chat foreshadow Stanley's ultimate frustration?

10. How does Stanley's apartment characterize him? Margaret wants to sprawl on the carpet and let Brahms flow over her... What is the connotation of the record getting stuck? Why is Stanley's analysis of the music funny—especially his comment on the "flute-like qualities of French horn," and his tone-poem about the young stag edging toward his doe?

> What are the symbolic connotations of the *sculpture* that they fondle? He feels the radiator and his tie; she feels his pillow... Why is their "touching game" absurd?

> "One touch of Cinzano, and I'm in Italy!" What is the significance of her sounding like a commercial?

> After all their chatter about "touching," why does she cry rape? Why is this predictable?

11. How does the *pigeon business* on top of the space needle serve as a transition to the next adventure?

> Why would George quote Proust? ("If you can stay up with a woman and listen to whatever garbage she has to say until ten past four in the morning, you're *in*.") what does this suggest about the actual goal of "intellectual" conversation between men and women?

> Through the telescope, Stanley sees Margaret and the Inspector fishing for his body. What is the significance of the time running out just as Margaret is about to speak?

12. WISH #2: Since intellect has gotten him nowhere, Stanley wishes to be a RICH BUSINESSMAN, with Margaret as his very "physical" wife. Why doesn't this work out as he intends?

Stanley arrives in his Rolls Royce as Randy is teaching Margaret to play *croquet*—why this particular game?

"Have you ever thought of making Margaret a charitable institution?" How is Stanley's conversation with George like the dialogue in a Pinter play?

"Your wife has a very beautiful body; you must be a happy man." Why is this ironic?

What does the BILLIARDS GAME symbolize?

Note Margaret's breasts in the mirror in the BATHTUB SHOT—"That Venezuelan deal: Do you want me to come in with you, or do you want to pull out?" What does this double-entendre imply about the business world?

13. Transition: What do George and his *wasps* symbolize in the lives of "those nice flower-people, grooving away quietly"? How does this relate to the "problem of evil"?

14. When Stanley gets tired of dancing around George's "throne," he asks, "Can't we change places?" How does this explain the fall of Lucifer?

15. Back at George's house, George and Stanley discuss "free will." Why does Stanley complain that he isn't really free? Why does Stanley *like* George?

16. LUST brings Stanley something to eat. Why is it appropriate that she offers him "honey" and "buttered buns"? Why does George interrupt and order her down to the Foreign Office?

17. WISH #3: Dressed like a ROCK STAR in a gold suit, Stanley shrieks, "Love me!" as Margaret screams and sobs. Why is it significant that Margaret is not looking at Stanley himself, but at his TV image? What is the purpose of the black-and-white split-screen effects?

Why is it predictable that he will be replaced by DRIMBLEWEDGE AND THE VEGETATIONS? How does this foreshadow David Bowie and punk rock?

"I don't care . . . You fill me with inertia." Why does George's indifference cause a stampede among the ladies?

18. In another transition, Stanley finds himself "up a pole." What does this symbolize?

George crosses telephone lines: "Mrs. Fitch? Abercrombie here... Your husband has just checked into a motel with..." How does this reflect the main theme of the film?

What is the significance of Li Quy Quat and the parable of the two tigers?

Changing pants in the van: "Excuse me, your ineffable hugeness, while we puny mortals change our drawers." What is the tone of this soliloquy?

While the old lady goes out to buy "Fruiney Green *Eyewash*," they eat her *raspberries*. How does this relate to the symbolism of the film?

George complains about last minute repentances: "Scusi, mille regretti," and Mussolini goes to heaven. How does this foreshadow the end of the film?

19. WISH #4: The film becomes a bit Kafkaesque when Stanley wishes he were a FLY ON THE WALL. What is the implication of his winding up in a morgue?

As Margaret checks out corpses, the Inspector complains that he has had three rapes on his hands that morning. Why is this an ironic setting for a seduction?

Why is it funny that the Vice Squad is having a party?

Note George's red feelers. How does this serve as a *leitmotif*?

What is the effect of the *subjective camera* as Stanley tries to fly? As he lies choking on the floor, Stanley finally blows his raspberry. How does the animation in this sequence contribute to its humor?

20. WISH #5: THE SIMPLE LIFE, with a cottage in the country. How does this parody *The Sound of Music* and other saccharine Julie Andrews films?

What is the significance of George's playing Margaret's husband as a "saintly" professor who reads Spinoza? Why is the idea of a "Giotto exhibition" absurd?

In the car: Why is it funny that Stanley and Margaret weep and talk about what a saint George is as they undress each other? They jump into the back seat, where she lies on his *pipe*(!) What does this symbolize?

21. Another Freudian transition: Stanley finds himself underwater, where George is drilling a hole in an oil tanker. What does this symbolize?

22. What is the implication of George's "having a giggle" about Job at a "summit conference" with God? What is the point of their playing a *game* to reach 100 billion souls?

23. George takes Stanley to the amusement park with Avarice and Gluttony. How do the roller coaster and the colliding cars symbolize Stanley's love-life? Gluttony eats constantly and doesn't say a word... How does this fit the general pattern of Stanley's dates?

24. Stanley finds Envy sitting in George's bed. What is the point of their conversation?

25. WISH #6: What is the loophole that allows George to transform Stanley into a NUN? Why doesn't Stanley's raspberry work any more, and why are his repeated attempts to end this wish funny?

> The "Order of Leaping Berylians" was actually founded by George. What does this imply?

> Stanley and Margaret "communicate" in guilty thoughts. How does this satirize "nun" films?

> The Ceremony: What is the effect of the nuns playing kettle drums for Stanley's initiation? What do the *trampolines* symbolize, and what is the significance of Stanley's being such a poor leaper? How is this a sexul metaphor? How does it also reflect his spiritual aspirations?

26. Dressed as a nun, Stanley goes to George's club, where he karate-chops Anger at the door. Why does this shock the priest?

> What is the effect of the *pan-down* from Lust grinding away, to Stanley sitting disgusted at her feet, drinking and smoking?

27. HEAVEN comes complete with a baroque elevator. Why is God's house set in Kew Gardens? What is the significance of its resemblance to the White House?

"I'll throw a bit of filth over myself—that should please him." How does the following dialogue characterize George?

"Hast thou swayed or wavered?" How do the echo chamber voice and the King James English satirize biblical films?

28. "You can't be *you* without your soul." Why have all Stanley's attempts to achieve love by adopting new *images* failed?

29. What is the point of George's final threat, and of the *zoom-out* shot of modern London?

BELLE DE JOUR (1967—French) Directed by Luis Bunuel; with Catherine Deneuve; cinematography by Sacha Vierny. Distributed by Hurlock Cine World.

When *Belle de Jour* opened in Paris, the film critic for *Le Monde* expressed astonishment that "such bad dreams could go on inside Catherine Deneuve's pretty head." Bunuel's point, of course, is that the psyche of a *grande bourgeoise* raised to be a painted doll is bound to overflow with masochistic fantasies. She may wear Chanel, but what is the purpose of perfume but to mask what one perceives as the stench of animal nature? For Bunuel, the smell of death pervades all bourgeois rituals and relationships. Like Strindberg's Miss Julie, Severine longs for someone to pull her down from her marble pillar and roll her in the mud.

***

1. Why would Severine fantasize about her gentle husband ordering two burly coachmen to bind and whip her? What do the coach and the cowbells symbolize, and why does Severine keep having this dream?

Severine is beautiful and rich. She loves her husband, a handsome young doctor who adores her and patiently caters to her every need. Why isn't she happy?

2. When Renee tells Severine that their friend Henriette works in a brothel, what is the significance of Severine's shocked fascination?

3. What is the reason for Severine's antipathy toward Husson? What does her dropping the vase of flowers symbolize? What is the visual effect of the sudden splash of *red* roses in what is a very cool setting?

3. "What's the matter with me today?" As the perfume bottle shatters on the floor, why does Bunuel flash back to Severine as a little girl being embraced by the plumber? (Note that the same actor plays one of the coachmen in Severine's opening fantasy.) Why would Freud say that this childhood incident causes her later problem?

4. After interrogating Pierre on the subject of sporting-houses, why does Severine suddenly stiffen and tell him to shut up? How does this reveal her inner conflict?

> "Won't you ever grow up?" Pierre asks. Why is he partly responsible for his own complaint?

5. After observing Severine talk with "the mysterious Henriette," why would Husson casually drop the name of his favorite brothel? Why does Bunuel repeat Husson's *voice-over?*

6. As Severine visits Madame Anais, why does Bunuel cut to her childhood memory of refusing communion?

7. How does Bunuel's brothel differ from the symbolic setting of Jean Genet's play *The Balcony?*

8. What is the significance of Monsieur Adolphe's being a *candy maker?* Why does Bunuel punctuate his vulgar song about "ham and sausages" with a popping champagne cork? How is Adolphe characterized by his *jack-in-the-box?*

> Severine resists doing her "job" with Adolphe until Anais orders her and pushes her into the room. Why does this rough treatment seem to *please* Severine?

> Why Does Bunuel have the other girls play cards while Severine is sporting with Adolphe? How does this metaphor allude to the ending of Bunuel's *Viridiana?*

9. Like Viridiana destroying her paraphernalia, Severine burns her underwear... Why does Bunuel make Severine's shift from one life to another appear so normal and rational?

10. Severine's dream: Why does Bunuel repeat the *cowbell* motif? What does the herd of bellowing bulls symbolize? How does Pierre's complaint about the soup being cold reflect his problem with Severine?

> When Pierre asks if bulls have names, Husson replies, "Yes. Most of those are called Remorse—except for the last one, which is called Expiation." How does this mirror Severine's attempt to resolve the split in her nature?

> Note that Severine is tied to the same tree in the Bois de Boulogne... Why does she fantasize about Pierre and Husson flinging *mud* at her? In the midst of this degrading ritual, why would she cry out to Pierre that she "loves" him?

11. Back in the brothel: Why is it ironic that Severine is disgusted by the Professor's masochism?

12. The Asiatic's "humming box"—why does Bunuel include this symbolic allusion to *Un Chien Andalou?*

13. As the Asiatic's bell tinkles faintly in the background, Bunuel cuts to Severine's motionless figure, then to a coach in the Bois de Boulogne... As Severine impersonates the Duke's dead daughter, what does his poetic ritual imply about sex, death, and religion? How does this sequence recall a similar allegorical scene in *Viridiana?*

14. As the Duke's butler rudely pushes Severine out the door into the rain, Bunuel cuts to Pierre and Severine's bedroom. Severine still insists that she "needs time" before she can make love with her husband. What is ironic about Pierre's constant apologies about forcing himself on her?

15. After Severine rudely refuses to speak with Husson, why does Bunuel include the surreal sequence of them crawling under the restaurant table as Pierre and Renee sit there trying to ignore them?

16. If this were a sixties Hollywood film, Marcel would be played by Paul Newman. Why does Bunuel make the object of Severine's passion so obnoxious and repellent? How do his *metal teeth* characterize him? When he discovers that Severine has a tiny birthmark, what is ironic about his ordering her to get dressed?

17. Vacation with Pierre: Why does Severine want to return to Paris? How do the deserted beach and the dead tree trunk on which she sits reflect her inner life?

18. Why wouldn't Marcel understand why Severine spends her afternoons in a brothel if she really loves her husband? As he climbs on top of her, why does Bunuel focus on their *feet* and the large hole in the heel of his sock?

19. As Pierre and Severine walk cheerfully from the hospital, why does Bunuel confront them with an empty *wheelchair?* How does this comment on his desire to have a child?

20. The inevitable meeting: After propositioning Severine shamelessly throughout the film, why does Husson now refuse to make love with her?

21. After the confrontation between Husson and Severine, why does Bunuel cut to the duel with Pierre? As Pierre fires, what is the symbolic significance of the cut to Severine—with a bullet wound in her temple? Why does Pierre then kiss her passionately?

> Note that she is tied to the same tree in the Bois de Boulogne.
> How does this fantasy sequence mirror the action of the film
> as a whole?

22. How does Marcel's revenge echo Godard's *Breathless?* How is Pierre Clementi different from Belmondo and Humphrey Bogart?

23. Pierre sits paralyzed in a wheelchair. As a symbol, how is he like Lady Chatterly's husband in the novel by D.H. Lawrence?

24. Why does Husson decide to tell Pierre about Severine's double life? Why doesn't Bunuel show us their conversation?

25. "What are you thinking about, Severine?"—How should we interpret the surreal ending? Is Severine fantasizing that Pierre is well? Is the entire film—right from the opening line—a dream?

> For those who have read *The Story of O.*, one intriguing
> possibility is that the gentle Pierre has deliberately plotted
> with his friend Husson, planting in Severine's mind the idea
> of spending her afternoons in a brothel. If so, why would he
> do this? What does this imply about the nature of love?
>
> As the cowbells sound, what is the significance of the coach
> being empty?

THE GRADUATE (1967—American) Directed by Mike Nichols; with Dustin Hoffman, Anne Bancroft, and Katharine Ross; music by Simon and Garfunkel. Distributed by Westcoast Films.

When Mike Nichols broke away from the Hollywood studio system to take full artistic control of *The Graduate,* he established himself as one of the most innovative American directors since Orson Welles made *Citizen Kane.* Like Welles, Nichols endured much criticism when his film first appeared, mainly because of its exaggerated, satiric tone—but also because Nichols had adopted from European directors advanced camera techniques that were still strange to American eyes. To intensify the satiric effect, Nichols used the kind of dialogue usually found in the plays of Eugene Ionesco and Edward Albee and other playwrights of the Absurd, combined with the deadpan delivery he had perfected in nightclub acts with comedienne Elaine May.

***

1. The camera zooms back from Ben Braddock's immobile face as the pilot of his plane announces their "descent into L.A." What are the connotations of this phrase? How is Ben characterized by his blank stare and his tightly buttoned suit?

2. Against the background of the aquarium, Ben "worries about the future." Why does Nichols keep referring to the aquarium?

3. As Ben runs for his room in panic, his mother reads aloud his successes from his college yearbook. How does this characterize his family and their way of life?

4. "There's a great future in Plastics." Why is this ironic?

5. After Ben takes Mrs. Robinson home, what is the purpose of the dreamlike tone of their conversation?"

6. Golfbag in hand, Mr. Robinson enters. As he puffs on his cigar, he urges Ben to "sow a few wild oats." What details make this scene ironic?

7. As Ben registers at the hotel, why does Nichols play upon his *toothbrush?*

8. "Sounds of Silence"—What is the purpose of this music? Why does Nichols juxtapose it against the shot of Ben sunning by the pool?

9. "April, Come She Will"—Nichols cross-cuts several shots here, including one of Ben lying in bed, blankly drinking a can of beer as Mrs. Robinson dresses and leaves. How do these shots advance our understanding of Ben's problem?

10. "Boy, what are you doing?"—"I'm just drifting here in the pool." Symbolically, how does this relate to Ben's earlier *scuba diving* act?

11. Ben's conversation with his mother is set in the steamy bathroom. How does this setting reflect on his mother's attempts to pry into his affairs?

12. Ben wants Mrs. Robinson to *talk* with him. Why does Nichols shoot most of their conversation in the *dark?* What is the purpose of her turning the light on and off? What is ironic in her being an art major in college?

13. When Ben visits the Robinsons, why does Nichols have the TV playing in the background (blaring a typical idiotic giveaway show)?

14. The date with Elaine: In the nightclub, what is the purpose of framing her against the belly-dancer?

15. Ben and Elaine "pig out" on hamburgers. How does this reflect on their new friendship for each other? After everyone at the hotel recognizes him as "Mr. Gladstone," Ben confesses to Elaine that his whole life is "just a waste." She seems slightly confused, but eats his french fries as they say goodnight. How do these incidents characterize their relationship?

16. In the pouring rain, Mrs. Robinson jumps into Ben's car and orders him to stop seeing her daughter. What does the setting contribute to the scene?

17. When Ben confesses to Elaine, what is the effect of the stark shot of Mrs. Robinson in *black* against the white walls?

18. Ben tells his parents about his intention to marry Elaine. Why does Nichols set this in the *kitchen,* with Ben's mother stirring the scrambled eggs? ("It's fully baked.")

19. Berkeley: How is Ben's landlord characterized by his fear of "outside agitators"? On the bus: Why does Nichols include the Other Lady? What is the purpose of the shots of the *monkey cage* at the zoo? (Note that this "zoo" metaphor is borrowed from Edward Albee.)

20. Where do your sympathies lie during Ben's confrontation with Mr. Robinson, and why?

21. Note the important details in the scene at the church: Ben hammering against the glass like a frantic animal...the hallucinatory faces of the wedding guests...Ben's action with the cross. What is the tone of this scene?

22. In the back of the bus: Note that Ben smiles for the first time. Why does Nichols use this setting to conclude the film?

KING OF HEARTS (1967—French) Directed by Phillippe de Broca; with Alan Bates, Genevieve Bujold, Jean-Claude Brialy, Pierre Brasseur, and Michel Serrault; music by Georges Delerue. Distributed by Walter Reade 16. The film is set in Senlis, France, in 1918.

1. In the opening shot of the clock tower, the knight emerges and strikes the bell. Why a *Knight?* Aside from the Last Judgment, what does he symbolize?

2. If the German soldiers in this film weren't so ludicrous, they would be quite sinister. When a funny little man with a Charlie Chaplin mustache bursts in shrieking, "Mein Kampf!" his commander dismisses him with "Later, Adolph." How does this comic digression establish the film's premise that the craziest people of all are the ones who govern us?

3. The English troops are actually Scottish, complete with *kilts.* How does this introduce the *masquerade* theme?

4. Charles reads Shakespeare to his pigeons ("Hippolyta, our nuptial hour draws on apace.") How do these particular lines from *Midsummer Night's Dream* foreshadow his romantic adventure?

5. How does the shot of Charles silhouetted against the sky carrying his pigeons establish his *alienation?*

6. In the Asylum: What does the *House of Cards* symbolize? Why does Charles fit right in with the lunatics? What are the connotations of his being the "King of Hearts"?

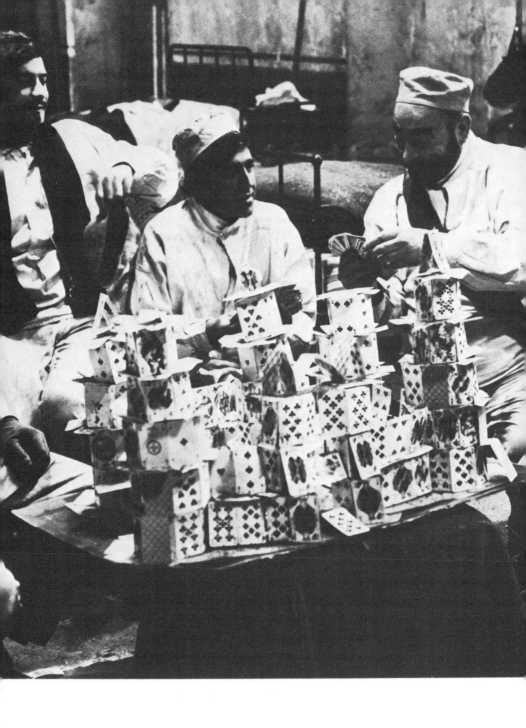

Civilization as a house of cards in *King of Hearts*.

7. Since the inhabitants have all fled, the lunatics take over the town. What is the significance of the fact that life goes on pretty much as usual? What does this imply about French culture?

8. The lunatics all act out their fantasies: one dresses up as a bishop . . . In a ruined house, Eglantine wipes the dust from a mirror and makes herself up as a whore . . . Michel Serrault puts on a wig and takes over the hairdresser's salon . . . General Geranium invades the circus and opens all the animals' cages . . . The Duke and Duchess of Clubs promenade in the town square . . . HOW DOES THIS SEQUENCE ASSERT JEAN GENET'S IDEA (IN *THE BALCONY*) THAT IDENTITY IS ALL A MATTER OF COSTUME?

9. Charles visits the hairdresser and tries the passwords: "The mackerel likes frying" and "The Knight strikes at midnight." Why is it significant that military passwords can't be distinguished from the disjointed ravings of schizophrenics?

10. Charles again tries the passwords (in vain) with General Geranium, who sits playing *chess* with a monkey. How does this game reflect military strategy?

> "The lion is used to being caged—he won't come out." What does the lion symbolize? How does he reflect the lunatics— and Charles himself?

11. Eglantine and her ladies open a Sporting House . . . Why are Charles' attempts to explain war to her *funny?*

> Eglantine "lives for the moment." How does this express the basic philosophy of the film?

12. What does the cross-cut from the lunatics in their firetruck to the Germans preparing to invade the town again in their armored half-track imply about the military?

13. The coronation carriage is pulled by a *camel.* What does this suggest about royalty?

14. The lunatics cheer the Germans and barrage their half-track with confetti. How does their attitude make them unconquerable? What is the effect of the *party hats?*

15. During the coronation, what is the *tone* of the entrance of the three Scottish soldiers? Why are their "camoflage" outfits absurd, and how do they reflect the film's masquerade theme?

16. The lunatics commandeer the German trucks and drive them in circles. How does this symbolize the nature of war?

17. As the three Scotsmen inspect the blockhouse, an elephant walks by, followed by the camel pulling a carriage. How does this symbolize the insanity of war?

18. Charles, again unconscious, is carried away on the strings of a piano. How do his repeated bouts of unconsciousness recall the earlier reference to *Midsummer Night's Dream?* How is he like Shakespeare's character, *Bottom the Weaver?*

> The lunatics decide that Charles needs a woman, a "beating heart, a clock" that will tick next to his. What is the significance of this metaphor?

> What is the implication of their finding a queen for him in the *brothel?*

19. What does Coquelicot's *tightrope act* symbolize?

20. "I'M A LONER, LIKE EVERYONE"—Why does Charles find it hard to accept Coquelicot's love? What is the significance of his leaving her to try to crack the blockhouse?

> When Charles crashes the truck into the blockhouse, the lunatics sit around and applaud, as though he were on a stage. What is the significance of their reaction to the idea of being blown up? ("Who cares?")

21. The parade begins to leave town. At the sound of gunfire, the lunatics turn back: "THERE'S A WALL BETWEEN US AND THE WORLD OUT THERE. YOU HAVE NO IDEA HOW DANGEROUS THEY ARE." Why is this ironic? How does it express the film's theme?

22. "Who made you a Duke?" Charles demands. "Yesterday you were in a nut-house." "And you, Mr. King," replies the Duke of Clubs, "You were out there with the *others.*" What does this dialogue imply about lunatics, soldiers, and kings?

23. "The world is so simple," Eglantine explains. "On one side the whores, on the other the generals." Well put. What does this surreal sequence suggest about the goal of warfare? How does it foreshadow the English "victory party" later in the film?

24. What is symbolic about the way Charles prevents the Knight from striking? Why is he unlikely to be injured in this encounter?

25. While the French lunatics perform their courtly dance, the Germans and the English prepare to invade. How does this reflect the position of the French during both world wars?

26. What do the *fireworks* symbolize?

27. What is the significance of the shoot-out in the town square? ("What funny people.")

28. "Thousands of soldiers are coming!" Who are they? "The Liberators." Why is this ironic?

29. Why do the lunatics return to their asylum and lock the gate, discarding their costumes as they do so?

30. Charles and his bird are given a medal and a kiss on both cheeks by the French commander. How does this echo his treatment by the lunatics?

31. Charles' new commander informs him that they're going to blow a German town sky-high. Why does Charles react to this by discarding his gun and uniform and returning to the asylum?

32. What is the effect of his standing by the gate wearing nothing but his bird?

PERSONA (1967—Swedish) Directed by Ingmar Bergman; with Bibi Andersson and Liv Ullman; cinematography by Sven Nykvist. Distributed by United Artists.

1. In classical drama, the *persona* is literally a *mask* worn by an actor to project his character. In what sense is this film about "masks?" How are the two women *personae* for Bergman himself, and how do they reveal opposing sides of his nature?

2. The pre-credit sequence in *Persona* is one of the strangest in the history of film, but its details are not as accidental as they seem. Like the first twelve lines of *Hamlet,* which introduce the ideas and images of the entire work, the prologue to *Persona* serves as the film's overture. It also reveals

Bergman's unconscious mind and recapitulates the themes of his whole artistic career. Consider the following questions:

(a) How does the closeup of the *carbon arc* lamp call attention to the filmmaker's art? What else does the glowing carbon symbolize?

(b) A strip of film snaps and springs from its sprockets. How does this mechanical breakdown foreshadow the film's theme?

(c) Cut from a cartoon figure (upside-down) washing her face by a rocky shore to a closeup of two hands washing. How does this allude to *Persona*'s setting?

(d) A fast-motion sequence from an old-time silent movie shows a man being pursued by a devil and a skeleton. How is this a self-parody of Bergman's earlier films?

(e) As the film spills from the projector, Bergman intercuts three symbolic shots: a *spider,* a dead *lamb* being slashed open and a closeup of its *eye,* and a spike being driven into a hand. What are the religious connotations of these images? How do these shots reveal the influence of Luis Bunuel?

(f) In the montage of closeups of bodies in a morgue, what does the *white room* symbolize? How does this setting recall Plato's Allegory of the Cave?

(g) A young boy gets up from under a white sheet. He gropes at the camera's lens. In a reverse-angle shot, he then moves his hand over a rear-screen projection of Bibi Andersson's face. How does he represent both Elizabeth's rejected son and Alma's aborted foetus? How is he like a soul waiting in some kind of limbo to be reborn?

Then the credits begin, intercut with a series of subliminal closeups ... the rest of the film is easy!

3. Why does Liv Ullman stop dead in the middle of a scene from *Electra?* Why this particular play?

Note that her name—Vogler—is the same as the magician's in Bergman's early allegory. Why does he also repeat the name (it means "bird") in *Hour of the Wolf?* What do *birds* symbolize for Bergman?

4. How is Bibi Andersson characterized by her straightforward autobiography? In what ways are Alma and Elizabeth opposites?

5. Alma turns on the radio... Why does Elizabeth react to the soap opera with laughter? Why does she get upset when the woman's voice suddenly becomes dreamlike ("Oh God, somewhere out there in the darkness...")? Why does Bergman insert this line from the end of *The Seventh Seal?*

6. Why does Bergman include the long closeup of Elizabeth's face with the Bach violin concerto in the background? Why does he juxtapose Alma's self-contented soliloquy about her fiance and her work?

7. Cut to Elizabeth pacing in front of the TV set. Why is she transfixed by the newscast of the immolation of the Vietnamese monk? What does this image symbolize for Bergman?

8. Alma reads Elizabeth's letter to her: "Have I wronged you without knowing it?" her husband pleads. "We must treat each other like shy children controlled by forces we don't understand." Why don't her husband's feelings move her? Why does she tear the photo of her son?

9. What do you think of the doctor's analysis of Elizabeth's refusal to speak? In what sense has her whole life been a "role?"

10. Alma and Elizabeth live together on the doctor's island. What does this setting symbolize?

> The two women happily collect mushrooms. What are the symbolic connotations of this activity? Why does Elizabeth "compare hands?"

> Why does Bergman dwell on the rocky shore while Alma reads existential philosophy about desolation and awareness?

11. "Imagine devoting your whole life to something..." Why is Elizabeth touched by Alma's idealistic attachment to her profession?

12. What is the significance of Alma's starting to *smoke* like Elizabeth?

13. Elizabeth listens intently while Alma agonizes over her first love affair. How have Alma and Elizabeth switched roles?

> Alma's long erotic soliloquy about her orgy on the beach with two young boys is a masterpiece of "emotion memory." What is the purpose of this guilt-ridden speech?

"Can you be *two* people?" What is the importance of this tortured question?

14. "I could change myself into you if I tried." Why is this ironic? Does Alma *imagine* Elizabeth telling her to go to bed? If so, what is the significance of the white-veiled shot of Elizabeth coming to her room? What is the meaning of the famous pose of the two faces leaning together and merging into one?

> The next day on the rocky shore, why does Elizabeth look puzzled when Alma asks her if she came to her room the previous night?

15. Instead of mailing Elizabeth's letter, Alma unfortunately reads it . . . "She complains that her ideas don't tally with her acts." What is the significance of Elizabeth's "studying" her?

> What is the point of the shot of Alma and her *reflection* in the water?

16. When Alma accidentally breaks her glass, why does she leave one piece for Elizabeth to step on?

17. As Alma and Elizabeth stare at each other in hatred, why does Bergman suddenly break the film and repeat the shots of the skeleton, the crucified hand, and the eye of the lamb? Why is the following shot of Elizabeth wandering through the house deliberately out of focus?

18. Alma confronts Elizabeth on the beach: What is the purpose of the identical black dresses and white hats? What is the effect of the stark white background and Alma's dark glasses? How has the style of this sequence been influenced by Resnais and Antonioni?

> As Alma is about to throw boiling water on her, Elizabeth cries, "No—don't!" (her only words so far!) Otherwise, why does Elizabeth merely laugh silently at Alma's threats?

19. "Can one live without lying?" how does this question relate to the film's theme?

> Alma accuses Elizabeth of being "rotten." How does this reflect her own changing self-image? When Elizabeth runs out onto the beach, why does Alma suddenly regret her words and pursue her to apologize?

> After this emotional sequence, what is the effect of the shot of Alma sitting silently among the boulders?

20. Why does Bergman juxtapose Elizabeth's *turning up the lamp* against her staring in horror at a photo of a little boy being herded to a concentration camp? How does this image explain her silence?

21. Cut to Alma struggling with a dream. How does this echo the opening of the film? She awakes and turns on the radio. Why does Bergman blend the static with a man's voice calling in the background?

> Why does Alma pore over Elizabeth's sleeping face? What is the effect of Elizabeth's suddenly opening eyes?

> What is the significance of Mr. Vogler's embracing Alma as though she were Elizabeth? Is this entire sequence a dream? If so, what does it mean?

> As Mr. Vogler lies beside her, Alma cries, "Leave me alone! I'm cold and rotten and bored!" Why the cut to Elizabeth's changing face?

22. "You hoped the child would be born dead..." Why does Bergman shoot this soliloquy *twice*, first focusing on Elizabeth's face, then on Alma's, but repeating the same words? How does the "long difficult delivery" Alma describes reveal her own guilt about her abortion? How is it also a metaphor for her transformation?

> What is the purpose of the composite of the two faces?

23. What is the meaning of the shot in which Elizabeth sinks her teeth into Alma's wrist? In what ways is *any* artist a vampire?

> What is the meaning of the incantatory "Nothing"?

> Alma awakes... If she has been dreaming this vampirish episode, what does her dream mean?

24. Alma and Elizabeth prepare to leave the cottage. While Alma stares in the mirror, Bergman briefly superimposes the famous pose. Then, as Alma puts on a black hat and walks stiffly to the bus, he cuts to Elizabeth filming *Electra*. What is the point of their exchange of identities?

25. Why does Bergman end the film by repeating the opening shots of the boy running his hands over the projection of Bibi Andersson's face, the film running through its sprockets, and the carbon arc lamp dimming out? How does this final image symbolize the human soul?

THE TAMING OF THE SHREW (1967—English) Directed by
Franco Zeffirelli; with Richard Burton, Elizabeth Taylor, and Michael
York; music by Nino Rota. Produced by Columbia Pictures; distributed by
Swank Films.

1. Since Shakespeare's language is poetic and rhetorical, rather than
naturalistic, what are some of the problems involved in adapting his plays
for the screen?

> Many directors regard Shakespeare as a mummified deity
> whose plays are scripture, not one word of which may be
> changed or omitted. In light of the way Shakespeare was
> seen by his own actors and contemporaries, why is this
> ironic?

> Since a film director must transform *verbal* images into
> *visual* images, why may it be advantageous that Zeffirelli
> doesn't speak English very well? Why are his two
> Shakespeare films visually more powerful than the films
> done by any English director . . . including Laurence Olivier?

2. The opening shows Lucentio and his servant riding through the rain.
What does the flock of sheep and goats symbolize?

> They come to Padua to "suck the sweets of sweet
> philosophy." What is the implication about college students
> in the cross-cut to the large-breasted lady hanging out the
> window?

3. What is the symbolic function of the carnival? What is the purpose of
details like the pig-bishop and the drunkard hanging in a basket?

> In the midst of the carnival, Lucentio and Bianca exchange
> eyes. What is the significance of their "loving" each other
> without speaking even once?

4. Lucentio and his servant exchange identities merely by changing cloaks.
What is the significance of this?

5. Lucentio pursues Bianca through the *laundry* as Katherine glares at them through a crack in the window. What does the setting symbolize?

6. Why is Katherine furious with her sister? When Bianca insists that she "never yet beheld *that special face*" that she could favor more than any other, what does this imply about her attitude toward love?

7. Petruchio's first move in Baptista's house is to check out the silver, which gleams with a beautiful soft light. How does this characterize him?

> Note that the interior looks like a Vermeer painting. How does this establish the social class of Baptista's home as wealthy bourgeois, rather than aristocratic?

8. What is the effect of Katherine shrieking and breaking furniture in the background while Petruchio plans what he'll say to her?

9. Why does Katherine lie laughing in the wool, munching a fruit? Why does Zeffirelli fill the love-pursuit with so many earthy symbols and sexual metaphors? Note the following:

> She sits on the trap door as Petruchio pushes it open with his head (!)

> As Petruchio performs his Tarzan act, how do the *salamis* curing on his swing comment on the nature of his love?

> He crashes through the railing, and when she bars the door, he bashes through the wall...

> What does their falling through the roof symbolize? What is the significance of their landing, and how does this image relate to the dialogue?

10. As they walk smiling across the balcony, Petruchio twists Katherine's arm behind her back. How does this characterize the Renaissance institution of courtship?

11. "She is not proud, but modest as a dove..." In what sense is Petruchio a "high mimetic" comic hero, creating his own reality and persuading others to live in it? How is he like Don Quixote in this respect?

12. The Wedding: "To *me* she's married, not unto my clothes." What is the thematic significance of this? (vs. Tranio wearing Lucentio's clothes)

> What is the purpose of Petruchio's coughing fit?

What is symbolic about the way Petruchio prevents Katherine from saying, "I will *not*...?"

Why does Zeffirelli include the effete little priest? In fact, how are *all* the men in Padua characterized, and how might this explain Katherine's bitchy nature?

"A woman may be made a fool, if she have not the spirit to resist." What is the function of the thunder and lightning that follow?

Petruchio carries Katherine out into the storm ... and leaves her in a puddle. How is this a metaphor for marriage?

13. The Homecoming: What is the effect of Katherine's donkey nosing its way through the door?

How is their homelife characterized by the series of cross-cuts as Petruchio calls for food?

How do the chickens twirling on the spit reflect their relationship?

Why does Zeffirelli make the servants so grotesque?

What does the *feast* symbolize? What is the purpose of the prolonged "grace" and the clearing of the table?

When Petruchio climbs into bed, how does Katherine's retaliation characterize their marriage?

14. How does Petruchio react as Katherine "re-decorates" his castle? What does her clearing away the cobwebs symbolize?

15. As his wife dresses his servants in fine clothes, Petruchio looks on ruefully, not quite sure how he lost control. How does this motivate his treatment of the tailor?

"It is the mind that makes the body rich ... Is the jay more precious than the lark because his feathers are brighter?" Why does Petruchio tear the gown to pieces, and how does this relate to the other incidents in the film involving *clothes?*

16. "How bright and goodly shines the moon..." Why does Petruchio insist that it is night when it is noon, and vice-versa? How does this relate to Shakespeare's obsession with Appearance and Reality?

17. On the road, Petruchio and Katherine meet Lucentio's father, Vincentio, whom she addresses as "young budding virgin." Why such an extravagant greeting? Why is Petruchio disconcerted by her sudden "agreement" with his poetic fantasies?

18. The "real" Vincentio confronts the fake—what is the point of this episode? Note that the servants, persisting in their masquerade, immediately deny their master. How does Lucentio's sudden shift into Reality characterize him?

In *Don Quixote,* "general opinion" creates reality unless *someone* is willing to declare that the emperor is wearing no clothes. How is this situation similar?

19. Why is Katherine unwilling to kiss Petruchio in the middle of the street?

20. The Wedding Feast: As Petruchio and Katherine drink their wine in silence, the children brawl on the floor. Biondello playfully picks up the smallest boy and gives him a horsey-ride on his dog to make him smile again. How does this action affect Katherine, and how does it motivate her tactic in her speech about women's duty?

21. The Wager: Bianca replies that she is "busy and cannot come." Hortensio's wife bids him come to *her.* Why does Katherine come when Petruchio *commands* her?

How are the three women characterized by their responses?

Why does Katherine make such an absurdly flattering speech about the obedience women owe their husbands? Does she mean it, or has she merely found the only way to manipulate him?

Note that while Petruchio basks in male contentment, Katherine suddenly disappears. What is the point of this?

ROMEO AND JULIET (1968—English) Directed by Franco Zeffirelli; with Olivia Hussey (Juliet), Leonard Whiting (Romeo), Michael York (Tybalt), John McEnery (Mercutio), Pat Heywood (Nurse), Milo O'Shea (Friar Laurence), and Robert Stephens (the Prince); costumes by Danilo Donati; music by Nino Rota. Produced by Paramount.

1. "Do you bite your thumb at me, sir?"—What is the symbolic function of the opening brawl? Why does Zeffirelli stress *dust* and *heat* through the film?

2. Enter Romeo, twirling a flower... Why does Zeffirelli replace his infatuation for Rosaline with an abstract, generalized yearning for love?

3. Cut to Paris asking Capulet for Juliet's hand in marriage... "Younger than she are happy mothers made." How does the zoom-shot of Capulet's wife slamming the window shut comment on his assertion? Why does Zeffirelli introduce Juliet running and playing like a little girl?

4. Why does Zeffirelli juxtapose the nurse's vulgar wit against Lady Capulet primping in the mirror?

> Marriage is "an honor that I dream not of," says Juliet. How does her attitude toward love differ from Romeo's?

> "I'll look to like, if looking liking move." How does this courtly word-play characterize her?

5. Cut to Romeo and his friends preparing to crash the party. John McEnery's Mercutio is *not* the courtly gentleman Shakespeare envisioned. Why does Zeffirelli stress Mercutio's cynicism and foreboding of death in his "Queen Mab" speech? Why does he shoot this sequence through the flames of the torches?

> Romeo's "mind misgives some consequence yet hanging in the stars." Why does Shakespeare keep emphasizing the stars? How does this allude to the role of *fate* in tragedy?

6. The Party: Romeo and his friends wear *animal masks*. What does this symbolize? How does Romeo, prowling like a hungry panther, contrast with Juliet's formal dance?

"She doth teach the torches to burn bright." What does Romeo's reaction to seeing Juliet for the first time tell us about his character, and about the nature of love?

When Tybalt demands that Romeo be ejected, why does Capulet insist that he be left in peace?

During the maresca that follows, what do the candles and the smoke symbolize? How does this wild, whirling dance foreshadow Romeo and Juliet's love?

7. "What is a youth?—impetuous fire; What is a maid?—ice and desire." Why does Zeffirelli insert Nino Rota's beautiful song about love and death?

Note the audience's mock-romantic reactions to the song while Romeo and Juliet search for each other. What is the effect of his seizing her hand and pulling her behind the pillar?

"My lips, two blushing pilgrims, ready stand to smooth that rough touch with a tender kiss..." What is the *tone* of the religious imagery in Romeo and Juliet's first conversation? Why does Zeffirelli frame Juliet's profile against the stained glass background?

8. As Romeo leaves, why does Zeffirelli cut from Juliet touching her lips—to Tybalt's scowling face?

9. Juliet's family and Romeo's drunk friends call their names in the darkness. How does this comic sequence emphasize the lovers' isolation?

10. The Balcony Scene: "What's in a name?" What is the thematic significance of Juliet's question? How does her speech relate to Shakespeare's concern with appearance and reality?

What does the balcony symbolize, and how does this setting express Romeo's concept of love?

"I take thee at thy word!" Romeo exclaims. Why does Juliet suddenly recoil?

Romeo reacts to Juliet's declaration of love by clambering up the tree and swinging from the branches like a monkey... How does this differ from the traditional interpretation of this scene?

What does Romeo's swearing his love by the *moon* symbolize? What is the moon's nature, and why does this bother Juliet?

As morning breaks, how does the closeup of their hands parting foreshadow the film's ending?

11. We first see Friar Laurence gathering herbs. How does this foreshadow the final tragedy? If he disapproves of Romeo's sudden love for Juliet, why would he agree to marry them?

12. Why does Zeffirelli include the vulgar routine between Mercutio and the nurse? How does his clowning foreshadow his death?

13. Why does Zeffirelli set the nurse's conference with Romeo in the *church?* Why does he include the exaggerated gestures over the holy water and the comic business with the poor-box? What is the effect of the nurse suddenly embracing Romeo and pulling him into her lap?

14. When the nurse returns with Romeo's answer, what is the significance of Juliet's impatience?

15. During the wedding ceremony, why does Zeffirelli stress the lovers' impetuosity and the friar's comic attempts to keep them from embracing? After the wedding, why does he focus on the mosaic of the *sun?*

16. Cut to Mercutio walking up the street with a handkerchief over his face. What does this image symbolize? What is the effect of his bathing in the fountain while Tybalt tries to pick a fight?

What is the significance of Mercutio's play on the word "consort," and of his sexual allusion to his sword as a "fiddlestick?"

17. At first, how does Mercutio interpret Romeo's declaration of "love" for Tybalt? Why does he then angrily draw his sword, and what is the *tone* of the duel that follows?

Note the zoom-closeup of the tip of Tybalt's sword. How does he feel about killing Mercutio?

"Ask for me tomorrow, and you shall find me a grave man." Why does Zeffirelli play Mercutio's death for comedy?

18. Why does Zeffirelli stress Romeo's rashness in challenging Tybalt? How does their fight differ from the usual polite Shakespearean duel? Why is their final "embrace" ironic?

19. Cut to the nurse grieving. Why does Juliet object when the nurse echoes her harsh words against Romeo? In what sense is Juliet's position in this scene *tragic?*

20. Why does Zeffirelli emphasize the riotous nature of the mob as both families agitate with the Prince for justice?

21. Cut to Romeo weeping about his banishment: "In what vile part of this anatomy doth my name lodge? Tell me, that I may sack the hateful mansion." How does this line allude to the "identity" theme? Why is Romeo unlikely to be convinced by the friar's logical outline of the reasons why he should be "happy?"

22. Cut to Romeo and Juliet awaking from their wedding night. As Romeo gets dressed, Juliet persuades him to return to bed. What is the significance of her confusing the nightingale and the lark, insisting "yon light is not daylight?" How does this scene develop the idea that their love thrives only with the darkness, and dies with the light of day?

23. While Juliet weeps, Lady Capulet plans revenge on Romeo. Why does Juliet react so violently when her mother informs her of her father's plan to marry her to Paris?

> How is Capulet characterized in his confrontation with Juliet? In what ways are father and daughter alike?

> Apparently, most women marry men who are like their fathers. How does Capulet reflect Romeo's main flaw?

> "I would the fool were married to her grave!" Why is this metaphor ironic? What is the significance of Lady Capulet's coldly refusing to help her daughter?

> Why would the nurse advise Juliet to forget Romeo and marry Paris? What does this say about her values, and why does Juliet conclude that she can no longer rely on her?

24. Cut to Friar Laurence and Paris as Juliet comes running... How is Paris characterized in this sequence, and why does Juliet rebuff him so coldly?

25. The friar is a modern man who thinks that all problems can be solved through the miracle of chemistry. What is the significance of his playing god, and concocting such elaborate plots?

> As Juliet runs out the door, why does Zeffirelli juxtapose the friar's worried face against the extinguished candle?

26. Why does Juliet feign repentance with her father? Why does Zeffirelli omit Juliet's debate with herself over drinking the potion?

27. The shot of Juliet swallowing the potion echoes the shot of her raising the glass to her lips in front of the stained glass window when she and Romeo first met. What is the purpose of this repetition?

28. "Death lies on her like an untimely frost upon the sweetest flower of all the field." Instead of the formal lamentation scene, Zeffirelli intercuts a single couplet with shots of Friar Laurence's messenger riding to Mantua. Why does he omit most of acts four and five?

29. Note Romeo's rash reaction to Balthasar's tragic announcement: "Then I defy you stars." What is the religious connotation of this line? What is the effect of Romeo's horse charging past the messenger's donkey and through the flock of sheep?

30. Why does Zeffirelli omit Romeo's duel with Paris?

31. What does Romeo's bashing in the door of the tomb symbolize?

32. Romeo drinks *poison* . . . Why this particular form of death? How does it relate to the love theme?

33. Cut to the friar approaching with a lantern . . . As he kneels beside Romeo's body, what is the effect of the closeup of Juliet's opening hand?

> "I dare no longer stay!" What is the significance of the friar's flight?

34. "Thy lips are warm . . . " What is the effect of the understated irony? What does Juliet's stabbing herself with Romeo's *knife* symbolize?

35. "All are punished!" The Prince's anger echoes through the piazza. Why does Zeffirelli end with these words? Instead of the traditional speech about "order" that concludes the play, why does he show the mourners embracing as they enter the church?

MIDNIGHT COWBOY (1969—American) Directed by John Schlesinger; with Dustin Hoffman and John Voight; music by Harry Nilsson and others, arranged by John Barry. Produced by United Artists.

In 1969, the overt sexuality of *Midnight Cowboy* distracted its audience's attention from its theme. Now that porno theaters have sprouted like mushrooms all over the country, the film no longer shocks, and its mythical qualities seem more impressive. In this allegory about the search for the American Dream, there are "no more westerns." The Cowboy of American myth meets rat-toothed reality in the badlands of New York City. In a pop-art world where poodles wear wigs and repressed homosexuals masquerade as fundamentalist preachers, can love exist? John Schlesinger finds hope only in Joe and Ratso's friendship, an archetypal relationship as true now as it was in the days of Don Quixote.

***

1. Joe Buck quits his job washing dishes in a Texas drive-in and heads for New York City to hustle after the American Dream. How is he a modern Don Quixote?

2. As Joe stares in the window of a beauty parlor, Schlesinger flashes back to him as a child massaging his grandmother's (?) neck. How has this childhood memory formed Joe's view of the world? What is ironic about his grandmother telling him he'll be "the best looking cowboy in the parade"?

3. "Do you love me, Joe?" What is the purpose of the slow-motion flashback to Joe's old girlfriend telling him, "You're the only one...You're the best"?

4. Why does Schlesinger include the broadcast of the fundamentalist advertising his "home worship kit?"

5. A well-dressed man lies flat on his face in front of Tiffany's as people walk by unnoticing. How does this characterize life in New York City?

6. "Do it for momma," a brassy lady in a short white skirt pleads with her poodle. How does the dog anticipate Joe's position in the ensuing scene?

To his opening line about the Statue of Liberty she snaps, "It's up in Central Park taking a leak." As a symbol, why does Schlesinger juxtapose this gross lady against the Statue of Liberty?

As they make love, what is the symbolic purpose of the rapidly changing TV channels? In particular, note the shots of Bishop Fulton Sheen intoning "And you think God is dead?", beans pouring into a bowl, and a slot machine disgorging. How does this sequence reflect the pop-art of the sixties?

When Joe raises the question of "business," note the ironic outcome of their liaison. Why is it obvious that he isn't going to make it in New York as a hustler?

7. Cut to Joe sitting at a bar beside Ratso Rizzo (Dustin Hoffman as a post-graduate). How do the two men contrast? How do they illustrate the Don Quixote/Sancho Panza archetype?

Joe can't tell that the "lady" who approaches them is a transvestite. What is the significance of his inability to distinguish appearance from reality?

8. "You need management," Ratso tells Joe as he takes him to see Mr. O'Daniel... who sits in a dingy hotel room wearing only a bathrobe. How do the double-meanings and misunderstandings in this confrontation recall the scene with the transvestite?

"Lonesome!" Mr. O'Daniel exclaims. "Why don't we get right down on our knees!" What does this ironic line imply about sex and religion?

Why does Schlesinger intercut the flashback to Joe's baptism with shots of the flashing statue of Christ?

9. What is the purpose of the black-and-white sections in the rapid montage of Joe looking for Ratso, fantasizing about strangling him?

When Joe returns to the bar, the surly bartender denies knowing Ratso, and the transvestite laughs. Why does Schlesinger intercut shots of him as a boy smashing the mirror?

10. Why does Schlesinger include the TV talk show sequence? How does the poodle wearing a wig reflect Schlesinger's view of women—and Joe's role as a hustler?

11. Joe walks 42nd Street. What is the significance of the virtual procession of "cowboys" there?

12. A student with thick glasses picks him up and takes him into a sleazy theater, where they watch a science fiction film. Why does Schlesinger juxtapose the ensuing act of oral outrage against the uncoupling space ship and the blaring sound track ("We've lost track of Captain Grace")?

> Why does Joe flash back to his girlfriend and the gang rape?

> What is the effect of the cut to the young man throwing up in the bathroom? Why does he deny that he has any money, virtually challenging Joe to hit him?

13. Suddenly Joe sees Ratso sitting in a coffeeshop. When Joe stalks off, why does Ratso invite him home? What does his living in a condemned building symbolize?

> Why does Ratso have a Florida poster on the wall? What does Florida symbolize for him?

14. As Joe sleeps, Schlesinger dissolves from Ratso's face to a black-and-white nightmare of the police arresting Joe in the gang rape. What are the ironic connotations of "He's the only one"? Why does Schlesinger include Ratso's face in these memories?

15. Why does Ratso insist that Joe's cowboy get-up is "strictly for fags?" What is Schlesinger suggesting about the American Cowboy Myth?

16. Why does Ratso go to the trouble of "grooming" Joe and stealing an address from the pocket of an escort? While he waits for Joe to complete his first job, why does Schlesinger include Ratso's fantasy of running with Joe on the beach in Florida?

> As the lady slaps Joe and the other men throw him out of the hotel, why does Schlesinger intercut the shots of the old ladies in wheelchairs converging on Ratso, pushing him into the pool?

17. Returning to their tenement, Joe and Ratso look out the window to see their building being torn down. What does this symbolize?

18. Why does Schlesinger fill the film with *commercial images*, cheerfully celebrating the materialism of the American Dream? Why are these images ironic? In particular, note:

(a) the commercial for "orange juice on ice"/vs. the frozen faucet

(b) the giant hissing deodorant can/vs. the blood bank on 42nd Street

(c) "Steak for Everybody" on the Florida airlines billboard/vs. Joe and Ratso's silhouettes crossing the bridge to the cemetary.

19. Ratso on reincarnation: "You could come back in a different body, as a dog or a president." Why does he want Joe to think about this?

20. Two strange people take Joe's picture and invite him to a party. How does the party satirize sixties psychedelia? How is it like a mythical descent into hell?

21. As Joe and Brenda Vaccaro match hands and kiss, why does Schlesinger bathe the screen in red light?

How does Ratso's rolling down the stairs foreshadow the end of the film?

Joe drives off with the lady, leaving Ratso standing alone in the snow. What does the setting symbolize?

22. "Maybe if you wouldn't call me ma'am, things would work out better..." What is the significance of Joe's impotence?

Why does she suggest that they play scrabble? What is the significance of his misspelling "MONY-MAN"?

"GAY ends in Y," she observes. "Is that your problem, baby?" Why does he react passionately to this?

23. Joe makes soup for Ratso, who is panicked about not being able to walk. What is the symbolic importance of this scene?

24. Why does Schlesinger cut from Joe's unsuccessful phone call to him *shooting* in a penny arcade?

25. After taking Joe back to his room, why does the elderly man spend the whole time on the phone with his wife? When Joe demands, "What do you want?" why does the man thank him for "helping him to be good"—and give him a St. Christopher medal? Why does he offer Joe only ten dollars, knowing that Joe will beat him up?

What does Joe's smashing the man in the face with the *phone* symbolize? Why does Schlesinger intercut shots of Ratso's sick face during this sequence?

26. Cut to Joe and Ratso on a bus to Florida ... "We're gonna tell all these new people that my name is *Rico.*" How does Ratso's desire for a new identity parallel Joe's cowboy act?

What is the significance of Joe's stuffing his cowboy outfit in the trashcan?

27. Why does Schlesinger close with Joe putting his arm around Ratso's shoulders?

THE WANDERER (1969—French) Directed by Jean-Gabriel Albicocco; with Brigitte Fossey; adapted from the novel by Alain-Fournier.

Alain-Fournier died in World War One at the age of twenty-eight, true to his philosophy that all happiness is ultimately doomed. In *The Wanderer,* his only published novel, Augustin Meaulnes pursues an ideal joy which can never be fulfilled and thus can never be lost. Jean-Gabriel Albicocco films Meaulnes' romantic yearning for perfection in a dreamscape that makes LSD hallucinations seem mundane by comparison. In this mannered, baroque fantasy, Albicocco charges his characters and their country environment with an inner light that heightens ordinary reality and blurs the distinction between dreams and real life.

***

1. Why is the story told from the viewpoint of a very ordinary, conventional young man? What is the significance of Seurel's being *crippled?*

2. Augustin Meaulnes' arrival at the village is "the beginning of a new life" for Seurel. What does their lighting *fireworks* symbolize? How is Meaulnes like the title character in Hermann Hesse's novel *Demian?* What is the significance of Seurel's following Meaulnes immediately and living

vicariously through his romantic adventure? How does their relationship echo the Don Quixote-Sancho Panza archetype?

3. The students enter the classroom like a military assault. How is Meaulnes different from the other boys?

4. How does Meaulnes' taking the donkey cart and charging into the woods—only to lose his way—establish the basic pattern of his life?

5. Meaulnes reappears in class after being missing all night. In his flashback to the "Lost Manor," note the hallucinatory perspective. What is the purpose of the visual distortion in the shot of the trees? Why does Albicocco fill the interior of the chateau with cobwebs of refracted light?

6. As Meaulnes tries to play several instruments lying around the room, he hears a harpsichord in the distance. How does this musical motif symbolize Meaulnes' pursuit of a romantic ideal?

7. "The kids are boss here," the clown's partner observes. Why would this be Meaulnes' idea of heaven?

8. How does the clown's "butterfly" act reflect Meaulnes' tragic search for happiness?

9. Why does Albicocco juxtapose the clown's performance against Meaulnes' wandering through the enchanted hallway to find the source of the harpsichord music? Similarly, why does he cut from the clown playing his trumpet (as he steps through a psychedelic dreamscape) to the shot of Meaulnes standing by the edge of the pond?

10. In a sequence straight out of a fairy tale, Meaulnes and Yvonne de Galais stare at each other as they float across the pond on a pair of lacy riverboats. How does their being on "different boats" foreshadow the tragic outcome of their relationship?

11. Both dressed in formal nineteenth century black, Meaulnes and Yvonne meet in the woods. How is this scene like a symbolist painting? How does the *fog* on the pond comment on their sudden love?

12. Why does Meaulnes' vision of the Romantic ideal center on Frantz? Why does Albicocco undercut this ideal by stressing that Frantz is a self-centered young man whose family "indulges all his whims"?

13. What does the "Lost Manor"—and Meaulnes' attempts to return to it—symbolize?

14. As though in a dream, Frantz suddenly appears at the school. Why does he lead a group of boys to steal Meaulnes' secret map? What is the significance of Meaulnes' not recognizing him? Why does Frantz say that he too "doesn't know the way back to the chateau"? Is he being metaphorical, or is he merely lying?

15. What does the *circus* symbolize? Why does Albicocco stress that the clown is both an artist and a chicken thief? How does this reflect on Frantz?

16. Meaulnes leaves for Paris. At his vigil beneath Yvonne's window, he meets a young lady, also "waiting in the cold." Why wouldn't it occur to him that she is Frantz's former fiancee?

> Valentine says she left her fiance because "he treated me like a princess." How does this explain her flight?

17. In the meantime, Seurel meets Yvonne. Why does he fight his attraction for her? What is ironic about her flirtatious observation that happiness usually waits right nearby?

18. If Meaulnes "lives for that strange affair," which he compares to being in heaven, why is he hesitant to see Yvonne when Seurel arranges their meeting?

19. Yvonne and her father arrive for the harvest festival on an old white horse, all that remains of their former glory. Yvonne tells Meaulnes that they've had to sell everything (because of Frantz's debts!) Why does this annoy Meaulnes? Why does he react so negatively when she asks if "the past can be reborn"?

20. Why is Frantz intent on having Meaulnes leave his sister to follow him? If Meaulnes has dreamed about Yvonne for years, why on earth would he leave?

21. "I met a girl in Paris I should have married." How does this motivate Meaulnes' determination to get Frantz and Valentine back together?

> Why does Albicocco intercut shots of Yvonne pursuing Meaulnes through the woods with his memories of Valentine?

> What does Yvonne's falling in the stream symbolize?

22. Why does Yvonne say it's *her* fault that Meaulnes has left? What does her mooning over someone she has known for only five days imply about the nature of love?

23. Only once in his life does Seurel get to hold Yvonne in his arms. In refusing to ever acknowledge his love for her, how is he like the film's two romantic heroes?

24. Meaulnes returns to bring Frantz and Valentine back to their play-house . . . and to claim his daughter, whom he kisses rather passionately (!) Why does the child shriek when confronted with her actual father? How does this reflect the other relationships in the film?

25. Why does the film end with Seurel weeping? In what sense is this film *his* tragedy rather than Meaulnes'? What questions does *The Wanderer* raise about the quest for Romantic ideals?

THE CONFORMIST (1970—Italian) Directed by Bernardo Bertolucci; with Jean-Louis Trintignant, Stefania Sandrelli, and Dominique Sanda; cinematography by Vittorio Storaro; music by George Delerue. Distributed by Paramount.

The baroque fantasies and art deco interiors of *The Conformist* evoke memories of Federico Fellini at his best. Like Guido in Fellini's *8½,* Marcello Clerici confuses "shadows" with reality. The similarity between the two characters ends here, however. Guido is a conventional chauvinist—pampered by his mother, searching for the perfect woman. There are no quests in Marcello's life. All he wants is to "fit in," and his repressed homosexuality is the main cause of his fascism. To accept the truth of this paradox, one need only observe the parade of young men wearing chains and leather in the streets of Florence and San Francisco.

***

1. The film consists of a series of flashbacks as Marcello Clerici rides through the snow to assassinate his former professor and friend. What questions does the flashback technique raise about Marcello's vision of reality? How do the car's *fogged windows* anticipate the "Allegory of the Cave" that becomes the film's central symbol?

2. In the first flashback, Marcello tells his friend Italo that he's getting married. How does the Felliniesque trio singing in the background comment on his announcement?

Why does Bertolucci juxtapose the man doing bird imitations against Italo's fascist sermon on the union of Italy and Germany? What does Italo's *blindness* symbolize?

3. Why is Marcello intent on being accepted by the fascists? Why does Bertolucci dwarf Marcello with the vast empty interiors? What is the effect of the huge symbols passing by? Why does Dominique Sanda appear briefly as a prostitute in this dreamlike sequence?

4. Flashback #2: Marcello visits his fiancee. Note that her black and white dress echoes the shadows that form "bars" across the room. What is the symbolic purpose of this striking interior?

Why is Marcello so passive when Giulia leaps on him passionately?

Her mother interrupts with a nasty letter implying that Marcello suffers from congenital syphilis (!) How does this sequence lead to Marcello's confrontation with his mother?

5. Why the tilted camera angle as Marcello's fascist shadow follows him to his mother's palazzo?

6. Marcello's aristocratic mother lies in bed wearing black eye shades. Why does Bertolucci repeat this "blindness" motif? What is the significance of her being a morphine addict?

"Does this look like a normal house to you?" Marcello fumes. Why is he upset by "decadence?" Why does he mock his mother as she calls her lover, and what is the purpose of the low-angle shot of the swirling leaves as he helps her into the car?

7. Marcello and his mother visit his father in the insane asylum. What is the effect of the stark white setting? How does the father's writing against "the individual's submission to the state" explain his being put in the asylum? When Marcello accuses him, why does he rise like a dignified old bird and summon the attendant to tie his straitjacket?

8. Why does Bertolucci cut from Marcello getting out of the car to the flashback of him as a child being molested by the other boys? How does this lead to his homosexual encounter with Lino, the chauffeur? Why does Bertolucci repeat this "chauffeur" motif? What do *cars* come to symbolize in the course of the film?

9. Why does Bertolucci intercut the confession sequence? Why is the priest so interested in the details of the episode in which Lino and the young

Marcello chase each other in the field and then go to Lino's room? What does the *pistol* symbolize?

> How does this childhood incident lead to Marcello's obsession with having a "normal" life? Why does he deliberately choose a fiancee whose head is full of "petty thoughts?"

> Why does the priest absolve Marcello immediately when he says he belongs to a group that hunts down subversives? What does this imply about the politics of the Catholic Church?

10. On the train to Paris, Giulia confesses to Marcello that she is "unworthy" of him. Why is this ironic?

11. As Marcello receives his orders to eliminate Professor Quadri, note that the fascist leader's desk is covered with *nuts* (!) What is the significance of Marcello's business with the pistol? What is the effect of the little old lady who wanders past the door?

12. Back on the train: While Giulia relates the story of her seduction, why does she have Marcello fondle and undress her? How does Giulia's reliving her adolescent memory reflect Marcello's motivation in the plot to assassinate Prof. Quadri?

13. Marcello and Giulia visit Prof. Quadri and his wife Anna. How is Anna characterized by her swagger, her chain-smoking, and her large dog? Why are the professor's friends dubious about Marcello's visit?

14. In the film's central symbolic sequence, Marcello closes the window shade and quotes Plato's "Allegory of the Cave." What is the effect of the backlighting in this sequence? Why is his reference to Plato's "prisoners in chains" ironic? In what sense is the entire film about "shadows and reality?"

15. While the men discuss philosophy, why does Bertolucci cut to Anna urging Giulia to crank the printing press? What are the erotic connotations of this action?

> Anna abruptly leaves the room and accuses Marcello of spying. Why does Bertolucci make their love scene so violent?

16. What is the significance of Anna's being a ballet teacher? When Marcello asks her to elope to Brazil, why does she hand him a letter from a friend in an Italian prison describing his torture? If she really thinks he's a "worm," why does she start to undress?

17. During the supposed shopping trip, Marcello returns to the hotel to find Anna fondling his wife's leg. Why does he quietly close the door and walk away without a word? How does this sequence further undercut his desire for "normalcy?"

18. As proof of friendship, Quadri gives Marcello a letter to deliver to friends in Rome. Why does Marcello abruptly get up and leave the table? What is the effect of the *swinging lamp* as Manganiello confronts him in the hall? Why does Marcello try to surrender his gun? What is ironic about Manganiello's speech about "honor" and "self?"

19. Bertolucci is famous for his dance sequences. What is the symbolic function of Anna and Giulia's tango?

> While everyone dances out in a long line, Marcello gives Manganiello the paper with the professor's travel plans. What does his separation from the dance symbolize?

20. Cut back to the car. Marcello tells Manganiello that he dreamed he was *blind* and that Prof. Quadri was operating on him. After regaining his sight, he eloped with the professor's wife. What is the significance of this dream? What does it imply about his flashbacks about his romance with Anna?

21. The assassination: What is the effect of the dreamlike fog and the backlighting as the assassins emerge from the woods? How does the professor's death echo the murder of Julius Caesar?

> While Marcello stares at her, Anna pounds on the window of the car like a frantic animal. How does this terrifying image express Bertolucci's idea of the relations of men and women?

> Why does Bertolucci use a hand-held camera for the chase through the woods? What does Anna's death in the snow symbolize?

22. Years later... Marcello's daughter tugs at him as the radio announces Mussolini's fall. Why does Bertolucci juxtapose the daughter's prayers against the ringing phone and Italo's plea for help?

> Why does Giulia suddenly ask about the long-repressed Quadri affair, and why isn't she satisfied by his explanation that he was just doing his duty?

23. As Marcello leads his blind friend across the bridge, what is the significance of his discovery that Lino is alive? What does Lino symbolize? As Italo listens in horror, why does Marcello accuse Lino of murdering

Quadri and his wife? Why does he suddenly turn on Italo and denounce him as a fascist?

24. Shadows flicker on the wall...What is the effect of the final shot of Marcello framed by the bars? How does this image recall the Allegory of the Cave?

25. In Platonic terms, how do Marcello, Quadri, Anna, and Giulia correspond to the division of the human personality into Self, Mind, Heart, and Body?

A CLOCKWORK ORANGE (1971—English) Directed by Stanley Kubrick; with Malcolm McDowell and Patrick Magee; music by Walter Carlos; based on the novel by Anthony Burgess. Produced by Warner Bros.

In this "Portrait of the Artist as a Young Punk," Stanley Kubrick transforms Anthony Burgess' philosophical allegory into a pop-art vision of hell. Though not tragic like the original novel, the film examines the same problem: the eternal connection between violence and art. Kubrick's Alex, a charming young conformist full of murderous impulses, represents Basic Man. But is he an artist? In a plastic civilization in which art is erotic kitsch and style has degenerated into fashion, Alex merely preserves the rhetoric of art. His poetic slang and white uniform symbolize the illusion of beauty in a "Brave New World" dehumanized by drugs and technology.

***

1. In cockney slang, a "clockwork orange" is a lunatic. What are the other connotations of this phrase as it describes Alex and his society?

2. For the opening credits, why does Kubrick use orange/blue jump-cuts in sync with electronic music?

3. Cut to a closeup of Malcolm McDowell's leering face...What does he symbolize? How do his stylish costume and makeup predict punk rock?

4. A zoom-out reveals the milk bar. What is the purpose of the stylized setting, with plastic ladies as tables?

5. What is the effect of the cut to the old drunk singing in the gutter? How does he symbolize the Old Order? Why would Alex resent his lack of "style?"

6. Cut to the baroque ceiling of a theater. Why does Kubrick set Billy Boy and his gang raping a girl on an *opera stage?* What does this imply about opera? What is the significance of the stylized movements and the Rossini music? Why is the gang fight *choreographed?*

7. Note the rear-screen projection as the four play "chicken" on country roads. How is this drive a symbol of their lives?

8. The Surprise Visit: Note that the doorbell chimes the opening bar of Beethoven's Fifth. Why the distorted hallucinatory perspective throughout this sequence?

9. Back at the milk bar: How does the *milk machine* reflect the contemporary treatment of women?

10. What is the significance of Alex's reaction to the lady singing Beethoven's "Ode to Joy?" Why does he hit Dim for interrupting?

11. Note the trashed condition of the modern flat-block in which Alex lives. How does this symbolize society in general?

12. How does the pop-art decor in Alex's bedroom characterize him? (Note his snake and the row of crucified Christs.)

> "It was gorgeosity made flesh..." Why would his hallucinations (inspired by Beethoven!) take the form of images from "B"-movies?

13. How is Alex's mother characterized by her vinyl dress and purple wig? What is the significance of his parents having no idea about what he does in the evenings?

14. What is the significance of Mr. Deltoid's hovering over Alex? What does the glass of false teeth symbolize, and how does it comment on his puzzling over the Problem of Evil? ("We've been studying it for damn well near a century.")

15. Alex picks up the two girls. What do their ice lollies symbolize? ("Cold and pointless?")

What is the purpose of the high-speed orgy? Why does Kubrick use the "Lone Ranger Theme" from Rossini's William Tell Overture? What does this mechanical approach to sex imply about modern love?

To make *Clockwork Orange* "acceptable" for teenagers, this sequence is eliminated in the "R" version. How does this change the *tone* of the first third of the film?

16. Alex's comrades drop by to surprise him. Why isn't Alex interested in the "big money?" What *is* Alex's interest in crime based on?

17. Why does Kubrick use slow-motion and Rossini music as Alex disciplines his gang? Why is this staged as a *ballet?*

18. Why does Kubrick introduce the Cat Lady doing a series of impossible exercises? Note all the very plastic erotic art. How does her taste in art reflect a general problem in this futuristic society?

19. Why the Rossini music and the choreographed steps as Alex and his gang scale the wall? How does this entire episode satirize the action of nineteenth century operas?

20. Note that the Cat Lady tries to hit Alex with a bust of Beethoven. Why does Kubrick use a hand-held camera with a wide-angle lens to film this comic battle between Music and Art?

"That's a very important work of art!" What is the significance of his smashing her with it?

21. How are the police characterized by their interrogation? Outside, the sergeant calmly sips tea. Why is their extreme politeness ironic? What is the purpose of the surreal, parabolic perspective as Deltoid and the cop hover over Alex?

22. Part Two: The Prison—After Alex signs in, he is known only as number "655321." What is the significance of the mechanical procedure? Why are *shelves of boxes* an appropriate setting for this sequence?

23. Cut to the Chaplain's sermon on hell. How does this satirize the famous sermon in Joyce's *Portrait of the Artist?* Why does Kubrick intercut the shots of the two convicts blowing kisses to Alex? Why are the prisoners amused by the Chaplain's sermon?

"I was a wandering sheep, I did not love the fold . . . " Why is the hymn ironic?

24. What is ironic about Alex's new interest in the Bible? Note Alex's daydreams about biblical adventures—whipping Christ, slitting an enemy throat in an Old Testament battle scene, and lounging on a couch with his "wife's handmaidens." How does this sequence satirize biblical films? What does it imply about violence and religion?

25. Alex is disturbed from his fantasy by the Chaplain's hand on his shoulder. What does this gesture insinuate?

> "I want to be good!" What is the significance of Alex's always brown-nosing authority figures?

26. "Goodness comes from within"—Why does the Chaplain disapprove of the Lodovico treatment? Why is *choice* a necessary element in morality?

27. Why does Kubrick use "Pomp and Circumstance" (the traditional *graduation* march) as the Minister of the Interior inspects the prison? Why would he take special note of the bust of Beethoven in Alex's cell?

> "Soon we'll need all our prisons for political prisoners." What does this imply about the true aim of all governments?

> "He's bold, enterprising, vicious"—Why is the Minister so *pleased* about finding Alex?

28. "An eye for an eye"—Why does the warden disapprove of reforming criminals? Why would he say it's unjust to turn bad into good?

29. Unlike the prison guards, the doctors who impose the Lodovico treatment are completely pleasant and technocratic. Why would Alex assume he can con them too—and why is he mistaken?

30. "It's funny how the colors of the real world only look real when you see them on the screen." Alex is impressed with the realism of the doctors' films. Why wouldn't it occur to him that the films *are* real?

> Dr. Branom: "You felt ill yesterday because you're getting better." What is the effect of the low-angle shot of her hate-filled face?

31. What is ironic about juxtaposing Beethoven's Ode to Joy against documentary films of the Nazi invasion?

> Why the cut to the closeup of Alex's *eye?* What is the meaning of his "primal scream?"

"It's a sin!"—Why the puzzled reaction from the doctors?

By wiping out Alex's love of violence they also destroy his love of music. What does this imply about the relationship of violence and creativity?

32. Why does Kubrick depict Alex's reformation on a *stage?* What is the significance of his licking the bully's shoe and falling at the girl's feet? What do the bows and applause imply about society?

Why does the Chaplain raise the question of *choice?* Why does the Minister contradict him, insisting that Alex will be the "ideal Christian?"

33. Alex goes home to P and M: What is the purpose of the tasteless decor and his mother's short red dress? How is Joe, the lodger, a mirror image of Alex? What is the significance of Alex's father being such a weakling?

34. On the bridge, Alex meets the Old Drunk again. What does his being beaten by the old men symbolize? What is the purpose of the hallucinatory perspective that makes them look like grotesques from a Bosch painting?

35. What is the significance of Dim and Georgie's new jobs? Why would they "baptize" him? What is the effect of the synthesized chords?

36. As lightning flashes, how does Alex's return "Home" reflect the Hindu idea of *karma?*

While Alex sings "Singing in the Rain," what is the purpose of the low-angle shot of Mr. Alexander in his wheelchair? What is ironic about Mr. Alexander's describing him as a "victim of the modern age"?

37. It's obvious that the Opposition Party is merely using Alex for political purposes. As they play the Ninth Symphony through the floor, note that Mr. Alexander looks like Beethoven. What is the significance of the politician's playing with the *pool balls?* Why does Kubrick juxtapose this game against Alex jumping out the window?

38. "I came back after a black gap of what might have been a million years." In a cast from head to toe, how does the mummified Alex symbolize the human race?

Why does Kubrick include the sequence of the half-dressed doctor and nurse? How are they like the other authority figures in the film?

39. Alex's mother's *hair* matches his father's lavender suit. Also note "Eat Me" in the picnic basket. How do these details undercut the sentimental tone of the dialogue?

40. Why does Alex's psychiatrist respond so sweetly to his violent reaction to her pictures? Why is his "recovery" ironic?

41. What does the Minister's *spoon-feeding* him symbolize?

42. "I was cured all right . . . " What does Alex's final hallucination imply?

THE LAST PICTURE SHOW (1971—American) Directed by Peter Bogdanovich; with Timothy Bottoms, Jeff Bridges, Ellen Burstyn, Cloris Leachman, Ben Johnson, and Cybill Shepherd. Distributed by RBC Films.

1. The film opens with shots of the gas pedal and the cracked windshield of Sonny's truck. What does the broken pedal symbolize? How does the circular crack in the windshield foreshadow Billy's death?

2. Early in the film, we see a scene from *Father of the Bride* (1950). What are some of the ironies in comparing Jacy with Liz Taylor as the "prospective bride?"

3. Later in the film, we see the closing scene of *Red River* (1948). How does the cattle drive allude to Billy's death, and what is the significance of this?

4. We also see and/or hear two television shows, one of which is called *Strike It Rich*. How does that title comment on the main story?

5. By 1951 most American homes had TV sets, and theaters were closing all over the country. What changes did this cause in our society? What does the closing of a small town's only theater symbolize for Bogdanovich?

6. At the pond, Sam tells Sonny about his past affair with Jacy's mother, Lois. This is preceded and followed by events at the swimming pool. How do these two bodies of water symbolically contrast? How does Jacy's performance on the diving board characterize her?

7. Since most of the action involves sex, it would not be surprising to find Freudian symbolism in the film. For instance—

> (a) What are the connotations of Jacy's losing her virginity (on the second try!) at the *Cactus* Motel?

> (b) Why does Jacy seduce Abilene, her mother's lover? Why does Bogdanovich set the seduction in the *pool hall?* (Note that she grasps the cue as the scene fades out.)

> (c) When Sonny and Ruth Popper first kiss, they are stuffing garbage into a can. What does this juxtaposition imply?

> (d) "Drill hard—you're better at oil wells anyway," says Lois to Abilene. What are the sexual connotations of oil wells, and what does this imply about Texan culture?

8. As the teacher tries to interest the class in the romantic poetry of Keats, why does Bogdanovich intercut the shots of the students passing a dirty book around, Jacy primping, and dogs copulating in the yard? What is the effect of the abrupt cut to Coach Popper bellowing "Run, you little pissheads!"?

9. At a football game late in the film, Coach Popper tells a linesman that you should never cheat—unless it's for a good cause. Why is it ironic that Sonny is listening? Why is the coach's name itself ironic?

10. Why does the film open and close with the same shot?

MURMUR OF THE HEART (1971—French) Directed by Louis Malle. Distributed by Walter Reade 16.

1. The film is set in Dijon in 1954, the year the French were expelled from Dien Bien Phu. Why, in 1971, would Malle make a film that hints constantly at defeat in Viet Nam? Where do his political sympathies lie? In his cynicism about religion and politics, how is Laurent (age 15) like young Americans in the seventies?

2. Although Laurent comes from a wealthy family, he "collects" for Indochina and steals records. Why? Although these are common activities among teenaged boys, why wouldn't a Hollywood film depict a young "hero" indulging in petty thievery?

3. Laurent is de-pantsed by his older brothers. As they "measure," the maid comes in. Again, why would this scene *not* appear in a Hollywood film? Why are French films more realistic in their depiction of teenagers?

4. What is ironic about Laurent's being an *altar boy?* The other boy munches communion wafers. Laurent's response: "Sacrilege doesn't interest me; to blaspheme means you still believe." Why is this so?

5. While walking with his little friend, Laurent sees his mother meet her lover. How does this affect him, and why?

6. Politics at the dinner table: the boys don't give a damn. Why not?

7. In the confession scene, the priest fondles him after asking him about his masturbatory habits. Why is Laurent so calm? Why does Malle include this scene? What is the implication of the print of Michelangelo's "God Touching Adam" hanging in the background?

8. Laurent's brothers play "spinach tennis." How does this game characterize them?

9. Laurent's brothers take him to the Sporting House. How does their behavior there characterize their relationship? Why are brothers frequently so cruel to each other?

10. Boy Scout Camp: How is the STORY OF THE ERL KING a metaphor for Laurent's inner problem?

11. What is the double meaning in Laurent's having a "heart murmur?" ("aortic insufficiency" in medical jargon)

12. Laurent and his brother play chess while their parents watch TV. How does this distinguish them. Why is it ironic that the father considers the two older brothers stupid?

13. Slicing the Corot: To what extent is the value of art just "capitalist speculation?" Why is it common for children in upper-middle-class families to parrot marxist ideas?

14. The Health Spa: Laurent and his mother are hopelessly bad tennis players. Why is this so endearing?

"You're flirting with a Royalist..." Why does Laurent *really* dislike Hubert?

15. Laurent's mother accuses him of being a "prying husband." Why are sons often more jealous and possessive than husbands?

16. Laurent is shocked that his mother is reading *The Story of O*. Why, when he has obviously read it himself?

17. Laurent stares as his mother lies naked in her bathtub. What is the significance of her reaction?

18. When Laurent's mother leaves with her lover, why does he lay out her underwear, stockings, and dress on his bed? Why does he try on her mascara and improvise a dialogue between his mother and her lover?

19. Hubert insists that France could have kept Viet Nam with American help. Why is this ironic?

20. What is the significance of all the references to *Proust?* How is Laurent like Proust as he depicts himself in *Remembrance of Times Past?*

21. Laurent's mother tells him that she left her lover because he wanted her to get a divorce. He didn't understand that "there are different ways of loving..." Laurent replies, "You'll find someone who loves you as you are." Why is this an unusual conversation for a mother and a son?

22. What is the significance of the *card game* that Hubert can't understand?

23. What is the symbolic function of the "Bastille Day" celebration? How does it relate to the themes of revolution and generational conflict?

24. After leaving his mother's room, why does Laurent go immediately to Helen? Then to Daphne?

25. Laurent appears, shoes in hand, as his father and brothers laugh. Why is this ironic?

WALKABOUT (1971—English) Directed by Nicholas Roeg; with Jenny Agutter, David Gumpilil, and Lucien John. Produced by Twentieth Century Fox; distributed by Films Inc.

1. How do the opening shots characterize the Modern City? (Note the stark white concrete and glass)

> The Girl's music class: Is their "breathing exercise" supposed to be primitive or absurd?

> Why are the trees in the park all labeled? What does this symbolize?

> As the boy leaves school, how does the parabolic shot of the giant tree assert the dreamlike nature of city life?

> The cheerful voice on the radio describes a "civilized" delicacy: a bird drowned in cognac, after it has stuffed itself with grain by trying to peck its way through to a light, which it thinks is the sun. How does this foreshadow their wandering in the desert? How is the bird like the human race in Plato's allegory of the cave?

2. HOW DOES THE PICNIC IN THE DESERT SYMBOLIZE WESTERN CULTURE?

> The radio chatters on: "You must distinguish between the fish fork and the meat fork." Immediately, the father turns and says, "Don't talk with your mouth full, son." What is the significance of this obsession with etiquette?

> Why does Roeg cut from the volkswagen to the hissing lizard? Why does he include so many shots of insects, scorpions, and lizards?

> After a silent meal, the Boy plays with his plane and water gun. What do these "war games" symbolize?

"The wheel's come off!"—In what sense does this also describe his father?

As the father shoots at them, he insists with cold malevolence: "... and bring *him* with you. It's getting late." Why doesn't Roeg provide motivation for the father's shooting himself and setting the car on fire? How might this scene be an *allegory* about the fall of Western Civilization?

3. CROSSING THE DESERT is the Girl's only alternative to leading her little brother back past their father's burning body. Apparently she doesn't know how far they'll have to walk to cross the Australian outback ... Or else Roeg wants her to reflect the western obsession with always pushing forward, away from our dead gods.

Why does Roeg dress them in private school uniforms?

Why do they carry their *radio* with them, and what does this symbolize?

The Boy finally lies down in the sand and plays with his car. How does he foreshadow the fate of California Culture?

4. What does the OASIS, with its fruit tree and parakeets, symbolize?

What is the significance of the *mechanical boat* (which is finally stranded in the mud)?

Why does Roeg cut from the radio program ("Captain Steel in another episode of 'Enemy'...") to a flashback of the Father in the burning car? How does this reflect the Aborigine concept of the "Dream Time?"

What is the significance of the oasis drying up? How does this foreshadow the future of the human race?

Why does Roeg cut from the parabolic shot of them lying there like corpses to a closeup of a large lizard eating a smaller one?

The electronic music (and noise) in the background stops dead when the Aborigine appears. What is the effect of the silence?

5. The ABORIGINE approaches with lizards (crawling with flies) hanging from his belt. Why does Roeg deliberately make his first appearance so disgusting to civilized eyes?

What is the significance of the Girl's attempt to communicate in *English* ("Where do they keep the water?")?

6. Why does Roeg intercut the shots of the Aborigine bashing kangaroos and the the butcher in the shop cutting chops? Why does he add the cut from the rabbit cooking to the volkswagen burning?

7. Why does the Aborigine put the little boy in the tree?

Note the sexual connotations of the tree limbs...

Why does Roeg intercut shots of the aborigines playing in the burned VW? (Note that the radio scares them: "If you have a good low-mileage car you'd like to sell...")

How does the Father in the tree foreshadow the Aborigine's death? In both cases, what is the significance of their crucified positions?

8. During the dreamlike shots of the sunrise, why does Roeg dub over the garbled radio transmission and the Father's voice saying "Come out now, and bring *him* with you..."?

9. As the Girl parades under her parasol, her little brother tells a story about a little boy who fell and broke his neck. Notice that she keeps correcting him, explaining that the Aborigine doesn't understand. Why does Roeg include this pointless story and their petty argument over its plot? Is there some symbolic connection between the story and the Aborigine's relationship with the Girl?

10. THE SACRED DRAWINGS: What is the significance of the Aborigine's painting their bodies?

"I think he's going to take us to Mars."—In what sense is this true? How does this line serve as a transition to the shot of the RED WEATHER BALLOON?

11. Why does Roeg include the scene with the researchers? Note how the men react when the lady crosses her legs... How does this scene parody Federico Fellini? How does it act as a *comic analogue* to the tragic relationship between the Girl and the Aborigine?

12. In a field of ashes (sulphur?), the Aborigine finds the red and black balloons. As the boy says "we'll be there today," the black balloon floats up. How does this foreshadow the end of the film?

13. What does the abandoned farmhouse surrounded by ant-cones symbolize?

14. After the discovery of the road, which is a symbol of civilization, why does Roeg include the scene with the White Hunter?

> What is the purpose of the freeze-frame repetitions of the buffalo's death and the startled reactions of the other animals?

> The Aborigine's reaction: Why does he walk past her without speaking? What has he realized about *her* civilization, and how does this motivate the scene that follows?

15. What is the symbolic purpose of the shots of the dead buffalo covered with maggots, the field of bones, and the Aborigine lying there painted like a skeleton?

> WHAT DOES HIS DANCE MEAN, AND WHY DOESN'T SHE UNDERSTAND? (...Or does she?)

16. WHY DOES HE KILL HIMSELF? (Don't assume the obvious. The fruit beneath his feet and hanging from the tree may suggest the aborigine ritual of seeking a new identity in the "Dream Time." This might be his only alternative after rejection by his "mate.")

17. THE ABANDONED MINING TOWN: What is the significance of the white man's lack of hospitality? ("Don't touch anything—it's private property!")

> What does all the *rusting machinery* symbolize? ("What's in the mine?" "Nothing. That's why they shut it.")

18. What is the effect of the cut from the rusty wagon crashing to the shot of her young husband?

> Note that he works in the same building her father worked in, and that they live in the same house. What does this imply?

> Why does Roeg intercut her husband's chatter about his new job and higher salary with her memories of swimming with the Aborigine?

Why does Roeg end with a quote about "the land of lost content"? Like all of Roeg's films, how does *Walkabout* deal with a "fall from innocence"?

CRIES AND WHISPERS (1972—Swedish) Directed by Ingmar Bergman; with Harriet Andersson (Agnes), Liv Ullman (Maria), Ingrid Thulin (Karin), and Kari Sylwan (Anna, the maid); cinematography by Sven Nykvist. Produced by New World Pictures; distributed by Films Inc.

1. Why does Bergman open with shots of light streaming through the trees, juxtaposed against closeups of a baroque clock?

2. How does the long, silent closeup of Agnes in pain contrast with the opening shots?

3. Why does Bergman dress the sisters in *white,* and place them in an *all red* room? How are they like ghosts in hell, or like characters in Poe's *Masque of the Red Death?*

> Note that the style of this film is *expressionistic,* highly reminiscent of Edvard Munch's painting, "Virginia Creeper." Also, Bergman once said in an interview that he always visualized the "membrane of the soul" as *red.*

4. What does the *doll's house* symbolize? (cf. the play by Henrik Ibsen, who wrote about the same kinds of relationships as Bergman.) Why the shot of Maria sucking her thumb?

5. The maid prays, then lustily eats an apple. How does this reveal the two sides of her nature?

6. In a transition to the past, Maria reminisces about her mother (who is also played by Liv Ullman). Why does Bergman have Liv Ullman play both parts? How does this explain Karin's sullen resentment, Maria's childishness, and Agnes' self-sufficiency?

7. Why does Maria try to seduce the doctor, and why does he resist? Why is his analysis of her indifference so accurate? (Maria: "You see it in yourself.")

> Why does her husband stab himself?

8. What is the significance of the love scene between Agnes and Anna? What does Anna symbolize?

9. What is the effect of the sudden cross-cut to Agnes in pain, unable to breathe?

10. What is the point of all the *ifs* in the priest's prayer over Agnes' body? Why has her suffering shaken his faith?

11. In the flashback to the BROKEN WINEGLASS scene, why does Karin's husband ignore the broken glass? What does the glass symbolize?

> "It's nothing but a tissue of lies ... " What does "it" refer to? How does her shocking gesture comment on the nature of sexuality?

12. Maria wants to be friends with Karin. What is the significance of their estrangement? Why does Karin hate any kind of contact (or say she does)?

> "I can't breathe any more because of all the guilt ... " How does this relate to her dead sister's illness?

13. Why does Karin say she hates Maria? Why is this outburst necessary before she can show real affection? Why the *cello* rather than the words of their affectionate conversation?

14. Anna: "There's someone weeping all the time. Can't you hear?" What is the significance of the subliminal weeping on the sound track as Anna goes back and forth between Maria and Karin?

15. Anna regards her hallucinatory conversation with the dead Agnes as "only a dream." Agnes wants Karin to hold her hands "until the horror disappears."

> Why would Karin refuse to have anything to do with her death?

> Agnes then asks Anna to bring Maria—who freaks out as Agnes' arms wrap around her neck and won't let go. How does this reflect Maria's fear of commitment?

Anna takes their place in the famous shot of her holding
Agnes in her arms. What is the *religious* connotation of his
pose?

16. The Funeral: Karin's icy husband offers Anna a token remembrance.
Why would she refuse it?

17. Karin: "You touched me. Don't you remember?"
Maria: "I can't remember every silly thing."

One assumes that Maria and Karin would become closer as a
result of their sister's death? What is the significance of their
failure to love each other?

18. Anna opens Agnes' diary: "It's wonderful to come together, like in the
old days...three good little sisters in white, sitting in the swing."

What is the significance of this "moment of perfection?"
Why is it ironic that Agnes, in her pain, would be the only
one capable of such humanity?

How does her death illustrate the philosophical "Problem of
Evil?"

HAROLD AND MAUDE (1972—American) Directed by Hal
Ashby; with Bud Cort and Ruth Gordon; screenplay by Colin Higgins;
music by Cat Stevens. Produced by Colin Higgins and Paramount
Pictures; distributed by Films Inc.

1. In the opening sequence, what does the wrought iron staircase
symbolize? Why does Ashby deliberately undercut the spooky atmosphere
with cheerful music by Cat Stevens? How does this set the tone for the rest
of the film?

Note the back-lighting and the stained glass as Harold lights
the candle. How is his ritual like a religious offering?

2. Harold's mother enters and calmly picks up the phone to cancel her hairdresser's appointment, pausing only briefly to say, "I suppose you think that's very funny." How does her stuffy reaction explain Harold's "suicides?" How does Harold's *position* in this sequence symbolize his family life?

3. The formal dinner: How is Harold's mother characterized by her endless chatter and her *wig?* Why does Ashby cut from Harold gobbling his *beets* to the blood-splattered bathroom?

4. Note that Harold and his psychiatrist are dressed exactly the same. What does this imply?

> "What gives you that special satisfaction?" "I go to funerals."
> What is the effect of Harold's monotone? Why is it unlikely
> that this psychiatrist will be able to help him?

5. Why does Harold buy the old hearse? What is the significance of his mother's reaction ("You can have any car you want . . . but that black monster is an eyesore.")

6. Why is it ironic that Harold's Uncle Victor was General MacArthur's "right-hand" man? What is the effect of the Nixon poster on the wall, and of Victor's artificial salute to *Nathan Hale?* How is Harold himself a parody of Nathan Hale?

7. What is the purpose of the classical music as Harold's mother goes for her swim? What is the significance of her ignoring Harold's floating body?

8. Harold's mother informs him of his *duty* to get married. How does the cross-cut to the *stained glass* serve as a transition from this discussion of *marriage* to Harold's favorite activity—funerals—and the minister intoning about the "bottomless pit?" What does this juxtaposition imply about weddings and funerals?

> From a rear pew, Maude tries to get Harold's attention:
> "Would you like some licorice?" How does her enjoyment of
> funerals differ from his?

> "I'll be eighty next week—good timing, don't you think?"
> How does this foreshadow the end of the film?

> What is the effect of the high school band marching by as the
> casket is carried out?

9. Harold's mother fills out the questionnaire for "computer dating." What is the significance of her actually answering all the questions *herself?*

> As she reads, "Do you believe in life after death," Harold loads a pistol and aims it at her. On "Did you have a happy childhood?" he turns the gun on himself and pulls the trigger. How do Harold's actions comment on the questionnaire?

10. Harold meets Maude at another funeral. How does her reckless driving reflect her lifestyle?

11. Maude lives in an old railway car. What does this symbolize? How does her overdecorated setting correspond to her inner life?

12. As Harold lies there like a corpse, his psychiatrist informs him that his mother is arranging dates for him. How does Harold's posture in this sequence communicate his attitude toward girls?

13. While Harold's first date laughs about her brother (a real comedian!) doing a newscast through an old TV, Harold sets himself on fire. How does his performance as a Buddhist monk comment on her story?

14. How does Maude's art collection characterize her—especially her "tactile" abstract sculpture and her machine that projects various smells? What is the effect of the *whistling kettle* as she urges him to caress and explore?

15. When Maude asks, "What do you do when you aren't visiting funerals?" Ashby cuts to a wrecking crew demolishing a building. Symbolically, why would this activity appeal to Harold?

16. Maude, in contrast, likes to "watch things grow." What does the field of daisies symbolize? They seem to be all the same, but they're all very different. Why does Maude say that this is the cause of the world's trouble?

> Why does Ashby cut from the daisy field to Golden Gate Cemetary? Why is the music—Cat Stevens singing "Where Do the Children Play?"—ironic?

17. Maude decides to transplant the tree from the city street to the forest. What does this act symbolize? How does it reflect her relationship with Harold?

18. Maude reminisces about her childhood in Vienna, and about going to dances at the palace. Her husband had been a doctor at the university.

What happened to all that, and how does this explain her anti-authoritarian attitudes?

19. What is the significance of the song Maude plays at the piano about human possibilities? Why does she insist that he must be able to play *something?* What does the *banjo* symbolize?

20. As Harold practices his banjo, his mother surprises him with a little present—a new jaguar. How do the two presents contrast?

21. When Harold and Maude drive across the Dumbarton Bridge with the rescued tree, a cop stops them: "Do you have a license, lady?" Why would Maude say, "I don't believe in them"? What does her driving circles around the cop symbolize?

> As Maude drives back from planting the tree, they run into the same cop, who charges them with "possession of stolen shovel." Why is Maude's method of escape funny and incongruous?

22. As they smoke hashish, Harold worries about indulging in vices. Why does he say that he has never lived?

> Harold tells Maude about his first brush with death in a school chemistry lab. His mother collapsed on hearing about the accident. How does this explain his subsequent "suicides?"

23. How does Harold and Maude's *waltz* contrast with his second date (She "supplies the whole southwest with chicken feed")?

> What does Harold's chopping off his hand on the table symbolize?

24. Why does Uncle Victor complain that we're not enemies with the Germans anymore? Why are the ruins of the Sutro Baths an appropriate setting for Victor's war stories?

> What is the tone of the sequence in which Harold raves about the "the taste of blood" and souvenirs of combat?

> "She took my shrunken head!"—How is Harold and Maude's masquerade designed to exempt him from military service?

25. Harold and Maude sit among the sculptures in the Berkeley mudflats. Why would this setting appeal to Maude? As Harold says his mother has arranged another date for him, why does Ashby cut briefly to a *number* tatooed on Maude's wrist?

Why would Hitler have approved of "computer dating?"

Why does Ashby cut immediately to Maude pointing at the seagulls?

26. Harold's date with "Sunshine": What is Harold insinuating in asking her, "Do you *enjoy* knives?" What is the effect of the creaking door? Why would she attempt to imitate his demonstration of hara-kiri, and what is ironic about her reciting Juliet's lines so badly?

27. The Amusement Park: how are Harold and Maude characterized by watching toy trains and playing with pinball machines?

Maude says Harold's ring is "the nicest present I've received in years." Why does she throw it in the bay?

28. How does the shot of the *fireworks* serve as a symbolic transition to Harold in bed, *blowing bubbles*, with Maude beside him? How do the two symbols relate?

29. When Harold announces that he's getting married, note the reactions of his three "father figures." How does the revelation of Uncle Victor's *last name* comment on Harold's announcement? How does the psychiatrist's analysis satirize Freudian psychology? (Note the portrait of Freud hanging behind him!) What is the significance of the minister's disgust? Why do most religions equate sin with *sex*, when there are obviously so many worse things happening in the world?

30. "Happy Birthday, Maude"—Why has Harold decorated the whole place with *sunflowers?*

"I couldn't imagine a lovelier farewell..." Why does Maude plan this particular finale? How does her attitude toward death differ from Harold's?

31. As Harold drives, Ashby intercuts shots of the hospital. What is the point of all the *paperwork?* Instead of dialogue, why does Ashby use Cat Stevens singing "Trouble" throughout this sequence?

32. What does the drive over the cliff and the *pan-up* mean?

33. What does the final banjo solo symbolize?

PLAY IT AGAIN, SAM (1972—American) Directed by Herbert Ross; with Woody Allen, Diane Keaton, Tony Roberts, Susan Anspach, and Jerry Lacy. Filmed in San Francisco. Produced by Paramount.

1. How does the title relate to Alan's hopeless love life? Why does the film start with the ending from *Casablanca?*

2. What is wrong with Alan's relationship with his wife, Nancy? (While they made love, "she used to watch TV and change channels with the remote.")

3. What is the significance of Dick's always being on the phone (even in bed)? Why is this funnier with each repetition?

4. Linda: "Can't you cook anything but TV dinners?"
Alan: "Who cooks them? I suck them frozen." How does this metaphor characterize Alan's bachelorhood?

5. Dick tells Alan, "You've invested your emotions in a losing stock." What does this metaphor reveal about Dick's view of love? (Note Alan's reply: "Who are you going to fix me up with—General Motors?")

6. Alan fantasizes about Nancy riding on a motorcycle with a Hell's Angel: "We're divorced two weeks and she's dating a Nazi." Why would his fantasy take this particular form?

7. When Alan complains, "Why can't I be cool? What's the secret?" his hallucination of Humphrey Bogart answers: "Dames are simple...I've never met one who didn't understand a slap in the mouth or a slug from a 45." Why is Alan's Bogart imitation funny? How does the contrast between Bogart and Woody Allen illustrate the change in values between 1940 and the present? What are the main differences between their world-views? In particular, how do they differ in their idea of what it means to be a Man?

8. How do Alan's performances with the hairdryer and the medicine cabinet establish his character as a *schlemiel?* What is the significance of his putting his jacket on backwards?

9. His date with Sharon: Why does he knock something over every time he makes a move (cf. the record over his shoulder)? Note how Sharon reacts to

his instruction on how to eat rice. Why is it funny that Alan thinks Sharon likes him?

10. Linda: "That's not real life; you set too high a standard." "You don't have to 'pick' anybody—you're you." In what sense is Linda the film's *raisonneur?* Why would Woody Allen put his "message" in the mouth of a neurotic female?

11. His date with Jennifer: After talking interminably about how sex is the only thing that interests her, she pushes him away: "What do you take me for?" Why is this predictable?

12. Alan tries to pick up the girl in front of the JACKSON POLLOCK in the San Franciso museum. When he asks her what this painting means to her, she replies, "It restates the negativeness of the universe . . ." How does this sequence satirize art criticism?

13. His date with Julie: "Let's get stoned and watch the freaks." Why is it predictable that his date will wind up as it does? What is funny about Alan's confrontation with the Hell's Angels?

14. Why is Alan's relationship with Linda so good? ("There's no pressure with Linda—I'm not trying to make her.")

> How do the cross-cuts between Dick's business deals and Alan's conversations with Linda establish the inevitability of their falling in love?

> "Just be yourself; the girls will fall in love with you."

> Why would Linda love the plastic skunk Alan gives her?

15. Alan's hallucinatory conversation with his ex-wife, Nancy:
"You're a dreamer—you're awkward and clumsy."
"Face it, Alan—you're sweet, but you're not very sexy."
Why does Woody Allen fill his films with such devastating self-criticisms?

16. In the supermarket, Nancy and Bogart argue about whether Alan should get involved with Linda. What does the *setting* symbolize?

17. Why the hallucinatory wide-angle perspective in the scene in which Alan imagines Dick leaving permanently for Alaska?

18. Why is the love scene funny?

19. Why does Linda ask Alan, "Do you think it's possible to love two people at once?" Why does her question take him by surprise?

20. Linda's comments on *rape:* Why are they funny? What questions would they raise in Alan's mind? Is this deliberate or unconscious on her part?

21. What is the effect of the frequent interruptions (e.g. Bogart's advice, Nancy's sudden appearance, the ringing phone, etc.)?

22. Why does Linda react as she does to the breaking of the lamp?

23. What is the *tone* of all the intercut shots of Alan and Bogart kissing the heroine?

24. Linda: "What did you think about while we were making love?" Alan replies, "Willy Mays." How does this response characterize him?

25. Alan's fantasies about how Dick will react: (a) two English noblemen in a stuffy British club, (b) the self-sacrificing husband walking into the sea ("A Star is Born")—both wish-fulfillments contradicted by (c) a revenge episode from an Italian neo-realist film set in a pizza parlor. Why are his fantasies all based on *films?*

26. In real life, Alan is surprised by running into Dick on a street in North Beach . . . "I've neglected her, and now she's involved with some stud." Why is Dick suddenly "in love" with his wife?

27. On the road to the airport: Why are Bogart's demonstrations of how to break up with Linda *funny?* What is the purpose of the distorted perspectives and the melodramatic lighting?

> (On the serious level, note that the *real* lesson of Humphrey Bogart emerges from this scene: "You're passing up a real tomato because you don't want to hurt a guy." How does this force Alan's hand?)

28. "Alan, do you realize what a wonderful thing has happened?"
"Linda, we have to call it quits."
"Yes, I know." Her response surprises him. How does he *expect* her to react?

29. Alan: "It's from *Casablanca*—I've waited my whole life to say it." Notice that every detail, even the cross-cut to the plane starting, parallels the ending of *Casablanca*. In what sense has Alan achieved a genuine identification with his hero in this scene?

30. When Bogart tells Alan that this is "the start of a beautiful friendship," what does he imply about Alan's past fantasies? Why is it likely that Alan will begin to relate to women more successfully?

THE RULING CLASS (1972—English) Directed by Peter Medak; with Peter O'Toole as Jesus and Jack the Ripper. Distributed by Westcoast Films.

1. How is this film a *triple allegory* with political, psychological, and religious overtones?

2. What is the function of the *gavel* that starts the film? How does it relate to the opening of a traditional English play? If this is a religious allegory, how does it establish the film as a symbolic Last Judgment on the human race?

3. In his anti-anarchist speech, Lord Gurney describes England as "this teeming womb of privilege." Why is this metaphor ironic?

4. How does the music ("God Save the Queen") prepare us for Lord Gurney's night-time ritual?

> He flings his clothes on the floor as he talks about the deaths of his sons. How do his gestures reflect the feeling behind his soliloquy? If Jack is the last remaining male heir, what does this suggest about the English aristocracy?

> What is the significance of Lord Gurney's being a *judge?* What does his tray of nooses suggest about the relation of judge and criminal? Like the judge in Genet's *The Balcony,* his entire life is a fantasy. How does his poetic language reveal this?

> How is he like an Old Testament God? How does his accidental death reflect Nietzsche's idea that "God is dead?"

5. Reading the Will: What is the effect of Tucker's tap dance? What is the function of the musical numbers in the film? How is this similar to Brecht's use of music in his "epic theatre"?

6. The camera zooms out as Jack announces his divinity. What is the effect of the *jump-cut* to Dr. Herder calmly asserting that "his lordship is a paranoiac schizophrenic"?

Dr. Herder's explanation of Jack's schizophrenia: "Jack's parents sent him at an early age to a primitive community of licensed bullies and pederasts." "You mean the public schools?"

Aside from the modern non-family, why is mass education the main cause of insanity in the world today?

7. When Jack is asked how he *knows* he's God, he replies, "When I pray, I find I'm talking to myself." What does this line imply about religion?

8. Whenever J.C. feels paranoiac, he climbs onto his cross. What is the significance of this?

9. J.C.'s Song and Dance: Why are the church ladies disturbed by his declaration that "God is Love"?

10. Dr. Herder: "If he ever answers to the name Jack, he's on the road to sanity." In light of the film's ending, why is this ironic? What does it imply about "normalcy" in the ruling class?

11. What do you think of Tucker's analysis: "The Gurneys are all crazy because they don't have any *work*...""?

12. Why does J.C. fantasize about being married to Marguerite Gauthier of *Traviata?*

When Grace Shelley appears singing and J.C. joins her in a duet, the scene instantly changes to a ballroom with crystal chandeliers. How does this transformation reflect the workings of J.C.'s fevered imagination?

What is the significance of this love-fantasy being engineered by Charles?

Like many films adapted from plays, *The Ruling Class* depends on its dialogue. Note all the implications in the repartee: Charles asks Grace, "Can you handle a man who thinks he's God?" She replies, "It happens all the time." What does this suggest about English noblemen, and about the male species in general?

Charles says to his son, "This is no *game,* sir—this is *real!*" What does this imply about the relationship of "games" and "real life"?

13. J.C. and Grace's Love Scene: What is the significance of their "bird act?" Why is he able to draw her into his fantasy?

> They sing "My Blue Heaven" while prancing through a formal garden. How does this sequence satirize thirties love-films?

> When Dimmesdale tells J.C. who Grace really is, why does he have a paranoiac attack and climb on his cross?

14. Dr. Herder wants a Guggenheim fellowship to study paranoiac-schizophrenic rats. What is being satirized here?

> Why does Medak cross-cut between Charles plotting with the bishop and Dr. Herder injecting a rat and explaining the chemical origin of schizophrenia?

> Claire easily seduces Dr. Herder, for whom the only "commandment" is "thou shalt not advertise." What does this imply about the medical profession?

15. J.C. blesses everyone and leaps from his cross. Why is the freeze-frame an appropriate transition to the wedding ceremony?

> On the wedding night, why does Medak juxtapose Grace's strip against J.C.'s entrance on a tricycle?

> J.C. and Grace reach toward each other while the orchestra blares away. How does this satirize Hollywood love movies?

16. Despite her original plot, why does Grace wind up falling in love with J.C.?

17. While Dr. Herder tries to cure J.C. with ink blot and lie detector tests, J.C. converts the lunatics. What does this say about the relative power of psychoanalysis and religion?

18. LIGHTNING provides the transition to Grace's labor pains, which J.C. shares. In what sense is this entire scene about birth, death, and rebirth?

> Dr. Herder wants J.C. to see the world in the "hard light of truth." Considering the outcome of this experiment, what does the film imply about the moral consequences of this obsession with "absolute truth?"

What is the significance of J.C.'s confrontation with the HIGH-VOLTAGE MESSIAH, who believes that "no God of love made this world ... "? How are they like Jesus and Jehovah? How does this confrontation reflect the dialectic in religions, both ancient and modern, between gods of love and gods of revenge?

Dr. Herder insists, "It's important to know which of you is telling the truth." How does this characterize the scientific attitude?

Why does Medak cross-cut from the Ape in the Top Hat to Grace giving birth to the baby being slapped on the rear?

At the moment his son is born, J.C. whispers, "JACK ... MY NAME IS JACK ... " What is the significance of this double birth? If all things give birth to their opposites, how do you expect Jack to change in the course of the film?

19. THE BURNING CROSS is a transition to the New Jack. What does this symbolize?

How is Jack characterized by the cross-cut from *baptism* to *haircut?*

While Dr. Herder brags about his "cure," Jack aims a shotgun at them. What does this imply about the results of psychoanalysis?

Jack calmly explains, "I've learned the RULES OF THE GAME." What is the purpose of this reference to Renoir's classic thirties film?

If "it's a sign of normalcy in our circle to slaughter anything that moves," what is the film implying about the "normal" man in our society?

20. When everyone leaves, Jack launches into his frightening soliloquy. What is the significance of his stammering? In a shot reminiscent of Hitchcock or Bergman, a flock of crows suddenly bursts from the tree—what does this symbolize?

21. Jack meets the Master of Lunacy. What does their old school rowing song imply about English education?

22. In the attic, Jack removes two masks and quotes Shakespeare's *Richard III,* describing himself as "deformed, unfinished, sent into this world scarce

half made up..." What is the significance of his confession? Why would someone who thinks he's Jesus Christ be likely to turn into Jack the Ripper?

23. At the hunting lodge, Jack makes a speech on the necessity of fear and punishment to hold society together. Why do people like Jack the Ripper always insist that crime be punished severely?

> What is the effect of the audience's suddenly bursting into song ("Disconnect them bones... and hear the word of the lord")?

> In the middle of the hunt, the fox stops to take a leak. How does this comment on Jack's speech?

24. Why does Medak transform the projected background to nineteenth century London as Claire tries to seduce Jack?

> "I always wanted the real thing." In what sense will she achieve her desire? ("Make me immortal with a kiss.")

> Why has Jack developed an intense hatred of women?

25. "Trust God's judgment." What is ironic in the bishop's leaning on Jack? In what sense does Jack still believe he's God?

> Why is Jack always quoting the Old Testament ("If thy hand offend thee, cut it off.")? How does this explain his betrayal of Tuck?

26. What does Jack's duel with Dr. Herder symbolize? ("You cured me! I was a pale moon-looney, and you turned me into a murderer.") Why does Dr. Herder go crazy?

27. Grace: "You were more loving when you were potty." What is the significance of his impotence? In what sense is his shriek a "primal scream?"

28. POMP AND CIRCUMSTANCE: What does Medak imply by the cross-cuts between Charles and the bishop being wheeled into the asylum, Dr. Herder in electroshock, and Jack being robed in parliament?

29. IN THE HOUSE OF LORDS, Jack kisses the bible and takes his oath. Why is this ironic?

> Note the speeches about increasing immorality, and the complaints about the demise of hanging and flogging. How does this characterize the English aristocracy?

While Jack speaks, why does his audience transform into a gallery of skeletons? What is the political implication of this?

"This is where I belong"—Why would Jack the Ripper feel perfectly comfortable in the House of Lords?

Jack berates his new colleagues: "You have forgotten how to punish," and he explains "the law of the universe: the strong survive, the weak soften into corruption." How has his world-view changed since the beginning of the film, and why?

What is the significance of their applause, and of their bursting into song with "ONWARD CHRISTIAN SOLDIERS"?

30. The ending is quite theatrical: a black background with Grace in the spotlight singing a love song. Why does Medak juxtapose her shriek, the baby's cry, and the childlike voice: "I'm Jack"? How does Jack symbolize the human race?

31. After such a chilling ending, why does Medak dub the "Varsity Rag" over an aerial shot of the castle?

AGUIRRE, THE WRATH OF GOD (1973—German) Directed by Werner Herzog; with Klaus Kinski. Distributed by New Yorker Films.

1. *Aguirre* is set in 1560, during Pizarro's conquest of Peru. Why does Herzog use the monk, Fr. Gaspar, as his *persona?*

2. The opening shot: What does the *fog,* moving into the valley in slow motion, symbolize?

3. Pizarro's army marches down a steep precipice, driving llamas, slaves, and pigs before them. What does this descent symbolize? What is the effect of the electronic music? What is the significance of the way Ursua's wife and Aguirre's daughter are dressed . . . and carried in a sedan chair?

4. The dreamlike mood of the opening sequence is shattered by the cannon, suggesting that the "play" is about to start. Why does Herzog then cut to a group of *pigs* wallowing in the river? What is the purpose of this juxtaposition?

5. Meanwhile, Pizarro and Aguirre agree: "From now on, it's all downhill." Why is this ironic? Why does Herzog cut to the *rapids* (shot in slow motion, using a telephoto lens)?

6. During the march through the jungle, what is the symbolic significance of the *cannon* getting stuck in the swamp?

7. As Pizarro introduces Aguirre, why does Herzog show him reaching into the carriage, grasping his daughter's hand?

8. Note the "representative of the royal house." How is Don Guzman characterized by stuffing himself with fruit?

9. On the river, one of the rafts gets caught in a whirlpool. What does this symbolize, and how does it foreshadow the end of the film? ("Those men must be sick—they're going around in circles.")

10. What is the significance of Ursua's obsession with bringing the dead soldiers back for a "Christian burial?" Why does Aguirre have his executioner "accidentally" blow up the raft?

11. Aguirre brings his daughter a baby sloth: "This animal sleeps its life away." How does the little creature reflect the human race? How does this sequence recall Plato's "Allegory of the Cave"?

> Why does Herzog cut to the soldiers waking to find that the
> river has risen in the night to sweep away their rafts?

12. What is ironic about the Indian playing a lively dance melody on his flute? What does he symbolize?

13. Dona Inez goes to the monk—her "last hope." He gives her a long sermon, filled with pious cliches, followed by "The Church was always on the side of the strong." Why does Herzog include this sequence? What is the relationship between religion and imperialism?

14. Why does Aguirre propose Don Guzman, the royal fop, as "leader?" Why doesn't he simply assume the leadership himself? How does this reflect power politics in the real world?

15. The Indian prince speaks of his past, and tells Dona Inez that there's "no way out of this jungle." Why does he say he's sorry for them?

16. As Dona Inez feeds Ursua through the bars, Aguirre's executioner *hums* over her shoulder. Why does Herzog repeat this little tune as a leitmotif throughout the film? How does it relate to the Indian playing his flute?

17. Why does Don Guzman weep when Aguirre puts him on his throne and declares their secession from Spain?

18. While Guzman gets his royal rubdown, Aguirre urges him to kill Ursua. Why would Guzman insist on a trial first? Why won't Ursua say a word at his trial?

> Don Guzman undercuts Aguirre's plan by *sparing* Ursua (but confiscating his property!) How does this conclusion reflect the eternal struggle between Royalty and Power?

19. In the jungle, a village burns. What is the significance of the conquistadors' stripping the Black slave and driving him forward first to frighten the natives? How does this echo Eldridge Cleaver's charge that the U.S. military *used* Blacks in Viet Nam?

20. Note the *skeleton* in the same pose as Edvard Munch's "The Scream." What does this grisly object symbolize? Why is it ironic that the soldiers are shocked at the thought of cannibalism?

21. The river becomes sluggish. How does the landscape reflect the conquistadors' plight?

22. After Dona Inez warns Aguirre that God will punish him, he turns without speaking, pushes the horse out of the way, and goes to fawn over his daughter. What is the significance of the way he sentimentalizes his daughter? Why does he hate Ursua and his wife so much?

23. Why does Herzog stress the *boredom* of war? What is the significance of Aguirre's firing the cannon into the jungle, while his soldiers are killed, one by one, by poisoned darts? How does this reflect the American involvement in Viet Nam?

24. Two natives approach in a canoe. What is the significance of the way the Spanish treat these potential allies?

> Notice the native's reaction to their bible. What is Herzog's attitude toward the monk's mission to "bring light to the world"?

> "It's hard work—these savages are difficult to convert." Why is this ironic?

25. Talking with the monk and Don Guzman, Okello declares, "All of us will get something from this." How do the three men represent the main forces that support fascist dictators? On a comic level, how are they also like the followers of Don Quixote?

26. Note the monk's reaction to any mention of *gold.* Why does Herzog juxtapose his greed against his fanatical religiosity?

27. How is Don Guzman characterized by going to the pottie so often? What is ironic about his "formally taking possession of all this land"?

28. As Don Guzman wolfs down fruit and complains about the lack of salt for fish, his men count kernels of corn. What do his enormous feasts symbolize?

> What does the rebellious horse symbolize? What is the significance of Don Guzman's ordering that it be put overboard? What is the effect of the shot of the horse's head staring at them from the jungle?

29. What does Don Guzman's death symbolize? Why does the audience usually laugh at the line, "The *Kaiser* is dead"? Herzog could have dubbed the film in Spanish. What is the purpose of having all these "conquistadors" speaking *German?*

30. Voices from the shore: "Fresh meat is floating by!" How does this undercut the pretensions of imperialists?

31. The soldiers grovel on the ground like animals, licking salt, while their comrades lie there with arrows in their heads. Why does Dona Inez walk calmly into the jungle?

32. "When I, Aguirre, want the birds to drop from the trees, they will drop..." Why is his godlike conception of himself ironic?

33. While the men eat snails, why does Herzog cut to the *sloth* taking her babies from their nest? What does the *butterfly* resting on the soldier's finger symbolize?

34. The monk complains to Aguirre, "We lose men, but never see the enemy. Until now, El Dorado has been just an illusion." What is the theological implication of this line?

35. The men suffer from fever and hallucinations. As Okello speaks of a ship with sails suspended in a tree, the monk tells him he's imagining things. Why does Herzog confirm Okello's vision as "real?" How does a ship "up a tree" symbolize their ill-fated journey?

Easily persuaded by the word of the church, Okello agrees: "That is no ship, that is no forest, this is no arrow." The monk continues the litany with "This arrow can't hurt me..." What is the significance of their loss of reality?

36. As Aguirre's daughter lies there with an arrow in her chest, the raft swarms with *monkeys*. What does this symbolize?

37. Aguirre, the monk, and the slave are the only ones left alive on the raft. What does this symbolize? How is their raft, drifting in circles, a metaphor for an imperialist society?

38. In an intense monologue, Aguirre picks up a monkey and declares, "I, the Wrath of God, will marry my own daughter and found a dynasty to rule this continent... Who else is with me?" How does the final whirlpool comment on his proclamation?

DISTANT THUNDER (1973—Indian) Directed by Satyajit Ray; with Soumitra Chatterji (Ganga) and Babita (Ananga). Distributed by Cinema 5.

1. Why does Ray emphasize the beautiful landscape throughout the film? How is the setting ironic?

2. *Ananga's hand* emerges from the water: What does this gesture symbolize? How is she like an Indian river spirit or fertility goddess?

3. How do the Japanese planes buzzing overhead symbolize their fate?

4. Ananga is frightened by her friend Chutki's underwater swim. How does her fear of swimming underwater characterize her? Why is Chutki's response ironic? ("I lead a charmed life.")

5. What does the Man from the Kiln symbolize? (Note that his face is burned on one side—what is the mythological and psychological significance of this?)

6. Ananga's former servant, Moti, visits—asking when *she* will be pregnant, like her cousins back in their old village. Note the shot of Ananga in shadow as she answers, "When the time comes." What does the troubled look on her face mean? How does this line foreshadow the end of the film?

7. How is Ganga, the young Brahmin, characterized?

> "These people are simple and ignorant; we must gather them in."

> Why does Ray introduce their meal with a shot of *ants* gathering crumbs among the flowers? How does this shot comment on the human condition, as well as on Ganga's pretentions to sophistication?

8. The village elders welcome their new minister with a bhong full of their best hashish. Why would this strike a western audience as odd?

> Why does Ray emphasize the respect all the peasants show their Brahmin?

> Note that they don't use money; the entire village is interdependent. WHAT IS THE SIGNIFICANCE OF THE DESTRUCTION OF THIS MUTUAL DEPENDENCE IN THE COURSE OF THE FILM?

9. THE CHOLERA RITUAL: Why doesn't Ganga just *tell* the villagers to stop drinking river water and to wash their hands—instead of performing such an elaborate ceremony? Why is the ritual important? What is the significance of the lack of ritual in our own culture?

10. The OLD BRAHMIN follows his ox-cart and and begs for food. Why does Ray make the old man ugly and unsympathetic, and sly besides?

> "I'll come and visit you someday."—What does the old man symbolize, and in what sense is he a mirror image of the young hero?

11. While Ganga and Ananga eat, they discuss how *planes* work. According to him: "Like kites—the higher you go, the harder the wind." How does this *mythological* explanation relate to the meaning of the film? How does this conversation connect with the *butterfly* metaphor that appears later?

12. The merchant has no more kerosene. Ganga's naive reaction: "It's hard to imagine not being able to get something if you've got money." How does Ganga's problem foreshadow our own energy crisis?

13. As Chutki monotonously pounds rice, the Old Brahmin visits Ananga and eats her lunch.

> When Ananga asks, "Isn't he a guest?" Ganga replies, "Be careful who you feed." How do their world-views differ?

> Why does Ganga thank Ananga for persuading him to allow the Old Brahmin to stay for the night? What has he learned from their conversation?

14. THE RICE RIOT: Note the shot of the rice being trampled underfoot. The young Brahmin is pushed to the ground when he tries to defend someone who paid for his rice. What is the significance of the change in the way the villagers treat him?

15. Why does Ray keep repeating the shot of the ORANGE BUTTERFLIES in a sea of caked mud? (cf. Ananga's orange sari)

16. While collecting pond snails, Chutki meets the Man from the Kiln... What is the symbolic significance of the *orange sari* that she has been given by Ananga? How does her apron full of snails comment on their meeting?

> The man will give her rice if she goes with him to the *Ruined House*. What does this house symbolize?

17. Ganga walks fourteen miles to buy rice. The merchant feeds him but won't sell him any.

> Why is the introduction to the *rape sequence* intercut with his lunch?

18. Considering that even *kissing* is taboo in Indian films, the rape sequence is extremely daring. Even so, Ray intercuts *symbols* (rather than actions) to communicate what has happened—i.e. the cigarette, the buzzing planes, the huge potato, and the blood flowing downstream. Why is this scene more powerful than a typical Hollywood sex-scene?

> Why does Ananga stare in the mirror and plunge into the river?

19. How does the shot of the orange butterflies serve as a transition to the scene with the Man from the Kiln waiting at the ruined house?

> What does the squirrel in the cage symbolize?

Why does Chutki finally go to him? Why does she give him a hard time if she intends to accept his rice?

Why does Ray cut to the *lizard* as he goes to get rice for her?

What is the significance of his being burned during the festival of KALI? What does Kali represent in Indian religion?

Note that both he and the rapist smoke *cigarettes* (rather than hashish). How does this characterize them? How are the two scenes parallel?

Why does Ananga refuse her friend's rice? How does this distinguish the two women?

20. Why does Ray intercut the man waiting at the Ruined House with the documentary shots of starving children, abstract forms in the mud, and Ananga's former servant Moti lying down to die by the roadside?

Why does Chutki elope with a man she loathes, and why would she ask Ananga for her blessing? How does the final appearance of the orange butterflies comment on her flight?

21. How does the shot of the butterflies also serve as a transition to Moti's death?

Note the slow zoom-shot, the freeze-frame of Moti's dead face with her eyes fixed on the sunset, and the silhouette of Ganga lifting her hand. Why does Ray make her death appear so beautiful?

The minute Moti dies, a watching child takes her bundle of food. Why does Ray include this incident? Why will the world food problem never be solved?

22. As Ganga resolves to cremate Moti's body, the old Brahmin and his family come down the road...

How has Ganga moved closer to his wife's view of life?

"We'll be ten instead of two."
"Eleven," Ananga replies. Why does she smile?

23. As the camera zooms back, the Old Brahmin and his family become a horde of marching peasants. What is Ray implying about India's future?

24. A title at the end of the film informs us that five million people died in this "man-made famine" of 1943. Why is this historical incident relevant today?

LAST TANGO IN PARIS (1973—International) Directed by Bernardo Bertolucci; with Marlon Brando, Maria Schneider, and Jean-Pierre Leaud; cinematography by Vittorio Storaro; music by Gato Barbieri. Produced by United Artists.

Art or trash? Critics will argue forever about the value of *Last Tango in Paris,* but there can be no doubt about Bernardo Bertolucci's artistic intent. He boldly asserts his claim as an artist during the opening credits by inviting comparison with the passionate, tormented paintings of Francis Bacon. Like Bacon's twisted figures, Marlon Brando and Maria Schneider tear at each other's guts with an eroticism born of alienation. Their world is the womb, symbolized by a bare mattress in an empty room. The orange light that filters into this cave of shadows transforms them into primal lovers for whom the outside world has no meaning.

***

1. Marlon Brando covers his ears as a train roars by. Why does Bertolucci use the passing train as a leitmotif throughout the film?

2. Inspecting a Paris apartment, Brando introduces himself to Maria Schneider rather abruptly. How does this sequence introduce Bertolucci's idea of "love?"

> Why does Bertolucci set the apartment on the Rue *Jules Verne?* Why the tongue-in-cheek reference to this explorer of fantasies?

> What are the mythological connotations of Jeanne's strange encounter with the concierge, who clings to her hand, laughing maniacally as she gives her the key?

3. Jeanne runs to meet her fiance at the train station . . . How does Tom with his ever-present camera satirize Francois Truffaut?

4. What is the effect of the cut to a bloodstained sheet? The bathroom in which Paul's wife killed herself looks like an Abstract Expressionist painting... How does Paul's painful private life contrast with Jeanne's?

5. What is the effect of the bongo music as Jeanne enters the apartment on all fours, stalking the cat? Why does she respond so quickly when Paul orders her around?

6. "I DON'T HAVE A NAME... " Why does Paul insist that he doesn't want to know her name or any details about her life?

7. Why does Paul react violently when his mother-in-law insists that Rose have a religious funeral? Why does he turn off all the lights in the hotel? How is the hotel like the flophouse in Edward Albee's *Zoo Story*—and how is it a metaphor for hell?

8. Considering how roughly Paul treats her, why does Jeanne return to the apartment?

9. When Jeanne says she'll have to "invent a name for him," why does Paul respond with an ape imitation? What is the significance of the animal noises that follow?

> What is the effect of the cut to Tom recording ducks quacking?

10. Why does Bertolucci include the sequence in which Tom sentimentalizes Jeanne's childhood? How does his "new wave" TV approach to love differ from Paul's brutal eroticism?

11. When Jeanne reminisces about her Father the Colonel, Paul exclaims that "EVERYTHING OUTSIDE THIS ROOM IS BULLSHIT!" Why does he resent her fantasizing about the past? How do Paul's childhood memories differ from Jeanne's?

> Note Jeanne's story about masturbating with her cousin at age thirteen—in separate trees! How does this comic image of alienation relate to the film's theme?

12. Jeanne accuses Tom of using her. Why does Bertolucci set their confrontation in a metro station, surrounded by billboards, as trains roar between them? How does their childish fight differ from the violence of her relationship with Paul?

13. Paul visits his wife's former lover. What is the significance of her giving them identical bathrobes?

14. *Butter* acquires new symbolic meaning in this film... Why does Paul force Jeanne to recite an anti-bourgeois litany while he sodomizes her?

15. Tom actually *films* his proposal. How does the sinking life preserver (from L'Atalante!) comment on his plans?

16. Jeanne puts on her father's uniform and points his pistol. How does this foreshadow the end of the film? What is the significance of her worship of her macho father? How is she like Strindberg's Miss Julie?

17. "For a pop youth, a pop marriage!" Tom declares. Why does Jeanne—still wearing her wedding dress!—suddenly run away, leaving him to parody *Singing in the Rain?*

> Why does Paul respond to her symbolic gesture by holding up a dead rat?

> "You're all alone," Paul insists, "until you find the womb of fear." Why does her declaration of love lead to their second strange ritual?

18. In a moving soliloquy over his wife's dead body, Paul reveals the cause of his bitterness: "Even if a husband lives two hundred years, he'll never understand his wife's real nature." Why does he try to wipe off Rose's makeup?

> What is the significance of his pain being interrupted by an insistent whore banging on the hotel door? Why does Paul pursue the whore's customer and beat him up?

19. Cut to Jeanne finding Paul's furniture gone. Why has he suddenly moved out of their apartment? Why does she tearfully phone Tom and suggest that he move in there with her? What is ironic in the apartment's being "too big" for Tom?

20. Paul again follows Jeanne in the street... After moving out on her, why does he break his own rule by telling her about his life? Why does Bertolucci dub Paul's autobiography over a formal tango sequence? If the tango is a ritual, as Paul says, how is this "Last Tango" the film's central symbol?

21. Now that Paul actually loves her, why does Jeanne run away? Why does she react so negatively to the *real* Paul?

> As she rises in the elevator, he runs up the staircase around her. What does her "cage" symbolize?

22. Paul puts on her father's hat and salutes: "How do you like your hero?" Why does Bertolucci connect him with Jeanne's father?

What is the significance of his wanting to know her name? Why is her response *tragic?*

Muttering "Our children," Paul's last act is to stick his gum on the balcony railing(!) What is the purpose of this absurd gesture?

23. Why does Bertolucci end the film with Jeanne repeating (over and over) "I don't know who he is . . . "? Considering that he is the only man with whom she has ever had real contact, why is this ironic?

PHANTOM OF THE PARADISE (1974—American) Directed by Brian De Palma; with Paul Williams, William Finley, and Jessica Harper; music by Paul Williams. Produced by Twentieth Century Fox; distributed by Films Inc.

Brian De Palma is one of the most literate of the so-called "movie brats," a group of young American directors who grew up on TV and Hollywood movies and who consciously parody and imitate the "old masters." In *Phantom of the Paradise,* De Palma satirizes shots from several famous horror films—including *Frankenstein, Phantom of the Opera,* and *The Cabinet of Dr. Caligari.* But he does more than that. He quotes Hitchcock's *Psycho* and Cocteau's *Beauty and the Beast* and other classic films, combining all these disparate references to create the cinematic equivalent of Brecht's epic theatre.

***

1. Swan, the president of Death Records, may be patterned on the famous rock producer, Phil Spector. How is Swan characterized in the introduction? What are the political and religious implications of his wanting to "inaugurate the Paradise"?

2. An important theatrical principle from Shakespeare to Bertolt Brecht is to begin a serious play with a *comic analogue*—an entertaining scene that foreshadows the main theme. How does the opening song about "Little Eddy" (who killed himself so his sister could have an operation) serve this purpose?

> Also note that the "Juicy Fruits" are supposed to be Sha Na Na, a nostalgic rock group from the early seventies, and that there are references in the song to the deaths of James Dean and Buddy Holly. Who *does* profit from the death of a young actor or singer, and how does this relate to the film's artist/society theme?

3. Philbin complains that his lead singer, "Annette," wants to sing benefits for "starving gook orphans." How does this scene characterize the rock music industry?

4. While Swan and Philbin scheme, Winslow Leach (at the piano) introduces the Faust theme. Aside from connecting him with Elton John, why would De Palma have him wear *thick glasses?*

> What Winslow wants most of all is a *voice* to sing his music. How does this provide Swan with the clue to tempt him?

5. Winslow and Philbin talk as the Juicy Fruits sing the suicide theme in the background. What is the purpose of this juxtaposition? Why is it ironic that Philbin wouldn't know who Faust was? Or that he couldn't care less? ("What is this, kid—school time?")

> In light of what happens to Winslow later, why is it ironic that he talks so academically about his "Faust" cantata?

6. One month later, Winslow approaches Swan's surreal office building. Note the low angle shot, his slow-motion expulsion, and the melodramatic music for his taxi chase. Why is this entire sequence stylized and dream-like?

7. Song: "Never Thought I'd Get to Meet the Devil." How does the Felliniesque stairway with its cacaphony of singers illustrate De Palma's vision of hell?

8. The audition on the round water bed introduces the *voyeur* theme. In what sense are *all* filmmakers voyeurs?

> What is the significance of the fact that Swan is completely *passive*, more interested in his telephone than in the female pulchritude that engulfs him?

9. Note the series of quick cuts as Winslow is beaten up, heroin is planted on him by the police, and he is sentenced to Sing Sing. What is the purpose of the extreme low-angle shots? What is De Palma's attitude toward authority figures?

10. In a scene reminiscent of Thomas Pynchon's novel *V.,* Winslow is "volunteered" to have all his teeth pulled (and replaced by stainless steel) by the Swan Foundation. Freudian castration complexes aside, why is this idea so frightening to most human beings? How does it relate to the idea of modern man becoming *inanimate?*

11. When Winslow hears the announcement of Swan's performance of his cantata, he goes berserk on the *assembly line.* What does this setting symbolize? How is he like Chaplin in *Modern Times?*

12. Note the paranoiac perspective as he breaks into Death Records. What is the symbolic significance of his being caught in the record press? Also note the moving camera backing away from him as he staggers away and slides into the river. How does this plunge relate to the death/rebirth theme?

13. Instead of showing the Phantom approach the theatre, why does De Palma use Hitchcock's *subjective camera* technique (with a rather shakily hand-held camera)? What is the effect of the loud breathing and the thudding footsteps?

14. Why the *red corridors?* Aside from the obvious reference to Poe's "Masque of the Red Death," how does this setting relate to the interiors of Bergman's *Cries and Whispers,* and to the expressionistic use of color in the paintings of Edvard Munch? What do all these artists have in common?

15. Song: "Carbureators, Man—That's What Life Is All About!" Why would Winslow be offended by this version of his "Faust" theme? What is the point of this parody of a group of aging Beach Boys? How does the explosion of their car symbolize the ultimate fate of California Culture?

16. What is the significance of Swan's slipping through *mirrors* all the time? (cf. Cocteau's *Orpheus*) What is ironic in the mirror scene in which Swan urges the Phantom, "Look at yourself"? How does this foreshadow the imagery of his *own* suicide?

17. Note the parabolic perspective as Swan plugs the Phantom into the electric piano. What is the purpose of this visual distortion? What is the significance of Swan's engineering the Phantom's voice to sound exactly like his *own* voice?

18. In the temptation scene that follows, what is the *tone* of all the legal jargon?

19. Song: "Beauty and the Beast"—In what sense are there *two* Beasts in this film?

20. Although it would be the easiest way to get the Phantom to work for him, why doesn't Swan let Phoenix sing? ("You know how I abhor perfection in anyone but myself.")

21. While the Phantom goes on writing, the auditions continue with parodies of major rock groups: Crosby-Stills-Nash & Young, James Taylor, the Pointer Sisters...

> Finally, Swan is impressed with *Beef*(!) What is the significance of his name, and what does he represent?

22. In a parody of *The Cabinet of Dr. Caligari,* Swan reveals Beef to the public: "The Juicy Fruits are a reflection of the past; I give you the future— BEEF." What are the cultural and political implications of this prediction? How does Beef foreshadow punk music of the late seventies? Why does decadence frequently lead to fascism?

23. While Swan plies the Phantom with pills to get him to finish the music on time, the *real* Beef is revealed in rehearsal:

> "You can sing it better than any bitch." "You don't know how right you are, Goliath." In light of his macho performance, what is the significance of Beef's being *gay?* What does his inability to get back up on his platform shoes symbolize?

24. The Phantom wakes to find his music stolen and the door *bricked over.* What does this symbolize (cf. Poe's "Cask of Amontillado")?

> As the Phantom bursts through the brick wall in slow motion, why does De Palma cut to Beef (in curlers!) shrieking, "This place is possessed!"? What is the effect of this juxtaposition?

25. Note the low angle and the music as Beef snorts cocaine and climbs into the shower: "I am your nightmare coming true." What details connect this with the famous shower sequence in Hitchcock's *Psycho?* What is the effect of the *toilet plunger,* and how does it comment symbolically on Beef's singing?

294   *Talking About Films*

26. For Beef's performance, De Palma combines the expressionistic sets of *Caligari* with the clown-white makeup used in Brecht's epic theatre. How does this set the scene for the ritual murder that follows?

> How do the "Undead" relate to the idea of Swan's Paradise actually being hell? How do they foreshadow the themes of punk rock?

> In their song, "Somebody Super Like You," they cut off limbs from members of the audience to create their ideal hero. What is the political implication of this? What is the significance of the audience's reaction to these mutilations? How does the rising of the coffin relate to the death/rebirth theme?

27. Beef's Frankenstein Act: In a parody of Rod Stewart and Mick Jagger, he sings "Life at Last." Why is this ironic? How do his "construction" and destruction reflect the main theme of the film?

28. Swan has a problem topping Beef's act, and it's hard to believe that Phoenix' song, "Old Souls," wouldn't be booed off the stage by such a crude audience. In any case, how do the lyrics of the song relate to the Temptation and Faust themes?

29. Swan enters her dressing room through the *mirror*-door. Why does De Palma shoot their conversation in the *mirror,* and how does this connect the scene with Swan's temptation of Winslow earlier in this film?

> Does Phoenix really like Swan, or is she just overwhelmed by the desire for fame?

> When the Phantom takes her up to the roof, why doesn't she believe what he says about Swan? ("Don't you hear them down there? Why should I give that up?")

30. In a repetition of the *voyeur* theme, the Phantom watches Swan and Phoenix through the skylight. Note the beautiful rear-screen projection on the skylight. What do the storm and the *rainy skylight* symbolize? (cf. *Citizen Kane*)

> What is the significance of Swan's *videotaping* the Phantom's reaction to their making love?

31. When the Phantom stabs himself, Swan goes to him on the rainswept roof and pulls out the knife: "This contract terminates with Swan." How does this strange plot twist reflect on the rock music business? In what sense are Swan and the Phantom "doubles"?

32. Another revelation: A middle-aged lady, who claims she went to school with Swan, appears with a locket containing his picture. He hasn't changed in twenty years. How does this derive from Oscar Wilde's *Picture of Dorian Gray?* How does it lead to the videotaped flashback that follows?

33. In the flashback of Swan's suicide attempt, he decides to kill himself because he's getting old and can't bear to see his beautiful features ravaged by time. How does this comment on American culture?

> Why does De Palma conceive of this temptation scene as a conversation with his own reflection?

> By asserting that Swan will die when the *videotape* is destroyed, what is De Palma suggesting about the relationship between the media and reality?

34. Why would Swan plan to assasinate Phoenix during a *wedding* ceremony? What is the significance of his wearing a *mask?*

> When the Phantom tears away Swan's mask, why is the face underneath so grotesque?

> Why does the Phantom's *own* wound open when he stabs Swan, and how does this establish their *psychic identification?*

35. As Phoenix finally recognizes Winslow, the camera zooms back to show the crowd going wild. What does this say about rock audiences?

36. "The Hell of It"—Why the juxtaposition of cheerful music and cynical lyrics during the final credits?

One interesting sidelight on *Phantom of the Paradise* is that both De Palma and William Finley worked together at Columbia University with the very talented director, Wilford Leech, who introduced them to Brechtian epic theatre. Since Leech appears transformed in this film as the Phantom, it is interesting to speculate whether De Palma himself has become a kind of Swan, absorbing his old teacher's identity and imposing his own voice.

THE SEDUCTION OF MIMI (1974—Italian) Directed by Lina Wertmuller; with Giancarlo Giannini and Mariangela Melato. Distributed by New Line Cinema.

1. The film begins and ends with a sound-truck roaring up to politicize a group of quarry workers. What is the purpose of this framework?

2. Rosalia washes Mimi's feet... What does this family foot-washing ritual imply about marital relationships in Italy?

3. Mimi and his family live in a hovel darker than Plato's cave. As the extended family snores all around them, Mimi berates his wife Rosalia for being frigid. How does this characterize him?

4. "What's the name of the man we've got to vote for?" How does this characterize Italian politics?

> As Mimi's friends insist that the vote will be secret, why does the camera zoom to the *three moles* on the face of Don Calogero, the reigning mafioso?

> Why is it predictable that when Mimi doesn't vote for Don Calogero, he can't find work anymore?

5. In Turin—The Communist Party Meeting: After Mimi's rousing speech about how they have to stick together and "name names," a "comrade" rises and challenges him to name the man who ran the Sicilian Brotherhood that exploited the workers in Catania. Why does Mimi back down when he notices that the man has *three moles* on his right cheek?

6. What is the purpose of the opera music as Mimi and Mariangela Melato see each other for the first time?

7. "First you beg for a kiss—then you try to rape me!" How do Mimi and Fiore's attitudes toward love differ?

8. After making Mimi swear that he'll never touch another woman, Fiore starts to undress. By juxtaposing opera music against his absurd insincere

promise, what does Wertmuller imply about the operatic idea of Romantic Love?

9. What is the effect of cutting from them making love to Mimi at his mirror wearing a hair-net?

10. While Mimi lounges with his mistress, his wife Rosalia writes that she's working in a factory. What is the *tone* of the shots of a machine pressing the crotch of a pair of pants, and of Rosalia getting on a motorbike emblazoned with decals of the Virgin Mary? Why does Mimi's father call her a whore, and why is this ironic?

11. As Mimi goes to get another bottle of champagne for his son's christening, gunmen invade the hotel's lounge. Announcing Mimi's name like a thundering Old Testament God, his three-moled antagonist shoots him in the head...fortunately the least sensitive part of Mimi's body. During the interrogation, why does Wertmuller intercut shots of Mimi's face and zoom-closeups of several men with three moles on their faces?

> Mimi declares that he "didn't see anything." Throughout the film, why does Wertmuller stress his refusal to testify?

12. At the factory, Mimi is accused of going over to the side of the bosses. Invariably caught between greedy capitalists and striking workers, how does he symbolize the desperate condition of the Italian economy?

13. Without his signature, Mimi is transferred back to Catania. What is the purpose of the Arabian music as Mimi and Fiore, all clothed in black, slip into town?

14. The General Manager at Mimi's new factory also turns out to have three moles on his face. What is ironic in his saying that Mimi has proved himself a "man of honor?"

> When Mimi accuses him of being an "errand boy for politicians," the Manager informs him that the politicians are actually *his* servants. In any political system, where *does* power lie?

15. Note the cut from Mimi pushing his men to work—to Fiore hanging a portrait of Lenin over their bed. How does this stress the impossibility of their relationship? What is the significance of his falling asleep as she lectures him on Marxist principles?

16. At the party, what is the effect of the closeups of all the insinuating smiles? Why do Mimi's friends challenge him with being gay? Why does this cause him to brag about his mistress?

17. In pairs, the overdressed friends go to meet Fiore. What is the effect of the portrait of Lenin hovering over their shoulders as they furiously stir their coffee?

18. Why is the second "car conference" funny? What does the setting (a sand pit) symbolize? When Mimi's friends hint at Rosalia's loneliness because of his neglect, why is he so slow to catch on?

> "This is your chance to show you're a good communist and a civilized man." Why is his reaction ironic and hypocrtical?

19. As Rosalia cowers in black, Mimi closes in on her with his smoky eyes. Note the comic, anti-heroic symbols in her confession: the Sergeant always gave her "sweets with honey-filled centers," and they made love in the cabin of a crane(!) When Mimi counters Rosalia's confession by bragging about his mistress, *she* grabs the knife. Why is their knife fight funny?

20. What Mimi fears most is that a rival's child will bear his name. What does Wertmuller think of his chauvinistic obsession?

21. Why would the gunman from the Tricarico family—a group of mafiosi taking control of the construction workers—offer his services?

22. When Mimi tells Peppino that he saw Tricarico's cousin kill four men in Turin, his friend asks why he didn't speak up. Why does Mimi immediately dismiss his best friend as a left-wing failure?

23. In a series of tracking shots, Mimi pursues his rival's wife. He finally corners her in a sewing factory. What does the warehouse full of *sacks* symbolize?

24. What is ironic about Mimi's meeting Amalia at church over a basin of holy water?

25. As Mimi and Amalia tango by the sea, note his expression. How has this sequence been influenced by Fellini and Bertolucci?

26. Note all the religious paraphernalia as Mimi wrestles Amalia onto the bed. Why is the setting ironic, and how does it echo Fiore's bed with its portrait of Lenin? What is the tone of the choreographed sequence as they undress to tango music?

27. Why does Wertmuller repeat the shots of Amalia slipping her panties down over her enormous rear end, intercut with zoom shots of Mimi's blinking eyes? What is the effect of the parabolic shot of her towering over him as he cringes at the other end of the bed?

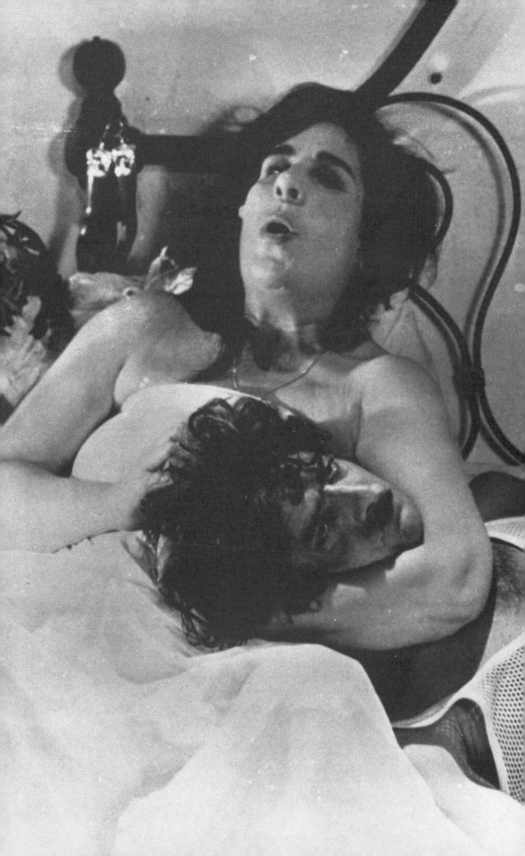

28. Amalia sings lustily afterwards, while Mimi lies in shock, clutched in her embrace. What is the significance of Mimi's throwing away both his wife and his beautiful communist mistress just to get revenge? How does this reflect the unconscious shift in his political attitudes?

29. Telling Amalia the truth behind his seduction, Mimi declares, "My *brain* understands things nowadays." Why is this ironic?

30. Mimi refuses to let his workers strike. How is this parallel to Amalia's insistence that he impregnate her on *principle?*

31. What is ironic in everything being confessed on the church steps, and of Mimi's bragging about being a "civilized man?" As Mimi stands there with a gun pressed into his hand, he looks up on the bridge and sees a Cardinal . . . with three moles on his face! What does this motif imply about the entire power structure?

32. Fiore: "Mimi asked what *honor* is . . . something ridiculously stupid." What is the significance of his now being accepted by the political machine because of his "crime?"

33. As Mimi emerges from jail, Fiore and his son await him to the accompaniment of opera music. What is the significance of their tearful reunion being interrupted by Amalia's *five* children? As he's engulfed by the children, why would he knock on the door to be let back into the prison?

34. What is the significance of Mimi's winding up on the sound truck working for Tricarico's election? Why does Fiore's face look so pained?

35. Note the final shot of Mimi chasing Fiore's truck across the wasteland as the camera zooms back, leaving him kneeling in the dirt. What does the setting symbolize? How does this sequence prefigure Raffaela's departure at the end of *Swept Away?*

36. At the end of the film, in what sense has Mimi been "seduced?" What is the significance of his primitive chauvinism causing him to wind up enslaved by the right-wing mafia?

> What is the connection between male-chauvinism and fascism, and why has the mafia thrived in the United States even more than in Italy?

ZARDOZ (1974—Engish) Directed by John Boorman; with Sean Connery, Sara Kestelman, and Charlotte Rampling; cinematography by Geoffrey Unsworth; music by David Munrow. Produced by Twentieth Century Fox; distributed by Films Inc.

John Boorman's *Zardoz* is a religious allegory masquerading as science fiction. The god of 2093 is a magician/clown who seeks death to relieve the boredom of immortality. In Boorman's attack on scientific utopias, Sean Connery symbolizes the carnal violence of the human race. As the "rough beast who slouches toward Bethlehem to be born," he provides the "gift of death" that allows the rebirth of humanity.

***

1. "Is God in Show Business?" What does Arthur Freyn's allegorical prologue suggest about filmmaking and religion?

2. The Exterminators gather to worship. What does the *flying head* symbolize? What is the significance of their all wearing masks in the image of their god?

> "The gun is good, the penis is evil... The gun purifies the earth. Go forth and kill." How does the shower of rifles reflect the Old Testament ethic?

3. Sean Connery aims his pistol at the camera and fires. Note his rather interesting costume: red diapers held up by a gunbelt. How does this symbolize imperialism? What does it imply about the military?

4. Cut from the flying head to a closeup of Zed's pistol emerging from the sand. In terms of evolution, what does Zed's hiding "buried in the head" symbolize?

5. "Fool! Without me you are nothing!" Arthur cries as he floats out of the mouth. What is the significance of Zed's shooting Arthur?

6. The Head lands in the Vortex, the domed dwelling of the Immortals. What is the significance of Zed's winding up in Arthur's room? How do the

astrological symbols and the wall-paintings of human evolution satirize the traditional concept of God?

7. Zed uses Arthur's magic ring to explore. What is the significance of his not knowing what a *flower* is? Why the hallucinatory crosscut to the nude lady on horseback?

8. May (Sara Kestelman) comes toward Zed as a reflection in the water. How does this image establish the film's concept of reality?

> Why does Zed think he has died and gone to heaven? Why is this ironic?

> May hypnotizes Zed to find out where he came from. Why does Boorman use a rear-screen projection for Zed's flashback to his work as an Exterminator among the Brutals? What is the significance of May's cold, clinical response to this frightful violence?

9. How are Sara Kestelman and Charlotte Rampling like Olympian goddesses? Why does May reject Consuela's advice that they kill Zed?

10. The Immortals regard the projected sufferings of the Brutals as "mere entertainment." How are they like the gods of Shakespeare and Euripides? What is Boorman also implying about *our* love of violent Hollywood movies?

11. "I wonder what's going on inside your pea-brain . . . " Why does Friend say he "likes" Zed? What does his gallery of classical statues symbolize? Why does Friend say that all these old gods "died of boredom"?

12. What is Boorman satirizing in the trial of the young man accused of "transmitting a negative aura"? Why does he finally exclaim, "I hate you all—especially me"?

13. In a land where death is impossible, the punishment for any departure from conformity is *aging*. "Renegades" are condemned to an eternity of senility. Why do they all want to die?

14. What do the "Apathetics" symbolize? What is the significance of their being aroused by Zed's violence?

15. What is the point of Consuela's lecture on the mystery of human sexual response? Why is passion impossible in the Vortex? What is the significance of Zed's reacting not to the erotic films but to Consuela herself?

16. Since the Immortals have achieved total consciousness, they no longer sleep . . . or *dream*. Why does Boorman link sleep, sex, death, and dreams?

17. May realizes that Zed is superior to them, and hence can destroy them. What is her actual reason for keeping him alive?

18. "The monster is a mirror. When we look on him, we look into our own hidden faces." How does this lead to Friend's breakdown and refusal to meditate with the group? ("I will not be one mind with you!") What is the significance of their casting him out as a renegade?

19. Why does Zed "seek Friend" in the dwelling of the renegades? How does this signify the evolution of his consciousness? Why do all the old people fawn on him when Friend tells them he brings the "gift of death?"

20. The Old Man who discovered immortality lies immobile in bed. Why is it ironic (and inevitable!) that he would ultimately be ostracized by his own people as a non-conformist?

21. When Zed says he wants the Truth, May replies, "It will burn you." What does she mean?

> Flashback: In the middle of an attack, Zed "lost his innocence." Why did Arthur Freyn lead him through a mysterious house and beckon him toward a child's spelling book? Why does Arthur want Zed to learn how to read if knowledge of "what the world was before the darkness" will cause him to become disenchanted with his god?

> "You murdered your own god!" What are the mythical overtones of May's startled announcement?

> Zardoz orders Zed to take prisoners and *farm* instead of just killing them. How does this mirror human evolution?

22. "You look behind the mask and you see the truth . . . " Note the identity of the "fatal book." Why does this revelation cause Zed to hide in the flying head?

23. "He made us killers!" Why does Zed's cry for revenge arouse May to passion? When Consuela interrupts them, what is the significance of their *tug-of-war?* What does his *blindness* symbolize?

24. Why the soft-focus photography as the Immortals restore Zed's sight? The priestess offers to help if he will "liberate" her when the time comes. What does she mean?

25. "This place is built on lies and suffering..." How do these wealthy survivors of a dying world reflect our own culture? Why does the priestess say, "You are the price...You have brought hate and anger into the Vortex"? Why does the mob attack Zed's plastic bubble?

26. As May and Consuela hunt him on horseback, Zed tries to hide among the Apathetics. What is the significance of their reaction to the taste of his sweat? ("We take life from you.")

27. Zed runs to the dwelling of the Renegades to find Friend. What are the mythical connotations of their disguising him as the "bride?"

28. May confronts Friend in his sculpture gallery. When Zed tells them they must die, why does May ask him to inseminate them instead to produce a new race? How is their projection of "all human knowledge" onto his brain analogous to the myth of creation?

29. In a flashback we learn how the Vortex evolved to its present state. Why is the former leader's sermon on immortality and perfection ironic? Why has his utopia failed? What is the significance of all the old scientists eventually becoming Renegades?

30. Gazing into the crystal, Zed admits, "I see nothing inside but my own perplexity." Why does this realization enable Zed to communicate with his "god?" Why does Boorman set their encounter in a gallery of costumed figures?

> "Would it have been worthwhile, to have bitten off the matter with a smile, to have squeezed the universe into a ball..." Why the quote from T.S. Eliot's "Prufrock"? What are the symbolic connotations of Zed's reply? ("I am Lazarus, come from the dead...I shall tell you all.")

31. Cut from Arthur throwing Zed the glass ball—to Consuela bashing down the door in slow-motion. As Zed stares into the ball, why does Consuela drop her knife?

> "He who fights too long against dragons becomes a dragon himself." After insisting all along that Zed be destroyed, why would Consuela suddenly "love" him?

32. "You have me in the palm of your hand." What is the significance of the *crystal* being god? How does Zed's refusal to join their society gain his admission to the center of the crystal, and what does his journey symbolize? What does his shooting his own masked image in the mirror mean?

33. Why do the Immortals destroy the statues? What is the significance of Zed's "reconstructing" these dead gods as he leads his friends to safety?

34. Why does Zed bring the crystal to the Old Man? Why does the society's founder declare that the Vortex is a "crime against nature" and hail Zed as a *god?*

35. When the priestess commands Zed to "liberate" her, why does he lower his aim ("All that I was is gone")?

36. "Kill me too..." What is the tone of the final massacre?

37. Zed and Consuela hide in a cave. As the camera pans over the bodies, why does Boorman cut from Zed's comrade crying his name to Consuela giving birth?

> Why the series of dissolves of the two with their growing son? How does this recapitulate the start of the human race? What is the meaning of the final shot of the two handprints on the wall of the cave?

THE MAGIC FLUTE (1975—Swedish) Directed by Ingmar Bergman; with Josef Kostlinger (Tamino), Irma Urrila (Pamina), Ulrik Cold (Sarastro), Birgit Nordin (Queen of the Night), Hakan Hagegard (Papageno), and Elisabeth Eriksson (Papagena); cinematography by Sven Nykvist; music by Mozart. Distributed by Films Inc.

Bergman's version of Mozart's *Magic Flute* may be the finest film of an opera ever made. Avoiding big-name stars, Bergman cast young singing-actors who actually look like the roles they play. His production in a small, elegant Swedish theater and his stylized stage show the opera as it would have been done as eighteenth century entertainment, rather than as Wagnerian music-drama. For the few scenes Bergman treats seriously, he relies on the dazzling cinematic technique of Sven Nykvist. Alternating from stage to dreamscape, Bergman combines the artifice of opera with the philosophical concerns of early masterpieces like *The Magician.*

***

1. In his fifties films, Bergman stresses the relationship between people and their landscape. How do the beautiful opening stills of swans on a pond, sunlight back-lighting the forest, and the old theater at dusk refer to this theme?

2. The Overture: How do the shots of classical sculptures (on the chords) echo Bergman's early "comedy of manners, " *Smiles of a Summer Night?* During the *allegro* section, why does he jump-cut the closeups of faces in the audience? What does the variety of faces symbolize? Why does he keep returning to the face of the Little Girl?

3. Bergman patterns the opening of Act One on Salzburg's Marionette Theater. Why does he use a comic-strip stage and a knock-kneed monster that looks like an overgrown toy?

> Note that Tamino sings straight out to the audience, as on an eighteenth century stage. Why is this more effective than any attempt at naturalism?

4. As the Three Ladies spear the dragon, he spews smoke and fireworks. Why does Bergman include such theatrical effects?

> In the trio over Tamino's unconscious body, note the formal choreography as the three ladies try to get rid of each other in order to enjoy the young man. Why do they finally agree to leave together?

5. Asleep in his dressing room, Papageno hears the cue for his entrance just in time. How does this characterize him? How does Papageno's "bird" metaphor relate to his problem in finding a girlfriend?

6. Note the scenery change as the Queen of the Night descends on a floating moon. Why does Bergman make the Queen look gray and sinister as she complains about her daughter's abduction?

7. In the locket, Tamino sees Pamina's face with Monostatos peering over her shoulder. What does Bergman imply about innocence and lust by repeating this famous shot from his film *Persona?*

8. The Ladies send Papageno along with Tamino to be his aide. How does their relationship echo Don Quixote and Sancho Panza?

9. Why does Bergman use placards to proclaim the words during the formal quartet? Why does he repeat this device whenever the actors step out of character to lecture the audience on the nature of love?

10. As symbols, how do the *Magic Flute* and the *Glockenspiel* contrast? How do they represent two different kinds of love? (Note the pornographic eighteenth century painting on the cover of Papageno's instrument!)

11. The Child Spirits descend in a balloon. What do they symbolize?

12. How is the Little Girl's startled face a transition to Monostatos' entrapment of Pamina?

13. How is Papageno characterized by stuffing himself with *cream-puffs* while talking with Pamina?

14. Papageno and Pamina pause in their escape to sing a duet about the beauties of love. What does the setting—on top of a wall—symbolize?

       Note their double-take at the end of the song. What is the effect of their almost getting carried away?

15. Tamino descends in the balloon with the Child Spirits, who counsel him to be "steadfast, silent, and obedient." Why does Bergman put this advice in the mouths of children?

16. "Where art is protected and beauty may dwell, the people are happy and the master rules well"—Mozart's philosophy, and undoubtedly Bergman's too. What are the problems with this idea, however?

17. When the old priest tells him that Sarastro rules in the beautiful temple, Tamino declares that "all must be hypocrisy." What is the significance of Tamino's inability to see through the Queen of the Night?

18. Tamino sings, "Oh endless night—When will the darkness ever brighten?" Voices answer: "Soon or never." Bergman uses this sequence also in *Hour of the Wolf*. Philosophically, how does the theme of this scene recall Bergman's early tragic allegories?

19. Tamino steps to the proscenium to sing about the wonders of the Magic Flute. What is the effect of the *animals* in what is usually done as a very serious scene? How is Tamino like Orpheus in Greek myth?

20. In a parallel scene, Papageno avoids capture by charming Monostatos and his devils with his magic bells. What does their dance symbolize?

21. With Sarastro's entrance, the opera takes a decidedly anti-female turn. As a filmmaker sympathetic to feminism, why doesn't Bergman bother modifying Mozart's misogyny?

22. How does Bergman use the *intermission* to develop parallels between the actors and the roles they play? Why woud Sarastro study the score of *Parsifal?* Why does Bergman include the little devil reading *Donald Duck* beside him?

> How is the Queen of the Night characterized by *smoking* under the "No Smoking" sign?

> How does Tamino and Pamina's *chess game* echo Shakespeare's *Tempest,* and what is the point of this allusion?

23. Act Two: Why does Bergman use the "Last Supper" setting for the meeting of Sarastro and the priests? Why does Sarastro want to leave his power to a worthy young *couple* instead of to a priest?

24. With Sarastro's hymn, the film becomes a conflict between Light and Darkness. How does this recall early Bergman films like *The Seventh Seal?*

25. What is the purpose of the *thematic analogue* as both Tamino and Papageno are sworn to silence? How does this sequence develop their "Don Quixote-Sancho Panza" relationship?

26. Monostatos' lustful song over Pamina's sleeping body is interrupted by the Queen of the Night. During the Queen's aria about revenge, what is the effect of the *blue light* glinting off the dagger and turning her face into a mask?

27. The House of the Dead: Papageno plays his bells and sings about how he wishes he had a girlfriend. How do the *skeletons* comment on his desire for love?

28. What is the significance of Papagena's disguise? Why does she reveal herself and disappear?

29. How does Tamino playing his flute among the skeletons repeat the Orpheus theme?

30. What is the significance of Pamina's desperate reaction to Tamino's silence? How does her pacing in the snow between two picket fences symbolize her inner state?

> As the snow falls, the Child Spirits descend in their balloon to prevent Pamina from killing herself. Why does Bergman undercut her anguish with the three children?

Why does he cut to the smiling face of the Little Girl as Pamina lays the dagger in the snow?

The formal quartet: What does their ascent in the balloon symbolize?

31. Why does Bergman introduce Papageno's "suicide" with a snowball fight among the angels? How does Papageno's suicide attempt differ in tone from Pamina's? What is the effect of the comic-strip trees? Note the way the Child Spirits prevent him from hanging himself.

32. The Spirits remind Papageno of his magic bells. What is the significance of the scene change as he starts to play? In the cheerful duet that follows between Papageno and Papagena, what is the effect of their *undressing* each other as they sing about all the children they plan to have?

33. Pamina takes Tamino's flute to him in the House of Trials. What does this symbolize? What is the significance of her accompanying him?

34. As soon as Pamina appears, the two guards with fire pouring out of their helmets suddenly take off their masks for a formal quartet. Why does Bergman change the tone of the scene so abruptly?

35. Note Sven Nykvist's beautiful cinematograpy as the young couple walk through the House of Fire. What do the naked bodies writhing in the flames symbolize? How does this sequence echo Orpheus leading Eurydice from hell?

What do the arms waving from the floor in the House of Water symbolize? And the bodies wreathed in fog?

36. The Queen of the Night's invasion looks like a sequence from a Fellini film. What does Sarastro's defeat of her army symbolize? ("The radiant sun overpowers the night...")

37. For the finale, why does Bergman return to the stylized stage for an eighteenth century dance? What is the significance of Sarastro's plucking his flute from the air as he leaves? Why does Bergman conclude with Papageno and Papagena dancing in front of the curtain with a whole brood of children?

THE STORY OF ADELE H. (1975—French/English) Directed by Francois Truffaut; with Isabelle Adjani; cinematography by Nestor Almendros. Produced by New World Pictures; distributed by Films Inc.

1. Do you consider Adele merely a silly lady, or can you identify with her in some way?

2. What kind of person is Pinson, and why on earth would Adele like him?

3. The opening shot of the map: Why does Truffaut frequently establish a *documentary* tone for his films? Why are "real" people often more unbelievable than fictional characters?

4. Why does the dialogue switch back and forth from English to French? Why does Truffaut set the story in two opposite climates (Nova Scotia and the Barbadoes)? How do the snow and heat mirror her inner problem?

5. Adele tells the doctor that she wants to find Pinson for her *niece* ("He is of no interest to me . . . "). Later, she tells her landlady Pinson is her cousin and is in love with her. What is the significance of her *pattern* of lies?

6. When Pinson shrugs and declines to read Adele's letter, Truffaut cuts to Adele's *dream of drowning.* How does this recurring dream serve as a metaphor for her passion?

> Why does Adele identify with her sister, whose husband "preferred to drown" since he couldn't save her?

7. Walking along the pier, Adele mistakenly stops another soldier . . . who turns out to be Truffaut! Why does Truffaut include this incident of confused identity, and how does it foreshadow the film's ending?

8. Why does Pinson visit Adele if he doesn't want to see her?

> Adele alternately fawns on him, threatens him, and bribes him with money. How does this characterize her?

> Pinson insists that her father despises him. Is this his real reason for not wanting her?

9. After Pinson weasels his way out the door, Adele writes an ecstatic letter expressing her joy about being "reunited" with her lover. What is the significance of her pouring all her feelings into her diary? How is she like her father, Victor Hugo?

> "Love is my religion"—Proust claims that people "believe" only because they *want* to. How is this also true of love?

10. Adele spies on Pinson as he climbs the stairs with the Dog Lady. Why does Adele *smile* as Pinson climbs in bed with the other lady? (Proust would suggest that jealousy *arouses* her. What do you think of this idea?)

11. As the landlady writes Victor Hugo's address in her book, Truffaut cuts to Adele *drowning* again. What does this imply about her relationship with her father?

12. Adele keeps leaving love-notes in Pinson's clothes—why, when she must know that her clinging behavior drives him away?

13. Why does Adele tell the little boy that her name is Leopoldine—and then after reading her father's letter of consent, go back to tell him her real name?

14. Adele disguises herself as a *man* to approach Pinson at a party. What does this reversal of roles imply?

15. Why does Truffaut set Adele and Pinson's conversation in a *cemetary?* How does this reflect on her father's letter of consent? Why does Pinson still refuse to marry her?

> Pinson makes the mistake of kissing her. Why? How does this characterize him?

> Truffaut cuts from the kiss to Adele at her shrine, in which she has put Pinson's picture. Why is it ironic that she considers him a god?

16. Why does Truffaut superimpose Adele's face against the *waves* as she tells her father they are married?

> Why won't Adele go home, even after her father writes that Pinson has written to him, refusing to ever marry her?

17. Why is Adele oblivious to the bookseller's affection for her? Why is she offended at his gift of books? (*Les Miserables* by her father!)

18. What is the ironic connection with the next scene, in which Adele sends Pinson a Lady as a gift? ("He deserves all the women in the world")

19. In what ways is the hypnotist's performance with the mountie a *mirror scene?* Note that he makes the mountie *row a boat* and *undress.* How do these grotesque sexual metaphors reflect the tragic action of the main plot?

> "I could force this man to leave the police and finish his life in a monastery." Why does Adele approach the hypnotist after the show?

> Why is their conversation shot in a *mirror?* Why does she write her father's name on the mirror?

> What is the significance of the mountie's turning out to be a fake? How does this reflect the role-playing that is the film's central theme?

20. Why would Adele write in her diary about herself as a "fraud of identity," born of an unknown father?

21. Adele goes to the father of Pinson's rich young fiancee . . . and tells him that she's pregnant. Is this mere slander, or does she believe it?

22. Adele approaches Pinson while he's on maneuvers with his troops. She offers him money. Then she pulls a cushion from under her dress and flings it on the ground. What does this gesture mean?

23. As Adele packs to leave, she maintains to the end that *she* rejected Pinson—why?

> Why does she pretend that she's going home? Why won't she tell her landlady that she's out of money?

24. When Adele goes to the bank for her mail, no one in the front office recognizes her. What is the significance of this, aside from showing that time has passed?

25. As Adele stands beneath Pinson's window, the dog bites at her dress and chases her away. What does this final humiliation symbolize?

26. Truffaut cuts to the Barbadoes. All in black, Adele walks swiftly through the empty streets as Pinson follows her. WHAT IS THE SIGNIFICANCE OF HER NOT RECOGNIZING HIM, EVEN WHEN HE FACES HER AND CALLS HER NAME?

27. Why the documentary anti-climax? After such a passionate story, why does Truffaut end with Adele returning to France and living until 1915, finally dying at the age of 85—long after her father has died?

SWEPT AWAY (1975—Italian) Directed by Lina Wertmuller; with Giancarlo Giannini (Gennarino) and Mariangela Melato (Raffaela). Distributed by Cinema 5.

1. Why does Wertmuller begin by showing Raffaela and her rich friends arguing about politics in the midst of such a beautiful environment?

> "The Right flirts with the Vatican": What is the significance of Raffaela's being a Social Democrat?
> "We're the ones who starve widows and orphans," Raffaela calls out when Gennarino glares at her.
> How do these political jokes establish Raffaela and Gennarino as *allegorical* figures, representing modern political forces?

2. Note that *food* becomes increasingly symbolic in the course of the film. Raffaela rejects reheated coffee, "soft" spaghetti, and anything else Gennarino cooks for her. Why does Wertmuller stress Raffaela's pickiness about food?

3. Raffaela's husband tells her to "drop the Marie-Antoinette bit" because "she sounds like a fascist." If Gennarino is a *communist*, what is Wertmuller suggesting about communists and fascists?

4. "The men go to bed early—the women stay up to drink and gamble. What a system!" Why would Gennarino disapprove? What is the significance of his attitude toward marijuana?

5. The rubber inflatable dinghy seems to establish a modern "ship of fools" metaphor as they "go against the current." The motor breaks down, and neither of them can get the boat running. When Gennarino finally fixes it, neither knows which way to go:

"Stop going in circles. You're wasting gas."
"Then *you* tell me which way to turn."
How does this symbolize the political situation in Italy?

6. Still regarding himself as her servant, Gennarino dutifully catches a fish for Raffaela to eat. Instead of eating the raw fish (or giving it back to him), she throws it overboard. How does this characterize her? What is the significance of her response to all his attempts to be kind?

7. When she notes that southern women look old and fat because they don't diet, he comments that they're on a constant diet: "poverty." How does this motivate his treatment of her later?

8. WHAT DOES THEIR ISLAND SYMBOLIZE? (Note parallels to the Garden of Eden, Robinson Crusoe, and Burt Lancaster in "The Pirate of Green Island.")

9. Raffaela complains, "There must be a law against witholding help." He replies that if there were, all the rich would be in jail. What is the political significance of their reversal of roles?

10. "When communists get power, they're worse than Hitler." Why do Raffaela and Gennarino always express their sexual animosity in *political* terms? Conversely, what are the political implications of the current battle between feminists and chauvinists in the United States? Why do these kinds of people always seem to *attract* each other?

11. What is the significance of her thinking she can *buy* food from him? Why does he insist that she wash his pants instead?

12. Gennarino shuts her out of his hut and almost starves her ... to what purpose? How is this like Shakespeare's *Taming of the Shrew?*

> "Women are meant to serve men, not the other way around."
> "Kiss your master's hand."
> "I like my water cold—like you and Brezhnev with the wine."
> Why does Wertmuller make Gennarino so extreme? Why does he continue to bully Raffaela even after he dominates her completely?

13. Why does Gennarino resent Raffaela and her friends sunbathing on the yacht? ("As if we weren't there")

14. After chasing her all over the island and beating her up, why does he *refrain* from raping her? ("You're already a slave, but I want you to be a slave of love.") *Does* she become a slave of love, or is she merely

pretending? If her love for Gennarino is real, is Wertmuller suggesting that all women like being battered this way . . . or only a certain *kind* of woman?

15. THE SKINNING OF THE RABBIT IS A HIGHLY SYMBOLIC EPISODE. As Raffaela watches Gennarino ram a *spit* up the rabbit's rear, why does she say she feels like the rabbit? Why does she kiss his feet?

16. In a shot taken directly out of "From Here to Eternity," they lie embracing in the waves. Why is this an appropriate metaphor for their passion?

17. What is the significance of her decorating him with flowers? (Has she been reading *Lady Chatterly's Lover?*) What does Gennarino imply by asking her if this is some kind of *shrine?* Is this scene meant to be comic or serious?

18. Why doesn't Raffaela signal to the passing yacht, and why does Gennarino hit her? How are they characterized by the "animal sounds" dialogue that follows?

> "You're a brute, my love, always hitting me." Does Wertmuller agree with Bernardo Bertolucci's idea that men and women *are* savage animals (like in *The Conformist* and *Last Tango*)? Or does this scene serve another purpose here?

19. As Raffaela and Gennarino lie by the fire in a scene that could be set in the caves of Lascaux, she describes him as a "basic man." Why the neolithic setting?

20. Why does she ask him to sodomize her? What is the significance of his failing to understand her "fancy words"—and of her inability to speak bluntly?

21. Note the shot of them against the rippled sand, curled up like a yin-yang sign. What is the purpose of this shot?

22. When the ship arrives, why does Gennarino insist on returning to civilization?

> "I want to know the truth."
> "But you've been reborn here."
> Why is she nervous about leaving their island?

23. Gennarino's bubbly wife has been waiting for him at the "Small Paradise" Hotel (ironic?). As she comes running to greet him, note the expression on Raffaela's face and the barely concealed irony of what she

says: "We'd never have met, if we hadn't been rescued." How does this confrontation determine Raffaela's decision to leave with her husband?

24. Reunited with her friends, Raffaela doesn't seem to chatter the way she used to. Why not? What does her startled husband realize from her silence?

25. What is the symbolic significance of the *ring* Gennarino buys with the two thousand dollars that Raffaela's husband gives him as a reward? How does this reveal Wertmuller's attitude toward the so-called "historic compromise" that the communist party has tried to establish with the Social Democrats for the last thirty years?

26. WHY DOESN'T RAFFAELA RETURN TO THE ISLAND WITH GENNARINO? Why couldn't their relationship work out in civilization, and what does this imply about Love in the modern world?

27. What does the *helicopter* symbolize?

28. Gennarino reverts to type, screaming "the rich will screw you every time." But is this what Raffaela is really feeling? Of the two of them, which one has grown as a person? Which one has achieved a tragic understanding from what has happened between them?

29. Why doesn't Wertmuller end the film with the shot of Gennarino throwing the earring into the sea? Why the anti-heroic ending with Gennarino and his wife tugging at the suitcase?

COUSIN, COUSINE (1976—French) Directed by Jean-Charles Tacchella; with Victor Lanoux (Lodovic) and Marie-Christine Barrault (Marthe). Distributed by Cinema 5.

1. Marthe's sister and her family drive to their mother's wedding. What is the significance of the husband's bitching? What does this opening suggest about the typical middle-class family?

2. The wedding is typically French: Marthe's mother chugs a liter—How does this characterize her?

A young man crawls beneath the table and fondles a girl's leg... The groom climbs on the table and drops his pants... Karine chews a straw as she tells Marthe's sister about her first lover (her psychiatrist!)... Nelsa tells the children scandalous stories of the family's past... Why is it logical, in the midst of this zoo, that Lodovic and Marthe would get together? What do they have in common?

What do the *squirrels in the cage* symbolize?

3. What is the significance of Lodovic's being a *dance teacher,* and of his wandering from job to job?

4. When Lodovic and Marthe dance, her bratty little boy interrupts and complains that he wants to go home. What does this tell us about her family life?

5. Pascal (Marthe's husband) and Karine (Lodovic's wife) return late with an improbable story about his car breaking down. Why do Lodovic and Marthe react calmly to their excuses?

6. Why does Pascal go around breaking up with his girlfriends? What is the significance of his having *six* lovers, and of their all being so different? (Note that he has a different line for each one.)

7. Lodovic seeks out Marthe because of his wife's suicide attempt. Why is he indifferent to his wife's affairs?

"To Pascal, in case I die"—Why does Marthe suggest that they burn the letter? What is the effect on Pascal and Karine's affair, and why?

8. How are Lodovic and Marthe characterized by their meal of *pastries?* (In what sense have they both been starved for "sweets?")

9. Pascal waits for Marthe. Why does he suddenly decide to tell his wife about his affairs?

As he confesses, they shop in a *supermarket.* How is this a metaphor for his love-life?

"My guilt is all gone," Pascal declares (conveniently in time for dinner). How does he expect his wife to react to his confession, and why doesn't she?

10. Marthe's mother and her new husband jog. What is the irony of his being active and healthy—digging a swimming pool, etc.?

11. Nelsa shows her wedding slides, which are vulgar, to say the least! When Marthe's mother insists, "You should see the pretty side of life," Nelsa responds with a slide of Pascal and Karine (half-dressed) climbing into a car. Why is Nelsa's attitude toward love so negative?

> What is the point of the juxtaposition of the slide of the groom dropping his pants—and dying of a heart attack?

12. Why does Tacchella continue this odd mixture of comedy and tragedy, even at the funeral?

13. Lodovic and Marthe go swimming and eat pastries again. What do these activities symbolize?

> He buys her a straw hat, and she buys him a hideous tie— why?

> Marthe comes home late: Pascal is wolfing his food, while their kid sits glued to the TV. How does this characterize their home-life?

14. Pascal meets a former lover on the street and starts to follow her home. Why does he suddenly drive in the other direction?

> Why does he shower Marthe with presents? Why does he decide he "loves" his wife? Similarly, why does Karine tell Lodovic that from now on she intends to devote her life to him?

15. Marthe goes to Lodovic's school with a picnic lunch. They discuss his wife and his lack of jealousy. Why do they plan to run into each other at a restaurant? Why does Pascal always complain throughout his restaurant meals?

16. Why do Lodovic and Marthe decide *not* to sleep with each other? Are they serious, or are they just playing games?

17. Jocelyn's Wedding: How is the setting at the *trout farm* a metaphor for sexual entanglements?

> How is Pascal characterized by his fight with the groom's father?

> At the bridal table, the groom blows cigar smoke in the bride's face, while Karine shows off imaginary scars. Why does she chatter non-stop about nothing? ("No one ever listens to me.")

Marthe's kid wants to wear a *rabbit costume* so he can be like the others. How does this characterize him? Why is the rabbit symbolism appropriate?

Lodovic and Marthe leave to visit his eccentric friend. How is Lodovic characterized by playing his trumpet in the street?

Meanwhile, Pascal fondles all the women as they try to fish, and he throws a huge rock into the lake. Why is he being obnoxious?

18. Lodovic and Marthe's mother charleston while Nelsa tells Marthe about her plans to kill someone. Why is Nelsa obsessed with death?

19. After intending to be platonic lovers, why do Lodovic and Marthe suddenly decide to spend the weekend in bed?

Note, by the way, that this tryst is a potential disaster. What is the significance of their looking for a building that isn't there?

How does their weekend characterize their relationship? (Note particular incidents and activities: breaking the lamp, cutting his toenails, lying under the covers as the madam brings their supper, taking a bath together, discussing a recipe for marinated rabbit...)

20. Sunday night, Pascal sits waiting at the dinner table, which is littered with dirty dishes. How does the setting characterize him?

He smashes the vase and fantasizes about shooting her. Why does he persist in such infantile chauvinistic behavior, even when it doesn't work? What is the significance of his refusing to get out of bed? (Note that he finally *has* to get up when he runs out of cigarettes!)

21. Pascal runs into a middle aged lady on the street. What is the significance of her reaction to his lovemaking?

22. Karine comes to Lodovic's school. Why would she want to relive their first date? Why does he look unexcited?

23. In bed again, Lodovic and Marthe *tattoo* each other. How does this activity characterize them? What is the significance of their not being able to wash it off?

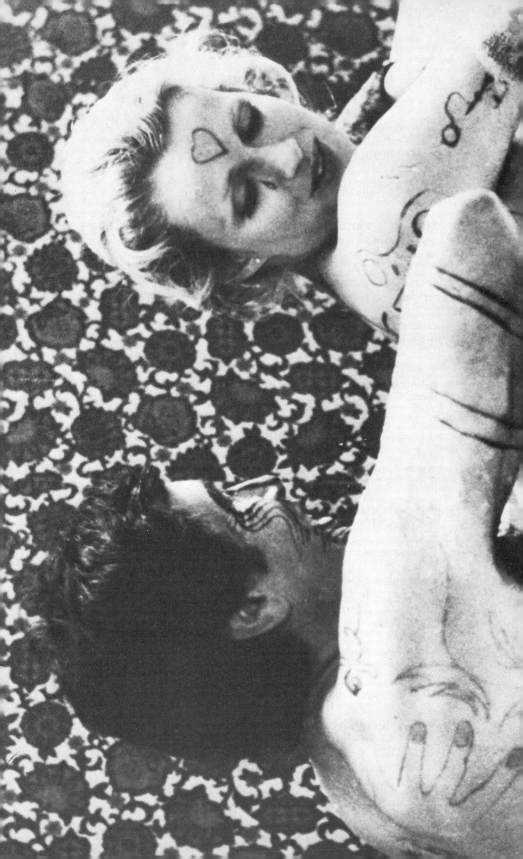

24. Why doesn't Marthe's mother hit it off with Lodovic's father when she stays with him? ("Your father is too kind—he's happy—he doesn't need anyone.") Her new boyfriend, Serge, is a *magician.* Why is he more suitable for her?

25. At the children's party, Pascal complains to Marthe's sister that "a man has to prove himself by sleeping with other women." What is ironic about his "respect for the family?" How does his approach to love affairs differ from Marthe's? ("In secret it's all right—it's decent.")

26. Lodovic and Marthe kiss passionately on the dance floor while the children stare and Karine gulps an apple. Why is the family scandalized by their behavior? (After all, everyone in the family seems to screw around all the time!)

27. Why would Karine leave a *lipstick* message on the mirror that she's leaving? Why does Lodovic react by packing away her paintings and sitting down to drink champagne with Nelsa?

> Were you surprised when Karine suddenly returned in tears? What is the significance of her wearing an outrageous new outfit every time she appears? How does this characterize her?

28. Christmas eve: Why does Pascal threaten to crash the car? How does this relate to his general behavior pattern?

> Lodovic and Marthe stay barricaded in the bedroom while everyone else watches midnight mass on TV. As Nelsa tells her grandfather about having sex with a boy, the priest on TV blesses everyone. What is the effect of this juxtaposition? How has Nelsa changed as a result of her experience?

> Why would Karine put on lipstick before attempting to slash her wrists?

> What is the significance of all the *monster masks?* Pascal staggers down the stairs with a *knife in his back.* How is this ironic touch a sign of his recovery?

> Serge's magic trick: What is the significance of his sawing Marthe's mother in half?

THE MAN WHO FELL TO EARTH (1976—English) Directed by Nicholas Roeg; with David Bowie, Candy Clark, Rip Torn, and Buck Henry. Distributed by Cinema 5.

1. Nicholas Roeg's films deal with a fall from innocence. In what sense is *The Man Who Fell To Earth* about lost paradises? How is Newton's landing in the lake a baptism?

2. The lady who buys his "wife's" ring warns him that he won't be able to buy it back. Why is this ironic? What does his collection of rings symbolize?

3. Why does Roeg emphasize Newton's thirst for *water?* As Newton drinks and prays by the river, he looks up to see a truck full of sheep being driven to the slaughterhouse. What does this juxtaposition imply?

4. Note that Newton's patents are written in mathematical equations that resemble an esoteric religious text. If this film is a religious allegory, how is Newton—with his advanced technological knowledge—a *god* of the modern age? What is the point of his eventual degeneration?

5. In an art book sent by his daughter, Prof. Bryce gazes at Brueghel's "Fall of Icarus." How does this painting relate to the film's theme?

6. Why does Roeg intercut shots of Newton watching an oriental sword dance with Prof. Bryce and a student taking pictures of themselves cavorting in bed? How are the two "performances" parallel? What is the implication of Newton's getting upset and rushing out of the theater?

7. Why does Roeg dwell on "Musee des Beaux Arts," W.H. Auden's poem about the fall of Icarus? How does this foreshadow Newton's ultimate failure and isolation?

8. How is Bryce's chairman characterized by his devotion to computer print-outs? Why does Bryce resign his professorship?

9. Returning to the site of his landing, Newton checks into a hotel. What does his trouble with the *elevator* symbolize? As blood pours from his nose, the chambermaid carries him to his room. How does her tending him while he throws up foreshadow their relationship?

10. During Marylou's unsuccessful attempt to seduce Newton, why does Roeg intercut the shots of Bryce in bed with various students? Why wouldn't Newton understand Marylou's heavy hints about spending the night with him? As he seems to "tune in" to Bryce's orgies, why does Newton appear appalled at the idea of sex? What is the significance of his preferring to watch TV? (four sets at a time, no less!)

11. As Bryce narrates his offer of a job with World Enterprises, why does Roeg include the comic sequence of him dropping his papers all over the lawn as a coed flirtatiously helps him pick them up? How is his leaving academia parallel to Newton's fall from innocence?

12. Marylou persuades Newton to go to church with her because "there has to be a God somewhere in space." Why is this ironic? How does the sentimental forties film on TV comment on her assertion?

13. A white horse rides by... Why does Roeg dub "Try to Remember" (from *The Fantasticks*) while Newton envisions being with his family when their planet was still green and beautiful? What is the effect of the cut to them crossing an endless white desert? What does this memory imply about earth's future? How does it also symbolize the relationships in this film?

> How does Marylou's memory of riding on a train when she was a child parallel Newton's vision of his former happiness?

14. Newton decides to build a house by the lake where he landed. As he stares at the water, Marylou cries, "Tommy, can you hear me?" What does this reference to the rock opera by The Who imply about Newton?

15. In his own world, Newton flashes back to his family and to a powerful memory of his landing. What is the significance of his inability to live in the present?

16. "Tommy, what's happening to you?" What is the significance of Newton's conversion from water to alcohol?

17. Why does Marylou get hysterical when Newton turns on all the TV screens behind her? What is the purpose of the montage of images: commercials, lions mating, a gangster film, a scene from *Billy Budd,* an Elvis flick, etc.?

> As Newton shrieks, "Get out of my life!" why does Roeg cut to Billy Budd on TV exclaiming, "God bless Captain Vere?"
> How is Newton like Billy Budd?

18. Why is Bryce puzzled at Newton's not knowing the motto "Per aspera ad astra?" How does this motto comment ironically on Newton's fate?

19. Mr. Peters, a large Black man, seems to be suggesting some kind of "merger" to Farnsworth. Why is Roeg vague about whether Peters is a gangster, a corporation executive, or a CIA agent?

20. Mr. Peters receives further instructions from his boss: "But remember, we're not the mafia...This is modern American Business and we're going to keep it that way." What does this disclaimer imply about American corporations and government agencies?

21. As Marylou clings to Newton to keep him from leaving, her oven alarm goes off (!) How does this affect the tone of this emotional sequence? Why does Newton knock the tray of cookies into the air? What is the meaning of the strange superimposition of bodies falling through space?

22. Why does Newton remove his contact lenses before letting Marylou see him again? Why does Marylou calm herself and try to join him? What is the significance of her failure? In what sense are *all* men and women "aliens" to each other?

23. "I don't hate anyone...I can't." Why does Roeg stress Newton's lack of strong or violent emotions?

24. During Newton's chaotic press conference, why does Roeg intercut the shots of Marylou refusing Farnsworth's financial offer? How does this scene recall Farnsworth's earlier scene with Mr. Peters?

25. Cut to two men in suits putting on motorcycle helmets...Why are they so businesslike? How does Farnsworth's "fall to earth" mirror Newton's?

26. What does the cut from Farnsworth's plunge to Mr. Peters diving into his pool imply?

> According to a Nicholas Roeg buff, the lady with him by the pool is the same actress who plays Newton's *wife*. This may imply that she has also come to earth with the same scientific knowledge. If so, how does her apparent contentment with her life and her swimming pool contrast with Newton's dream-world?

> What is ironic about Mr. Peters being a "family man?"

27. What is the significance of Arthur (Newton's chauffeur) now working for Mr. Peters? As Peters threatens Bryce ("You don't know how all this effects *you!*"), why does Roeg cut to Newton being examined by doctors, then to Bryce having dinner with Marylou?

What does Roeg imply with the intercut shots from the forties gangster film ("They asked me to help take him.")?

As Marylou exclaims, "Save him—from what?" why does Roeg cut back to the doctors?

28. Marylou enters the ruined house and goes through the secret door to Newton's room. Why has he been sealed in—and by whom?

29. While Newton stirs his drink with a *pistol,* she asks him what he fantasizes about. Why does Roeg have them shoot each other with blanks while they make love? How does this recall Bryce making love with his students, and how does it reveal Roeg's attitude toward heterosexuality?

30. Why on earth does Roeg include the comic ping-pong game? What is the effect of the abrupt change of mood as she flings the ring away ("It doesn't fit!")? How are they like a typical suburban couple?

31. What is the significance of the doctors' "changing Newton's eyes?" As he cries, "They're stuck!" what is the effect of the shot of the doctors' smiling faces?

32. "I can't get them off!"—In a mysterious series of cross-cuts, Newton says goodbye to his wife, a spaceship blasts off, and Newton's children lie beside their blood-splattered house. What is the meaning of these intercut shots? Is this a vision or a fantasy?

33. Roeg cuts from Newton lying in bed filling his glass with gin to Bryce standing over him while he lies unconscious. Why does Bryce unseal the front door? Why would the Corporation (or the government?) no longer care if Newton goes or stays?

34. Years later, Marylou shops for Christmas in a liquor store (!) Why does Roeg costume Bryce as Santa Claus? What is the significance of their winding up together? What does Roeg imply by cutting from their sentimental Bing Crosby Christmas to a vision of Newton and his wife?

35. Bryce tracks Newton through his record "The Visitor." What is the significance of Newton's being drunk? What is the point of his degeneration? In what sense has he become totally human?

Newton made his record for his wife, so she'd hear it on the radio. What is ironic about his continuing to send signals to a love who may not even be there?

36. "I think Mr. Newton has had enough." Since Sir Isaac Newton discovered the theory of *gravitation,* what does this ironic line imply about the Newtonian world-view and the technology it has produced?

SEVEN BEAUTIES (1976—Italian) Directed by Lina Wertmuller; with Giancarlo Giannini. Directed by Cinema 5.

Lina Wertmuller's first four films with Giancarlo Giannini explore the same set of paradoxes: that men who lack honor are the most obsessed with it; that macho strongmen are generally impotent; and that fascism—like chauvinism—stems not from superiority but from insecurity. Wertmuller's tragi-comic chauvinists are very stupid men who exaggerate their masculinity because they're afraid of being put down. Like Mimi the Metal worker and Gennarino in *Swept Away,* Pasqualino "Seven Beauties" is a coward who craves the appearance of honor and respect. He pursues sex (rather than love) merely to prove he's a man, even if it involves performing for someone thoroughly grotesque. By analogy, he is a natural fascist: a man who screws on principle will also kill on command. What are Wertmuller's alternatives to this macho code? Love and Anarchy—the only two forces that can counteract the "order" of the systems that dehumanize us.

***

1. Why does Wertmuller dub the cynical voice over the intercut shots of battle explosions and the newsreel of Hitler and Mussolini shaking hands? How does this voice introduce the character of Pasqualino?

2. Cut to two soldiers lost in the woods. Pasqualino has deserted after faking a wound. How does this epitomize his way of life? How do his political views differ from his comrade's, and what is the significance of this? Why does Wertmuller consider people like Pasqualino responsible for the rise of Mussolini?

3. The beautiful pan-shot across a forest shrouded in fog ends with a zoom to a procession of naked bodies being lined up and machine-gunned very methodically. Why does Wertmuller stress the *order* of this ritual? Why does she set it in such an idyllic place?

4. As Pasqualino boasts, "I killed a man before the war—for a woman," Wertmuller flashes back to a sleazy nightclub dance. Why does she make the performer so gross?

> Cut to Pasqualino's feet descending the steps. How does his pimp-outfit project his self-image?

> Pasqualino confronts his sister in the *mirror* of her dressing room. What is the significance of his obsession with "family honor?" Why does he think he'll gain respect by shooting her lover?

> Why does Wertmuller include the shot of the *clown* as Pasqualino walks down the steps after harassing his sister?

5. While all the women stuff mattresses in the family factory, Pasqualino perfumes himself and loads his pistol. How does this sequence symbolize male chauvinism in Italy?

6. Pasqualino swaggers through town flirting with all his ladies. What does the young street-singer symbolize? Why does Wertmuller pose the *parrot* right over Pasqualino's shoulder while he gives the girl a line about being his fiance?

7. The mafioso growls that he can't respect Pasqualino because his sister "wears red bows on her shoes." Why does Wertmuller stress the puritanism and chauvinism of the mafia?

8. Note the low camera angle as Pasqualino confronts his sister's seducer. What is the effect of the whirling fans in the background? How is this scene, with its distorted perspective, like a sequence from a "spaghetti western?"

9. To get revenge, Pasqualino shoots the man while he lies defenseless in bed. How does this foreshadow the sequence with the woman in the asylum? What is ironic about his doing things like this to prove he's macho and to gain respect?

10. Cut back to the two soldiers lost in the woods ... Pasqualino sneaks into an elegant old house, where a large half-naked lady sings ecstatically at the piano. How does she symbolize German culture? How does she contrast with Pasqualino's "performance" in the kitchen?

11. As Pasqualino stuffs his face, he looks up to see German soldiers standing over them. How is he characterized by being caught with a mouth full of food?

12. Why does Wertmuller use Wagner's "Ride of the Valkyries" as background music while the prisoners line up naked in the concentration camp? Note the shots of the prisoners gowned in gray and the rows of corpses. How is this sequence like Guido's "descent into hell" in Fellini's *8½?*

> The music climaxes as the huge lesbian commandant marches up with her guards to herd out a group of prisoners. How does this grotesque lady symbolize the connection between fascism and sexual chauvinism? As an authority figure, how is she like the Big Nurse in Ken Kesey's *One Flew Over the Cuckoo's Nest?*

13. Fernando Rey plays a "failed anarchist." In what sense is he Wertmuller's *raisonneur?* What is ironic about Pasqualino's asking him "how the world got this way?"

14. Why does Wertmuller juxtapose two prisoners playing violin while several of their comrades are shot? How does this dreamlike image illustrate a basic paradox in nazi "culture?"

15. As Pasqualino catches the commandant's eye, he flashes back to his mother singing a song about how all women live only for a man to love them. How does this childhood conditioning form Pasqualino's fantasy that he can seduce the commandant? Why are women like Pasqualino's mother responsible for much of the male-chauvinism that afflicts modern Italy?

16. Why does the old prisoner mock Pasqualino's obsession with surviving and cranking out children? What does he mean by saying that a "new man" must be born? Why does he stress the need for *disorder?*

17. Why does Wertmuller cut to the flashback of Pasqualino being criticized by his mafia boss, who has an elaborate, organized code for gaining respect?

> Don Raffaele: "We invented everything here in Naples." Why does Wertmuller stress the mafia's *efficiency* in disposing of corpses? What is the implied parallel between fascism and the mafia?

18. What is comic about Pasqualino's attempt to dispose of his victim's body? How does his "operation" on the body satirize nazi death camps?

19. As Pasqualino calls to inform Don Raffaele that he has shipped his victim to three different cities, Wertmuller cuts to a riot in the factory as the

police chase him across the rooftops. How does this comic sequence undercut Pasqualino's idea of his own cleverness and imagination?

20. Cut back to the concentration camp, where a prisoner is being whipped. Why does Wertmuller include the shot of Pasqualino "fixing himself up?" What is the meaning of the shot in which Pasqualino stands with his hands behind his head while the commandant drives around him in her jeep?

21. As Pasqualino stands there, why does he flash back to his trial? "I'm a man of honor...I won't be a clown." Why does he refuse to deny the murder or to plead insanity?

> Why does Wertmuller juxtapose Pasqualino's sentimental reunion with his family against the revelation that his sister is now sleeping with the lawyer to get him out of jail? Why does this cause Pasqualino to compromise his macho code and let the lawyer get him off?

22. What does Pasqualino's Mussolini imitation imply?

23. At the trial, note all the admiring faces of the ladies. Instead of dialogue, why does Wertmuller dub sentimental music for this sequence? How does this characterize the Italian judicial system? What do the closeups of Don Raffaele imply about the influence of the mafia on the court?

24. In the train station: Why does Wertmuller observe that the socialist has been sentenced to the asylum for *twice* as long as the "Monster of Naples?" What is ironic about Pasqualino's admiring Il Duce ("He gave us respect.")?

25. What is the significance of Pasqualino's setting himself up as a manipulator in the insane asylum? How does his rape of the female patient (while she's tied down!) fit his general pattern of behavior?

26. Cut to Pasqualino being hosed and beaten as he too is tied down to a bed. Why does Wertmuller intercut the closeups of human *brains* as he's being electroshocked?

27. What does the doctor's offer to get him transferred from the asylum to the army imply about the army?

28. As Pasqualino declares, "I'll do anything to live," what is the effect of the cut to him standing in the concentration camp with his hands behind his head? Why does he start singing? Why does this lead the commandant to have him brought to her office?

29. As he crawls on the huge swastika, giving her his "seductive" line, how does he symbolize Italy's relationship with Hitler?

30. When Pasqualino fails to "perform" for her, the commandant feeds him like a dog...so he can try again. How does this sequence undercut his macho assumptions?

31. Why does Wertmuller cut from the Blue Angel parody to Pasqualino's flashback of his sister singing and his seductions of other women in the past?

> As Pasqualino gives it a second try, what is the purpose of the cut to the sixteenth century Florentine painting (Bronzino's "Allegory")? Why does the commandant fix her gaze on the portrait of Hitler?

32. When Pasqualino is finished, why does the commandant say his "love of life" disgusts her? Why would she regard him as a "subhuman worm without any soul or ideals," and why does this lead her to put him in charge of his barracks?

33. Pasqualino's moral problem: he must choose six men for execution, or she'll send them all to the ovens. Why does the old prisoner volunteer to die? When Pasqualino refuses to name him for execution, why does the old man stand up, shout that he's free, and jump into the *latrine?* What does this act symbolize?

> Why does Pasqualino's friend also revolt...and why does he insist that Pasqualino shoot him? What is the significance of Pasqualino's surviving only by shooting his friend?

34. Why does Wertmuller have them all freeze as she pans the lines of prisoners and Pasqualino standing there silently with the gun? What is the effect of the romantic music dubbed over, then the cut to Italy being rebuilt?

35. Similarly "reconstructed," Pasqualino returns home to the adoration of his seven sisters. Why does Wertmuller cut to the closeups of all the *dolls?* What do they symbolize?

36. The young street-singer, heavily made up, appears at the door. What is ironic about Pasqualino's saying, "Even you have become a whore?" How does her transformation mirror his?

37. Pasqualino echoes the old anarchist without understanding his point: "Soon we'll all be killing each other over an apple." Why does he insist on

their having lots of children so they can "defend" themselves? How has life as a capo in a concentration camp affected Pasqualino's world-view? How does his attitude reflect the cultural values of post-war Italy?

38. As Pasqualino's mother tells him not to worry, that he's beautiful and alive, what is the effect of the multiple images in the mirror?

39. "Yes ... I'm alive"—As Pasqualino stares into the mirror, what does the long final closeup of his face mean?

THE TENANT (1976—English/French) Directed by Roman Polanski; with Roman Polanski (Trelkovsky), Isabelle Adjani (Stella), and Melvyn Douglass (Mr. Z.); cinematography by Sven Nykvist. Distributed by Films Inc.

1. Why does Polanski begin with a shot of lace-web curtains with faces peering out, followed by a shot straight *down* from the window?

2. How is Trelkovsky like the main character in Kafka's novel, *The Trial?* There are a lot of good actors in Europe ... Why would Polanski choose to play the part himself?

3. How is the *dog* that nips Trelkovsky like the dog in Albee's *Zoo Story?* How does this establish the decaying apartment building as a kind of *hell?*

4. What is the effect of the shot *up* the spiral staircase? What does this Dantesque image symbolize?

5. Apparently, the only way to get an apartment in Paris is if the previous tenant jumps out the window ... Trelkovsky visits the hospital, where he meets Stella, who is visiting her dying friend, Simone. ("Simone, don't you recognize me?") Note that this simple line develops nightmarish overtones in the course of the film.

> How is Trelkovsky characterized by dropping his oranges all over the floor?

WHAT IS THE SIGNIFICANCE OF THE MUMMY-PATIENT'S SHRIEK? (cf. EDVARD MUNCH'S PAINTING, "THE SCREAM")

6. Stella, who seems to get excited by violence, takes Trelkovsky to see a *Bruce Lee* film. What is the effect of the sound of crunching bones coming from the screen as she grabs him by the crotch? Why does Polanski include the *voyeur?*

7. Trelkovsky sees Stella again at Simone's funeral. Why does his vision become distorted as the priest talks excitedly about putrifaction? Trying to escape from this maniacal sermon, Trelkovsky finds the door locked. What does this symbolize?

(cf. Sartre's *No Exit* and Bunuel's *Exterminating Angel*)

8. The Housewarming Party: Why is Trelkovsky always apologizing? How is he characterized by standing there with his arms full of garbage?

9. A face stares at him from the bathroom opposite. What is the effect of the repetition of this motif?

10. He finds a *tooth* in a hole in the wall. Why is this image so disturbing?

11. As Trelkovsky picks up Simone's bra, there is a knock on the door. Why would he suddenly feel guilty?

At the door stands an old woman, who is worried about a complaint about her daughter's clumping foot. How is this like an episode in a Kafka novel? Why does Polanski include so many instances of physical deformity in his films?

12. Trelkovsky's vulgar co-workers plan revenge on his neighbors. Why would this idea make him very nervous?

13. Trelkovsky visits his friend, who deliberately plays loud military marches to upset his meek neighbors. How does this reflect the film's main premise that the world is made up of persecutors and victims?

14. After going out drinking with "Simone's friend," Trelkovsky comes home to find his apartment ransacked. Why does the landlord warn him not to contact the police?

15. At the cafe, Trelkovsky meets Stella and her friends. He is informed, "She was looking at *you* when she screamed." Why do they all stare at him? (Or does he imagine this?)

What is the significance of Trelkovsky's acquiring Simone's books?

16. "AT WHAT PRECISE MOMENT DOES A PERSON STOP BEING WHO HE THINKS HE IS?" How does this relate to the film's main theme?

"If you cut off my head ... do I say me and my *head* or me and my *body?*" Why would he have such a bizarre thought while a beautiful woman is performing oral intercourse on him?

WHERE IS THE *SELF?* WHERE DOES *PERSONAL-ITY* LIE? (Having nudged millions of rats through mazes, behavioral psychologists insist that these are both fictional concepts, and have no more reality than God or Santa Claus. What do *you* think about Trelkovsky's question?)

17. Note that Trelkovsky's shirt is buttoned all the way up to the neck as he leaves Stella's bed to throw up ... How does this characterize him? What is his attitude toward sex?

18. Trelkovsky gets the *Egyptian postcard* in the mail. What does this symbolize? If Simone's soul has indeed invaded his body, what does this have to do with the cult of Isis and Osiris?

19. Mme. Dioz comes with a petition to evict one of the other tenants. Why does this intensify his already Kafkaesque paranoia?

20. What does his fantasy about *strangling* symbolize? (cf. Truffaut's *Story of Adele H.*)

21. The police inspector warns Trelkovsky against "disturbing the peace." Why is this ironic?

22. What is the significance of Trelkovsky's painting his nails?

23. What is the implication of the *Egyptian hieroglyphs* in the bathroom? When Trelkovsky looks over at his own window and sees *himself* looking through binoculars, what does this do to his sense of his own identity?

24. As unearthly light pours through his window, Trelkovsky looks across and sees the *mummy* unwrapping herself. What does she symbolize? How does this mocking apparition foreshadow the end of the film?

25. While watching the workmen repair the tiles below, Trelkovsky hears people laughing. Why would he imagine that they're laughing at *him?*

26. As the dreamlike incidents pile up, why does Polanski make it so difficult to determine whether Trelkovsky is being driven to suicide or whether he is merely becoming increasingly paranoiac? Note the following incidents and details:

> He puts on Simone's makeup and buys a wig. How is he like the main character in Hitchcock's *Psycho?*

> When he wakes, he finds blood on his hand and his missing *tooth* in the hole in the wall... Why the *same* missing tooth as the mummy in the hospital?

> The severed head bounces outside the window...

> The crippled child, wearing a *Trelkovsky-mask,* points up at his window. Is there some kind of satannic ceremony going on in the courtyard?

27. Trelkovsky visits Stella again. She wakes him ("You do recognize me, don't you?"), and he shrieks. How does this foreshadow the film's ending?

> As he looks through the peep-hole, the doctor's face transforms into the face of Mr. Z. What is the significance of this?

> Why does he wreck her apartment?

28. The Car Accident: Why does he insist that they're trying to kill him when they offer to take him home?

29. That night, all the neighbors (including Stella) appear on the roof, *applauding*... very much like a crowd in New York urging a suicide to jump.

> What is the effect of the oriental carpets, and the balconies that look like opera boxes? How does this comment on Polanski's image of *himself* as a filmmaker?

> What is the significance of Trelkovsky's hallucinatory perspective as the neighbors appear to have hissing tongues and distorted faces?

30. The Ending in the Hospital: How has the action come full circle, and what is the meaning of this?

> Possibly, this strange film is an allegory. If so, in what sense is the soul merely the *tenant* of the body?

If souls are indestructible, and if the whole world is just a torture chamber full of persecutors and victims, what is Polanski's chilling implication about death?

Of couse, the film may simply be a sick existential joke.

ANNIE HALL (1977—American) Directed by Woody Allen; with Diane Keaton, Tony Roberts, and Paul Simon. Produced by United Artists.

PROLOGUE: "I would never belong to a club that would have me as a member." How does this explain Woody Allen's film-relationships with women?

1. As a child, Alvy Singer was depressed because "the universe is expanding." His doctor assured him that Brooklyn won't expand for a long time, and that we should enjoy life while we can. How does this sequence establish Alvy's obsession with death?

2. What does Alvy's childhood home being *under the roller coaster* symbolize? How are his teachers characterized? What is absurd about the little girl's lecture on "latency periods?" When Alvy's classmates explain where they are today, why are their recitations funny? ("I was a heroin addict; now I'm a methadone addict.")

3. As Alvy and Annie stand on line for the film, an intellectual phony behind them criticizes Fellini as "indulgent." Why does Alvy get upset? Why does Woody Allen identify with Fellini? What is the effect of his introducing Marshall McLuhan?

4. In bed, they discuss *The Sorrow and the Pity*. Why does Alvy keep returning to this particular film, and how does this relate to their sexual problem?

5. Flashback to Alvy meeting his first wife, Alison, at a Stevenson rally: Why is his stereotypical characterization of her funny? How does his joke at the rally reflect the main action of the film? (He "dated an Eisenhower

woman, trying to do to her what Eisenhower has been doing to the rest of the country.")

6. Years later: As Alison wants to make love, Alvy insists on discussing the Kennedy assassination. She calmly observes, "You're using this conspiracy as an excuse to avoid having sex with me." Why does Alvy resist such a warm, witty, lovely, intelligent woman who loves him—and how does this echo his statement at the beginning of the film?

7. What does the business with the *lobsters* symbolize?

8. Alvy and Annie confront the image of her and her former boyfriend, a pseudo-hip young actor. Why would Alvy disapprove of him?

9. Flashback to Alvy's second wife, a neurotic academic: Why does he flee the "intellectual" party to watch the Knicks play basketball on TV?

> "You're using sex to express hostility," she claims. How is she different from Alvy's first wife?

> She can't make love because she has a headache... "like Oswald in *Ghosts.*" Why is her scholarly comparison funny?

10. If New York City is the "victim of an anti-semitic plot," as Alvy claims, why does he insist on staying there?

11. Flashback: Alvy and Annie meet in a tennis game... What is the significance of their both being such terrible players? How do her *clothes* characterize her? Why would Alvy become interested in a lady whose conversation is as incoherent as her clothing?

12. What does their confusion over "who is driving" symbolize? What is the significance of her being such a terrible driver? How does her method of parking foreshadow their relationship?

13. "You're what Grammy Hall would call a Real Jew"... During their "intellectual" conversation, what is the point of the subtitles?

14. Alvy goes to hear Annie sing at a nightclub audition. What is the effect of the interrupting noises and the oblivious audience?

15. They wind up in bed: What is the significance of her having to smoke marijuana before making love... and of his dislike for "stimulants?"

16. When Annie decides to move in with Alvy, why does this bother him?

17. As Alvy and Annie make love, a double-exposure of her gets up from the bed and observes. How does this foreshadow difficulties in their relationship?

18. How does Alvy's comic delivery differ from the corny nightclub comedian who interviews him?

19. Meeting Annie's family: Why the hallucination of Alvy as a rabbi? In the split-screen sequence, how is Annie's family different from Alvy's?

20. As Annie's brother Duane confesses his suicidal urges, why is his grim, deadpan delivery funny? Why does Alvy say he has to go (he's "due back on planet earth")? What is the effect of the cut to Duane driving them home in the rain?

21. After urging Annie to take night courses, why does Alvy freak out over her friendship with her professor?

22. Alvy and Annie break up: Trying to understand, he asks an old lady on the street what the problem is. "Love fades," she says. How to stay together? A very straight-looking middle aged gentleman tells him that he and his wife use a vibrating egg (!) A beautiful young couple who look like they've just stepped off a magazine cover explain that they're happy together because they're both completely shallow. Why does Woody Allen include these surreal interviews?

23. The animation sequence: Alvy complains that in *Snow White* he always fell for the wicked queen. How does this reveal his basic problem with women?

24. What is the tone of Alvy's date with the *Rolling Stone* reporter who adores the Maharishi?

> She tells him that making love with him is a *Kafkaesque* experience. How does this metaphor reveal Alvy's self-image? How does it echo the sequence with the *lobsters?*

25. As Alvy lies in bed with the reporter, Annie calls him. What is the significance of her "emergency" being a *spider* in the bathroom?

26. How does the hallucination of the 1945 party relate to the film's "Old Times" theme?

27. Note that Annie sings much better than she used to. How has she changed since she and Alvy first met? What is the importance of Frank Sinatra "smothering" her in her dreams...and of Alvy's last name being "Singer?"

When Tony Lacy approaches them, why does Alvy reject his party invitation? (Note his reaction to the word "mellow.")

Why would Alvy rather go back to "The Sorrow and the Pity," a depressing film about Nazi collaborators?

28. The split-screen of Alvy and Annie in analysis is a lesson in relativity theory. How do they both interpret making love "three times a week?"

29. What is the point of the cocaine joke? What is the effect of the cut from his sneeze to "We Wish You a Merry Christmas" and the shot of Hollywood palm trees? Why does Woody Allen juxtapose the Christmas music against images of hot dog stands and plastic taco palaces?

30. As Rob engineers laughs for his TV show, why does Alvy react so negatively?

31. "I forgot my mantra"... What is the point of all the pseudo-hip chatter at Tony Lacy's party? What is the significance of Annie's conversion to the California lifestyle?

32. On the plane, both Alvy and Annie worry about "hurting" each other by breaking up. Why is this ironic? Why is his "shark" metaphor funny?

33. When they divide their books, what is the significance of all the books on death being *his?*

34. Alvy tries going out with other women. What is the significance of his date not understanding his "lobster" joke? How does this lead to his calling Annie again?

35. Alvy flies to Los Angeles. At the sidewalk cafe, he orders alfalfa sprouts and a plate of mashed yeast. How does this satirize California culture? How does the roaring traffic comment on their meeting? Why does Alvy call Los Angeles "munchkin land?" Why won't Annie return to New York?

36. As Alvy crashes back and forth, what is the purpose of the intercut shots of the bumper-cars in the amusement park?

37. Rob bails him out... Alvy interrupted him in the middle of an orgy with 16-year-old twins (!) Why would he rather live this way than perform Shakespeare in Central Park?

38. For his first play, Alvy rewrites his goodbye scene with Annie. How has it changed? How does this shift in modes reflect on the film itself, which deals with Woody Allen's "real-life" relationship with Diane Keaton?

39. Why does Allen end the film with a montage of their past, juxtaposed against Annie singing "Old Times?" Why does he give the audience a "choice" of endings?

40. What is the meaning of his final comment on "relationships?"

PROVIDENCE (1977—English) Directed by Alain Resnais; with John Gielgud, Dirk Bogarde, Ellen Burstyn, David Warner, and Elaine Stritch. Distributed by Cinema 5.

Rumor has it that Clive Langham, the venomous old novelist who rules over Providence, is modeled on H.P. Lovecraft. As a portrait of the artist as a constipated old man, Clive could also be a self-parody of Alain Resnais. In this wickedly funny film, Resnais returns to the love-triangle of *Last Year at Marienbad:* an icy husband, a sleepwalking wife, and a star-gazing lover who may (or may not) be real. *Providence* is even more complicated than *Marienbad* because Resnais uses his omniscient *persona* to intrude on his characters. Clive comments on their dialogue, imposes his own voice, and even orders one of them to leave (having accidentally written him into the wrong scene!) The result is a religious allegory about predestination and free will, as well as a philosophical examination of the nature of reality. It's also a bitter black comedy about the creative process. As mythical God and dying artist, Clive Langham is the ultimate Primal Father thundering about the bourgeois complacency of his children.

***

1. The film begins with a crumbling old castle and a slow zoom to its name-plate: "Providence." "Damn!" Clive Langham mutters as he spills his drink. In what sense does John Gielgud "play God" throughout the film? How does this sequence satirize the opening of *Citizen Kane?*

2. How does the sequence of the soldiers hunting the old hermit in the woods satirize horror movies?

3. In court: Claud insists, "Surely the facts are not in dispute!" How does this ironic line establish the film's theme?

When Kevin protests that the old hermit was turning into an animal, Claud sarcastically asks if he was a "werewolf." How does this *transformation* reflect what Clive is doing to his family?

In what sense is writing novels a vampirish activity?

How does the dying old man reflect Clive's self-concept?

4. As Clive narrates, why does Resnais cut to a corpse being dissected, then to his son drinking wine?

5. Why does Sonia bring Kevin (the accused!) to join Claud for lunch?

6. "That's right, children—go in," Clive urges as Sonia takes Kevin home with her. She starts to undress... only to find that his feelings are less than passionate. Why does Clive keep stressing that both men in Sonia's life are virtually asexual?

7. Cut to Claud dictating a bitchy letter to his father attacking him for taking such a long time to die. How does this fantasy-letter project Clive's own feelings about life?

8. As Clive drinks bitterly, he chooses a new mistress for his son from the crowd on a plane. What is the significance of Helen's looking just like Claud's mother, Clive's dead wife?

9. Kevin ignores Sonia's seduction to soliloquize about the psychological problems of astronauts... "Why do you go on about the astronauts?" Sonia cries. Why does Resnais juxtapose Clive's own voice against Sonia's?

"Up there in the icy universe there's nothing." Why does Clive despise Kevin's preoccupation with astrophysics? What is the theological implication of his declaration?

10. Clive arranges for Claud to walk in on his wife while she's with Kevin. "I don't smell any sex. Hasn't there been any?" Claud asks coldly. Then he retaliates by telephoning the "mistress" his father has just created for him. When Sonia demands, "Who's Helen?" Claud puzzles, "I don't remember." How does this absurdity comment on the relationship of character and writer?

11. As Claud sits in his car, an old man collapses on the street in front of him. How does his non-response characterize him? Why does Resnais cut from a wrecking-ball shattering a building to Clive "soothing his tired rectum?" What does Clive's *constipation* symbolize?

12. Claud stares as an old werewolf is put into an ambulance. Why does Resnais include this dreamlike sequence?

13. As Kevin walks into Helen's room (!) Clive exclaims, "Out! Out!"... having accidentally written him into the wrong scene. Note the embarrassed expression on David Warner's face as he leaves hurriedly. How does this absurd sequence call attention to Resnais as a filmmaker?

14. TAKE TWO: Observing the witty artifice of his dialogue, Clive quotes his critics' complaint that he has substituted style for feeling. His reply: "Style *is* feeling." In what sense does Resnais intend this as his own self-defense?

> Helen's first words: "I'm dying." Clive has already mentioned that Helen looks like Claud's mother. What is the significance of Clive's dead wife Molly intruding on his writing, making herself a character in his novels against his will?

15. Claud characterizes his relationship with Sonia as "a silent scream." Why would he develop self-control as a defense against his father?

16. "We must do something about father." Cut to Clive being dragged across the lawn, then to Claud in court condemning stacks of his father's books. Why does Clive keep emphasizing his son's hatred?

17. In the kitchen, Claud and Sonia soliloquize past each other. Why does Sonia say she's not a person but merely a "construction?" What is the double-meaning of this?

18. Kevin is mugged while pondering sub-atomic particles. How does this characterize him? When Claud asks him what he thinks of his wife's body, she interrupts with "It isn't the point!" Why does she resent Claud's icy self-control? How is the dialogue in this scene reminiscent of Harold Pinter?

19. As Claud walks out the door, he appears in a different scene—on a sunny patio lunching with his mistress. How does this illogical shift in setting call attention to Resnais' own art?

20. As Clive soliloquizes about spewing out his rage, there is a knocking sound. Why does Resnais cut frequently to the steps of a gloomy stadium where Clive's dead wife Molly lies huddled? How does this setting symbolize the afterlife?

21. As Claud arranges to have Kevin bundled out of the country, note that his cool tone finally erupts in anger: "Do you disapprove of violence? So do

I—it reeks of spontaneity." Why does Resnais cut to Clive sitting on the toilet?

22. Why would Claud have Kevin fitted for an expensive suit?

23. "Molly wore white gloves like that . . . " Why does Resnais dub *Clive's* voice as Kevin talks with Sonia?

> "I have an erection."
> "Ooh—Is it urgent?" Sonia asks hopefully.
> "It isn't mine!"
>
> How does this absurd dialogue illustrate Clive's projection
> of his own feelings onto his characters?

24. Claud cooks *beans* for Kevin while the three of them drink white wine. How does this image comment on bourgeois dinner parties? How does it reflect Clive's excremental vision of the world?

> "Do you like the way he masticates?"
> "I'm more interested in the way he fornicates."
> What is the effect of Clive's sudden burst of laughter?

25. Cut to Clive: "How darkness creeps into the blood . . . " Why does he urge his children to show a little more venom?

26. The four-way conversation: Sonia describes Claud as tragically incomplete because he feels no rage. Helen claims she's merely *using* Claud for the novel she's writing. How do both female characters project Clive's own feelings about his son?

> The scene suddenly converts to a cocktail party out of
> *Marienbad!* Why does Resnais refer so overtly to his earlier
> film?

27. Claud asks his secretary if the words addressed to his father offend her. She storms out exclaiming, "He had me more than once! Why shouldn't I be fucked by a genius?" Since Clive is writing this about *himself,* how does it connect him with Freud's idea of the Primal Father?

28. Clive remembers his son as a child lecturing him on the necessity of finding a "moral language." Why does Resnais repeat this phrase several times in the film, each time attributing it to a different character?

29. Helen and Kevin talk over a glass of wine. Why does Resnais keep referring to the "white wine" motif? Why does he punctuate their conversation with terrorist bombs in the background?

Why does Helen speak as though she were *Molly?* When Clive remembers Molly's accusing words about his coldness, why does he beg her to get out of his mind?

30. Claud and Kevin fire pistols. What does the setting symbolize? How is it a metaphor for family life?

Why does Kevin speak in *Claud's* voice accusing his father of making people's lives hell just so he can turn them into fiction?

31. While Clive dreams again about the dark stadium, why does Resnais cut to worms revealed beneath a rock, then to Claud pursuing Kevin with a pistol? As Claud chases Kevin, note that Resnais intercuts three highly symbolic sequences:

(1) In a flashback, Claud is introduced to Kevin, who observes that we can't attribute all our problems to childhood. "What we're searching for," he insists, "is a moral language."

(2) In a shot reminiscent of *Marienbad,* Claud remembers Sonia swinging in a *white hammock.* What is the purpose of the surreal beach scene?

(3) Helen reads a telegram for Clive: "My son is an emotional cripple... Descend on him if it amuses you."

32. As Claud corners Kevin in the woods, Kevin starts turning into a werewolf—just like the old man he shot in the beginning of the film. What is the significance of this transformation as victim, murderer, and prosecutor exchange roles?

"HOW YOU'VE DRIVEN MY MOTHER!" Claud declares. What is the double-meaning in this dreamlike confrontation?

33. What is the effect of the cut to bright sunshine and flowers as Clive rests in his chair?

Why the flashback to the autopsy?

As Clive regrets the night of booze and nightmares, Claud arrives. Why does Clive flash back to discovering his wife's suicide?

34. What is the tone of the reunion, and what does this imply about the "real" Claud and Sonia? What is the significance of Kevin's true identity? How does this explain the love-triangle?

"How's the new book going, father?" Claud asks. "Whom are you disemboweling this time?" Why is this ironic? How does it recall the repeated shot of the autopsy?

How does Claud's excusing his mother's suicide relate to the trial for mercy-killing that starts the film?

Sonia jokes with Claud that his father thinks they're a bit "unreal." Why would Clive find her "opaque?"

35. As they laugh over dinner, why does Resnais emphasize the peacefulness of the lush green estate?

36. Clive reacts to Claud's bourgeois credo with: "Is he naive or just a hypocrite?" As Claud responds with a toast ("Live long"), what does the troubled look on his face mean?

37. Why does Clive tearfully ask them all to leave without a word or a gesture? As he sits there alone, what is the significance of his last line ("I guess it won't hurt to have one more.")?

THAT OBSCURE OBJECT OF DESIRE (1977—French)
Directed by Luis Bunuel; with Fernando Rey, Carole Bouquet, and Angela Molina. Produced by First Artists; distributed by Films Inc.

"Of all perversions," the Marquis de Sade once said, "the worst is chastity." Luis Bunuel explores this paradox using *two* actresses alternating in the role of a young lady who pursues Platonic Love as though it were an act of terrorism. The rich old man who desires her doesn't seem to notice that she's "two different people," just as the spoiled, wealthy society he represents is oblivious to the dual nature of terrorism. The analogy is complete when we examine the basic question of the film: Does she really love him? Is she trying to reform him the way revolutionaries say they want to reconstruct their society, or is she merely in love with danger and hungry for power over him? Bunuel has made the object of Mathieu's desire so obscure that our answer to this problem would only reveal our own values.

***

1. Seville: How do the shot of the phallic palm trees and the Flamenco guitar music symbolize the two main characters?

2. After arranging a first class sleeper to Paris, Mathieu Fabert (Fernando Rey) returns to his mansion. Note the smashed vase on the floor and the blood on the pillow. What does his *burning* a woman's shoes and panties symbolize? Throughout the film, why does Bunuel dwell on *fetishes?*

> His butler's philosophy: "If you go anywhere with women, carry a big stick." What are the erotic connotations of this line? How does the misogynistic butler act as Bunuel's *persona?*

3. Cut to a wealthy businessman getting into his car ... Suddenly the car explodes. "Terrorists again," Mathieu remarks calmly. What is the significance of his indifference? How does the exploding car reflect his own inner state?

4. On the train to Paris, Mathieu meets one of his rich neighbors from Paris and a judge from his cousin's law court. How does this dreamlike coincidence set the tone for the rest of the film?

5. Looking very bruised, Carole Bouquet walks up the platform. After asking someone to go the lavatory with a bucket, Mathieu pours it on her when she tries to board the train. What does this act symbolize, and why do Mathieu's companions pretend not to notice?

> The dwarf is curious about why he did it. What is the significance of his being a psychologist?

6. Matthieu's story begins in Paris. He was visiting his cousin the judge, who was bemoaning the fact that a priest connected with a terrorist group had received a mere eight-year jail sentence for blowing up a church. Throughout the film, why does Bunuel use absurd initials to identify competing terrorist organizations?

> Why does he juxtapose their discussion of R.A.I.J. (The Revolutionary Army of the Infant Jesus!) against Concita's appearance over a vase of roses?

While the judge fumes that "terrorists are fascinated by danger," Concita calmly goes through the motions of serving them. Why does Bunuel hint that she's *not* actually a professional maid?

7. As Mathieu prepares to receive Concita for a midnight tryst, a different actress (Angela Molina) walks through the door. Why does Bunuel use *two* actresses to play this part? What is the significance of Mathieu's talking with her as though she were the same person? What does this imply about the way men perceive women?

Despite Concita's sultry exterior, she insists that she was raised "the old-fashioned way." How is this contradicted by her *laugh* as she rebuffs him and leaves the room? Why does she quit the next morning without explanation?

8. Three months later in Switzerland: What does the flock of swans gliding peacefully on the lake symbolize? Why does Bunuel undercut this image with Mathieu's encounter with the young men in the park? Why does their wanting only 800 francs confuse him? Why does he pause instead of telling the gendarme that he was robbed?

9. While Mathieu enjoys his breakfast in a cafe, Concita One sits down at his table. Why does she return his money? If she objects to his being "too affectionate," why does she give him her address?

As she walks away, he picks up her handkerchief. Symbolically, how does this recall her shoes and panties in the film's opening scene?

10. Mathieu finds Concita's flat in Courbevoie. Judging from her sideways looks, what does she think of her mother's spending all her time in church? Why does she bite her finger and look upset when he slaps a thick wad of money on the table?

"I'm not that kind of girl," she says ... but what does the expression on her face imply? What does her box of candy symbolize?

11. The next time Mathieu returns to the flat, Angela Molina is performing a fiery Spanish dance. Unlike Concita One, who seems cold but leers lasciviously, Concita Two appears to be very sexy ... She undresses and bathes in front of him, for instance. How do the "Two Concitas" represent opposite ways of driving men insane with frustration?

"I think about you all the time," Mathieu pleads.
"So do I" is her reply. Why is this ironic?

Concita sits on Mathieu's lap and kisses him passionately,
but when he pushes things further, she lectures him on her
virginity. How is this calculated to lead him on?

12. "Two women alone are so exposed," Concita's mother complains, "but
our souls are straighter than St. John's finger." Why are her protestations
ironic?

13. As Mathieu kisses Concita's hand, what is the effect of the cut to the
"Chapel of the Annunciation?" How does their "affair" reflect the
relationship of the wealthy and the Church?

14. Mathieu sends for Concita's mother: "I would like to unite our lives," he
declares. How does the *mouse* caught in the trap comment on his desire?
What is the significance of the mother's taking his money without any
hesitation?

15. Mathieu goes to the door with a rose in his hand. Instead of Concita, her
friend appears with a letter. Why does Concita refuse to come to him?

Rushing to their apartment, Mathieu finds them gone. What
are the possible interpretations of their sudden disappearance?

16. Two months later, Mathieu again joins his cousin for dinner. As he
complains about his passion for Concita, why does Bunuel put a *fly* in his
martini?

17. By dreamlike coincidence, Concita One is checking hats at the
restaurant. As she discourages Mathieu's advances, her boss chastises her
for talking with the customers. How does her abrupt resignation reflect her
character?

"You tried to buy me like a piece of furniture ... just when I
was about to give myself to you." Do you believe her? Where
do Bunuel's sympathies lie in this scene?

"I can live on nothing ... I'm not like you." Throughout the
film, what is Concita trying to tell Mathieu about his values
and his life?

18. When Concita declares, "I'll be your mistress in that house!" does she
mean it, or is she just leading him on? If this film is a political allegory, how

does their relationship reflect the uneasy "marriage" of conservatives and socialists in European governments?

19. Mathieu and Concita Two are stuck in traffic because the power plant has been blown up by terrorists. How does this foreshadow the love scene that follows?

20. Mathieu's mansion: Why would Concita refuse to sleep in the bed where his dead wife slept seven years ago?

21. After asking him if he'll always love her, Concita goes to "get ready" for bed. What is the significance of her transformation into Concita One as she emerges from the bathroom?

> Standing in front of the mirror, she bares her breasts—then says, "I'm not in the mood." When he gets infuriated and leaps on top of her, why does she stop resisting and tell him to put out the candle? What are the connotations of his gesture as he does so?
>
> WHAT DOES CONCITA'S RATHER UNUSUAL SLEEPING GARMENT SYMBOLIZE?
>
> Why does Bunuel interrupt the love scene to have the lady on the train send her daughter away? What does the lady's fascination with Mathieu's story imply about the bourgeoisie?
>
> Back in bed: Noting Mathieu's frustration, Concita admits, "I don't like what I'm doing either." What are the various things she might mean by this?

22. At lunch: "If I marry her, I'll be completely helpless," Mathieu tells his cousin. What does he mean?

> Why does Concita One turn down the maitre'd when he offers her champagne? How does this reflect her treatment of Mathieu?

23. Concita Two photographs Mathieu by the river, where she asks him why he's so intent on making love... What does the burlap *sack* he's carrying symbolize?

24. Cut to Mathieu reading a newspaper article about a hijacked plane being blown up. How does this incident comment symbolically on his state of mind?

25. Preparing for bed again ... Concita One lies in Mathieu's arms. Why does she say that if she gave in to him he wouldn't love her anymore?

> He retaliates by accusing her of just wanting him for his money. Why wouldn't this appear to be so? Why does she insist that she isn't attracted to younger men?

> What is the significance of the assassination on the street below?

> When she pleads with him to give her more time to get used to him, he angrily pushes her out the door. Why does Bunuel stress Mathieu's total disregard for Concita's needs?

26. How does the shot of Concita Two leading her friend through the dark hallway undercut her sincerity?

> Mathieu climbs on a ladder to look through the transom. How is he like the *pantaloon* in Renaissance commedia del arte?

> When Concita assures Mathieu that her friend merely needs a place to sleep and that they lie back-to-back, he throws them both out. If she *is* telling the truth, how do their value systems differ?

27. Mathieu's cousin urges him to *travel* to forget her. In the meantime, what is the significance of his using political connections to have Concita and her mother deported as undesirable aliens? How does this underscore the film's political theme?

> Note that the girl's actual name is "Conception" (!) Aside from the obvious connotation, how does she also symbolize Bunuel's relationship with his art?

28. How does Mathieu's game of *blind man's bluff* with the map characterize his whole approach to life? After going through this charade, why does he actually return to Seville?

29. The gypsy reads his palm ... What does the lady with the *pig* symbolize, and how does she reflect his problem with Concita?

30. Mathieu and Martin visit Gaudi's cathedral, which inspires Martin to quote the standard religious idea that women are "sacks of excrement." Why does Bunuel include this extreme Augustinian view of women's nature?

As Mathieu goes out that evening, the servant reminds him: "Monsieur, you forgot your sack." What does the *sack* symbolize? What is the purpose of this surreal sequence?

31. How does the *funeral procession* comment on Mathieu's meeting Concita Two again? What is the effect of the shot of them reaching toward each other through the *bars?*

32. What does Bunuel imply by cutting from Concita offering him her *hair* through the bars to the wild Latin dance at her club?

> "I'm not the same, you'll see"—How does her upstairs job comment on her assertion?

> What is the effect of the shot of Mathieu staring at her through the bars of the window?

> Why doesn't Concita's job necessarily contradict her claim of virginity?

33. She offers to quit dancing if Mathieu gives her a small house ... which he does. The first action of Concita One is to install a *locked gate.* How does this relate to the film's imagery?

> "That's all I ever wanted," she coos as he hands her the deed. "Now nothing can come between us." How does this lead to the next scene with Concita Two?

34. When Mathieu returns at midnight, Bunuel provides us with a very simple explanation of Concita's motivations. She has him kiss her hand through the gate—then tells him to go away: "Mateo, you fill me with horror ... " Echoing every man's worst nightmare, she tells him that the touch of his body fills her with disgust. Should we take this at face value, or is Bunuel just setting Mathieu up for another of her capricious games?

> Why does she know that Mathieu will return to the locked gate?

> "The guitar is mine. I play it for the one I want." If Concita really *does* love Mathieu, what is the meaning of her performance with the young man?

35. Mathieu's chauffer stops his car for a man lying in the road. How does this sequence parallel what Concita has just done to him?

36. As Mathieu has breakfast in the park, Concita One calmly sits at his table—just as she did in Switzerland. "I thought you loved me enough to

commit suicide," she mocks. If the house is all she wants, why does she bother seeing him again?

37. Why does Bunuel cut from them leaving to Mathieu entering his mansion with the more sultry Concita Two?

38. When Concita reproaches him—"You just don't understand women"— he responds by beating her up. Lying on the floor with blood pouring from her nose, she sighs, "Now I know that you really love me." Why does she give him back the key and tell him to visit her whenever he likes?

39. "You agree she deserved this chastisement?" Mathieu asks his companions on the train. Cut to Concita One walking up the aisle with a bucket of water. How does the repetition of this motif symbolize their relationship?

40. As Mathieu pursues Concita One, she turns around—transforming into Concita Two. What is the purpose of this rapid identity switch? Why does Bunuel cut from her sticking out her tongue at him to the two of them exiting in Paris, arm-in-arm?

41. While Mathieu and Concita One walk along the Rue de Rivoli, why does Bunuel dub the loud-speaker announcement about the formation of a strange terrorist alliance (R.A.I.J. has apparently gotten together with P.R.I.Q.U.E.)?

> How does this campaign of violence reflect the love theme?
> How does the paralyzed Monsignor in the news report correspond to Mathieu?

42. WHAT DOES THE *LACEMAKER* SITTING IN THE WINDOW SYMBOLIZE? Note that she is drawing material from the same *sack* Mathieu was carrying earlier in the film?

> Why the bloodstains? Why does Mathieu stare compulsively into the window? How does the *torn lace circle* the lady is trying to stitch reflect Mathieu and Concita's relationship? How does it also relate to the film's *bondage* imagery?

43. Instead of letting us hear what Concita and Mathieu are saying, why does Bunuel dub opera music from Wagner's *Walkure?*

44. Concita One leaves in disgust, transforming suddenly into Concita Two, who shrugs Mathieu off and walks away...WHAT IS THE MEANING OF THE FINAL BOMB BLAST THAT FILLS THE SCREEN? How is their relationship a metaphor for the class struggle that rocks their society?

DAYS OF HEAVEN (1978—American) Directed by Terrence Malick; with Sam Shepard, Brooke Adams, Linda Manz, and Richard Gere; cinematography by Nestor Almendros; music by Ennio Morricone. Produced by Paramount.

Despite the beautiful European-style music and photography, the opening stills in black and white make *Days of Heaven* a very "American" film, closely associated with the innocent period of our history just before World War One. This film is not merely a period piece, however. Like Steinbeck's *East of Eden,* it is archetypal—a religious allegory resounding with Old Testament imagery, a visual poem about people who live in the Promised Land but don't know it.

***

1. Chicago: While Abby picks garbage by the polluted river, Bill shovels coal into a blast furnace. How do these two symbolic actions foreshadow the film's tragedy? What is the significance of Bill's getting into a fight with one of the other workers?

2. In a film about a love-triangle, what is the purpose of Linda Manz' deadpan narration? Note that she is attracted to "characters," and that she judges no one. How does she represent Malick's own approach to his material?

> Why does Malick include her description of the fundamentalist preacher who lectures her on the Second Coming, assuring her that "the people who have been good will escape all that fire?" How does Linda's sardonic reference to the apocalypse foreshadow the climax of the film?

3. A dignified Victorian house stands alone on the Texas Panhandle. As a symbol, how is this lonely mansion like a house in a painting by Edward Hopper? How does the house establish the aristocratic young farmer's isolation? What does his *sickness* symbolize?

4. Bill and Abby pretend to be brother and sister so they can travel together. How does this echo the relationship of Abraham and Sarah sojourning

with the Pharaoh in the *Old Testament?* How are the farmworkers like ancient Israelites in bondage in Egypt?

5. Why does Malick *backlight* all the shots of the farmworkers harvesting and swimming? Instead of developing the characters in depth, why does he dwell on the landscape? In the midst of this beautiful country, why does he keep emphasizing the machines and the ruthless way the masters exploit the workers?

6. Linda and her friend try to catch grasshoppers in the field: ("I don't think they like us.") Why is this ironic?

7. What is the significance of Abby's running into the farmer while she's chasing *pheasants?* What do pheasants come to symbolize in the course of the film?

8. Bill overhears the doctor telling the farmer that he has only a year to live. Why does he urge Abby to stay on the farm after the harvest? Why does Malick set this dialogue in the *river?*

9. Abby agrees to stay with the farmer. What are the symbolic connotations of the *square dance* and the huge *bonfires* during this sequence?

10. Why does Abby hesitate when Bill pushes her to marry the farmer...even though it seems certain that he will die soon from some unnamed "sickness?"

11. While Abby and the farmer honeymoon, Bill cautiously inspects the house. Why does Malick focus on the decanter of wine and two glasses? What is the significance of the farmer's sickness vanishing as a result of marrying Abby?

12. History intrudes briefly as Woodrow Wilson's train passes through. How is the aristocratic farmer like President Wilson on the eve of World War One?

13. Amidst symbolic baseball games and pheasant-shoots, Bill and Abby slip out to go down to the river. As Abby continues her double life, why does Malick focus on details like the *weather vane* and the *wine glass* at the bottom of the river?

14. The Flying Circus: The big man and the little man are always fighting, and their lady belly-dances. How does this comic sequence reflect the tragic action of the film? How is the "flying circus" a metaphor for love?

15. Why does Malick include the clips from silent films—especially the one of Chaplin in *The Immigrant?* How do these images relate to the farmer's seeing Bill and Abby's intimate silhouette on the curtain?

16. Bill realizes that Abby is growing to love the farmer. Why is this ironic? What does his leaving with the Flying Circus symbolize?

17. Even though the innocence of their former love is dead, Bill unfortunately decides to return. Frankly blaming himself, he admits, "I didn't know what I had with you." How does this connect the love theme with the idea of Lost Eden?

18. As Abby again says goodbye to Bill, the farmer stands on the roof watching them. How does the *weather vane* symbolize his inner state? What is the effect of the low-angle closeup of his reaction?

19. What is the significance of a *locust* appearing in Abby's wash-basin? What does the swarm of locusts symbolize? What is the effect of the extreme closeups of them devouring the wheat?

20. While the workers vainly try to burn the locusts, why does the farmer attack Bill with his lantern? Why does Malick associate Bill's return (on his little red motorcycle!) with the coming of the locusts?

21. The firestorm turns their "Days of Heaven" into a night of hell. What are the religious connotations of this stunning sequence? How does the fire reflect the unconscious feelings of the three main characters?

22. As the farmer surveys his burned fields, why does Malick juxtapose the *exotic bird* walking through the ashes?

23. What does the murder weapon symbolize? Why does Malick cut from the dying farmer to the white horses silhouetted against the smoke?

24. Why does Malick stress the beauty of the landscape as Abby, Bill, and Linda escape down the river? How does the leisure of this sequence contrast with the traditional western escape?

25. How does the foreman's pursuit echo *Bonnie and Clyde* and *Butch Cassidy and the Sundance Kid*, as well as Malick's earlier film *Badlands?* Why does Malick use the *river* for the final shootout?

26. Why doesn't Malick end the film with Bill's death and Abby's grief?

27. After putting Linda in a boarding school, Abby leaves in a train full of *soldiers.* What does this imply about her future? How does this reference to

the nation's fall from innocence in World War One recapitulate the theme of the film?

28. Linda escapes through her window to go on the road again with her girlfriend ... "This girl didn't know where she was going or what she was doing. Maybe she'd meet up with a character." Why does Linda attach herself to losers and live vicariously through their disasters?

GET OUT YOUR HANDKERCHIEFS (1978—French) Directed by Bertand Blier; with Gerard Depardieu, Patrick Dewaere, Carol Laure, and Riton; cinematography by Jean Penzer; music by Georges Delerue; distributed by New Line Cinema.

Get Out Your Handkerchiefs is one of the finest French films to appear since Truffaut's *Jules and Jim*. Like Truffaut, Blier stages his war of the sexes on a mythological battleground. Both directors view women as fertility goddesses, mystifying to the men who love them. But while Truffaut's Catherine dominates her lovers—like a liberated lady should!— Blier's Solange outrages modern feminists by knitting, scrubbing floors, and refusing to conform to the new cliches. Blier has no part in his film for Ms. Virginia Slims, the Unmarried Woman who smokes cigarettes and sports designer jeans to prove she's free. His Earth Mother doesn't "find herself" by clawing her way to the presidency of a corporation. And she certainly doesn't wind up with Mr. Right, as determined through Hollywood market research. True to life, to the chagrin of her friends, she loves the "wrong" person. Why does this happen? Blier thinks our emotional lives are governed by infantile desires, unconscious needs that subvert all ideologies, whether feminist or chauvinist. The little old ladies of both sexes who hiss *Get Out Your Handkerchiefs*—while ignoring the pornography that clogs our theatres—obviously react so strongly to Blier's films because they feel threatened by the truth of his vision.

***

1. In a Paris cafe, Raoul berates himself publicly over his wife's supposed frigidity. Meanwhile, Solange stares glassy-eyed, nibbling her sauerkraut strand by strand. What does her loss of appetite symbolize? Is she catatonic because her husband is heavy-handed, or vice-versa?

2. "If you get her to smile, you'll be my pal . . . " Raoul and Stephane's bond is based on the macho assumption that Solange's happiness depends on *their* sexual prowess. What does Blier think of this attitude? Why does he stress that neither of these self-assured studs makes any emotional contact with Solange?

> After offering his wife to a stranger, Raoul stops a passerby at random and brings her into the restaurant. Why does Blier include the perspective of the second woman? How does the comedy of this sequence echo Truffaut and Woody Allen?

> If Solange is indifferent, why does she cry when Stephane gets up to leave? Why does she faint when the two men argue?

3. When Raoul stereotypes the barmaid as "Bernadette," she responds with an erotic soliloquy about appearance and reality. How does this speech foreshadow the revelation of Solange's true nature?

4. Raoul and Stephane soliloquize over Solange's sleeping body, poeticizing her nervous system: "Isn't it our job to protect this marvelous machine?" How does Raoul's metaphor reflect the medical profession's response to Solange's fainting fits?

5. Stephane has walled his room with a collection of every *Livre de Poche* novel ever printed. He prides himself on being able to recite any title if given its serial number. He also has a complete Mozart collection—but knows zero about any other composer. Why is it ironic that he considers himself an intellectual?

> Raoul, on the other hand, likes "breaking down walls . . . " If he and Stephane respectively symbolize Body and Mind, what is the allegorical meaning of their attempts to satisfy Solange?

6. Why does Solange collapse in hysterics as she shuttles between her two lovers? If she doesn't want to leave the hospital, why does she suddenly embrace Raoul when he slaps her?

7. Raoul's rhapsody about Mozart climaxes with a knock on the door. How does Michel Serrault's sudden appearance undercut their fantasy? Why do the men treat him as though he *were* Mozart, ritualistically offering him a drink and plunking him in Solange's bed?

> What does Solange's fainting at the Mozart concert imply about culture?

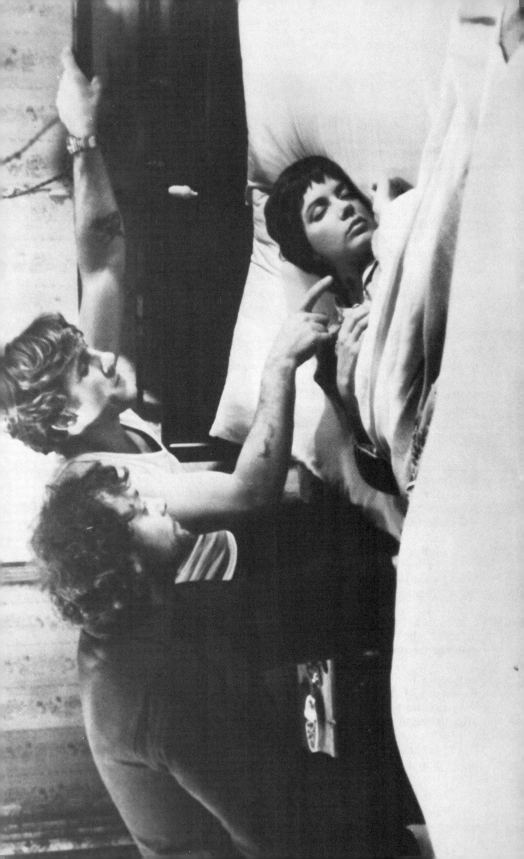

How are the three men characterized by stuffing their faces while arguing loudly about Solange's infertility? What is the effect of the cut to her leading a troop of small boys up a country road?

8. The first half of *Get Out Your Handkerchiefs* is a kinky Keystone comedy—and possibly a parody of the New Wave. How does the film's tone change as the *menage a trois* moves from the city to the country? How does the mythology of part two resolve the questions presented by the Pierrot-Harlequin farce of part one?

9. Christian's wealthy parents have sent him to a camp for the underprivileged so he'll know how to deal with them when he takes over his father's factory. Why does he dismiss his parents as "creeps?" Why does Blier include the episode in which the other boys pelt him with their desserts?

10. As an I.Q. test, Christian has Raoul and Stephane "draw a tree." What is the significance of Solange's laughter?

> Note that after the other boys molest Christian, he hides in a *tree-house* in the forest. What are the erotic and religious connotations of this "tree" symbolism?

11. Earlier, Raoul and Stephane joked about offering Solange to Mozart. How does Christian, a manipulative brat with a high I.Q., embody the spirit of Mozart? In his seduction of Solange, how is he like Cherubino in Mozart's *Marriage of Figaro?*

> Why is Solange moved by his urging her not to have children—but rather to care for the ones who already exist?

12. Christian's parents pack him off to a boarding school. How is the late-night dormitory scene like an episode from a mythological romance? Why does Blier juxtapose this dreamlike sequence against the farcical chase scene, the kidnapping, and the car crash?

> How does Mrs. Beloeil's *amnesia* and consequent seduction parallel Solange's "awakening?"

13. Solange knits identical sweaters for both husband and lover—then for Christian, and finally for Mr. Beloeil. What is the meaning of this leitmotif? How is she like Penelope in the myth of Odysseus?

14. In the film's brilliant conclusion, Raoul and Stephane stare longingly through the bars that enclose the mansion. Inside, Solange knits

contentedly. What is the symbolic purpose of Schubert's "Hungarian Rhapsody?" What does Christian's *billiard* game symbolize? How does Mr. Beloeil's position in the wheelchair echo the themes of Bunuel's *Tristana* and *Belle de Jour?*

15. In *The Sirens of Titan,* Kurt Vonnegut theorizes that the primary human bond is not between husband and wife, but between mother and son. How does *Get Out Your Handkerchiefs* support this view of kinship? What is ironic about Stephane's theory that Solange just "needs a child?"

16. Pauline Kael describes *Get Out Your Handkerchiefs* as a "sleeping-beauty fable, but told from the point of view of a man's erotic fears." What does she mean?

17.Why does Blier stress that Solange's inner self is *opaque*—not only to her two bumbling lovers, but to us, and even to himself? How does his view of women contradict the pat feminist formulas of films like *An Unmarried Woman?*

LA CAGE AUX FOLLES (1978—French) Directed by Edouard Molinaro; with Ugo Tognazzi (Renato) and Michel Serrault (Albin). Distributed by United Artists.

La Cage Aux Folles is not merely a gay joke, but a philosophical examination of the nature of the theatre, which uses sets and costumes to manipulate appearance and reality.

1. The film opens with a dance number in a "typical" cabaret. How does the removal of *wigs* at the end of the dance establish the film's *masquerade* theme?

2. How do the following lines characterize Renato and Albin as a typical middle-aged couple?

"I can't take any more—I'm going to kill her!"

"Every night the same thing—I taped it yesterday."

"Indifference is the most awful thing, Renato. I dieted for two months, and you didn't even notice."

3. How is Jacob, the Black maid, characterized by the blond wig and heart-shaped apron?

4. A handsome young man enters while Albin is on stage. What do you assume about his relationship with Renato ("It's Jacob's night off—we're all alone.")? Why does the director keep us waiting before revealing their actual relationship?

5. What is the immediate effect of the change in color and lighting in the cross-cut to Andrea, who is also informing her parents? When she tells them Laurent's father is a cultural attache, her mother declares, "He's one of us!" Why is this ironic? How does it foreshadow the film's ending?

6. What is the effect of the cross-cut to Albin shopping?

7. "He's too young—he'll ruin his life!" How is Albin's reaction like that of a typical possessive mother?

8. How are Andrea's parents characterized by sitting at opposite ends of a long, formal dining table? While Mr. Charrier records a political speech attacking welfare recipients as "degenerates," he gets so flustered from his wife's nagging that he dunks the microphone in his coffee. How does this comic image relate to the "tragic" phone message that the president of the Moral Order is dead? What does this sequence imply about conservative politicians who are obsessed with morality?

9. Mrs. Charrier's solution: "a big white wedding to reaffirm tradition." How does Molinaro comment on this assertion by cutting to Albin on stage trying to rehearse with a new partner? Albin bulges out of his corset, while Salome dresses in black leather and chews gum. How does this satirize the concept of "young love?" Why is this sequence juxtaposed against Laurent's problems with his approaching marriage?

10. Why does Laurent suggest sending Albin away for a few days? Why does he insist on censoring the apartment? To what extent do people's settings reveal their natures?

11. "Yes, I'm an old fag—but I know who I am." In this respect, how does Renato differ from Mr. Charrier? In spite of his offended feelings, why does Renato agree to go along with the masquerade?

12. What does Mr. Charrier's position on the *ladder* symbolize? Trapped by the press, he announces, "I'm off to organize an event that epitomizes

the meaning of our order." What does the cut to Renato's *phallic sculpture* imply?

13. The scene in the cafe—Renato tries to teach Albin how to butter his toast and drink his tea without extending his little finger: "It's important to react like a Real Man." How does this lead to the Spaghetti-Western parody of Renato striding through the saloon doors ("just like John Wayne")?

14. Why does Renato go to see Laurent's mother? As the red light flashes over the office door, the "outraged wife" barges in. How does this reversal of roles satirize "executive" love scenes?

15. Under Albin's direction, Jacob redecorates the apartment. What is the effect of the dark new decor, especially the gigantic crucifix? How does this "set change" allude to one of the basic concepts of the theatre medium?

16. How does Albin's farewell satirize *Uncle Tom's Cabin?*

17. Preparing for their conservative guests, Jacob wears a tuxedo . . . but no shoes! How does this parody racial stereotypes?

18. What is the effect of the dark suits, and the antique chairs placed miles apart? How do Albin's *pink socks* undercut the illusion?

19. *"Mon pere . . . "* What is ironic about Renato's dignified pose beneath the crucifix? His handshake is so firm that Mr. Charrier winces. Why is this funny?

20. When Mr. Charrier observes, "I like the severity of this place," Laurent goes on to describe his father's house as "a monastery, a place for meditation." What does this masquerade suggest about the problem of distinguishing appearance from reality? (And what, incidentally, does it imply about monasteries?)

21. Mrs. Charrier gushes, "You've seduced my husband, Mr. Baldi." Why is this ironic?

22. What is the significance of everyone's reaction to the popping champagne?

23. Why does Albin decide to dress as a woman? Why isn't his performance as convincing as it would be on a stage?

24. Dinner: What do the *soup plates* symbolize, and what is the significance of Mr. Charrier's not being able to see them clearly without his glasses?

("They're young men playing together, aren't they?") How does this reflect the main action of the scene?

25. What is the symbolic connotation of Mrs. Charrier's having the Lord in her arms?

26. What does Albin's shifting wig symbolize? Why does Renato finally grab it and refuse to let Albin return to the table?

27. The truth comes out of the closet when Mr. Charrier searches for the key in the "nook" to admit Laurent's "real" mother. When the shocked deputy asks, "Your son, Mr. Baldi, has how many mothers?" Renato quietly but firmly replies, "One—Albin." What does this sequence imply about "real" mothers?

28. How does the anniversary party comment on Renato's assertion? Note the deputy's stricken face as they all kiss him. How is his realization a comic *catharsis*, similar to the epiphanies that end great tragedies?

29. Andrea refuses to leave. How is this a sign of her growth?

30. What is the significance of the deputy's final masquerade? "White makes me look fat—I wanted black!" What does this imply?

31. Laurent and Andrea get their White Wedding. Why does Molinaro include the gay priest? Why does he end the film with a *freeze-frame* of Albin throwing another tantrum? What does this suggest about the future?

32. Many people assume that a child raised by gay parents will wind up being gay himself. Why is it equally possible that he will turn out like Laurent—rigidly normal and conventional, intent on marrying young?

VIOLETTE (1978—French) Directed by Claude Chabrol; with Isabelle Huppert and Stephane Audran. Distributed by New Yorker Films.

In Claude Chabrol's elegant *Violette,* style *is* meaning. Violette's nightly metamorphosis from a dumpy schoolgirl into a bird of prey reflects the filmmaker's art. Chabrol's exercises in style, like Violette's affectations of fashion, hint at deep sensitivities. Is anything really there? Violette Noziere's lovers and critics, who refuse to believe that she would murder her parents merely to provide her wastrel boyfriend with money, insist on seeing her as a symbol of revolt. But maybe Chabrol is just setting us up. He loves to tantalize his audience with possibilities, just as Violette implies unique delights concealed beneath her banal glamor.

***

1. The opening credits: As Violette slips down the stairs into the night, why does Chabrol make the gate of her apartment look like prison bars?

2. How are Violette and her girlfriend characterized by putting lipstick on the statue of Claude Bernard?

> "We need a Hitler..." Note her girlfriend's reaction to the students' pseudo-intellectual chatter: "Such bores with their politics!" Why does Chabrol link Violette's dissolution with the rise of fascism?

3. Before entering her apartment, Violette must duck into the lavatory in the hall to remove her makeup and change into her schoolgirl's clothes. What is the significance of her transformation?

4. Forcing Violette to scrub off her sinful perfume, her mother confronts her with a love-letter she found in her drawer. Why is Mrs. Noziere's snooping ironic and hypocritical?

5. Note Violette's bored expression as she and her parents play cards. How does this game foreshadow the tragic climax? Why does Chabrol stress Violette's stifling bourgeois homelife?

6. Violette listens while her parents lie in bed joking about the photos in their sex manual. "Get the cloth—You'll dirty the sheet," Violette mouths... a moment before her father speaks. Why does Chabrol include this Freudian "primal scene?"

7. Why does Chabrol cut from Violette's disgust at her parents' lovemaking to her doctor informing her that she has syphilis?

8. Violette goes to bed with an African student. After refusing his offer of payment, why would she try to steal the money from his wallet? Why does she balk when he cheerfully tells her to keep the money?

9. What is the meaning of Violette's flashback to herself as a little girl waving goodbye to her father as he drives off on the locomotive? What does this blatant surrealist symbol imply about their relationship?

10. Violette and Jean Dabin both suffer preconceptions when they meet. He thinks she's rich; she sees him as the lover of her dreams, emerging from the sea. "I love you like an animal," Violette tells Jean. Why does Chabrol make the object of her passion such a creep?

11. Why is Violette obsessed with going to the Sables d'Olonnes ("in a Bugatti")? What does the seashore symbolize for her?

12. Although Mrs. Noziere is rather prudish with her daughter, she too hides a packet of old love-letters. Violette uses them to blackmail her mother's former lover, implying that he's her actual father. How does this relate to the film's appearance-reality theme?

13. "Swear you love only me..." What is the significance of Violette's soliloquy in the mirror? Also note the beautiful shot of the couple in the mirror as Jean promises to take her to America some day. Later, Violette finds a message in lipstick on the mirror that Jean has gone to check out the Sables d'Olonnes: "I'm waiting for you and your promise." Why does Chabrol repeat the mirror motif? Why does he balance his Freudian analysis of Violette's nature with this very simple motivation for her crime?

14. Despite her own past—and her promise to Violette—why does Mrs. Noziere reveal Violette's love-letters to her husband? How do the two parents contrast in this sequence? Why does Violette tear up the letter and run out?

15. As Violette's parents prepare dinner for Dr. Deron's fictitious sister, Chabrol cuts to Violette's flashback of being picked up. Afterwards she goes home to find her parents lying on the floor. Why does Chabrol take this oblique, fragmented approach to the "fatal dinner?"

16. Why does he cut from the neighbor's announcement of her father's death to the screaming locomotive and her father calling her name?

17. While Violette lies in bed, why does Chabrol juxtapose the surreal broadcast about Nazi fashions against Violette's nightmare vision of her mother veiled in black?

18. The rich young man who picked her up obviously expects to pay her. Why does she pull a wad of bills from her purse, drop it on the bed, and leave?

19. "God is empty," Violette tells the maid. How does the maid's simple reply, "You love Monsieur Jean too much," undercut the "philosophical" explanation of her crime?

20. Cut to headlines reporting Violette's crime as a young man propositions her in the park. When he observes, "You look just like Violette Noziere," note her bold lie. Why does Chabrol stress her tendency to create elaborate fantasies?

> Why is it ironic that someone who propositions a woman on the street would feel a "moral" obligation to hand her over to the police?

21. "I would like to understand," claims the police inspector. How does his chauvinism connect him with the other men in the film?

> Violette insists that killing her father was an obsession with her. Is her fantasy about her father's incestuous attacks merely a tactic to avoid punishment, or does she really believe it for some psychological reason?

22. In the flashback to the fatal dinner, note how carefully Violette lights the three candles after handing her father the three packets of "medicine." What is the significance of Violette's blank expression as her parents drink the poison and collapse on the floor?

23. Violette is brought to the hospital to confront her mother. Why does she collapse in hysterics? As they sedate her, why does Chabrol cut to her vision of Jean (with a hypodermic needle!)—then to Violette as a little girl waving goodbye as her parents drive off in a cart?

24. While Violette writes to Jean, Chabrol flashes back to him telling her not to cling to him all the time—then to her as a child pushing her mother away. How do these two incidents illuminate the conflict in her character?

25. Mrs. Noziere tearfully decides to prosecute her daughter. Why does Chabrol cut to a flashback of Violette as a child riding on her father's knee while her mother stands ominously in the background? What is the significance of her mother's slapping her when she observes her parents making love? Why does Chabrol stress the Freudian implications of these memories?

26. What is the purpose of the Christ-like image of Violette washing her cell-mate's feet?

> She declares that the disgusting things she saw her parents do ruined her appetite for pleasure. How does this explain her promiscuity?

> Why doesn't Violette care about the outcome of her trial?

27. What is the the purpose of the circus atmosphere that surrounds Violette's trial? Why does Chabrol juxtapose the ballad singer's lurid song about Violette's cruelty against her impassive face as she sits quietly in a gray prison cell? What is the purpose of this simplistic fictional interpretation of her character?

28. When the judge announces that Violette will be decapitated, why does she react by looking for her necklace?

29. After the verdict, why does Mrs. Noziere decide to try to save Violette's life? How is this motivated by Violette's refusal to talk about her mother's old lover?

30. Waiting for the guillotine, Violette calmly embroiders. What does this symbolize? What is the purpose of this allusion to Isabelle Huppert's earlier film *The Lacemaker?*

A cool documentary voice explains that after being pardoned, Violette married and had five children. Why the anti-climactic ending? Why the stop-frame shot of her staring blankly at the camera?

WOYZECK (1978—German) Directed by Werner Herzog; with Klaus Kinski and Eva Mathes. Distributed by New Yorker Films.

Werner Herzog peoples his nightmare world with sleepwalkers, solitary dreamers drifting against the stream of time. In *Heart of Glass*, he literally hypnotizes his actors to achieve the proper catatonic effect. In *Nosferatu*, he engulfs them in hallucinogenic fogs. But perhaps the worst nightmare is reality itself—the stark, flat, banal world of Woyzeck, to whom the earth shrieks its dreadful message.

***

1. Why does Herzog open the film with a pan-shot of a pond by a sleepy nineteenth century village? What does the "still pond" symbolize? Why is the apparent peace ironic?

2. Woyzeck enters running high-speed, like a character in a silent movie. He stands at attention and goes through rifle exercises, finally crawling toward the camera with a pained expression on his face. How does his comic entrance characterize military life?

> While he tries to do pushups, his commander steps on his back. What are the political and sexual connotations of this particular exercise? How does Woyzeck's position in this sequence reflect his inner state?

3. Note the *speed* with which Woyzeck shaves Captain Hauptmann. What is the effect of his suddenly snapping to attention?

> Why are the captain's meditations on time and eternity amusing?

> "You're a good fellow—you just lack morals." Why is it funny that the captain lectures Woyzeck on his illegitimate child at this particular moment? Why is it difficult for a poor man like Woyzeck to bother much with nineteenth century "virtue?"

4. Standing beside the pond with his friend Andres, Woyzeck hears singing and insists that the ground is hollow (!) How do the *sticks* they're sharpening symbolize Woyzeck's frustration? How does this activity also foreshadow the end of the film?

5. Cut to Marie, Woyzeck's mistress, looking out the window as the drum major marches up the street. How does this robust bully satirize the "ideal man" in German culture? Why does Herzog juxtapose the nervous Woyzeck complaining about the "hot breath of the spirit on his back?"

6. Woyzeck apparently spends his whole life standing at attention. Next he visits the doctor, who berates him for "pissing on a wall." What does Woyzeck's inability to provide the doctor with a urine sample symbolize?

> What is the significance of the doctor's regarding "Nature" as superstition? How is he a parody of the German scientific establishment?

7. The village square: What do the *goats* and the *carousel* symbolize? How does the uniformed monkey ("a creature as God created him") express Herzog's view of mankind? How does the ringmaster mirror the other authority figures in the film?

8. Marie takes the drum major home with her. How does this prancing oaf with his desire to spawn a brood of drum majors represent Herzog's concept of basic man?

9. Cut to the doctor performing an experiment. How does his dropping the cat out the window relate to the previous scene? What is the significance of the cat crapping all over Woyzeck when he catches her?

> The doctor displays Woyzeck as a man who has eaten nothing but *peas* for three months (!) What does the doctor's absurd experiment imply about science?

10. Marie's lullaby warns her baby about the gypsy coming to take him in the night. Why does Herzog juxtapose her song against the shot of her in the mirror admiring her new earrings?

11. If Woyzeck understands where Marie got the earrings, why doesn't he protest? Why does she weep as he cracks his knuckles, drops his paycheck, and leaves?

12. As Woyzeck runs past, the captain jokes, "You're running through creation like an open razor—you're liable to cut someone." Why is this ironic?

13. How does Woyzeck's examination of Marie echo Hamlet's famous confrontation with Ophelia?

> "A man is an abyss. You get dizzy looking in," Woyzeck mutters and walks out. How does this foreshadow the end of the film?

14. The dance at the White Horse Tavern: Why does Woyzeck insist on going to watch Marie dance with her new admirer? As he looks through the window, Marie cries, "Don't stop!" How does Woyzeck interpret her enthusiasm for the dance?

15. Cut from the musicians to Woyzeck running through a poppy field. What does the setting symbolize? Why does Herzog shoot this sequence in slow-motion through a telephoto lens?

16. The drum major forces Woyzeck to drink. What is the symbolic importance of this humiliation? How does this sequence connect Woyzeck with Stroszeck and Kaspar Hauser—Herzog's archetypal "Mystic Fools" victimized by conventional bullies?

17. Why does Herzog cut from Woyzeck "hearing voices" to Marie reading the bible? What is ironic about her relating to the story of Christ saving the woman taken in adultery?

18. Marie tells the children a story about a little girl who longs for the moon and the sun because everything on earth is dead. What does her parable mean, and how does it reflect her inner state?

19. Why does Herzog shoot the murder in extreme slow motion? In place of normal sound, why does he repeat the fiddle music from the dance? What is the effect of the clarinet concerto during the long closeup of Woyzeck clutching Marie's dead body?

20. Covered with blood, Woyzeck returns to the tavern. When the girl grabs him, why does he dance so violently?

"What are you staring at me for? Stare at yourselves in the mirror!" In what sense is Woyzeck the "shadow" of all these respectable citizens?

21. Woyzeck wades into the pond to throw the knife out farther. How does his drowning reflect his jealous passion?

22. Instead of showing Woyzeck's death, why does Herzog cut to the little girl skipping rope?

As the children run to see the dead lady, the authorities examine the murder site. Why the slow-motion and soft focus with Vivaldi's peaceful guitar concerto dubbed over?

HAIR (1979—American) Directed by Milos Forman; with Treat Williams (Berger), John Savage (Claude), and Beverly D'Angelo (Sheila); book and lyrics by Gerome Ragni and James Rado; music by Galt MacDermot; choreography by Twyla Tharp. Produced by United Artists.

1. Opening shot: A farmhouse on the prairie in Oklahoma. Claude, complete with cowboy hat, goes with his father to meet the bus that will take him to New York to enlist. Why does Forman juxtapose the zoom-

closeups of Berger and his friends burning their draftcards? How does this opening sequence illustrate the basic cultural split during the sixties?

2. "Age of Aquarius": Note that even the *police horses* dance to Twyla Tharp's choreography... As Sheila rides by on her horse, she and Claude exchange glances... Fresh from the farm, why does Claude look so astonished as the Black singer revolves through space?

2. Berger and his friends approach the ladies on horseback to ask for spare change. How does this encounter symbolize class conflict in the United States? Why do the hippies use *all* their change to rent a horse? When Woof rides up beside the rich ladies singing "Sodomy," what is he implying about their lifestyle?

4. Hud's song about being Black is a string of racist epithets. Why is this funny rather than offensive? Why does Forman stress the love between White and Black hippies?

5. "Ain't Got No"—The hippies singing and dancing this great production number are beautifully costumed and have elaborate, styled hair-dos. Why does Forman cut from this glamorized picture of the sixties to Claude awaking in the cold light of dawn?

6. Berger takes a leak on a newspaper story about Sheila's debutante party in Short Hills. How does this communicate Forman's attitude toward High Society?

7. What does their crashing Sheila's party symbolize? How do the elderly waltzers and the young ladies in formal gowns contrast with the hippie culture in the previous scene? Why are Claude and his friends' attempts to "blend in" funny? How is Sheila's fiance Steve characterized?

8. The formal dinner: Sheila's father couldn't care less if Claude is going to Viet Nam to fight for *his* riches. What is the significance of this?

9. When Sheila's mother exclaims that he's "got a helluva nerve," Berger responds by dancing on the table. What does his dance symbolize, and why does the matronly lady in pink applaud and join him?

10. To get the money for bail, Berger stops Sheila and Steve in their Continental. Why is Sheila secretly pleased by Berger's commandeering the car?

What is the significance of Berger's finally getting the money from his middle-class Jewish mother?

11. Why does Sheila go looking for them at the Central Park love-in? What is the significance of LSD being administered as a communion ritual?

12. Why would Claude's LSD hallucination take the form of a formal wedding with Sheila in his prairie chapel? Note the forest of candles, the floating Krishna, and the horse neighing at the church door. How do these symbols relate?

13. The swimming party: When Sheila insists that she wants to go home alone, Claude walks away and jumps in the water. Why does Sheila follow him? What does this act symbolize?

14. The Induction: How does the sequence in which the young man won't remove his *socks* lead to the "White Boys-Black Boys" number? Why does Forman have *recruiting sergeants* sing the choruses? Why is the *food metaphor* funny?

15. While the chorus sings "Walking in Space," why does Forman intercut the face of the angelic Vietnamese singer with the shots of Claude's training? How do individual shots like Claude struggling across a stream and crossing a rope-bridge symbolize his inner state?

16. "Easy to be Hard"—Why does Forman put this song in the mouth of a Black lady with a small boy? What is the significance of "Lafayette's" name-change?

> What is ironic about Hud's affecting "cosmic love and consciousness" while abandoning his straight girlfriend and his child?

> Why can't Jeannie and Hud's girlfriend agree on the importance of "who the father is?"

17. The general's address is interrupted by loud electronic rock music. Why are the men so unruly? What does the army's solution—shooting the speakers—symbolize? Why does Forman intercut the shots of the dance in front of the Washington Monument?

18. Meanwhile, Berger and his friends drive to Nevada. How does "Good Morning Starshine" contrast with the music of the previous scene?

19. What is the irony of the final impersonation . . . and of no one noticing the switch?

MANHATTAN (1979—American) Directed by Woody Allen; with Diane Keaton, Michael Murphy, Mariel Hemingway, and Meryl Streep; cinematography by Gordon Willis; music by George Gershwin. Produced by United Artists.

1. "Chapter One: He adored New York City... He romanticized it all out of proportion..." What is the significance of Woody Allen's constantly revising his introduction, undercutting his critical remarks with apologies? In what sense is New York a "metaphor for the decay of contemporary culture?"

2. Why is the film shot in very *dark* black and white? In the "New York Montage" set to Gershwin music, what do the *fireworks* symbolize? How does this sequence serve as an overture to the action of the film?

3. Cut to Woody Allen and Michael Murphy arguing about art. Why is this pseudo-intellectual discussion set in Elaine's?

4. "She's seventeen—I'm old enough to beat up her father." Why does Isaac *really* back away from his relationship with Tracy? Later in the film, why does he prefer to pursue a woman who is obviously screwed up?

5. How does Isaac react to Yale's confession about having an affair—and why?

6. Isaac confronts his ex-wife over the book she's writing about their relationship. She angrily declares, "It's an honest account of our breakup." Why is this ironic? In what sense could this film be considered Woody Allen's reaction to Paul Mazursky's sentimental portrayal of a divorcee in *An Unmarried Woman?*

7. Why is Isaac surprised that Tracy has already had *three* affairs? Why does he work so hard at discouraging her?

8. At the art gallery, Isaac and Tracy run into Yale, who is obviously nervous about being seen with Mary. Mary thinks the photography exhibit is derivative: "straight out of Diane Arbus, but without her wit." On the other hand, she likes the stainless steel cube because of its "negative capability." Everything else she dismisses as "bullshit." How do her

statements on art characterize her? What is the significance of her opinions being the opposite of Isaac's?

9. Why does Isaac take offense at Yale and Mary's "Academy of the Overrated," in which they put people like Mahler, Van Gogh, Carl Jung, and Ingmar Bergman? What do these great geniuses have in common that would cause them to be disliked by fashionable New York intellectuals?

10. Although Mary dislikes Bergman ("all that Kierkegaard"), she loves the TV show Isaac writes for. What does this say about her taste? After fuming about how obnoxious Mary is, why would Isaac fall for her?

11. Note the parody of "Saturday Night Live." Why does Isaac quit his job? ("All you guys do is drop quaaludes and percodans—naturally it seems funny.")

12. The reception at the Museum of Modern Art: How are the socialites characterized by their chatter about orgasms ("I had an orgasm once, but my doctor told me it was the wrong kind.")? Why does Isaac compare them to the cast of a Fellini movie?

> After deriding several great artists as "overrated," what is ironic about Mary's considering Denis, the young director, a "genius?" (He's the one who wants to make a film about a guy who "screws so great" that all the women die!)

13. Isaac and Mary discuss their divorces: After putting down his relationship with Tracy, she declares that she says whatever is on her mind—and anyone who doesn't like it can just "fuck off." How is Mary like Isaac's ex-wife?

> When Mary insists that two women can raise a child just fine, Isaac replies that it's hard enough to survive *one* mother. How do his jokes about his mother ("The Castrating Zionist") explain his difficulties with women?

14. Mary calls her psychiatrist "Donnie" and she refers to her dachshund as a "penis substitute." Why wouldn't even a great dane cure her of her neuroses?

15. Why is Bloomingdale's an appropriate setting for Yale and Mary to discuss their relationship?

16. As Isaac picks up his son, he again berates his ex-wife: "My analyst warned me, but you were so beautiful I got another analyst." Why does he repeatedly get involved in impossible relationships?

17. When Mary can't get together with Yale, she calls Isaac. What is the significance of her inability to be alone?

18. As Mary exclaims, "Its such a beautiful day," cut to a lightning storm in Central Park. How does their drenching foreshadow the outcome of their relationship?

19. Isaac and Mary take refuge in the Planetarium. What does the setting symbolize? As they walk among the planets, why does Mary rave about how sexy her ex-husband Jeremiah was? When she starts an intellectual game about naming the planets, why does Isaac tell her she lives too much in her head?

20. Why does Isaac urge Tracy to go to London to study acting? Why does he always joke about his sexual powers?

21. Isaac and Tracy ride around Central Park in a carriage. How is Tracy "God's answer to Job?"

22. What is the purpose of the cut from this peaceful, romantic scene to Yale and Mary arguing? ("I'm beautiful and I'm bright and I deserve better!") How do the dachshund yapping at Mary's heels and the constantly ringing phone reflect her state of mind?

23. Tension builds with the cut to Isaac moving into his new apartment. What is the significance of Isaac's complaining as he and Tracy lie in bed? How does "brown water" symbolize his love-life?

24. At an avenue cafe, Yale breaks up with Mary. Why is she so upset when *she* suggested breaking up in the first place? How is she characterized by saying she could sleep with the entire faculty of MIT . . . except that she's so screwed up?

Why does she turn immediately to Isaac?

25. How is Isaac and Tracy's relationship characterized by eating Chinese food in bed?

26. Yale and Isaac play racquet ball. How does this game symbolize their relationship? Why does Yale urge Isaac to date Mary?

27. As Isaac and Mary wander through the Museum of Modern Art, she complains that she's both "attracted and repelled by the male organ." How do the modern sculptures comment on her assertion? Why does Isaac pursue her despite such dingbat statements?

28. Isaac's first wife was a kindergarten teacher who "tried drugs, moved to California, got into EST—She's with the William Morris Agency now." How does this sum up the fate of a whole generation of sixties' "radicals?"

29. When Isaac accuses Tracy of being too young to know what love is, she replies, "We have laughs together; I care about you; your concerns are my concerns; we have great sex." Why is Isaac incapable of appreciating such a simple, wholesome definition of love?

> How does Tracy's assertion distinguish her from Mary? Why does she cry when Isaac tells her she should go out with guys her own age? Why wouldn't she be interested in dating "Billy and Biff and Scooter?"

30. As Isaac and Mary row in Central Park lake, he dips his hand in the water . . . and withdraws it seconds later to find it covered with muck. How does this reflect on their relationship?

31. After splitting with Mary, why would Yale buy a Porsche?

32 The artificial double-date: Note the three faces sneaking glances at each other during the Mozart concert. What does this imply?

33. Why does Allen cut to an old building being torn down? How does this image also introduce the meeting with Mary's "oversexed" ex-husband Jeremiah?

34. Mary types a "novelization." Why does she waste time on something so trivial when she's bright and talented?

> When Yale calls, why does she lie and say it was an offer of "dance lessons?" Why is Isaac's response ironic?

35. Isaac's friends jokingly read aloud what his ex-wife says about him in her book. She mocks his "Jewish-liberal paranoia" and derides his fear of death as "mere narcissism." Why does Woody Allen include such a devastating self-analysis in his film?

36. What is the effect of the cut to Mary telling Isaac she's seeing Yale again? Why is it predictable that she would still be in love with Yale? When Isaac says he gives the whole thing with Yale four weeks, she replies she "can't think that far in advance." How does this characterize her? Why does she want him to get angry?

37. Isaac confronts Yale in his classroom at Columbia. As might be expected of someone named after one ivy league university and teaching in

another, Yale is smooth, handsome, and successful. What does the *ape skeleton* imply about his inner state, however? How is he like the rival in Woody Allen's other films?

38. Isaac's conversation with Emily: What is ironic in her blaming *him* for introducing Yale to Mary?

39. Alone in his apartment, Isaac talks into his tape recorder about people who "create unnecessary neurotic problems for themselves because it helps them avoid more *serious* problems about the universe." How is he like the old man in Samuel Beckett's *Krapp's Last Tape?* Why does he try to list things that make life worth living? How does this contrast with Yale and Mary's "Academy of the Overrated" earlier in the film? Why does he end his list with "Tracy's face?"

What does the harmonica symbolize?

40. When Isaac rushes to find Tracy, she's just about to leave for London. Why is their reversal of roles ironic? Why does she now insist on leaving?

41. "Everyone gets corrupted," Tracy says, meaning to be reassuring. "You've got to have a little faith in people." What does the final closeup of his face imply about her optimism and about their future?

How is this final shot like the ending of Chaplin's *City Lights?*

THE MARRIAGE OF MARIA BRAUN (1979—German) Directed by Rainer Werner Fassbinder; with Hanna Schygulla. Distributed by New Yorker Films.

1. As Hitler's portrait is shot down, Maria is married to a Nazi officer. How is this ceremony in the midst of a bombing raid a metaphor for marriage? What is the effect of juxtaposing classical music against explosions and a baby crying? What is the purpose of the stop-frame shot of Maria and Hermann lying there in the rubble? How does this foreshadow the end of the film?

2. With a sign on her back, Maria searches for her missing husband. What is the significance of her devoting her life to a man she has known for only one night?

3. How is Maria's mother characterized by giving Maria her *brooch* in exchange for cigarettes? Why does Fassbinder juxtapose an accordian playing Germany's national anthem against Maria trading the brooch for a sexy dress to entice Americans?

4. To work in a nightclub, Maria goes to her family doctor for a health certificate. What does his being a drug addict symbolize?

5. The Nightclub: How does Maria's performance on the *parallel bars* reflect her relationships with men?

6. Betti's husband Willi returns. When he informs Maria that Hermann is dead, why does she immediately go to the bar to dance with "Mr. Bill?" What is the political significance of Maria's affair with an American soldier? Why does Fassbinder cast a very polite, middle-aged Black man in this role?

7. While Maria and her American lover undress each other, Hermann appears in the doorway... After slapping Maria, he rushes to the table to grab a cigarette. How does this characterize him?

> After all the extravagant things Maria says to Mr. Bill about how great he is, why does she hit him on the head?

> Why does Hermann take the blame for the American's death?

8. Maria visits her husband in prison. What do their positions on opposite sides of the bars symbolize?

9. When Maria hears there is a wealthy Frenchman in the first class car, why does she change into her nightclub dress? After blatantly picking him up, why does she pretend to ignore him?

> What does the drunken American soldier barging into the first class car symbolize? How does he contrast with her former lover? What is the significance of Oswald's not understanding what she says to the soldier to drive him off?

10. What is the political significance of Maria's working her way into the businessman's confidence? Why does his associate Senkenberg object to her?

11. Why does Maria tell Oswald so bluntly that she wants to sleep with him? What does she mean when she says, "You're not having an affair with me; I'm having one with you."? (Note how gracefully she slips into a discussion of salary.)

12. BY JUGGLING HER PRACTICAL AND EMOTIONAL LIVES, HOW DOES MARIA REPRESENT THE MODERN "LIBERATED" WOMAN?

13. While Maria explains things to Hermann, why does Fassbinder focus on the guard fingering his keys? What does this image imply about her inner life?

14. Why does Maria say she'll be Oswald's mistress, while also insisting that she'll never marry him? In what sense is this a political metaphor?

15. Maria describes herself as a "Mata Hari of the economic miracle . . . a capitalist tool by day, an agent of the proletarian masses by night." How does Maria symbolize the postwar recovery in Germany?

16. Maria's relationship with Oswald is obviously better than what she has ever had with her "husband." Why does she maintain the reality of her fantasy marriage?

17. Why does Fassbinder cut from Oswald confronting Hermann in prison to Maria and Betti exploring the *ruins?*

18. "I want you to have everything, so you'll feel independent," Maria tells Hermann. Why does he refuse her money and ask to be taken back to his cell?

19. While Maria is being informed of Hermann's release, why does she fuss compulsively with the *adding machine?* How does this machine symbolize her inner life?

20. Why does Hermann go away instead of waiting for Maria to pick him up at the prison?

21. Willi and Maria discuss his breakup with Betti while they explore the ruins. Why does Fassbinder keep returning to this setting?

22. Why does he cut to a *rose* lying on Maria's doorstep? What does the vase of dead roses symbolize?

23. How does Maria's lighting her cigarette on the gas burner foreshadow the end of the film? Why does Fassbinder cut from Maria phoning Oswald

to tell him she "wants someone to sleep with..." to Senkenberg announcing Oswald's death?

24. As Maria sits in a drunken stupor, the bell rings...and Hermann appears. How is he characterized by sitting coldly in his chair listening to the sportscast, while she runs around in her negligee and garter belt?

> How is Maria characterized by offering Hermann a "contract" as they undress?

25. Why would Oswald leave half of his property to Hermann, and why does this bother Maria?

26. What does Maria's final accident in the kitchen symbolize? Why does Fassbinder undercut this tragic ending with an ecstatic announcement that Germany has won the world soccer championship?

27. How do the portraits of German chancellors assert the film as a political allegory?

NOSFERATU (1979—German) Directed by Werner Herzog; with Klaus Kinski, Isabelle Adjani, and Bruno Ganz. Distributed by Twentieth Century Fox and Films Inc.

1. Why does Herzog begin with a pan shot of a gallery of *mummies,* possibly former Count Draculas, all shrieking in pain? How do they reveal Herzog's view of history and his conception of human nature?

> What is the effect of Popol Vuh's electronic music?

2. Cut to a *bat* flying in slow-motion, then to Lucy awaking with a scream as the bat flies out her window. How does this establish the film's dream-framework? Why does Herzog juxtapose the shot of two kittens playing with a locket containing Lucy's portrait?

3. The Harker kitchen is all white. How do the setting and the soft natural light characterize them?

4. Jonathan ought to notice that his boss is a bit strange. Why would he undertake a commission that might "cost him some blood?" How is this a metaphor for capitalism?

5. Jonathan describes Wismar (=Amsterdam) as a city whose canals "double back on themselves." What does this symbolize? Why is the story set in Amsterdam, a prosperous middle-class city that considers itself liberal and progressive?

6. As Jonathan and Lucy walk on the beach, what is the effect of the wide-angle lens? What does their walk symbolize?

7. As Jonathan leaves Lucy in his family's care, why does Herzog fill the left side of the frame with a horse's rear end?

8. The Gypsy Village: Note the look on the peasants' faces as Jonathan says he's going to visit Count Dracula. How does this satirize old horror movies?

9. The gypsies believe that there is no castle—that it's a hallucination. When Jonathan tries to hire a coach, the coachman declares that he has no coach and no horses. How do these bizarre conversations establish Herzog's idea that life is a dream?

10. Jonathan climbs uphill, framed against a telephoto slow-motion shot of the *rapids* . . . What do the rapids symbolize?

11. As the fog moves into the valley, note the shot of Jonathan framed against the sky like a medieval knight, and the sudden silhouette of a ruined castle. Why does Herzog accompany this sequence with music from Wagner's *Das Rheingold?*

12. Dracula has prepared a feast for Jonathan. How does this echo Cocteau's *Beauty and the Beast,* and what does it symbolize?

13. What does Dracula's *clock* symbolize? Why does Herzog juxtapose this against Jonathan cutting his finger?

14. Lucy wakes to find a bat climbing her bedroom curtain. How does this foreshadow the climax of the film?

15. In a daze, Jonathan wanders through the castle until he finds his room. How does this foreshadow the end of the film?

16. Looking in the mirror, Jonathan notices a bite on his neck. Why does Herzog cut to a gypsy boy playing violin in the courtyard below?

17. Why does Herzog cut from a silhouette of the castle with *fog* moving in fast-motion—to Lucy walking along the shore, watching the *tide* come in? What do the fog and the tide symbolize?

18. Jonathan writes in his diary that he has had a "bad dream. . . . Sometimes the castle itself seems to be a dream." How does this reveal Herzog's view of reality?

19. Cut to dinner with Dracula: How does Kinski's lonely, alienated Dracula differ from the original interpretation of the role? Why does he insist that it's terrible not to be able to grow old and die?

20. "What a lovely throat . . . " How does the shot of Dracula lingering over Lucy's locket establish this as a "love" film?

21. Despite his suspicions about Dracula, Jonathan still agrees to sell him the house next to his. How does Jonathan's willingness to "sell his country to vampires" reflect Herzog's attitude toward capitalism?

22. As Dracula approaches Jonathan's bed, why does Herzog cut to Lucy *sleepwalking?* How does this recall Jonathan's statement that life in Dracula's castle is "like a dream?" How does Lucy's "double image" in the canal reveal her inner nature?

23. As Lucy shrieks Jonathan's name, Herzog cuts to Dracula lifting his face from Jonathan's throat. What is ironic in Dr. Van Helsing's insisting that it "isn't serious?"

24. Note the high-angle shot of Dracula loading coffins onto a wagon. Why does Herzog stress such a hallucinatory perspective?

25. Jonathan drops from the wall. He wakes to find the gypsy boy playing his violin over his body. Why does Herzog repeat this motif?

26. What do the coffins swirling down the rapids symbolize?

27. The customs official allows the coffins full of rats to board the ship merely because "the documents are in order." What is Herzog implying about bureaucracy?

28. "Blood is Life!" What does Renfield symbolize, and why isn't Dr. Van Helsing capable of dealing with him?

29. How is Lucy characterized by sitting in the *cemetary* all the time? How does this motivate her decision later to take Dracula into her bed?

30. As Herzog intercuts the shots of the ship and Jonathan riding home, everyone on the ship seems to be dying. What does the ship symbolize? What is the *political* significance of the captain's not being able to figure out the cause?

31. When Lucy reproaches Renfield for sending her husband to Transylvania, he laughs and declares, "The Master is coming!" What are the political and religious connotations of his announcement?

32. As Jonathan gallops home, how do the *windmills* symbolize his mental state?

33. Why does Herzog cut from the peaceful, lyrical shot of the ship landing in Amsterdam to Renfield celebrating in his cell? How does his insanity reflect the inner life of the city?

34. When the town officials examine the ship, what is the significance of their ignoring the obvious presence of thousands of rats? What do the rats swarming off the ship symbolize?

35. What does Dracula's putting his coffins in an *abandoned church* symbolize? Why the Wagner music?

36. As Dracula's shadow spreads over the city, Herzog cuts to Jonathan's carriage approaching. How does the mirror shot in the canal recall the earlier shot of Lucy sleepwalking? Why does Herzog repeat this device?

37. What is the significance of Jonathan's not recognizing Lucy? Note that the sun hurts his eyes . . . Why?

> Lucy: "Is it possible that we've all gone mad and will wake up some day in strait jackets?" How does this relate to Jonathan's observation that life in Dracula's castle is like a dream?

38. Cut to Dracula running through the town square. What does his shadow falling across the Harker House symbolize?

39. As Lucy fixes her hair in the mirror, the door creaks open and Dracula's shadow appears. What does the mirror symbolize?

> Why is Dracula so polite? How is he like the Beast in Cocteau's classic film *Beauty and the Beast?*

40. Lucy: "Rivers flow on after we are gone . . . Only Death is certain." Why does Herzog stress her obsession with death? Ironically, how does Dracula finally achieve his wish to "share the love she has with Jonathan?"

41. As Lucy reads about Nosferatu, note Jonathan laughing in the background. What is the purpose of this?

42. When Renfield approaches Dracula, why does the Master shoo him away? What is the implication of his running off crying, "amen?"

43. The parade of coffins: What is the significance of no one listening to Lucy when she declares she knows the "cause of the evil?"

> "We live in an enlightened era; science has swept aside such superstition," Dr. Van Helsing replies. Why is this ironic, and what does it imply about our own scientistic culture?

44. As Lucy approaches the church, the steps swarm with rats. What does this symbolize?

45. What does the party among the coffins symbolize?

46. Why does Herzog make the climactic scene between Lucy and Dracula so erotic?

> Cut to the bat flying in slow-motion. What is the purpose of this leitmotif? How does it emphasize Dracula's alienation?

47. What is the significance of Dracula's being destroyed by *sunlight?* What does the "crowing of the cock" symbolize? How does this sequence reveal Herzog's ambivalence toward sex?

48. What is the point of Dr. Van Helsing's "conversion" and of his resorting to superstitious methods to solve the Problem of Evil?

49. Why does Jonathan clutch his heart as the doctor pounds the stake into Dracula? Why does he tear Lucy's locket from his neck? What is the significance of Jonathan's transformation?

50. Note the hallucinatory final shot of Jonathan riding across the fog-swept desert. What is the purpose of the religious music *(Sanctus)?* In what sense is the film an allegory about the coming of the Anti-Christ?

51. The film may also be interpreted as a "Jungian Fairy Tale." In which case... How do Jonathan, Van Helsing, Lucy, and Dracula correspond to Jung's "four parts of the personality?" (i.e. *self, ego, anima,* and *shadow*)

THE TIN DRUM (1979—German) Directed by Volker Schlondorff; with David Bennent, Angela Winkler, and Charles Aznavour; screenplay by Gunter Grass; music by Maurice Jarre. Produced by New World Pictures; distributed by Films Inc.

1. The film begins in a potato field in 1889, with Grandma Anna Bronski hiding a fugitive under her skirts. How is she characterized by spearing and eating *hot potatoes?*

> As the soldiers stick their bayonets into baskets of potatoes, Joseph creates Oskar's mother. Why does Schlondorff juxtapose these images? What is the purpose of the electronic music?

> Throughout the film, why does Schlondorff link *food* and *sex?*

2. Oscar narrates the family history: Why does Schlondorff film the sequences about the grandfather's escape to America and Agnes' romance with her cousin, Jan Bronski, in the style of a silent film?

3. How does Alfred Mazerath's *feeding soup* to Agnes foreshadow their relationship and her eventual death?

4. Why does Schlondorff dwell on the basket of *fish* as he introduces Jan and Alfred's friendship? How does the *mushroom* Alfred fondles comment on their conversation? What does their loving the same woman symbolize? (Note that she is Kashubian, while the two men are Polish and German).

5. Oskar's birth: What is the meaning of the hallucinatory shot of Oskar, staring inside his mother's womb? Why the *subjective* camera angle as Oskar is being born? Why does Schlondorff film Oskar's first glimpse of his family *upside-down?* Why does he intercut the lightning storm with closeups of Oskar's crying bloodstained face?

6. When Oskar hears his proud father proclaim that he will take over the family shop when he grows up, why does he immediately reject the idea of being born? Why does he look forward only to getting a *tin drum* on his third birthday? What does this drum symbolize?

7. Why does Schlondorff intercut shots of Agnes and Jan's love duet with closeups of Oskar's glaring face? What does the drunken feast symbolize?

8. Note Oskar's expression when the Scoutmaster tells him he's getting bigger. Why does he resolve not to grow up?

9. While everyone plays cards, Jan slips his foot between Agnes' knees. How does this motivate Oskar's calculated plunge down the cellar steps?

> Why the subjective camera angle?

> Why is it ironic that Agnes blames her husband for "leaving the trap open?"

10. Whenever anyone tries to take Oskar's drum, he shrieks until he breaks glass. What does this symbolize? How is he like a character in a Kafka story? How does he represent the Modern Artist?

11. Why does Schlondorff show Oskar's parade crossing in front of a group of Nazis?

12. Why does Schlondorff include the Scoutmaster's ecstatic rhapsody over *potatoes?* ("always conceiving new shapes, and yet so chaste")

13. Oskar's first day at school: Why do all the children behave so badly in such a rigid, authoritarian classroom? Why does Schlondorff make the teacher look so masculine? What is the significance of Oskar's shattering her glasses when she threatens him?

14. In the doctor's office: What is the purpose of the slow-motion shot of the foetus spilling on the floor? What is Schlondorff's attitude toward the doctor's joyful proclamation that he's going to write a scholarly article about Oskar?

15. How does the "soup" the children feed Oskar echo the theme of perverted "spiritual nourishment" in Kafka? In both cases, what does this forced meal symbolize? How does it foreshadow the sequence with the eels?

16. Agnes and Oskar visit Markus the toyseller, who watches Oskar while his mother spends a busy half-hour with her cousin Jan. Why does Schlondorff make their "love" meeting so animalistic?

> Why does he cut to the eighteenth century pastoral scene on the wall above them, then to horses dragging a cart, then to a bicycle rider falling and spilling *fish* all over the street?

Why does Oskar respond to their love-making by shattering all the windows in the town hall?

17. What does Schlondorff imply by cutting from the rise of Nazism to a group of *midgets* performing in a circus?

18. What does Bebra's performance with the glasses symbolize, and why is Oskar drawn to him? When Oskar says he prefers to sit in the audience, why does Bebra insist that their sort must always get up on the *stage?*

19. Why does Schlondorff cut from Bebra announcing, "*They* are coming!" to a group of children playing with a Nazi flag? What is the significance of Agnes and Alfred's unveiling a *radio* as they replace Beethoven's portrait with a picture of Hitler? How does Jan react to this scene, and why?

> "The stew is on," Alfred declares as he leaves for a Nazi meeting. What does this food metaphor imply?

20. Why does Schlondorff shoot the Nazi meeting in a cold blue light? What does Oskar's upsetting the "rhythm" of the meeting symbolize?

21. On the beach: What does the horse's head swarming with eels symbolize? Why does Agnes throw up as the fisherman brags about pulling eels out of dead bodies after the battle of Jutland? In what sense is this scene an *epiphany* for her?

22. As Alfred cleans the eels, why does Schlondorff focus on their twitching heads? What does his forcing Agnes to eat the eels symbolize, and how does this lead to her insanity?

> Note how Oskar, hidden in the closet, reacts to Jan's method of persuading his mother to eat the eels... Why does she now insist on eating the whole plate? What does her "surfeit of eels" symbolize?

23. What is ironic in Markus' urging Agnes to stick with Alfred (the German) rather than go with Bronski (the Pole)?

24. Oskar in church: What does his confrontation with the sculpture of Jesus symbolize? Why does he hang his drum around the statue's neck?

> As Agnes confesses that she already feels the "consequences" of her affair with her cousin Jan, what is the effect of Oskar's sudden burst of drumming?

25. What are the sexual implications of Agnes' glutting herself with fish?

26. Oskar responds to his mother's death by crawling under his grandmother's skirts. Why does Schlondorff repeat this motif? Why does he intercut the shots of Jan playing cards?

27. What does Markus' death symbolize? What is the significance of his no longer being around to supply Oskar's drums?

28. Why does Oskar feel that he "drummed his mother to her death?" Why does he also feel responsible for his uncle Jan's death? What is the Oedipal significance of his considering Jan his actual father?

29. September 1, 1939: What is the significance of the destruction of the Polish post office? What does Jan's "house of cards" symbolize? How does it recall the earlier "card game" with Oskar's mother? Why would Jan persist in playing cards with a dead man?

> As Jan is arrested and lined up against the wall, why does he flash the Queen of Hearts?

30. Maria, Oskar's cousin, is also his first love. What are the connotations of their "fizz-powder" ceremony?

31. As Oskar slams the door so confidently, why does Schlondorff cut to the sequence of Alfred and Maria screwing violently? Why does Oskar jump on top? What is the significance of Alfred and Maria berating each other afterwards? Why does she turn against Oskar when he offers her fizz-powder to make things better?

32. Maria, pregnant, tries on one of Agnes' dresses. Why does Oskar threaten her with the scissors? How does this reveal Schlondorff's attitude toward love?

33. Oskar visits the Scoutmaster's wife, who takes him into her bed. What does the Scoutmaster's "loving boys more than girls" imply about Nazism?

34. As Alfred and his friends feast, they rejoice over "starving" their enemies. Why is this ironic?

> How does Oskar feel about having a little brother? As the baby shrieks, why does Oskar promise him a drum when he turns three?

35. Oskar again meets Bebra, who now wears a uniform. What is the significance of his performing for the Propaganda Ministry?

> How is Roswitha Raguna like a Fellini character?

As Oskar looks up at the Eiffel Tower, why does he think of his grandmother's skirts?

36. What is the significance of Oskar's "breaking glass" to entertain the army? What does their performance on top of a Normandy pillbox symbolize? Why is their picnic ironic?

37. At the Nazi party in a French chateau, what does Oskar's breaking the officer's champagne glass imply? How does Bebra on his unicycle symbolize the Nazi movement?

The soldiers' song about "the witch as black as pitch" is a reprise of the song of the "soup-children" earlier. What does this imply? How do the sudden air raid sirens and the blackout comment on their party?

38. The evacuation of Paris: What is the significance of Roswitha's being blown up when she returns for a cup of coffee? How does this continue the film's *food* metaphor?

39. Oskar returns to Danzig just in time for his "son" Kurt's third birthday... and for the Russian invasion. Why does Oskar press the Nazi pin into his father's hand? What does Alfred's trying to *swallow* the pin symbolize, and how does this echo his wife's death?

40. As Alfred is buried, little Kurt throws stones at the crosses... How does this characterize him? Why does Oskar throw his drum into the grave? What is the significance of Kurt's hitting him in the head with a rock, and of his falling into his father's grave? Why does he "decide to grow?"

41. Why is everyone except the old grandmother loaded into a boxcar? For Oskar, what does this separation from his grandmother mean?

BEING THERE (1980—American) Directed by Hal Ashby; with Peter Sellers, Melvyn Douglas, and Shirley MacLaine; adapted from the novel by Jerzy Kosinski. Produced by United Artists.

Hal Ashby is an "absurdist" with a gift for orchestrating non-sequiturs and for making repulsive people amusing and sympathetic. His approach to humor extends back through his film *Harold and Maude* to Mike Nichols' *The Graduate,* and ultimately to Buster Keaton, the first blank American anti-hero. In creating the role of "Chance the Gardener," Peter Sellers had an enormous problem—how to depict an empty-headed character without giving a boring performance. Ashby helped by surrounding him with interesting character actors, against whom he could act as straight-man. The Pinteresque dialogue that follows, filled with twists and pauses, is the most brilliant and subtle work Peter Sellers has done in his entire career.

***

1. In the opening shot, Chance is almost literally a person plugged into his TV set. In what sense is he a modern Everyman?

> How do the shots of Chance in his garden, intercut with the TV orchestra, serve as an *overture* to his adventure?

> What is the importance of his old-fashioned clothes?

> Chance clicks channels frequently. What is the significance of his short attention span, and of his total immersion in whatever happens to be on the tube?

2. We never do learn whether Chance was "created," or whether he merely "evolved." Politically and theologically, what does the Old Man's death symbolize?

> Why does Ashby intercut the shots of Big Bird singing cheerfully on TV?

3. While the Old Man lies there dead, Chance switches on the TV. Why is the *posturepedic* commercial ironic? Why does Ashby cut to the racist film about the Old South? How does this relate to the maid's farewell?

4. As the two young lawyers enter, Chance watches a *game show* and a newscast about the President. Symbolically, how do these programs foreshadow his later adventures?

> How are the young lawyers characterized by their legalistic treatment of Chance?

5. "EVER SINCE I WAS A CHILD, I'VE WORKED ON THIS GARDEN." WHAT DOES CHANCE'S EXPULSION SYMBOLIZE?

6. As Chance goes out the front door, we see that the house is in the middle of a ghetto. How does this reflect the relationship of rich and poor, of the

U.S. and the rest of the world? Why is it ironic that Washington D.C. is one of the worst slums in the country?

7. The jazzed up version of Richard Strauss' "Thus Spake Zarathustra" sounds like the theme song from some TV cop program. How does this prepare us for Chance's encounter with the Black gang? How does this sequence differ from the way Blacks are ordinarily depicted on TV? When they threaten him with a switchblade, why does he flick his TV remote? How does this relate to the problem of Appearance and Reality?

8. Chance stops in front of the White House and tells a guard that a tree is very sick and needs care. What is the significance of the guard's reaction?

9. How is Chance, walking up the center strip of a freeway, like a character in a painting by the surrealist master, Rene Magritte? In both cases, what does the bowler-hatted figure symbolize?

10. Chance gets confused by seeing his own image on a giant TV screen. How does this reflect the film's view of "political images?"

11. As Chance backs away from the TV screen, Shirley MacLaine's car hits him. How is this a metaphor for success?

12. Chance's reaction to his first car ride: "This is just like television, but you can see further." How *do* these two symbols of our culture relate? How does Chance's observation reflect Marshall McLuhan's idea that we tend to live "looking in the rear view mirror?"

13. Chance chokes on the drink Mrs. Rand gives him. How does this foreshadow their relationship?

> Note that his name gets garbled as he chokes. Why would she hear his name as "Chauncey Gardiner?" How does his 1929 English suit influence her judgment of him, and what does this imply about appearance and reality?

14. In the elevator, Chance and the butler talk past each other. What does the setting symbolize? What is the significance of their lack of communication? How is this conversation, and other absurd misunderstandings throughout the film, like the dialogue in a Pinter play?

15. Why does Ashby cut from a Gatorade commerical to Mrs. Rand embracing her husband, who lies sick in bed?

16. MR. RAND WANTS "FRESH BLOOD FOR DINNER." HOW DOES HIS NEEDING TRANSFUSIONS TO STAY ALIVE SYMBOLIZE AMERICAN CAPITALISM?

17. Mrs. Rand and the doctor attribute all kinds of qualities to Chance that he doesn't possess. How is he like TV personalities in this respect?

18. Why does Chance ask the Black doctor if he knows "Raphael?" How does this reflect American racial perceptions, both Black and White?

19. When Chance complains that his "House" was shut down, why does Mr. Rand launch into a tirade about government interference?

20. Chance says, "I would like to work in your garden." Why would Mr. Rand take this as a metaphor and elaborate on it in a string of political cliches? ("A productive businessman is like a worker in a vineyard.") Why is it so easy for Mr. Rand to project his own political philosophy onto Chance?

21. Mr. Rand and Chance talk past each other about "That Room Upstairs." Why does Mr. Rand assume that Chance's responses are "philosophical?"

22. What is the significance of Mrs. Rand's first name being *Eve?* How does this continue the garden metaphor from the beginning of the film?

23. "Nobody likes a dying man . . . " Audiences frequently expect to dislike Mr. Rand because of the ruthless political views he represents. Why does Ashby make him so sympathetic as a *person?*

24. What is the symbolic connotation of the two *wheelchairs* that follow Ben and Chance as Ben expresses his political philosophy?

25. The meeting with the President: "As long as the roots are not severed, all will be well in the garden" is Chance's response to the President's very complicated debate with Ben. Why do Ben and the President take Chance's cliched "season" analogy so seriously?

26. Chance copies Ben, embracing the President and addressing him as "Bobby." Why is the President so unnerved by this?

27. The President assumes that *everyone* must have a "file." What does this imply about the American way of life? What is the significance of the CIA and FBI not being able to find data on Chance, and of the way they interpret this lack of information?

28. Ben wants Chance to head his proposed foundation for businessmen. What does this suggest about the directors of Foundations?

29. Eve shows Chance around the garden. Why does she interpret his "liking to watch the young plants grow" as a romantic flirtation?

30. Note that Chance's cliches appear in the President's TV speech. What does this say about the intellectual level of political speeches?

31. Chance is distracted from his phone conversation with the Washington *Post* by an exercise show on TV. What is the significance of his copying everything he sees on TV? How is he *like* the audiences that laugh at him?

32. Chance's TV interview: "Do you realize that more people will be watching you tonight than have seen theatre plays in the last forty years?" "Yes," Chance deadpans... "Why?" What is the point of Chance's reply? What does this suggest about the general level of taste and intelligence in our country?

> When Chance says, "There is plenty of room for new trees and flowers of all kinds," what is the significance of the audience's wild applause?

33. What is the significance of the President's *impotence?*

34. Why would Eve be drawn to Chance? How does she interpret his unemotional response to her kiss, and why does this excite her?

35. Eve enters while Chance eats breakfast in bed. What is the purpose of the idiotic TV song in the background ("You are my friend")? Why does he clutch the remote while she kisses him? Why would she admire his lack of response?

36. Chance tells the press that he doesn't read newspapers—he only watches TV. What is the cultural implication of this and of the reporter's enthusiastic response?

37. With the Russian ambassador, Chance says, "We are not so far from each other. Our chairs are almost touching." Why would the ambassador like this idea, and why does he interpret Chance's remark as profound?

38. While Eve gushes about Chance's ability to communicate—even in Russian—why does Ashby cut again to the impotent president?

39. Chance tells the publisher who wants him to write a book (for six figures!) that he doesn't read or write. How does the publisher interpret this, and why? What does this sequence imply about values in the world of publishing?

40. When Chance says, "I love to *watch,*" the homosexual exclaims, "You wait here—I'll go get Warren!" How is a TV addict like a *voyeur?*

41. Why does Ben encourage Eve's feelings for Chance?

42. As Eve enters, Chance watches a TV commercial showing people kissing. Why do we *all* base our ideas of Romance on TV images and toothpaste commercials?

> "I like to watch..." What does Eve's performance on the bearskin rug imply about "love" in the modern world?

> How does the soundtrack on the TV comment on their love scene?

> What is the symbolic implication of the TV exercise he does, standing on his head?

43. As Ben dies, he asks Chance to stay there with Eve and take care of her. Why doesn't the doctor speak up, even though he knows that Chance really *is* just a gardener?

44. Ben's funeral: While the President reads Ben's words, the *pallbearers* decide that *Chance* will be our next president. What do the pallbearers symbolize in our political process? What is the relationship between the media and our choice of political leaders?

45. During the President's speech, Chance walks in the forest. What is the significance of his final walk across the lake and the business with the umbrella?

46. What is the purpose of the out-takes? Why can't Sellers repeat the Black street-punk's line with a straight face?

47. Chance is an extension of his TV set, a "media-made man," whose perceptions are formed completely by commerical TV. What does this imply about the rest of us?

KAGEMUSHA, THE SHADOW WARRIOR (1980—Japanese) Directed by Akira Kurosawa; with Tatsuya Nakadai as Lord Shingen and the Nameless Thief. Distributed by Twentieth Century Fox and Films Inc.

1. The Prologue: How is Kurosawa's "Double" like a character in a Dostoyevsky novel? How does the idea of a "shadow" warrior reflect the psychology of Carl Jung?

2. "WHO IS WICKED?"—How does Kurosawa differ from his Hollywood contemporaries in the treatment of this philosophical theme?

3. In an impressive display of self-knowledge, Shingen admits, "I banished my father and killed my own son." How do lines like this connect him with Zeus and Jehovah? How is this prologue like a council of Olympian gods?

4. Why, philosophically, does Shingen decide to make the Thief his Double? Why is it significant that the Thief's punishment was originally going to be *crucifixion?*

5. How does the shot of exhausted warriors on the *steps* serve as a symbolic landscape?

6. What does the *flute* inside the castle symbolize? What is the significance of its being interrupted by a *shot?* Why does Kurosawa place this tragic action *offstage* instead of showing the shooting?

> Apparently the bravest and best samurai can be killed very easily by a Nobody hiding with a rifle. Why does Kurosawa dwell on ironies like this?

7. How do Shingen's two rivals differ in their reactions to his reported death?

8. Before Shingen dies, he warns his clan not to attack. Why? How does this establish his image as the "mountain?"

9. Shingen emerges from his little box, proclaims his ambition to conquer Kyoto, and dies. How does this symbolize the brevity of man's life? What are the *religious* connotations of this sequence?

10. Note the composition of the shots of the armies marching in long, curving lines. Why does Kurosawa deliberately echo Eisenstein's *Alexander Nevsky?*

11. Shingen's brother, Nobukado, has the Double enter from behind a *curtain.* How does this establish the film's theatre metaphor? What does the howling *wind* symbolize?

12. After riding triumphantly past the troops, the Double falls off his horse. How does this foreshadow his own fate, and the destruction of the Takeda clan?

13. What is the significance of the Double's reverting to thievery? How does he symbolize the human race?

> He breaks into Shingen's funeral urn and comes face to face with himself. How does this lead to his unwillingness to continue?

> Why does he say, "It all seems meaningless?" How does this echo Nietzsche's idea that "God is dead?"

> "This role is for someone who can die for the Takeda clan." What is the significance of his *acting* metaphor?

14. Shingen's funeral at Lake Shuwa: What does the boat disappearing in the fog symbolize?

> "I want to be some use to him . . . " What is the religious connotation of the Double's position at the edge of the lake? How does it foreshadow the end of the film?

15. How is the NOH PERFORMANCE a "mirror scene"? How does it comment symbolically on the three spies' attempt to find out if Shingen is really alive?

16. The Welcoming Ceremony: Why does Kurosawa include the comic business with the *brooms,* as the servants try in vain to cover their tracks?

17.The little boy immediately declares that the Double is not his grandfather ("He's changed—I'm not afraid of him any more.") Why do children understand what adults don't even notice?"

18. The Double finds that he always has three guards with him. ("These people know who you really are.") Why are *all* rulers actually prisoners of the systems they command?

19. "The shadow of a man can never desert him." As Shingen's brother, why is Nobukado so aware of this?

20. "Study the structure of the mansion. Don't get lost in your own house." What is the political meaning of this metaphor?

21. The Double impresses his guards by doing an impersonation of Shingen in a thoughtful pose, stroking his beard. Why is he able to understand this aspect of Shingen's nature?

22. Shingen's horse is even harder to fool than his grandson. The problem of Shingen's *mistresses* also arises, but the Old General solves this problem, declaring, "Our master has been ill—He must refrain from *riding*." How does this comic metaphor foreshadow the tragic conclusion of the film?

> Why do the women laugh when the Double admits bluntly that the "Play" is over, and that he is an impersonator?

23. Shingen's banner identifies him with the elements of the *I Ching:* mountain, wind, fire, forest. How does this identification reflect Shingen's concept of himself as a *God?* Why does this "impersonation" make *him* a "Double" too?

24. When Shingen's son, Katsuyori, forces the Double to speak, he replies that "a mountain does not move." In what sense has he absorbed the character of the dead warlord?

25. Why does Shingen's brother say that "living another man's life" must make the Double feel like he's "on a cross." How do these lines imply that the film is an allegory about the death of God?

26. In the Double's nightmare, what does Shingen's bursting from his jar symbolize? Note the intense colors as Shingen pursues him across an hallucinatory field of snow. What is the significance of his plunge into the lake, "surrounded by a million enemies?"

> As the Double wakes, note the Hokusai wave on the wall behind him. How does this foreshadow the end of the film?

27. While castles fall, Shingen's grandson plays with his *top*. On a tragic level, how does the top reflect the Double and the role he's playing? How does it also foreshadow the destruction of the clan?

28. Why does Kurosawa shoot the first big battle at *night?* What symbolic purpose does this serve? Why does he make the soldiers look like swarms of black ants?

29. The Double is ordered to sit silently on his *director's stool* while his guards are shot one at a time around him. Nobukado says, "They died protecting you. Imagine you're already crucified—don't move." How does this episode reflect Kurosawa's consciousness of *himself* as a director? How do Lord and Thief represent polarities in Kurosawa's own nature?

30. Shingen's young rival drinks *European wine.* What does this symbolize? What is the significance of his older ally's "not liking the taste of it?" How does this reflect his earlier ambivalence about Shingen's assassination?

> How do the *guns* stacked in the background relate to this
> odd communion ritual?

31. "When the original is gone, what happens to the Double?" What is the theological implication of this line?

32. What is the significance of the Double's being thrown by Shingen's horse?

33. "The *play* is over—Katsuyori is our master now." What does this metaphor imply about politics and religion?

34. What is the effect of the cross-cut to the Double leaving in the rain? Why is he slow to take the generals' money? What is the significance of his being cast out like a leper without even an umbrella?

> The servants throw rocks at him as he leaves. How does this
> relate to his image as a saint or messiah?

35. The Double looks through the bars at Shingen's funeral. How has his relationship with Shingen's grandson changed him? In what sense is he observing his *own* funeral?

> What is the purpose of the young rival's NOH performance,
> in which he chants about the illusory nature of life?

36. "The Mountain has moved" . . . and the Takeda clan takes the offensive. On the shore of the lake, the Old General warns Katsuyori that the unearthly light is a warning from his dead father to stay home and guard his domain. Why does Katsuyori ignore this advice and determine to attack?

37. "The Takeda clan can't fight without horses." What do the *horses* symbolize, as opposed to the *guns* of the younger generation?

38. The Double watches helplessly as the horses rush past. What is symbolic about his position in the middle of the field?

39. We don't see any actual killing. Why does Kurosawa emphasize the Double's *reaction,* rather than the blood and guts of the usual Hollywood battle scene? How is this in keeping with his conception of the film as a *classic drama?*

40. After the battle ... What is the purpose of the long slow-motion shots of wounded soldiers staggering around as if in a dream? Why does Kurosawa dwell on the *horses?* As symbols, how are they like the horses in Picasso's "Guernica"?

41. Why does the Double finally charge across the battlefield?

42. What is the meaning of the final sequence in the lake?

43. In twenty-seven films, now, Akira Kurosawa has indeed been a "shadow" warrior, casting images on the wall through the prism of reality. His main projection in *Kagemusha* is *himself*—as God, King, Director, and Thief. How does this reflect his early concern with the nature of reality in *Rashomon?*

STARDUST MEMORIES (1980—American) Directed by Woody Allen; with Charlotte Rampling (Dorie), Marie-Christine Barrault (Isabel), and Jessica Harper (Daisy); cinematography by Gordon Willis. Produced by United Artists.

1. How does the opening sequence of Woody Allen on a train, surrounded by grotesques, parody the opening of Fellini's *8½.* What is the effect of the *ticking clock?*

A party (costumed in *white*) passes on a train headed in the opposite direction. What does his concluding that he's "on the wrong train" symbolize?

2. As he pounds on the window trying to get out, the cut to birds flying over the beach suggests symbolic death and resurrection (as in *8½*). Why does Woody Allen undercut this image by having the procession on the beach confront a heap of garbage? How does this image symbolize Woody Allen's view of contemporary culture? How does it reflect his persona's self image?

3. What is the effect of the cut to *shadows* in front of the screen, a cacaphony of voices criticizing him as "indulgent ... not funny anymore?" Why wouldn't the studio like the sequence he has just shown them?

4. As Sandy bickers with agents and secretaries, what is the point of the background mural of a Vietnamese execution? How does it relate to his not wanting to be "funny" anymore?

5. How does the fire in the oven symbolize his inner state? Why his aversion to eating *rabbit?*

6. The arrival at the Stardust Hotel: As his car is surrounded by Felliniesque grotesques, all shrieking absurd questions, why does Sandy hallucinate a vision of his childhood self as *superman,* flying away? What is the significance of his being a *magician* as a child? How does this relate to his playing God as a filmmaker?

7. The screening of Sandy in a song-and-dance film: "What were you trying to say in this picture?" Answer: "I was just trying to be funny." What is ironic in critics' attributing all kinds of "meaning" to Woody Allen's early films, while rejecting his recent attempts to say something meaningful?

8. Marie-Christine Barrault is extremely earthy and maternal. How is she different from Sandy's former lover, Dorie, played by Charlotte Rampling? What is the point of this contrast, and of Sandy's involvements with women who are too neurotic to relate?

9. Dorie accuses him of flirting with her kid-cousin. How does this sequence characterize her? (Note the word "incest" on the wall.)

10. As Sandy's sister complains about her children hitching to Texas and selling stolen cameras, her husband rides his exercise machine. What does this absurd image symbolize?

11. The people from the train wind up in "Jazz Heaven." Why does Sandy object to this as an ending for his film?

12. "You may be the Perfect Woman": How does Sandy's parody of a Frankenstein film relate to his personal problem? (In the operation, he wants to put the mind of one woman into another's body.)

13. As Isabel's children shriek for ice cream, Sandy looks out the window to see an *elephant* on the beach. What is the point of this hallucination? How does it relate to his sudden memory of standing on the beach with Dorie, who gives him a flute for his birthday?

> Symbolically, how is this gift like the *harmonica* in *Manhattan?*

14. At the Felliniesque UFO party, what is the symbolic significance of his magic trick, levitating Jessica Harper's body?

15. In the flashback to the last time he saw Dorie, how do the jump-cuts of her face allude to Bergman's *Persona?* What does this technique imply about her mental state?

16. Dorie accuses Sandy of always looking for the Perfect Woman. Why does this prevent her from being close to him?

17. In Sandy's hallucination of an "encounter of the third kind," the space invaders tell him, "We have to go—we can't breathe your air." How does this metaphor comment on his view of life?

> "If you want to do mankind a real service, tell funnier jokes."
> How does this sequence satirize science fiction films?

18. During Sandy's love scene with his "muse," Jessica Harper, what is the symbolic effect of the hot-air balloons landing behind them?

> She warns him that she's nothing but trouble, as he must realize from overhearing her phone conversation earlier. Why would he be attracted to someone so much like Dorie?

19. "You're my idol"—BANG! How does this echo the Vietnamese mural early in the film? How does this sequence prefigure the death of John Lennon?

20. Cut to Sandy being wheeled into a hospital, where he *dreams* about people's reactions to his death. What is the effect of juxtaposing a nurse munching an apple against an existential psychologist proclaiming, "Too much reality is not what people want"?

21. During the testimonials, Sandy's shadow complains, "What good is it if I can't pinch any more women?" Why does he include this joke before his serious final speech? ("I was looking for something to give my life meaning...") What is the point of the long shot of Dorie smiling with Louis Armstrong playing in the background? How is this like the sequence with the tape recorder near the end of *Manhattan?*

22. As Sandy wakes from his faint calling Dorie's name, Isabel flees. Why, when she was so hesitant about living with him in the first place?

23. Alluding to the beginning of his film (being trapped on the wrong train), Sandy tries to assure Isabel that he has thought of a "better ending." How does this reflect his realization that he must change his cycle of relationships?

24. With the cut to the audience applauding, we realize that this *is* merely the forced "happy ending" of a film, or a wish-fulfillment. Or is it another fantasy, like his hallucination about being shot?

> What is the purpose of the alternative endings? How does this echo the conclusion of Fellini's *8½*?

> Why does the film end with Sandy staring at the empty screen and walking away?

BEAU PERE (1981—French; Directed by Bertrand Blier; with Patrick Dewaere, Ariel Besse, Nicole Garcia, Maurice Ronet, and Nathalie Baye; music by Philippe Sarde. Distributed by New Line Cinema.

An English wit once observed that French girls are *women* from birth, while French men are always little boys. In Bertrand Blier's *Beau Pere,* Patrick Dewaere is very much a child. He's a charming, conventional loser who worships music and hides in the Blues because he lacks the depth to cope with the precocious step-daughter who loves him. As his eternal child-lover, Ariel Besse is no Brooke Shields in tight blue jeans, but a real teenager—bony, awkward, intense—trying to deal rationally with her feelings. Unfortunately, her intellect also causes the emotional isolation that prevents her from loving anyone but the man who raised her. What saves *Beau Pere* from being either sentimental or sordid? Bertrand Blier's ironic detachment. Without moralizing, he delves into myths and archetypes, turning incest taboos on end and daring us to judge the characters in his "subversive fairy tale."

***

1. How does the tone of Remy's opening monologue echo Truffaut's *Shoot the Piano Player?* What is the significance of his being a second-rate musician, old-fashioned, and hung up on the Blues?

2. "Even the car is on my side..." Why is this ironic? Before the tragic crash, why does Blier include the comic business with Remy pushing Martine's car?

3. Instead of telling Marion about her mother's death, Remy puts a letter on the table and leaves. What is the significance of his cowardice? Why does Blier pose him with a bag full of groceries in front of the "sale" signs at the supermarket?

> Note the large photograph of Martine sitting on the floor.
> Why does Blier repeat this visual motif throughout the film?

4. If Marion's alcoholic father never gives her a thought, why would he insist on his authority over her?

5. "You can't count on anyone," says Marion. Why does she walk so stiffly to her father's car? How does her emotional isolation mirror the incest theme?

> Why does Blier repeat the car-pushing motif?

6. Why does Blier punctuate Remy's comic gloom with his friend Nicholas' documentary narration? What is the significance of his being a *bass* player, coaxing Remy from the dinner table by giving him the beat?

> What is the symbolic purpose of the jazz transition as Remy
> stops by the phone booth? Why won't Marion speak to him?

7. Back in the nightclub, why does Remy just sit at his piano, not playing?

8. As Remy drowns in his jazz collection, the doorbell rings... "You can't even be miserable in peace..." Why does Remy savor his unhappiness?

> Why is Marion so calm about the expected visit from her
> father? Why does Blier stress that *she* is the strong one in the
> ensuing confrontation?

> How does the tragi-comic fistfight echo *Shoot the Piano
> Player?* Why does Blier have the two men sit like abject little
> boys while Marion kneels at their feet to patch their wounds?

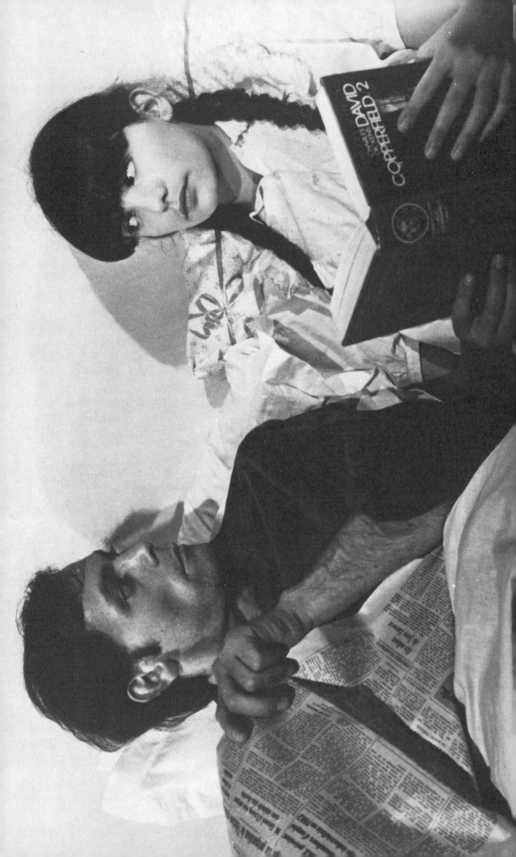

9. Why does Blier cut from the father warning that "boys will be sniffing around..." to Remy and Marion happily playing the piano? What does their duet symbolize?

10. Remy summons Marion to his bed to lecture her on baby-sitting so late. Why is his fatherly concern ironic?

> What is the effect of Remy's hands slowly rising as Marion confides her "problem?" Why does Blier make Remy's protestations so unconvincing?

> "You're only fourteen, and I'm nearly thirty!" wails Remy. "So what?" Marion snaps. Why does Blier cut abruptly to Remy jamming on the piano with his friend?

11. Remy returns home to find Marion in his bed. "What am I lacking as a woman?" she demands. Why does Blier juxtapose Marion's seriousness against Remy's conventional cliches?

12. Ever persistent, Marion climbs back into Remy's bed, this time armed with Dickens' *David Copperfield* (!) She calmly explains that she wants him to be the first: "I know you want to make love to me ... Why lie?" Why does Blier stress her cool rationality?

13. When Marion leaves for vacation, note how ingeniously she gets Remy to kiss her goodbye. What is the meaning of the expression on her face as the train pulls out?

14. How does the cut to Remy being evicted comment on the previous scene? What does his struggle to carry the piano down the stairs symbolize?

15. How does Remy's drive through the snow echo *Shoot the Piano Player?* Why does Blier include the reflections of the snowcovered mountains in the windows as Marion steps onto the balcony?

16. Why is Remy so "correct" with Marion when she returns to Paris? What is the significance of their living in an old building that is about to be torn down? Why does he still insist that she sleep in a separate room? Why does he claim that "nothing special" happened between them?

17. Why does Blier include Remy's sardonic monologue about the rich old ladies stuffing their faces?

> He returns home to find his house full of teenage boys... How is the party part of Marion's tactic to make Remy love her?

18. Cut to Remy and his friend playing the Blues... What is the symbolic function of this musical interlude? What is the effect of the lone motorcycle appearing on the final chord?

> Why does Remy back away from Marion's door instead of confronting her? How is she characterized by her blunt description of her evening ("I expect a visit")?

19. The birthday party: What is the significance of the young man ignoring Remy's music to flip on the stereo? Why does Remy insist on leaving instead of accepting his hostess' proffered leg of lamb?

> "Midnight wasn't possible..." Why does Marion deliberately stay out all night—and then fend off the advances of the boy who drives her home?

20. As Marion vows to help Remy forget the Blues, her father drives up... How does his suggestion that the three of them live together echo Truffaut's *Jules and Jim?*

21. Charlotte (Nathalie Baye) gives her sick little girl a suppository as Remy looks on. Why does Blier focus on Marion's troubled face while Remy and Charlotte talk? What is the effect of the *thunder* in the background as Remy looks around the apartment?

22. Remy and Marion walk home in the rain. What does the setting symbolize? Why does Remy have so little to say? Why does Marion tease that as soon as she turns her back, he'll return to check on the little patient?

23. What is the symbolic purpose of the cut to Charlotte passionately attacking her piano? What is the significance of her being a much better pianist than Remy? Considering his worship of music, what does she symbolize to him?

> Why does Remy stand outside Charlotte's door, listening instead of knocking? As she invites Remy in for tea, what does his position in the *elevator* symbolize?

> Why doesn't he admit that he plays piano?

24. When Remy returns home, Marion sits peeling apples. What does this activity symbolize? What is the meaning of her gesture as she stands and wipes her hands on her apron? (Note that she looks just like the young girl in Edvard Munch's painting "Puberty.")

25. "My poor love," says Marion. "You sure do make yourself miserable." What does she mean? Why does Blier include Marion's soliloquy? ("Maybe

some day I can give him a baby... He can't be a step-father all his life, raising other people's children.") How does this speech foreshadow the film's ending?

26. Cut to Charlotte playing in a concert... then to Remy and Charlotte enjoying dinner as Marion wanders through a disco. What do the contrasting settings symbolize?

> What is the effect of the red lighting as Marion approaches her father? Why does she return to him, and what is the meaning of their embrace?

27. Remy dashes home to find Marion gone. "Martine!" he sighs, staring at the photograph... then "Charlotte" as he runs to her apartment. Why is it funny that he says the three names in the same despairing tone of voice?

28. Charlotte exclaims, "I'll cure you, you'll see!" What does she mean?

> WHAT IS THE SYMBOLIC MEANING OF THE SERIES OF ZOOM SHOTS OF LITTLE NATHALIE AS THE FILM ENDS? How does this Freudian punchline bring Remy's life full-circle?

MEPHISTO (1981—German/Hungarian) Directed by Istvan Szabo; with Klaus Maria Brandauer, Rolf Hoppe, and Karin Boyd; cinematography by Lajos Koltai; adapted from Klaus Mann's novel; an Analysis Films release.

Can a political toady become a great artist? Probably not—but it is certainly possible for him to be a success. Hendrik Hofgen's lust for success borders on the obscene. His manipulation of women and his self-righteous conformity, coupled with his image of himself as an "incredible villain," render him as contemptible as his limp handshake. His naivete, however, eventually causes us to feel sorry for him. For all his posturing, he is upstaged by the truly Mephistophelean Prime Minister whom he thinks he has seduced. The political implications of Istvan Szabo's allegory should be clear to any artist—on either side of the Iron Curtain.

***

1. What is the allegorical function of the opening sequence? How does the lady with her courtiers symbolize Hendrik's aspiration?

> How does Hendrik's tantrum in the dressing room foreshadow the final shot of the film?

2. Why does Szabo ritualize Hendrik's relationship with his mistress by making her his dance teacher?

> Juliette calls him "Heinz," mocking him for not even being able to order a beer without sounding like he's acting. In what sense is she his *anima?* How is she also a projection of his conscience—possibly even his soul?

> "You comical picture of misery!" Why does she laugh at him? As he kisses his image in the mirror, she jokes, "You love only yourself—and even then not enough." What does she mean?

> "An actor is a mask among human beings!" Hendrik exclaims. How does this principle motivate his actions throughout the film?

> What is the implication of the cut from them about to make love—to Dr. Kroge blowing his nose?

3. Intent on success, Hendrik courts a wealthy society lady... "I can't talk anymore. So many thoughts are just parts I've played." How does Hendrik's proposal to Barbara actually reflect his inner self?

> When Hendrik tells Juliette he's getting married, why does Szabo shoot their conversation in a mirror? Why the business with the pistol?

4. Hendrik meets Barbara's wealthy family. What is the effect of the Felliniesque smiles as Nicoletta von Niebuhr declares that she is Barbara's best friend? Why does Szabo refrain from characterizing the two women, leaving their motivations vague? How does this cause the audience to identify with Hendrik's self-centered perception of the world?

> What is the significance of Hendrik's coughing fit during the engagement dinner?

5. With the help of his wife's money, Hendrik plans his Brechtian street-theatre. "An end to passive audiences!" he rants. "The public must play an active part." Why does Szabo stress that Hendrik begins his career as an ardent communist?

If communists and fascists are mirror images of each other, why is it predictable that Hendrik will later swing to the other side with equal enthusiasm?

6. Over dinner, Hendrik derides Lotte Lindenthal, asserting that her list of lovers has led to her success. Why is this hypocritical of him? When Miklas springs to her defense, why is it ironic that he calls the Nazis murderous thugs and insists that Miklas be dismissed from the company?

7. As Dr. Kroge bows to Hendrik's ultimatum, why does Szabo cut to a can-can number danced by an angel in white? How is this sequence, with Hendrik joining the dance, an analogy for the action of the film as a whole? How does it allude to the ending of Goethe's *Faust?*

8. Hendrik in Berlin: "In real life I may seem non-descript . . . " How does his boasting of his ability to "transform himself" relate to the theme of the film? Why do actors frequently seem to lack personal identities?

9. In his cabaret act, Hendrik attacks the bourgeoisie for their greedy exploitation of the poor. How does the cut to the Nazis beating a man in the alley comment on this scene? What is the significance of Hendrik's refusal to intervene?

10. Why is Hendrik's communist anthem ironic? Why does Szabo juxtapose it against a montage of his entrances in various roles? What is the significance of his shifting identities?

11. Why the cut from Miklas training the Nazi youth group—to Hendrik as Mephisto exclaiming that "Blood is a very special juice?"

12. "YOU'RE IN THE END EXACTLY WHAT YOU ARE!" Mephisto declares. Why is this line ironic, and how does it relate to Hendrik's inner life?

13. Having established himself in Berlin with his wealthy wife, Hendrik quietly arranges for a flat so Juliette can live nearby. How are his personal relationships analogous to his professional and political life?

14. While the Nazis are voted into power, Hendrik *sleeps* to recover from an orgy with his mistress. How does he symbolize Germany as a whole? Why doesn't he care that the "Austrian clown has become chancellor?"

"This is my answer—Hamlet! Shakespeare!" Why is Hendrik's worship of Shakespeare ironic?

Why does he reject his friend Otto's plea to form a united front against the Nazis? Instead, why does he quietly accept an offer to make a film in Hungary?

15. When Hendrik's old girlfriend Angelika intercedes with Lotte Lindenthal, why does he decide to return to Germany? Why does Szabo dwell on his hesitation as he steps from the train?

16. "The role of elegant friend and seducer won't cause you any difficulty," Cesar mocks. Why does Szabo cut to Hendrik rehearsing with Lotte? What is the significance of his fawning over a lady he formerly scorned as a "cow?"

17. When Hendrik learns that he has not been cast in *Faust,* he asks Lotte to intercede with Cesar. How does this undercut his insistence that he lives outside politics?

18. What is the symbolic significance of Hendrik's playing Mephisto—to Miklas' Faust!—and instructing him in the art of seduction? How does Miklas represent the average German citizen?

19. Why is the Prime Minister fascinated with Hendrik's performance as Mephisto?

>   "It's all going like clockwork!" Hendrik gloats. Why is this ironic?

>   "The mask is perfect—so evil—yet your handshake is limp." Why does the Prime Minister dwell on this paradox?

>   What is the symbolic implication of Mephisto and the Prime Minister shaking hands in the box as the audience stares?

20. Why is it ironic that Hendrik considers himself an "incredible villain," manipulating politicians to achieve success?

21. "Isn't there a bit of Mephisto in every German?" the Prime Minister asks. What is the effect of the green lighting and the Romantic painting hanging on the wall behind them? How does the setting connect Hendrik with Faust?

22. Why the series of low-angle shots as Hendrik attends the reception?

23. "What sort of man are you?" the sculptor asks. How does this question relate to the main theme of *Hamlet?* ("What a piece of work is man?")

>   How do all the floodlights during this sequence foreshadow the end of the film?

24. The Prime Minister praises Hendrik's unpredictable effects: "I think I'm learning from you, Mephisto." Why does he flatter Hendrik's acting?

"Building the role is all-important," Hendrik explains. What are the political implications of their conversation about theatre?

25. Why does the Prime Minister smile as he agrees to release Hendrik's friend Otto?

Why does Szabo make Hendrik's reunion with Otto so lyrical? Why does he juxtapose the cut to the absurd idealized sculpture?

What is the symbolic function of all the false images in the art gallery and of Hendrik's flowery speech about them? Why does Juliette object to his speeches?

26. Miklas—who always seems to be on the "wrong" side—asks Hendrik to sign a protest. By resigning from the Nazi party, how is he Hendrik's *foil?*

What is the significance of Miklas' fate and of Hendrik's reaction? ("Would the government deem a mere actor worthy of a fake car accident?")

27. Reviewing Hendrik's file, the Prime Minister sings mockingly about Hamburg—then raises the matter of Juliette Martens. What is the significance of the shift in tone?

28. Threatened by the loss of his mistress, the desperate Hendrik cries, "I have to find a freind!" Considering the nature of his relationships, why is this ironic?

As Nicoletta von Niebuhr offers to help, why does Szabo cut to the police hustling Juliette out of Berlin—then to Hendrik enthusing over his new job?

29. Hendrik scurries through the theatre confiscating anti-Nazi handbills. How does this sequence undercut the importance of his position as Director of the Prussian State Theatre?

30. Cut to Hendrik on a cultural mission to Paris. Why does he refuse to stay there with Juliette? Why does Barbara reject his argument that "someone has to safeguard our values?"

Standing in front of the Odeon, Hendrik asks, "What would I be able to do here? Freedom! What for?" Why is his question ironic? What does his descent into the underground symbolize?

31. At the engagement party, why does the Prime Minister teasingly call Hendrik "Hamlet?"

32. In an ecstatic rhapsody about the purity of his art, Hendrik does some soul-searching—and concludes that he deserves all he's got! How does the Prime Minister's contemptuous dismissal of his appeal for Otto comment on Hendrik's perception of his own importance?

33. Lotte gives Hendrick the official line on Otto's fate. Why does Szabo shoot their conversation in a mirror? How does the imagery in this sequence echo Hamlet's famous confrontation with his mother?

34. What is the significance of Hendrik's revisionist interpretation of Hamlet as the representative of Nazi ideals?

35. How does the Prime Minister's birthday party assert the government's attitude toward theatre and the arts?

> The look on Hendrik's face reveals his tragic knowledge of Otto's fate and his own position. Still, he can't resist making speeches: "Without patrons, art is like a bird with broken wings..." How does Hendrik's "performance" reveal his inability to perceive reality?

> If the Prime Minister and Lotte are like Shakespeare's Claudius and Queen Gertrude, why is it ironic that Hendrik considers himself a "Hamlet?"

36. What are the implications of the final sequence in the amphitheatre?

> "Well, Mephisto, what power is looking down on you?" How does this echo Hamlet's being led up onto the battlements by the ghost of his father? How does it also allude to *Faust?*

> "This is the real light, isn't it?" What is the meaning of the final shot?

> "What do they want of me? After all, I'm only an actor!" Why are Hendrik's final words ironic?

COUP DE TORCHON (1981-French) Directed by Bertrand Tavernier; with Philippe Noiret, Isabelle Huppert, and Stephane Audran; music by Philippe Sarde. Set in Bourkassa in 1938.

Morally, *Coup de Torchon* leaves the audience on shaky ground. Most of us are probably pleased that the lethargic old sheriff finally turns on his tormentors, encouraging their own worst impulses to cause their self-destruction. We have second thoughts, however, when he kicks a dying man or manipulates his pathetic little mistress. "What does all this mean?" we ask, thinking perhaps of a similar representative of colonial power in George Orwell's "Shooting an Elephant." If Sheriff Cordier does indeed symbolize God or imperialism, Tavernier doesn't allow us any comfortable conclusions.

***

1. While a vulture circles, cut to a group of emaciated children digging for termites in the sand. Lucien Cordier watches from a distance, looks up at the vultures, then lights a fire for the children as it gets dark. As sheriff in the African town of Bourkassa, how does he represent both western authority and God in his relationship with the human race?

2. What does the outhouse just below Lucien's window imply about his authority? How does it also reflect his relationship with his wife and her "brother?"

3. While Lucien wonders what to do with his life, cut to Marcaillou beating his wife. Why does Lucien get up so slowly from the barber's chair to stop him?

4. The two pimps entertain themselves by shooting the bodies drifting down the river. "You can always be bought," Le Peron chuckles as they push Lucien in the river. What does this sequence imply about power and government in Third World countries.

5. Lucien visits Marcel to ask his advice in dealing with the pimps. Why does Tavernier set their conversation in a pool room, and why does he stress Marcel's racism? Why does Lucien take Marcel's "lesson" so cheerfully?

> As he leaves on the train, Lucien tells Paulo, "Thank Marcel for telling me what to do. Now I'm covered." What does he mean?

6. On the train, Lucien meets the new schoolteacher. How does his peeling fruit for her foreshadow their relationship? What does the blind man symbolize?

7. In the middle of the night, Lucien again meets the pimps by the river. Why does he make them sing a bawdy song?

8. Why does Tavernier include Lucien's dream about the spiders? When Marcel wakes him to ask if he killed the two pimps, why does Lucien take him to the brothel and get him drunk?

> What does Marcel's being carted away in the wheelbarrow symbolize? What's ironic about his bragging "I took care of your two pimps?"

9. "Are you going to arrest me for hitting a nigger?" Marcaillou demands indignantly. What is the meaning of the look on the schoolteacher's face as Lucien lets him go?

10. As the priest nails Christ on the cross, he urges Lucien to get rid of the poisonous elements, one at a time, starting with Marcaillou. Ironically, how does this motivate the scene that follows? Why does Lucien kick Marcaillou as he lies bleeding on the sand?

11. "Good thing Christ is cast iron." What do the crosses eaten by termites symbolize? How do they reflect Lucien's relationship with Rose?

12. What is the significance of the natives watching the French war movie backwards while Lucien falls asleep on the schoolteacher's shoulder? What does the sudden dust storm symbolize?

13. During the night, Lucien saws through the boards in the outhouse. How does the comic consequence parallel the tragic action in the film?

14. During dinner with Huguette and Nono, why does Lucien suggest that

Rose get a gun?

15. Lucien sees Nono peeking through a woman's window. How does the "pretend" beating foreshadow the film's conclusion?

16. "What's good, what's evil? It doesn't make much difference here," Lucien tells the schoolteacher. What does he mean, and why does he need to confess to her?

17. What is the effect of the tracking shot through the trees as someone approaches Rose's house? What is the significance of Marcaillou's reappearing in the doorway and falling on top of her? How does Rose's unfortunate slip of the tongue motivate the scene between Lucien and Friday?

18. "I'm tired of taking the rap for doing what everyone wants me to do," Lucien tells Rose and walks away. What does he mean?

19. If Lucien *sees* Nono watching them in the mirror, why does he kiss Rose so passionately?

20. What is the effect of Le Peron's twin brother suddenly appearing in town? Why does Lucien take him to the river, where they drink the dead brother's ratafia? Why is it ironic that Lucien and George get along so well together?

> What does Lucien mean when he says, "I'm not a policeman—I'm Christ."? Why would he feel that "All crimes are collective. We *all* shot your brother—and maybe I did."?

21. As George sits perplexed in the train, why does Tavernier repeat the motif of the blind man?

22. "God told me to kill them," Lucien has written on the schoolteacher's blackboard. What does this imply about his mental state? Why does she tell the children it's the Marseilleise?

23. When Nono tries to blackmail him, Lucien calmly tears the room apart and tells him to clean it up. Why does he then carefully check the pistol in Rose's drawer before leaving his hat on the table?

24. "If I offer temptation, people don't have to be tempted. Normally, I should crack down on the rich and powerful, but the rich and powerful won't

allow that." How does Lucien's callous treatment of Rose reflect the larger philosophical problem of evil?

25. How does Lucien's parable about dogs reflect human behavior?

26. Cut from Rose's curse to the dance. "Thousands are unhappy, and I'm alone," Lucien tells the schoolteacher. "What happens isn't important because I've been dead for a long time." What are the political and theological implications of this line?

27. The film ends, as it began, with the children eating termites. This time, why does Lucien raise his pistolthen lower it in despair? What does this imply about Africa's plight?

EATING RAOUL (1982-American) Directed by Paul Bartel; with Mary Woronov, Robert Beltran, Susan Saiger, and Buck Henry. Released by Twentieth Century Fox International Classics.

With its stock characters and flat visual style, *Eating Raoul* is a parody of TV sitcoms—except, of course, that no TV show would ever be allowed to joke meaningfully about sex. It's also a classic comedy developed by theme and variation, as Paul and Mary Bland bump off one social stereotype after another, giving the bodies to their partner Raoul to be ground up for dog food. Like many classic comedies, *Eating Raoul* is a masquerade involving an imposter, an ironist, and a scapegoat. Mary dresses up to deceive her victims, only to find herself deceived by her own desires. Paul represents the cool, ironic voice of reason. And the unfortunate Raoul of the title is the scapegoat who suffers for their sins, literally becoming the object of their communion in the end. This low-budget satire, shot on borrowed film, proves that you don't need a lot of money to make a good comedy. Just a solid comic structure and a sense of humor.

***

1. How does the theme song ("Exactly Like You") establish the film's tone?

2. "Big weenies are better." After the travelogue voice stressing the connection between food and sex, cut to Paul urging a customer to buy a good bottle of Beaujolais (instead of "Mountainbrook"), then to Mary feeding hospital garbage to a patient trying to put the make on her. What do these grotesque food metaphors imply about love and sex in southern California?

3. In contrast, Paul and Mary dream of opening a restaurant: Chez Bland! How does the name characterize them, and how is this impression reinforced by their "fabulous fifties furniture," twin beds, and stuffed pets?

4. Paul and Mary's financial woes are interrupted by a lost swinger, who throws up on their rug, nearly drowns in the toilet, and finally expires on the chicken cacciatore. Why is all this graphic imagery amusing?

5. "I don't mind a little hugging and kissing, but *that*!" How does Mary's physical appearance belie her prudishness, especially in her scene with Mr. Leech?

6. "I suppose one takes what one can get in this life." Why does Bartel intercut the "sale" of the wine with Mary's attempt to get a loan at the bank? How is their conclusion a comic restatement of the problem of job?

7. "This city is full of rich perverts." How does Mary's scheme to make money represent the revenge of the middle class on the sexually liberated? How does it also satirize middle class values?

8. What is ironic about the *real* Doris the Dominatrix feeding her baby while advising Paul and Mary on placing ads in the *Hollywood Press*? Why the cut to the laughing baby as his mommy declares that she "draws the line at golden showers"?

9. How do the swingers Paul and Mary bash with their frying pan represent specific social stereotypes in American culture?

10. What does their choice of murder weapon symbolize?

11. What does the scene with the spoiled brat who hates his mother imply about the nature of the sexual revolution?

12. How does the sequence with the Nazi torturer satirize forties war films?

13. What does Raoul's being a "locksmith" symbolize? When he slips into Paul and Mary's apartment to discover their scam, how does the sequence with the flashlight foreshadow his affair with Mary?

14. Mary as Minnie Mouse: When Raoul protests, "I hate to see a beautiful woman degraded," Paul snaps, "We don't choose these fantasies. *They* do!" What is the significance of this particular fantasy?

15. "I don't fuck with the King!" Sounds like Raoul is dealing with the Mafia. Why is this ironic?

16. Why is it ironic that the hippie becomes violent, and that Raoul has to strangle him with his own love beads?

17. The seduction scene is genuinely erotic. Why would someone as uptight as Mary be attracted to Raoul? Nevertheless, why does she insist, "I'm not about to risk my marriage for the sake of some low animal attraction."?

18. "I'm a hot-blooded, emotional Chicano!" How do Raoul's romantic outbursts make him a comic figure? How is the love-triangle a comic version of the conflict between Apollo and Dionysus?

19. How do Doris' performances as a blind nun, an immigration officer, and a health inspector relate to the film's theme?

20. At the swingers' party, what is the significance of Howard the DJ serving Mountainbrook as his house wine? How have Paul and Mary changed by the time they must deal (again) with Mr. Leech and the hot-tubbers?

21. What is the significance of Paul's trading his fifties Buick for a little yellow sports car?

22. Outraged that Paul is selling cars without giving him a cut, Raoul outlines his ambitious plans: "I'm going to expand this business and bring in some sexy young chicks while my wife is home having my babies." How does Raoul's speech motivate Mary's decision in the kitchen?

23. Cut to James the real estate agent, enjoying his meal:
"I hope you make this a permanent item on your menu. French?"
"No—Spanish."
"So tender!"

"Yeah..." Mary sighs.

"It's amazing what you can do with a cheap piece of meat," Paul comments sardonically. What are the double-entendres in the final scene? Why does Bartel reveal the ending from the very beginning in the title of the film, instead of letting the audience figure it out from the dialogue?

FANNY AND ALEXANDER (1983-Swedish) Directed by Ingmar Bergman; with Bertil Guve, Ewa Froling, Jan Malmsjo, Harriet Andersson, Erland Josephson, and Pernilla Allwin; cinematography by Sven Nykvist.

After *The Serpent's Egg* in 1978, many critics worried that Ingmar Bergman had lost his way in soap opera and political melodrama. In *Fanny and Alexander* he proves us all wrong. He returns to the themes and images of his classic films: the idyllic feasts of *Wild Strawberries* and *Smiles of a Summer Night*, the magic theater of *The Magician*, and the powerful double portrait of *Persona*. Bergman even brings back many of his former actors, aging now, to explore the problem of evil and the relation between imagination and reality. Like the last mythical plays of Shakespeare and Ibsen, *Fanny and Alexander* is the farewell of a great artist who wants to leave us some of his secrets before he goes.

***

1. The opening title shots show Alexander and his puppet theater, and the statue moving her arm when Alexander looks at her from under the table. How does this establish the tone of the film? Why does Bergman want us to see the story through the eyes of a child?

2. The story begins with the Ekdahl family Christmas pageant and feast. How does Oscar's speech about the "little world" of the theater reveal Bergman's attitude toward his art? Later, how does the grandmother reinforce his idea when she says, "We play our parts, some with negligence, some with care. Everyone is acting, some parts nice, some not. The thing is

not to shirk."?

3. Oscar's goatish Uncle Gustav courts Maj. Why doesn't his wife Alma seem to mind? How do Gustav and Bishop Vergerus, with the worlds revolving around them, suggest the traditional polarity between Dionysus and Apollo?

4. How is Uncle Carl characterized by his performance with the candles? How does this comment on the Bible reading that follows? Why does Bergman then cut from the story of the Holy Family to the pillow fight?

5. Why does Bergman include the gentle romance between Isak and Grandma Ekdahl?

6. Cut to Gustav and Maj slurping oysters, then to Carl and his wife. How do the two relationships differ? In his self-loathing, how is Carl a typical Bergman husband? How does he foreshadow Bishop Vergerus' treatment of Emilie?

7. What is ironic about Oscar's stroke while playing the ghost of Hamlet's father? Later in the film, what are the parallels between Alexander and Hamlet?

8. After the stark funeral supper, why does Alexander take refuge in his magic lantern? How does this motivate the children's seeing the ghost of their father playing the harpsichord?

9. Bishop Vergerus seems to be a cross between Ibsen's fanatic Brand and Bergman's own father. "Can you tell me what a lie is, and what is the truth?" he demands. In his obsession with "truth" how is the bishop different from Alexander's father? Why does Alexander instinctively hate him?

> Why has Alexander been telling his classmates that his mother has sold him to a traveling circus?
>
> Why are his mother and the bishop intolerant of his imagination?

10. While the bishop prays, why does Alexander again see the ghost of his father? How does this allude to the confessional scene in *Hamlet*?

11. In its austerity, how does Alexander's new home differ from his father's

house, and what do the two settings symbolize? Specifically, how do the settings allude to Bergman's earlier films?

12. How does the bishop's bedridden sister Elsa reflect his inner state?

13. What does the bishop's playing the *flute* symbolize, and what is paradoxical about the eroticism of his relationship with Emilie?

14. Why does he insist that the children may not bring their toys to his house? What are the religious connotations of his command?

15. Why does Grandama Ekdahl have misgivings as she watches the new family walk off stiffly into the snow? Why does Bergman cut again to the turbulent stream?

16. How does the bishop's servant Justina, played by Bibi Andersson, parody the gloomy gothic figures of Bergman's early classic films?

17. In Alexander's story of the bishop's dead wife and her drowned children, is he motivated by malice or imagination? Is the whole thing a dream? Why does Alexander have a hard time distinguishing fantasy from reality?

18. "The love I feel for you is strong and harsh," the bishop smiles. Why does Bergman dwell on the other faces during the sadistic whipping sequence? Why is it ironic that the bishop insists he has punished Alexander "out of love?"

19. Emilie bursts into the attic to comfort her bleeding son. Why does Bergman juxtapose Grandma Ekdahl's lecture to Gustav on Maj's future? How does the comic subplot reflect the main theme?

20. Cut to the stream, then to the bars on the children's window, as Isak visits the bishop on the pretext of buying a chest. Why does Bergman include the bishop's anti-semitic explosion and the hallucination of Emilie insisting, "Don't touch them!"?

21. How does Isak's shop with its masks and puppets represent the world of the imagination?

22. Why does Bergman cut from Oscar's ghost telling Alexander, "You must be gentle with people," to the bishop's guilt-tormented scene with Emilie?

"You once said you were always changing masks, so you didn't know who you were. I have only one mask, and it is branded into my face." What is tragic about his realization? How does it foreshadow the end of the film?

What does the drugged cup symbolize, and how does it recall the conclusion of *Hamlet*.

23. Cut to Alexander, waking as "God speaks to him from behind the door." What is the meaning of Aaron's puppet performance, and how does it reflect the bishop's agony?

24. What does the breathing mummy symbolize, and why does Bergman cut to the bishop's sick sister turning toward the lamp?

25. "Perhaps we are the same person, with no limits," Ishmael says, reading Alexander's mind. What does the androgynous young man symbolize, and why does Bergman intercut his incantation with the sister in flames?

26. Cut to Emilie's peaceful, sleeping face, then to the account of the police as Alexander listens in the background. Why does Bergman include both gothic and factual accounts of the bishop's death?

27. Why does Bergman cut to the two babies and Gustav's upbeat speech about the importance of the "little world?"

28. "You can't escape me." What is the meaning of Alexander's final vision of the bishop, and how does it reflect Bergman's own preoccupations in his films?

29. Why does Bergman end the film with a quote from Strindberg's *Dream Play*? ("Anything can happen, anything is possible. Time and space don't exist on this flimsy ground of reality. Imagination spins out and weaves new patterns.")

THE GODS MUST BE CRAZY (1980/1984-South African)

Directed by Jamie Uys; with Marius Weyers, Sandra Prinsloo, and N!xau. Released in this country by Twentieth Century Fox in 1984.

Shot in Botswana in 1980, *The Gods Must Be Crazy* wasn't released here until four years later, presumably because it didn't mimic Hollywood formulas or feature stars like Burt Reynolds as the anthropologist or Eddie Murphy as the bushman. Avoiding Hollywood cliches, Jamie Uys mocks civilization without sentimentalizing primitive culture. He also depicts the brutality of military dictatorships without glorifying the thugs who call themselves "freedom fighters." In his absurd world, the heroes are the little people, clumsy with machines and inarticulate in love, rather than macho movie stars. As a result of Uys' originality, this unpretentious little comedy has become the biggest foreign box-office hit in history.

***

1. "The bushmen of the Kalahari Desert," the narrator tells us, "must be the most contented people in the world... They never punish their children or even speak harshly to them, so naturally their children are well behaved. They have no sense of ownership... They live in a gentle world where nothing is as hard as steel or concrete." How does this prologue parody a National Geographic special?

2. How does "civilized man" six hundred miles to the south contrast with the bushman? How do the shots of freeways and assembly lines characterize life in South Africa, and what is the narrator's attitude toward clocks and calendars?

3. Why has Uys chosen the *coke bottle* as the symbol of modern civilization? How does this particular object represent the effect of our meddling in Third World countries?

4. What is the tone of the guerrilla attack on the cabinet of the Black military government? How does the shoot out in the banana patch characterize both the revolutionaries and the army?

5. What does Stayn's collecting elephant dung imply about Ph.D. research?

6. What is amusing about Stayn's attempts to be a gentleman with Miss Thompson? How is he like his land-rover, whose brakes don't work? Why does Uys repeat the business with opening and closing gates?

7. How does the land-rover's getting stuck in the river and ultimately winding up a tree reflect Stayn's success with women?

8. Why does Uys include the surreal episodes of the wart-hog charging Stayn's red underwear, the rhino stamping out the fire, and the two travelers being "grabbed" by the bushes? ("You get these sudden urges. . .")

9. "She was the ugliest person he had ever seen. She was as pale as someone who had crawled out of a rotting log." What do the bushman's observations imply about western ideas of beauty? What is ironic about his conclusion that maybe these two aren't gods after all?

10. The Great White Hunter roars up in his tour bus to rescue Kate as the land-rover is being towed across the desert. How are the two men characterized by their vehicles?

11. The bushman is shot by a policeman and arrested for slaughtering a goat. What is ironic about the cop reading him his rights? What is the point of the trial sequence that follows? Why does the narrator point out that in Xi's language there is no word for "guilty"?

12. Why is the high-speed chase with the lion funny, and how is Jack Hind characterized by abandoning his two guides? How does this incident foreshadow the showdown with the guerrillas?

13. What does the bushman's learning how to drive symbolize?

14. Why does Uys contrast the way Stayn and the bushman spot the *people* below?

15. How is Sam Boga, the Cuban revolutionary, characterized by his treatment of the hostages? What's the effect of the echo as Kate argues with him?

16. What is the significance of the bushman's immobilizing the heavily armed guerrillas with his primitive bow?

17. How is Kate characterized by shooting it out with the last two guerrillas? While Stayn uses nature to defeat them, why does Uys cut to the bushman driving the land-rover backwards?

18. "The marines have landed." How is Jack Hind characterized by taking the credit while Stayn tries to control the runaway land-rover?

19. "It's an interesting psychological phenomenon." Why does Kate react as she does to Stayn's clumsy explanation?

20. Why does the bushman scatter the money across the desert? What is the effect of the long-shot of him standing on the edge of the cliff? ("He thought he would never get to the end of the world.") How does this draw us into the bushman's view of reality?

VERTIGO (1958/1984-American) Directed by Alfred Hitchcock; with James Stewart, Kim Novak, and Barbara Bel Geddes; music by Bernard Herrmann.

Apologies to Hitchcock! When this book was first published in 1983, *Vertigo* had been out of circulation for twenty years, and I had forgotten what a truly great film it is. *Vertigo* is Hitchcock's obsessive masterpiece, arguably better than any other film released in the eighties. Its re-emergence to general acclaim, in fact, proves a general aesthetic principle: that film style moves in cycles, just like Hitchcock's acrophobic hero trying to recreate his lost love.

***

1. How does the opening closeup of a hand grasping an iron bar symbolize

Hitchcock's view of man's position in the universe? Why doesn't he bother showing us how Scottie gets down from the roof?

2. Cut to Scottie balancing a *cane* while Midge draws an advertisement for a *bra*, followed by their conversation about his *corset*. How do these symbols reveal the repression typical of Hitchcock's characters?

3. At Ernie's, we first see Madeleine from behind, as a voyeur would. What does this imply about Hitchcock's view of his art and his audience?

4. Madeleine visits a grave at Mission Dolores. How does the setting reflect Scottie's inner state and foreshadow their relationship?

5. Scottie tracks Madeleine to a Victorian hotel surrounded by the urban renewal of the Western Addition. How does the hotel represent both the unconscious mind and the grip of the past?

6. "Her blood is in Madeleine." Elster stresses that Madeleine doesn't know who she is. How does this reflect Hitchcock's view of history and psychology?

7. What does Madeleine's plunge at the Golden Gate Bridge symbolize? How does it foreshadow both her relationship with Scottie and the ending of the film?

8. What is the effect of the ringing phone as Scottie touches Madeleine's hand to take her coffee cup?

9. "I remembered Coit Tower; it led me straight to you." Why does Hitchcock include Coit Tower in the background as Scottie and Madeleine talk by the fire? What does the tower symbolize, and how does it foreshadow the end of the film?

10. "Only one is a wanderer. Two together are always going somewhere." Why is this line ironic? Why does Hitchcock set Scottie and Madeleine's mystical conversation in a redwood grove ("always living—forever green")? How do the redwoods contrast with the symbolic towers?

11. "And then I died. It was only a moment for you—you took no notice." Why is this ironic?

12. From the crash of the surf as Scottie and Madeleine kiss, cut to Midge painting. How does her portrait express the film's Pygmalion theme?

13. In the bell-tower at San Juan Bautista, what are the symbolic connotations of Scottie's inability to "make it to the top"? As he descends, how is the shot straight down the stairwell supposed to affect us?

14. How does the judge's summary at the inquest contribute to Scottie's sense of guilt? Why does Hitchcock make this sequence strangely humorous? Why is it ironic that Elster sympathetically pulls Scottie aside and tells him, "You and I know who killed Madeleine"?

15. As Scottie roams through San Francisco, why does he see Madeleine everywhere? When he finally finds a brunette who looks just like her, what is the significance of her transformation into someone coarse and earthy? What are the psychological and political implications of her living in the *Empire* Hotel?

16. After Judy's flashback to the tower and the chase, she packs to leave. Why does she change her mind and tear up the letter?

17. Why does Scottie take her to Ernie's? What is the effect on her when he looks up as a pretty blonde walks by?

18. "You certainly know what you want, sir." Why does Scottie dress Judy and try to make her over? What does this imply about all human relationships, including the director's relationship with his actors?

19. When Judy pleads, "Couldn't you like me—just me—the way I am?" Scottie exclaims, "The color of your hair!" How does the symbolism relate to the blonde/brunette archetype in American literature dating back to James Fennimore Cooper?

20. "If I do what you tell me, will you love me?" Why can Scottie love Judy only when her hair is blonde and *up*? Why would he be unexcited by a dark-haired lady who "lets her hair down?"

21. Note Judy's profile silhouetted against the neon green of the window. As they kiss, why does Hitchcock revolve the background to the carriage house, then back to the hotel room? What does this do to our sense of time and space?

22. As Judy puts on her black dress to go to Ernie's, note the closeup of her necklace. What is the effect of the cross-cuts to Scottie's reaction and to the portrait of Carlotta?

23. "Oh, Scottie, I do have you now!" Judy exclaims. Why is this ironic? Why does he decide to drive to the Mission instead of going to dinner? (Note his smile: "One final thing I have to do, and then I'll be free of the past.")

24. Why does he drag her up the steps of the tower, telling her about Madeleine's death?

> "I tried, but I couldn't get to the top!" What are the sexual
> and psychological connotations of this line, and what is tragic
> about his obsession with the past?

25. "You're my second chance, Judy." Like Jean-Paul Sartre in *No Exit*, why does Hitchcock think "second chances" are doomed to failure?

26. What does the sudden appearance of the *nun* symbolize? What does the final shot of Scottie tottering on the edge imply about the human condition?

DESPERATELY SEEKING SUSAN (1985-American) Directed by Susan Seidelman; with Rosanna Arquette, Madonna, Aidan Quinn, Mark Blum, and Robert Joy. Music by Madonna. Released by Orion Pictures.

It has been a convention in romantic comedy since Mozart's *Marriage of Figaro* that one woman may "become" another merely by putting on her clothes. In seeking Susan by adorning herself with Susan's magical talismans, Roberta Glass ironically finds herself. Her metamorphosis in the Magic Club is one of the most delightful transformations in the history of comic Doubles and the power of the Imagination.

***

1. What is the purpose of the opening sequence of Roberta having her legs shaved and her toenails painted? Why does she fantasize about the

personals? ("It's romantic to be desperate.") How is she different from her sister-in-law?

2. What is the effect of the rock music as Seidelman cuts to Susan lying on the floor photographing herself, and how does this shot allude to the act of making a film? How do the details in the first two scenes stress the contrast between the two main characters?

3. Note Susan's overstuffed hatbox that pops open at two crucial moments in the film. Symbolically, how does it relate both to Pandora's box and to the Freudian purses common in Hitchcock?

4. Gary and Roberta's party: Why does Seidelman cut from the news report about stolen Egyptian artifacts to Gary's hot-tub commercial in which "all your fantasies can come true"? Why does Roberta stare at the George Washington Bridge?

5. How is the "Atlantic City Plunge" analogous to Roberta's romantic adventure?

6. What does Susan's jacket with the pyramid on the back symbolize? What is the significance of Roberta's wearing it?

7. What does the *key* dropping from the pocket symbolize, and how does Des' helping her find the locker foreshadow their relationship?

8. "People *live* here?" How is Des' loft with its Bruce Lee murals different from what Roberta is used to? What does his job as a projectionist symbolize?

9. "You are not at all what I expected." After everything Des has heard about Susan from Jim, why is he perplexed? Why would he not be likely to fall for the real Susan?

10. On opposite sides of the partition, why are both Roberta and Des unable to sleep? Why does Seidelman cut to the mobster sitting in the car outside, then to the cat licking his chops over the fish in the tank?

11. Just because of the jacket, the diner owner sees Roberta as Susan and throws her out. How does this advance the idea of her shifting identity?

12. "This one's worse than the other one!" What is the significance of Roberta's inept performance at the Magic Club? Why does Seidelman

juxtapose Gary's appearance at the punk bar?

13. The neon street scene, complete with sleeping drunk, looks like a George Segal sculpture. How is Roberta characterized by her flight, bird cage in hand?

14. When she takes refuge with the night watchman, his TV blares Gary's commercial—in Spanish! "All your fantasies can come true." What is the effect of the surreal repetition?

15. Why does Roberta's costume lead to her arrest for prostitution? Why does Seidelman cut to Susan testing Gary's bed, checking out Roberta's self-help books, and asking Gary, "Between you and me, what do you really know about Roberta?"

16. Cut from Roberta's mug shot to Gary smoking pot with Susan and waxing philosophical: "What's it all about?" Why is his question ironic? Why does Seidelman intercut Gary's scenes with Susan with the sequences showing Roberta and Des getting together? How are the two relationships different?

17. "I'm not who you think I am." Why does Des think Roberta is joking when she finally remembers who she is (the wife of a hot-tub salesman in New Jersey)?

18. Note Susan's judgment of Roberta's diary: "It's gotta be a cover. Nobody's life could be this boring." On the other hand, Des tells Jim, "I can't see her settling down. She's too wild." What do these antithetical views imply about Roberta's identity?

19. "You're in for a real surprise." Why does Seidelman set the final confrontation in the Magic Club? How does the magician's cutting Roberta in half reflect the main theme of the film? How is the revelation of identities like the ending of *A Midsummer Night's Dream*?

20. Why does Seidelman intercut Susan's kidnapping with Gary's quarrel with Roberta?

> "Look at *me*, Gary." Why does she refuse to go home with him?

21. "Our defenses are at their weakest. A successful mutant attack is likely." How do the lines from the sci-fi film in the background effect the tone of the love scene, and what does the burned out frame symbolize? Why does Seidelman cut to Susan and Jim eating popcorn in the audience?

22. "What A Pair!" How does the final headline clarify the symbolism of the Nefertiti earrings?

23. How do Susan and Roberta represent the two sides of Susan Seidelman, or of any female artist? In contrast with the two female characters, why are the men so two-dimensional?

THE PURPLE ROSE OF CAIRO (1985-American) Written and directed by Woody Allen; With Mia Farrow, Jeff Daniels, Danny Aiello, and Diane Wiest; cinematography by Gordon Willis. Orion Pictures.

The Purple Rose of Cairo, Woody Allen's most philosophical film, explores the conflict between illusion and reality by borrowing a scene from Pirandello: a debate between an actor and the character he plays about who is "real." Of course, the viewer smugly concludes, neither man is real. Reality is Cecilia's brutal husband Monk, who drinks and gambles and beats up on her. But isn't he, too, just acting a part in the script of the Great Depression? Maybe Cecilia is right to smile as she sits in the dark, watching her fantasies flicker on the big screen.

***

1. "Heaven, I'm in heaven," sings Fred Astaire. Why is this an ironic theme song for a film set in the Depression?

2. As Cecilia stares dreamily at the movie poster, a letter falls from the marquee and almost hits her. What does this symbolize?

3. While Cecilia and her sister gossip about the stars, dropping dishes left and right, her husband Monk pitches pennies. "You like sitting through that junk," he tells her. "I like to shoot crap." How does this characterize their marriage?

4. Why would Cecilia be fascinated by a movie about a lot of bored, rich phonies? What is ironic about Tom Baxter's line, "It's so impulsive, but I'll come. A fortune teller predicted I'd fall in love in New York"?

> "Ours could be a different sort of love affair." How does Kitty's song at the Copacabana foreshadow the main action of the film?

5. Cecilia goes home early to find her drunken husband with another woman. When she complains that all he does is beat up on her, he objects, "I never just hit you—I warn you first." How does her real-life relationship contrast with the world of her imagination? After looking in the tavern, why does she go home again?

6. After losing her job, why does Cecilia take refuge in the movies? Why the repetition of Tom's line about the "madcap Manhattan weekend" (twice!)?

7. "My god, you must really love this picture!" Why does Tom come down from the screen?

8. Trading barbs with the audience, the movie characters argue about the meaning of the film. How is this like Pirandello's *Six Characters in Search of an Author*? Why do the lines suddenly seem more real, and what does this imply about art and reality?

9. "They sit around and talk," a customer complains. "No action? I want my money back." What does the audience's reaction suggest about the American public? Why *is* it "comforting" to see the same fantasies and cliches over and over?

10. Tom and Cecilia talk in an abandoned amusement park. What does the setting symbolize?

11. While the studio executives go berserk, Tom and Cecilia go dancing. "Where I come from," Tom tells her, "people are consistent. They never disappoint." Why does Cecilia reply, "It's not like that in real life."? What is Allen's point about film and life?

12. Cut to Gil Shepherd being interviewed about his career. How is Gil different from his double?

13. Back in the nightclub, Tom pays for their champagne with stage money, and when they jump in the car to escape, he has no key. How does this characterize their relationship?

14. As Cecilia exclaims, "You kiss perfectly!" Tom wonders, "Where's the fadeout?" What is Allen saying about love in the movies?

15. When Cecilia bumps into Gil in a coffee shop, what is the point of her confusing him with Tom? What is the significance of the confrontation between the actor and his character? Why does Allen stress Gil's obsession with his career, while Tom keeps insisting he loves Cecilia? How does this symbolize the relationship between actor, character, and public?

16. Why does Allen set the confrontation between Tom and Monk in an empty church? Why does Cecilia refuse to go home with her husband? What is the significance of Tom's having no conception of fighting dirty? ("That's why you'll never survive in the real world.")

17. What is ironic about Cecilia's praising Gil's lonely, heroic qualities? ("You've got a magical glow.") What is the point of his actually being a cab driver with a made-up stage name?

18. Why does Allen juxtapose the scene with Tom and the prostitute? Why are the ladies in the bordello moved by his speech about childbirth? Why doesn't he understand where he is, and why can't he make love with them?

19. "I love my baby, and my baby loves me." Why does Allen include Gil's performance in the music store? What does the ukelele symbolize, and why is the song ironic?

20. "I won't be going south with you this winter." How do the lines from Gil's movie foreshadow the end of the film?

21. Why is Cecilia confused when Gil kisses her? ("I just met a wonderful new man. He's fictional, but you can't have everything.")

22. "Let's redefine *ourselves* as the real world," a character on the screen exclaims, indicating the audience. "*They're* fictional." The old actress replies, "You've been flickering on the screen too long." How is the debate on the screen parallel to Cecilia's inner struggle? ("You're some kind of

phantom.'' vs. ''I'm not going to argue about what's real and what's illusion.'')

23. When Tom leads Cecilia back onto the screen so they can eat, why do the movie characters get upset?

24. Tom wines and dines Cecilia in a perfect screen romance, until Gil bursts into the theater and demands that she make a choice. What is the philosophical importance of the debate that follows? For instance, when Tom argues, ''I'm honest, dependable, and a great kisser,'' Gil snaps, ''And I'm *real*.'' Why is this ironic?

25. Why does Gil plead with Cecilia to leave with him for Hollywood, and what is the significance of her decision?

26. Cecilia runs home to pack. ''It ain't the movies, it's real life. You'll be back!'' Monk shouts after her. Why does Allen virtually repeat their earlier argument, the last time she walked out?

27. Cut to the title of the movie being removed from the marquee. What does this symbolize, and why does Allen repeat the film's opening? Why is it ironic that Gil is going to play Charles Lindburgh?

28. Cut from Cecilia's stunned face to Gil on the plane, then to Fred Astaire singing ''Cheek to Cheek.'' Why does Cecilia return to the movie theater, and why does her expression soften as she watches Fred Astaire whirl Ginger Rogers around the dance floor?

RAN (1985-Japanese) Directed by Akira Kurosawa. With Tatsuya Nakadai and Mieko Harada; photography by Takao Saito. Produced by Serge Silberman.

The title of the film, ''Ran,'' is the Japanese word for *chaos*, an important theme for both Kurosawa and Shakespeare. Specifically, what are the parallels to *King Lear*? Why has Kurosawa made certain changes, like transforming Lear's three daughters into *sons*? Why has he replaced Shakespeare's thematic analogue of Gloucester's tragedy with the subplot about Lady Kaede's revenge? Finally, What artistic adjustments follow from the decision to change a tragedy into an *epic* suitable for the screen?

After asking yourself these large questions, please examine the film in detail.

***

1. How does the hunt for the wild boar foreshadow the main action of the film? What is ironic about Hidetora's joking that the old boar is too tough to eat? (''Like *me*, old Hidetora. . .'')

2. What is the significance of Hidetora's falling asleep in the middle of his feast for Ayabe and Fujimaki?

> How is Saburo characterized by cutting down a tree to shade his sleeping father?

> What does Hidetora's nightmare about being alone in a vast wilderness symbolize? What is the meaning of his bursting through the curtain, like an actor on a stage? Why is it ironic that he's comforted by the sight of his adoring sons?

3. ''You are either senile or mad!'' Why does Saburo react angrily to his father's abdication, instead of humoring the old man's clichéd lesson about the sheaf of arrows?

> ''What kind of world do we live in? One barren of loyalty or feeling.'' Why does Saburo's cynicism offend his father?

4. Why does Tango defend Saburo's arrogant words? What is the significance of Hidetora's banishing him as well?

5. Although Saburo is an outcast, why does Fujimaki offer him his daughter in marriage?

6. Lady Kaede insists that Hidetora's concubines make way for her entourage. How does this characterize her? Why does the Fool call Hidetora a scarecrow?

7. Why does Kaede insinuate that Taro is merely a shadow if he doesn't have his father's banner hanging on the wall?

8. "A gourd in the wind. . ." When the Fool is about to be killed for taunting Taro's soldiers, what is the meaning of Hidetora's reaction? How does this precipitate the crisis with Taro?

> When Hidetora demands, "Who am I?" what is the significance of Kaede's response? ("The father of my husband.")

> Why is Hidetora angered by having to sign a pledge that merely restates what he previously proclaimed?

> "The hen pecks the cock," Hidetora observes astutely and storms out. What does he mean? Why, at this point, does Kaede reveal that Hidetora had murdered her father and brothers, and that her mother committed suicide in that very room?

9. Cut to Jiro worrying that his father is coming. He's resentful that he must "grovel at Taro's feet" just because he was born a year later. How is he like Edmund in *King Lear*? What are the connotations of the extended *hunting* metaphor?

10. In contrast, how is Jiro's wife Sué characterized by her shrine and her song to Buddha? Why does Hidetora seek her before speaking to his son, and why does she intimidate him?

11. Why does Jiro refuse to allow Hidetora's warriors inside his castle walls? What is the visual effect of the massive gates closing behind Hidetora as he leaves?

12. Cut to the blazing sun as Hidetora sits rigidly in a barren field. Why does Kurosawa consistently fill his chaotic world with geometric patterns of soldiers?

13. Why is it ironic that, at the very moment Hidetora is refusing to go to Saburo, Saburo's followers are relinquishing the Third Castle to Taro?

14. Disguised as a peasant, Tango brings Hidetora a horse laden with food. How is Hidetora characterized by commanding that the peasants' houses be burned? What is the effect of the sound of the *locusts* as Tango tells Hidetora

that Taro has banished him?

15. Why does the Fool deride Hidetora's plan to go to Castle Three now that Taro's men have occupied it? How does Hidetora's reaction display his faulty judgment?

16. Hidetora wakes to find the castle under attack by Jiro's troops. Why does Kurosawa shoot the bloody battle sequence in silence, with only music dubbed over?

17. What is the effect of the streams of red and yellow banners? Why does Kurosawa costume the armies in the three primary colors?

18. With a single symbolic gunshot, the sound track of the battle returns. What is the meaning of Hidetora's sitting impassive in the citadel as bullets and flaming arrows blaze past him?

19. Trailing his broken sword behind him, Hidetora descends the steps in a trance. Why does the army part to let him by? What is the effect of the long-shot of the citadel burning?

20. "The die is cast. Do not falter," Kurogane advises when Jiro has second thoughts about driving out his father. By persisting in evil, how is he like a Shakespearean villain?

21. As Hidetora walks out into the wasteland, what does the dust storm symbolize? What is the effect of the long-shot as Tango and the fool ride up to him in the swirling grass?

22. As Hidetora gathers flowers, the Fool comments, "In a mad world, only the mad are sane." What is Shakespearean about this paradox? Why does he sing about a "phantom army in this withered plain"?

23. As the three wanderers knock at the door of a hovel, an androgynous young boy inside sits in the darkness. What is the significance of his identity, and what does his blindness symbolize?

24. What does Tasumaru's *flute* symbolize, and why does Hidetora stare in horror as he plays?

25. Cut to Jiro presenting Kaede with his brother's *hair*. What does this symbolize, and what is the significance of Jiro's wearing his brother's armor?

26. Why does Jiro banish the two vassals who helped him kill his brother to achieve power?

27. "I am not blind. . ." After slicing Jiro with her knife, why does Kaede lick his wounds? How are they both characterized in this "love" scene?

What does her kicking the helmet with her foot symbolize?

What is the meaning of her squashing the insect as she cries, "You're mine! No one else will have you!"?

28. As Kaede demands that Jiro kill his wife, cut to a field of flowers, then to a destroyed castle. How do the settings relate to Kaede's demand? How does the Fool's crowning Hidetora with reeds and flowers comment on the action?

29. Why does the Fool lie down beside Hidetora in the ruins, even though his common sense asks, "Why stay with this mad old man!"

30. Ordered by Kaede to bring Sué's head packed in salt, what is the meaning of the object Kurogane places before her?

31. "Who am I?" Hidetora asks again, this time ironically. As the Madman and the Fool continue their one-sided conversation, what is the meaning of the Fool's parable of the serpent's egg, and how does it answer Hidetora's question? ("Stupid bird.")

32. Why does Kurogane urge Jiro to let Saburo have their father instead of risking war? Why does Jiro ignore his good advice to adopt Kaede's treacherous plan? At this point, how is Jiro like Shakespeare's MacBeth?

33. "Men always travel the same road," the Fool philosophizes. Why does Hidetora respond by jumping off the cliff, and what does his plunge symbolize? What do Sué and Tasumaru standing above him represent?

34. "Is this a dream? No, this is hell!" Hidetora cries as he runs across the black, barren plain with the Fool chasing after him. How do the setting and his words express the main themes of the film?

35. As the red and blue armies confront each other, Ayabe's horsemen line the mountain above. What does Kurosawa imply by cutting to Sué and Tasumaru on the wall of their ruined castle? Why is it ironic that Sué gives him an image of the Buddha to protect him while she's away?

36. Saburo finds his father staring at the clouds: "Is this paradise?" In calling himself a "stupid old fool," how is Hidetora like King Lear?

37. Cut to Jiro's cavalry attacking, while Saburo's men fire at them from the woods. What is the tone of the slow-motion carnage? Why is Saburo's victory ironic?

38. "We will talk, father to son. . ." Hidetora rides behind Saburo as the second symbolic shot rings out. What does Saburo's death symbolize? "Is this justice?" Hidetora cries. Why is his question tragic?

39. "Are you so bored and cruel that it amuses you to crush us like ants?" When the fool berates the gods, Tango tells him not to blaspheme: "It's the gods who weep. They can't save us from ourselves." Does Kurosawa take sides in this debate, or does he leave it up to us?

40. "Look at them in the First Castle! They revel in bloodshed!" As Tango continues, cut to Jiro, surrounded by the black banners of Ayabe's army, then to Sué and her maid lying in the field of flowers. Why does Kurosawa juxtapose these two scenes?

41. Kurogane confronts Kaede, who calmly reveals her motivations. . .

42. As Hidetora and Saburo's bodies are carried from Azusa Plain, cut to Tasumaru standing on the edge of the castle wall, tottering on the brink. What is the significance of the scroll of Buddha tumbling over the edge? What does the long-shot of this solitary figure symbolize?

43. A final question: Why doesn't Kurosawa use any closeups in this film? How do all the long and medium shots affect the *tone* and establish Kurosawa's stance toward his creation?

BLUE VELVET (1986-American) Written and directed by David Lynch; with Kyle MacLachlan, Isabella Rossellini, Dennis Hopper, and Laura Dern. Produced by Dino De Laurentis.

David Lynch's dreamlike film about corruption in Plasticville U.S.A. is part film-noir, part hallucination. From the moment Jeffrey Beaumont finds a severed ear in a field, to the final shocking sequence in which dead men still stand, we know that something isn't quite right in this slumbering mill-town with white picket fences. The blond heroine's stare is a bit too bold, and the clean-cut young hero is a little too anxious to spy on naked ladies. To Jeffrey's anguished question, "Why are there people like Frank?" Lynch would only reply, "Look inside."

***

1. Why is the sentimental fifties theme song ("Blue Velvet") ironic?

2. What does the opening shot of a red rose on a white picket fence symbolize? What is the purpose of the dreamlike cut to the fire engine, the pistol on TV, and the school children crossing the street? Why does Lynch shoot this opening sequence in false fifties technicolor?

3. Why does Lynch intercut Mr. Beaumont's heart attack with the close-ups of the sputtering hose? Why does he include the dog biting the hose, and the toddler wandering in the background?

4. What are the connotations of the banal radio announcement? ("This is a sunny day in Lumberton, so get those chainsaws out.")

5. Why does Lynch include the surreal sequence with Jeffrey's father in the hospital bed, hooked up to machines and tubes?

6. Walking through the field, Jeffrey finds a severed ear, crawling with ants. What does this disturbing image out of Bunuel symbolize? How does it introduce the film's voyeur theme?

7. When Jeffrey takes the ear to Detective Williams, why does Williams order him to tell no one about his discovery? How is he characterized by wearing his gun at home?

8. "Are you the one who found the ear?" Sandy asks, emerging from the shadows. "It's a strange world, isn't it?" Jeffrey exclaims when she tells him what she has overheard. Why would this seemingly innocent girl prompt him to his adventure?

9. What does the blind man in the Beaumont hardware store symbolize? How does he reflect Jeffrey?

10. "There are opportunities in life for gaining knowledge and experience." Why does Sandy reply that Jeffrey's naive plan gives her the creeps? Why is she also fascinated enough to agree to help him?

11. How does Jeffrey's masquerade as a pest control worker relate to the film's imagery? What does his stealing Dorothy's *key* symbolize? Why does Lynch intercut the zoom close-ups of the man in the yellow jacket during this sequence?

12. Aside from singing "Blue Velvet" badly, how is Dorothy Vallens different from Sandy? How are they both American archetypes, illustrating a standard fifties polarity?

13. "I don't know if you're a detective or a pervert." In the context of this film, why is Sandy's observation ironic? Why does she stare at Jeffrey so intently while they drive to Dorothy's apartment?

14. Why does Dorothy react as she does to finding Jeffrey spying from her closet? After sticking him with her knife, why does she make him get undressed?

15. How is the sequence that follows with Frank, while Jeffrey hides in the closet, like a primal scene? ("It's Daddy, you shithead! Where's my bourbon?")

16. "Mommy, mommy. . ." Frank screams as he inhales nitrous oxide. Why does he alternate between infantile babble and abuse as he rapes

Dorothy on the floor? How does this shocking sequence reveal the dark side of American family life.

17. After embracing Jeffrey passionately, why does Dorothy plead with him to hit her?

18. Why does Lynch include all the sequences of Jeffrey going up and down the back stairs?

19. Why does Lynch cut to Jeffrey's dream of Frank's face snarling like an animal and Dorothy sighing, "Hit me"? What is the effect of the repeated extreme close-ups of her lips?

20. Why does Lynch intercut Jeffrey and Sandy's phone conversation with the workers in the hardware store examining an *axe*?

21. "Why are there people like Frank?" Jeffrey asks Sandy. How does this allude to the problem of evil?

22. How does Sandy's dream about the dark world illuminated by thousands of robins parody middle class values?

23. "I'm seeing something that was always hidden." Why is Jeffrey intent on pursuing his investigation, even though he doesn't know what he's going to do with it? Why does he also say that *Sandy* is a "mystery?"

24. "Are you a bad boy? Do you want to do bad things?" Why does Jeffrey keep returning to Dorothy's apartment? Why does he wind up hitting her, and why does Lynch intercut the shots of the flames and the animal roars from his dream?

25. Why does Frank keep playing with the word "neighbor?" Why does Lynch include the Felliniesque visit with Frank's friend Ben? While Dorothy talks with her son behind the closed door, why does Lynch cut to Ben pantomiming "Candy Colored Clown"?

26. The Joyride: Putting on his gas-mask, Frank mutters to Jeffrey, "You're just like me." What does he mean?

27. "Pretty, pretty..." sounds like the witch from *The Wizard of Oz*. Why does Frank *kiss* Jeffrey, then command his men to play "Candy Colored Clown" ("In dreams I walk with you, in dreams you're mine") ...before he beats him up?

28. Jeffrey wakes bleeding in the daylight. Home on his bed, why does he hallucinate Dorothy crying "Hit me!" and "Donnie, Mommie loves you," along with nightmarish details of making love and being beaten? What has he learned about himself?

29. Back at the police station, what is the significance of the identity of the man in the yellow jacket?

30. Picking up Sandy for a date, Jeffrey again sees the man in yellow. Sandy's father warns, "Easy does it, Jeffrey. Behave yourself. Don't blow it." Why does Lynch make the detective's advice deliberately ambiguous?

31. The pursuit: Why would Jeffrey think it's Frank? What is the significance of its being Sandy's drunken boyfriend? What is the effect of Dorothy's sudden appearance on Jeffrey's front lawn?

32. "He put his disease in me." What does Dorothy mean?

33. Why does Jeffrey return to Dorothy's apartment, and what is the meaning of the dreamlike scene that greets him there? What is the effect of the close-up of the man with the severed ear, and the dead man still standing with the police radio playing in his pocket?

34. "Here I come, ready or not!" What does the final confrontation in the *closet* symbolize?

35. Jeffrey looks up from his lawn chair and blinks. What does this imply about the action of the film? What is the meaning of the robin on the windowsill eating a bug? What does the robin's being fake imply about the ending?

36. How do the four main characters (Jeffrey, Sandy, Dorothy, and Frank) correspond to Jung's model of the personality: Self, Soul, Anima, and Shadow?

37. If you've seen David Lynch's earlier films, *Eraser Head* and *The Elephant Man*, how does this film compare, particularly in its depiction of normal, middle class life?

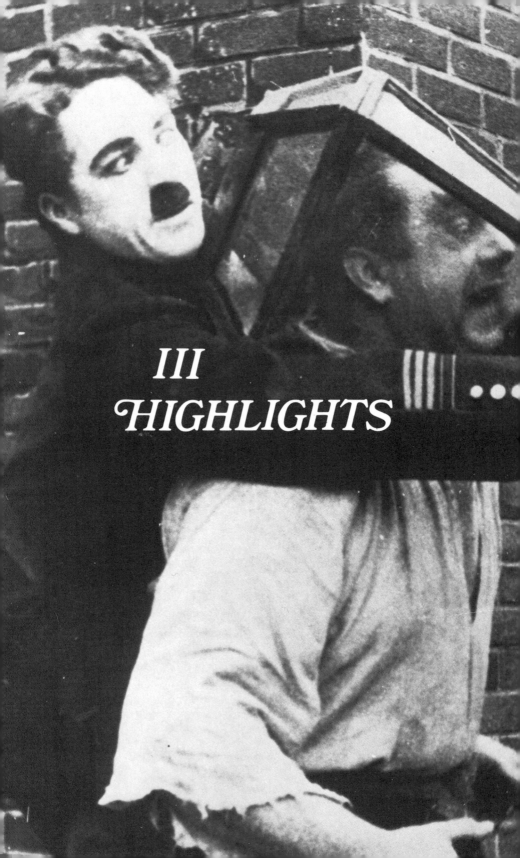

III
HIGHLIGHTS

HIGHLIGHTS IN THE HISTORY OF FILM

This catalogue attempts to make some sense of the many movements in Film History. Compiling lists of this kind *does* present several problems. First, what to include? All lists hide philosophical biases, and I hope no one will be upset at my leaving out his favorite Kung Fu films. There is also the "international" problem: Movements become ambiguous when filmmakers work in several languages, and especially when they start influencing each other. Finally, the best directors have been producing films for many years, and their work spans decades. Luis Bunuel, for instance, has been making films in various languages and styles from 1928 to the present. I have chosen to "place" him in the seventies because that's when I think he reached his artistic peak. For the same reason, I have placed Bergman in the fifties, and Fellini and Truffaut in the sixties. Where do Resnais and Kurosawa fit in? I'm inclined to throw up my hands and declare, with Henry Ford, that "History is Bunk!"

Granting these objections, I have merely hoped to provide a context for the individual masterpieces—indicated in boldface—discussed at length in the text. *All* these films are worth seeing, and most of them are better than Hollywood's current Top Forty. A "new" film, remember, is any film you haven't seen. And a "good" film—by definition—is one that gets better with each viewing.

Talking About Films

THE ORIGINS OF CINEMA

EARLY INVENTIONS:

Peter Roget's theory of the "persistence of Vision" (1824)
Louis Daguerre's photographic process (1839)
George Eastman's Kodak Camera (1888)
Thomas Edison and William Dickson's Kinetoscope (1889)

FRANCE: EARLY EXPERIMENTS

The Lumiere Brothers: chase and trick films (1900-1907)
Georges Melies, *A Trip to the Moon* (1902)

AMERICA: THE DEVELOPMENT OF NARRATIVE

Edwin S. Porter, *The Great Train Robbery* (1903)
D.W. Griffith (from 1907)—Major films: *The Lonely Villa* (1909), *Enoch Arden* (1911), *Judith of Bethulia* (1914), *THE BIRTH OF A NATION* (1915), *Intolerance* (1916)
Charles Chaplin (from 1914)—Major films: *The Tramp* (1915), *Easy Street* (1917), *The Immigrant* (1917), *The Kid* (1921), *The Pilgrim* (1923), *THE GOLD RUSH* (1925), *The Circus* (1928), *CITY LIGHTS* (1931), *MODERN TIMES* (1936), *The Great Dictator* (1940)

THE TWENTIES: THE SILENT CLASSICS

EUROPE: THE NIGHTMARE OF HISTORY

Robert Wiene, *THE CABINET OF DOCTOR CALIGARI* (1919)
F.W. Murnau: *Nosferatu* (1922), *The Last Laugh* (1924)
Carl Dreyer, *The Passion of Joan of Arc* (1928)
Luis Bunuel and Salvador Dali: *Un Chien Andalou* (1929) and *L'Age D'Or* (1930)

AMERICAN NATURALISM

Robert Flaherty (documentaries): *Nanook of the North* (1922) and *Man of Aran* (1934)
Erich von Stroheim, *Greed* (1924)
Buster Keaton, *The General* (1927)

RUSSIA: REVOLUTION AND MONTAGE

V.I. Pudovkin, *The Mother* (1925)
Sergei Eisenstein: *POTEMKIN* (1925), *Alexander Nevsky* (1938), *Ivan the Terrible* (1946)

THE THIRTIES: MYTHS AND ARCHETYPES

First sound film: *The Jazz Singer* with Al Jolson (1927)

GERMAN EXPRESSIONISM

Josef von Sternberg, *THE BLUE ANGEL* (1930)
G.W. Pabst, *THE THREEPENNY OPERA* (1931)
Fritz Lang, M. (1931)

HOLLYWOOD AND THE AMERICAN DREAM

Busby Berkeley—dance numbers (from 1930)
The Marx Brothers: *The Coconuts* (1929), *Animal Crackers* (1930), *Duck Soup* (1932), *A Night at the Opera* (1935), *A Day at the Races* (1937), and others
Cooper and Schoedsack, *King Kong* (1933)
Mae West: *She Done Him Wrong* (1933) and *I'm No Angel* (1933)
W.C. Fields: *It's a Gift* (1934), *The Bank Dick* (1939), *My Little Chickadee* (1940—with Mae West), *Never Give a Sucker an Even Break* (1941)
Walt Disney (1901-1966): *Snow White* (1937), *Pinocchio* (1939), *Fantasia* (1940), *Bambi* (1942), *Cinderella* (1949)
Frank Capra: *It Happened One Night* (1934), *Lost Horizon* (1937), *You Can't Take It With You* (1938), *Mr. Smith Goes to Washington* (1939)
John Ford: *The Informer* (1935), *Stagecoach* (1939), *Grapes of Wrath* (1940), *Mister Roberts* (1955)
Ernst Lubitsch, *Ninotchka* (1939—with Greta Garbo)
Victor Fleming: *THE WIZARD OF OZ* (1939) and *Gone With The Wind* (1939)
George Stevens: *Gunga Din* (1939) and *Shane* (1953)

ENGLAND: MYSTERY AND SUSPENSE

Alfred Hitchcock: *The Thirty-Nine Steps* (1935), *The Lady Vanishes* (1938), *Rebecca* (1940), *Suspicion* (1941), *Lifeboat* (1944), *To Catch a Thief* (1955), *Vertigo* (1958), *North by Northwest* (1959), *Psycho* (1960), and others

FRANCE: A CLASSIC STYLE

Jean Vigo, *Zero for Conduct* (1933)
Rene Clair: *The Italian Straw Hat* (1927), *A Nous la Liberte* (1931), *Le Million* (1931)
Jean Renoir: *GRAND ILLUSION* (1937) and *THE RULES OF THE GAME* (1939)

THE FORTIES: FROM ROMANCE TO REALISM

FRANCE: ROMANTIC FANTASY

Marcel Carne: *Le Jour Se Leve* (1939) and *CHILDREN OF PARADISE* (1945)
Jean Cocteau: *Blood of a Poet* (1930), *The Eternal Return* (1943), *BEAUTY AND THE BEAST* (1946), *ORPHEUS* (1949)
Jean Delannoy, *Symphonie Pastorale* (1947)
Rene Clement, *FORBIDDEN GAMES* (1951)

ENGLAND: THE THEATRICAL TRADITION

Powell and Pressburger, *THE RED SHOES* (1948)
Carol Reed, *The Third Man* (1949)
Laurence Olivier: *Henry V* (1945), *Hamlet* (1948), *Richard III* (1956)

AMERICA: THE ART OF ACTION

Orson Welles: *CITIZEN KANE* (1941), *The Trial* (1962)
Michael Curtiz, *Casablanca* (1942)
Howard Hawks: *The Big Sleep* (1946) and *Red River* (1948)
John Huston: *The Maltese Falcon* (1941), *The African Queen* (1951), *The Red Badge of Courage* (1951)

ITALY: "NEO—REALISM"

Roberto Rossellini, *Open City* (1945)
Vittorio De Sica: *Shoeshine* (1946), *THE BICYCLE THIEF* (1949), *Umberto D.* (1952), *Two Women* (1961), *The Garden of the Finzi-Continis* (1971)

THE FIFTIES: THE CINEMA OF IDEAS

AMERICA: THE SILENT GENERATION

Joseph Mankiewicz: *All About Eve* (1950), *Julius Caesar* (1953), *Sleuth* (1972)

Fred Zinnemann: *HIGH NOON* (1952), *From Here to Eternity* (1953), *A Man for All Seasons* (1966), *The Day of the Jackal* (1973), *Julia* (1977)
Elia Kazan: *A STREETCAR NAMED DESIRE* (1951), *ON THE WATERFRONT* (1954), *East of Eden* (1955), *A Face in the Crowd* (1957)
Nicholas Ray, *Rebel Without A Cause* (1955)
Delbert Mann, *Marty* (1955)
Billy Wilder: *Witness for the Prosecution* (1957) and *Some Like It Hot* (1959)

FRANCE: A TOUCH OF SOPHISTICATION

Max Ophuls: *La Ronde* (1950) and *Lola Montes* (1955)
Jules Dassin: *Rififi* (1955) and *Never on Sunday* (1959)

JAPAN: TRADITIONAL ARTISTRY

Akira Kurosawa: *RASHOMON* (1951), *Ikiru* (1952), *Seven Samurai* (1954), *Throne of Blood* (1957), *Yojimbo* (1961), *Dersu Uzala* (1977), *KAGEMUSHA: THE SHADOW WARRIOR* (1980)
Kenji Mizoguchi, *UGETSU* (1953)
Teinosuke Kinogasa, *GATE OF HELL* (1954)
Hiroshi Teshigahara, *WOMAN IN THE DUNES* (1965)

SWEDEN: GUILT AND METAPHYSICS

INGMAR BERGMAN has made more than forty films, including: *Monika* (1952), *SAWDUST AND TINSEL* (1953), *SMILES OF A SUMMER NIGHT* (1955), *THE SEVENTH SEAL* (1956), *WILD STRAWBERRIES* (1957), *THE MAGICIAN* (1958), *The Virgin Spring* (1959), *Through A Glass Darkly* (1961), *Winterlight* (1962), *The Silence* (1963), *PERSONA* (1967), *Hour of the Wolf* (1968), *Shame* (1968), *The Passion of Anna* (1969), *CRIES AND WHISPERS* (1972), *Scenes from a Marriage* (1973), *THE MAGIC FLUTE* (1975), *Face to Face* (1976), *Autumn Sonata* (1979), *From the Life of the Marionettes* (1980)

INDIA: A CHANGE OF PACE

Satyajit Ray has made more than twenty films, including: *Pather Panchali* (1955), *Aparajito* (1956), *THE WORLD OF APU* (1958), *The Music Room* (1958), *Devi* (1960) *Two Daughters* (1961), *Charulata: The Lonely Wife* (1964), *Days and Nights in* the Forest (1970), *DISTANT THUNDER* (1973), *The Middleman* (1975), *The Chess Players* (1977)

POLAND: REVOLUTION

Andrej Wajda: *Generation* (1954), *Kanal* (1956), *Ashes and Diamonds* (1958), *Man of Marble* (1980), *Man of Iron* (1981)

THE SIXTIES: NEW EXPERIMENTS

FRANCE: THE "NEW WAVE"

Francois Truffaut: *The Four Hundred Blows* (1959), *SHOOT THE PIANO PLAYER* (1960), *JULES AND JIM* (1961), *Stolen Kisses* (1968), *The Wild Child* (1969), *Day for Night* (1973), *THE STORY OF ADELE H.* (1975), *Small Change* (1976), *The Last Metro* (1980), *The Woman Next Door* (1981)
Jean-Luc Godard: *Breathless* (1959) and *Weekend* (1967)
Alain Resnais: *HIROSHIMA MON AMOUR* (1959), *Last Year at Marienbad* (1961), *Stavisky* (1974), *PROVIDENCE* (1977), *Mon Oncle D'Amerique* (1980)
Claude Chabrol: *Les Cousins* (1959), *Les Biches* (1968), *La Femme Infidele* (1969), *Le Boucher* (1970), *VIOLETTE* (1978)
Serge Bourguignon, *SUNDAYS AND CYBELE* (1962)
Claude Lelouch, *A Man and A Woman* (1966)
Philippe de Broca, *KING OF HEARTS* (1967)
Jean-Gabriel Albicocco, *THE WANDERER* (1969)

ITALY: POETIC REALISM

Federico Fellini: *The White Sheik* (1952), *I Vitelloni* (1953), *LA STRADA* (1954), *Nights of Cabiria* (1957), *La Dolce Vita* (1960), *8½* (1963), *JULIET OF THE SPIRITS* (1965), *Satyricon* (1970), *Roma* (1972), *Amarcord* (1974), *Casanova* (1977)
Michelangelo Antonioni: *L'Avventura* (1960), *Red Desert* (1964), *Blow-Up* (1966), *The Passenger* (1975)
Luchino Visconti: *Rocco and His Brothers* (1960), *The Stranger* (1967), *Death in Venice* (1971)
Pietro Germi, *Divorce Italian Style* (1961)

THE NEW ENGLISH CINEMA

Jack Clayton, *Room at the Top* (1959)
Tony Richardson: *Look Back in Anger* (1959), *The Entertainer* (1960), *A Taste of Honey* (1961), *THE LONELINESS OF THE LONG DISTANCE RUNNER* (1962), *Tom Jones* (1963), *The Loved One* (1965), *Hamlet* (1969)

Stanley Kubrick: *Paths of Glory* (1957), *DR. STRANGELOVE* (1964), *2001* (1968), *A CLOCKWORK ORANGE* (1971), *The Shining* (1980)

Richard Lester: *A Hard Day's Night* (1964), *The Knack* (1965), *How I Won the War* (1967), *The Three Musketeers* (1974), *Robin and Marian* (1976)

Peter Brook: *The Beggar's Opera* (1953), *LORD OF THE FLIES* (1963), *Marat-Sade* (1967), King Lear (1971)

Joseph Losey: *The Servant* (1963), *King and Country* (1964), *Accident* (1967), *The Go-Between* (1971), *A Doll's House* (1973)

John Schlesinger: *Billy Liar* (1963), *MIDNIGHT COWBOY* (1969), *The Day of the Locust* (1975)

Michael Cacoyannis, *ZORBA THE GREEK* (1964)

Silvio Narizzano, *GEORGY GIRL* (1966)

Karel Reisz: *MORGAN* (1966), *The French Lieutenant's Woman* (1981)

Franco Zeffirelli: *THE TAMING OF THE SHREW* (1967) and *ROMEO AND JULIET* (1968)

Lindsay Anderson: *If* (1968), *O Lucky Man* (1973)

AMERICA: SOME INDEPENDENT DIRECTORS

Frank Perry, *DAVID AND LISA* (1963)

Mike Nichols: *Who's Afraid of Virginia Woolf?* (1966), *THE GRADUATE* (1967), *Catch-22* (1970)

Arthur Penn: *Bonnie and Clyde* (1967), *Alice's Restaurant* (1969), *Little Big Man* (1970)

Dennis Hopper, *Easy Rider* (1969)

Bob Rafelson: *Five Easy Pieces* (1970), *The King of Marvin Gardens* (1972), *The Postman Always Rings Twice* (1981)

CONTEMPORARY FILMMAKERS

THE ABSURDISTS

LUIS BUNUEL has made more than thirty films, including: *LOS OLVIDADOS* (1950), *Nazarin* (1958), *VIRIDIANA* (1961), *The Exterminating Angel* (1962), *Diary of a Chambermaid* (1964), *Simon of the Desert* (1965), *BELLE DE JOUR* (1967), *The Milky Way* (1969), *Tristana* (1970), *The Discreet Charm of the Bourgeoisie* (1972), *Phantom of Liberty* (1974), *THAT OBSCURE OBJECT OF DESIRE* (1977)

Milos Forman: *Loves of a Blonde* (1965), *Fireman's Ball* (1968), *Taking Off* (1971), *One Flew Over the Cuckoo's Nest* (1976), *HAIR* (1979), *Ragtime* (1981)

Mel Brooks: *The Producers* (1968), *Blazing Saddles* (1974), *Young Frankenstein* (1974)

George Roy Hill: *Butch Cassidy and the Sundance Kid* (1969), *Slaughterhouse Five* (1972), *The Sting* (1973), *A Little Romance* (1978)
Hal Ashby: *HAROLD AND MAUDE* (1972), *BEING THERE* (1980)
Woody Allen: *Bananas* (1971), *PLAY IT AGAIN, SAM* (1972), *Sleeper* (1973), *ANNIE HALL* (1977), *MANHATTAN* (1979), *STARDUST MEMORIES* (1980)

VISIONARIES

Roman Polanski: *KNIFE IN THE WATER* (1963), *Cul-de-Sac* (1966), *Rosemary's Baby* (1968), *MacBeth* (1971), *Chinatown* (1974), *THE TENANT* (1976), *Tess* (1980)
Alexandro Jodorowsky, *El Topo* (1971)
Nicholas Roeg: *Performance* (1970), *WALKABOUT* (1971), *THE MAN WHO FELL TO EARTH* (1976)
John Boorman: *Deliverance* (1972), *ZARDOZ* (1974)
Terrence Malick: *Badlands* (1973), *DAYS OF HEAVEN* (1978)

ITALY: ACTIVISTS

Bernardo Bertolucci: *The Spider's Strategem* (1970), *THE CONFORMIST* (1970), *LAST TANGO IN PARIS* (1973), *1900* (1977), *Luna* (1979)
Lina Wertmuller: *Love and Anarchy* (1973), *THE SEDUCTION OF MIMI* (1974), *SWEPT AWAY* (1975), *SEVEN BEAUTIES* (1976)

AMERICA: THE "MOVIE BRATS"

Peter Bogdanovich, *THE LAST PICTURE SHOW* (1971)
Francis Ford Coppola: *The Godfather* (1972), *The Conversation* (1974)
George Lucas: *American Graffiti* (1973), *Star Wars* (1977
Brian de Palma: *Sisters* (1973), *THE PHANTOM OF THE PARADISE* (1974), *Obsession* (1976), *Dressed to Kill* (1980)

FRANCE: FREUDIAN FANTASIES

Louis Malle: *The Lovers* (1959), *Zazie* (1960), *MURMUR OF THE HEART* (1971), *Atlantic City* (1981). Malle has also directed several serious films on social themes: *Phantom India* series (1970), *Lacombe, Lucien* (1974), *My Dinner With Andre* (1981)
Eric Rohmer: *My Night at Maud's* (1970), *Claire's Knee* (1971), *Chloe in the Afternoon* (1972), *The Marquise of O.* (1976)

Jean-Charles Tacchella, *COUSIN COUSINE* (1976)
Edouard Molinaro, *LA CAGE AUX FOLLES* (1978)
Bertrand Blier: *Going Places* (1974), *GET OUT YOUR HANDKERCHIEFS* (1978), *BEAU PERE* (1981)

GERMANY: NEO-EXPRESSIONISM

Werner Herzog, *AGUIRRE, THE WRATH OF GOD* (1973)
Stroszek (1977), *WOYZECK* (1978), *NOSFERATU* (1979)
Rainer Fassbinder: *Fox and His Friends* (1975), *Despair* (1978), *THE MARRIAGE OF MARIA BRAUN* (1979), *Lola* (1981)
Volker Schlondorff: *THE TIN DRUM* (1979), *Circle of Deceit* (1981)
Istvan Szabo, *MEPHISTO* (1981)

POSTSCRIPT TO THE SECOND EDITION

Since 1981, a number of my film students have volunteered discussion questions about their favorite films. In addition to their unanimous selections, which I've included in this second edition, they've been particularly impressed by: Beineix' new-wave thriller, *Diva*, Wim Wenders' *Paris, Texas*, Bertrand Blier's *Menage*, Woody Allen's *Hannah and Her Sisters*, *My Life as a Dog*, and Louis Malle's *Au Revoir Les Enfants*. Have I left out anything wonderful? If so, please let me know by writing to me at De Anza College.

Finally, I can't conclude this postscript without expressing my appreciation to my friends and colleagues at De Anza and San Jose State University for sharing their ideas with me, waking me from my dogmatic slumbers. I'd especially like to thank: Will Crockett, Brock Kreiss, Zaki Lisha, Mark Mollander, Stuart Roe, Soumen Sanyal, Russell Simmons, Robert and Karen Lane, and my wonderful, supportive office-mate, Kim Walters. I'm also deeply indebted to my deans, Don Barnett and Lou Lewandowski, without whose encouragement the second edition of *Talking About Films* would not have been possible.

AFTERWORD

Will the film industry continue to roll along in its groove, like the monstrous stone in *Raiders of the Lost Ark?* Just as the seventies repeated the mythology of the thirties, the eighties will probably recreate the romantic machismo that accompanied World War Two. It's already clear that both *Raiders* and *Reds* consciously echo *Citizen Kane,* and that the lovers in Lawrence Kasdan's *Body Heat* try to walk in the footsteps of Lauren Bacall and Humphrey Bogart. For those who admire *The Maltese Falcon* and the macho heroes of the forties, this will be a happy decade of spin-offs from *Raiders of the Lost Ark.* The rest of us can only hope that Bertrand Blier will be the new Truffaut, and that Werner Herzog will develop into the Ingmar Bergman of the nineties. Although the rough beast invariably slouches towards Bethlehem to be born, the wheel will certainly come full circle once again.

ROBERT SELINSKE received his A.B. and M.A. from Columbia University in New York City. He has taught Film Appreciation courses in the San Francisco Bay area for many years. He currently teaches English and Film Analysis at De Anza College in Cupertino, California.